D0083448

ECONOMICS:
THE AMERICAN ECONOMY

ECONOMICS:
THE AMERICAN ECONOMY
from a Christian Perspective

Tom Rose

American Enterprise Publications
RD 6 • Box 6690
Mercer, PA 16137

Copyright © 1985 by Tom Rose

Scripture taken from King James Version

ISBN 0-9612198-0-7
Library of Congress Catalog Card No. 83-72165

Printed in the United States of America

Typography by Thoburn Press, P.O. Box 6941, Tyler, Texas 75711.

Contents

Preface

For of him, and through him, and to him, are all things; to whom be glory forever and ever. Amen.

Romans 11:36

THE excellent reception so graciously bestowed on my earlier work, *Economics: Principles and Policy (from a Christian Perspective)* has made it possible to produce this companion text, *Economics: The American Economy (from a Christian Perspective)*.

The former work deals primarily with **micro**economic topics, while this one deals primarily with **macro**economics (although it is impossible to neatly divide the science of economics into absolutely separate compartments). I wrote the **micro** text first because, in my own teaching, I prefer to introduce students to man and his environment first—starting from the individual consumer/producer, then to the firm, next to individual markets and finally to the economy as a whole. Instructors who use the same approach will want to use *Economics: Principles and Policy* the first semester and *Economics: The American Economy* the second semester. Those who like to approach the study of economics from the larger view and then gradually work down to the individual consumer/producer will encounter no difficulty in reversing the order.

Now a word about the perspective from which this book is written. This book views economics from a Christian—that is, a biblical—perspective. I make no apology for this fact, for this textbook, like its earlier companion, is dedicated to the honor and glory of God. It is in Him that all wisdom and knowledge is centered, and it is to His word that all must go who seek truth. The Bible can be used as a "benchmark" from which to judge all learning and all science, including the science of economics.

If there is one great fault that the Christian community has been guilty of, it is the failure of Christians to do "intellectual battle" with secular scholars who leave out all consideration of God from their thinking. For the secular community is wedded to the humanistic view of man which omits God from their presuppositions. This decidedly anti-Christian view has become so pervasive in our day that most scholars accept it as a norm. But it produces a type of scholarship in which man has no outside foundation on which to build his values. Man's activities thus come to be judged only by man and only according to whatever values happen to be popularly held at the time.

As a result of this secularizing trend, the reins of scholarship have for too long been in the hands of people who are dedicated to building a world system that is out of harmony with biblical precepts. This world system tends to enthrone man instead of God, and it tends to build state-directed economies which end up by enslaving the mass of citizens instead of guaranteeing their freedom of action as individuals responsible to God.

For too long Christians have meekly accepted the false view that a natural dichotomy exists between the study of science and the word of God. But the Bible does not compartmentalize man into a spiritual aspect on the one hand and a physical or worldly aspect on the other. No, the Bible indeed does just the opposite. It instructs the Christian that God's holy word is useful, even necessary, for bringing the whole world into conformity with the mind and will of God. As Christians we are to transform the world, and not to be conformed to it. The Apostle Paul admonishes us:

> *I beseech you therefore, brethren, by the mercies of God, that ye present your bodies a living sacrifice, holy, acceptable unto God, which is your reasonable service.*
> *And be not conformed to this world: but be ye transformed by the renewing of your mind, that ye may prove what is that good, and acceptable, and perfect, will of God.*
>
> *Romans 12:1-2*

As Christians we are to renew our minds by frequent referral to God's word, and we are to bring the whole world — the world of science and all the world's social institutions — into conformity with the mind and heart of Christ.

One Christian scholar, in speaking of knowledge gained from a Christian perspective, had this to say:

> . . . The mind of man is finite and knows only by thinking God's thoughts after him. But what it knows it then knows truly. It has at its disposal the revelation of God. This revelation does not hide God while it reveals him; it reveals him truly, though not exhaustively.[1]

This same scholar also said:

> . . . But if man is not autonomous, if he is rather what Scripture says he is, namely, a creature of God and a sinner before his face, then man should subordinate his reason to the Scriptures and seek in the light of it to interpret his experience.

[1]Cornelius Van Til, *The Defense of the Faith* (Philadelphia: Presbyterian and Reformed Publ. Co., 1955), p. 148.

. . . The objects man must seek to know are always of such a nature as God asserts they are. God's revelation is always authoritarian. This is true of his revelation in nature no less than of his revelation in Scripture. The truly scientific method, the method which alone can expect to make true progress in learning, is therefore such a method as seeks simply to think God's thoughts after him.[2]

Another Christian scholar in an essay entitled "Can Scholarship Be Christian?" writes:

Now the way in which a Christian's mind is to be dedicated to Christ in reasonable service as a living sacrifice unto God is twofold.

Negatively, the Christian is not to yield his mind to be conformed to the world—he is not to allow his intellect to be molded by worldly or non-Biblical teaching.

Positively, the Christian is to yield his mind to be transformed by the Holy Spirit—to be transformed by the renewing of his mind, so that he may prove what is that good, acceptable, and perfect will of God. This renewal will necessitate the Christian's development and advocacy of a specifically Biblical perspective in mathematics, mechanics, physics, biology, psychology and everything else!

This does not mean that the Christian will never be exposed to the non-Biblical interpretation of the arts and sciences. But it does mean that he must develop discernment—knowing that in spite of the limited truth contained therein by God's common grace, the non-Biblical approaches to any and every discipline are basically incorrect. And it also means that, rather than *conform* to those non-Biblical perspectives, the Christian will use his mind and actually try to *transform* them into a systematic life and world view by evaluating them in the light of God's true revelation in nature and especially in Scripture. For only in this way, can all of life be viewed from a BIBLICAL perspective.[3]

This is what *Economics: The American Economy* attempts to do—to investigate the science of economics from a decidedly Christian viewpoint.

It appears to me that there are two contrasting motivations for studying economics. One is to learn how man thinks and acts economically so that one can better serve his fellowmen. That is, so the producer can adjust his own productive efforts to the demands of the marketplace, thus increasing productive efficiency.

The other motivation is aimed at discovering how men react to outside

---

[2]Ibid., p. 125.
[3]Nigel Lee, *Can Scholarship Be Christian* (Memphis: Christian Studies Center, n.d.), [pp. 3-4].

stimuli with the objective of learning how to manipulate them in order to more easily attain predetermined ends.

The former view, in the author's opinion, constitutes a legitimate course of endeavor for Christians, who are admonished "to love your neighbor as yourself." But it seems that the latter view of economics—the manipulative view—predominates in most economics textbooks today. This view goes hand-in-hand with the current humanistic view of man which sees man as a chance evolutionary "happening" rather than a precious and purposefully created being. But if there is nothing sacredly precious about man, and if he was not created to fulfill a specific purpose, then why should not a self-appointed intellectual elite sit at the head of government and manipulate and control the supposedly less-intelligent masses of men in order to lead them into a wordly Utopia?

But the Bible teaches that man indeed is a precious, God-created being. It teaches that man indeed does have a God-ordained purpose. And it also teaches that man is personally responsible to a holy and righteous God rather than to an all-powerful state. In this text, therefore, we will investigate not only the theories of economic science and present economic structures (a positive process), but we will also have occasion to evaluate them from a biblical perspective to determine if what exists is indeed in conformity with biblical precepts (a normative process). So as we proceed in our study, let us begin with the presupposition that, from God's viewpoint, there is an ideal method men should use in the exchange of goods and services. Our goal as Christian scholars is to discover the mind of God, to measure present systems against the "benchmark" of His word and to conform our activities and practices to the heart and mind of Christ. "Let this mind be in you, which was also in Christ Jesus" (Phil. 2:5).

I owe a debt of gratitude to the able librarians at the Grove City College Library for their valuable assistance in researching many items in this book.

Finally, my warm thanks to Ruth and Karen Rose for the many hours they spent in typing and editing the manuscript. It is much better as a result of their valuable input.

TOM ROSE

1

Workers, Labor Unions and Collective Bargaining

Whoso keepeth the fig tree shall eat the fruit thereof: so he that waiteth on his master shall be honoured.

Proverbs 27:18

IN a free market economy—that is, in an economy in which prices are free to fluctuate in response to the unrestricted buying and selling activities of free and self-responsible individuals—economic production cannot help but be consumer oriented. This does not mean that consumers will play a **direct** role in managing the productive processes in the millions of producing firms which supply the public with goods and services—for indeed they will not. This does mean, however, that the economic activity which takes place in these firms must, if it is to be profitable, result in products that the public wants at prices the public is willing to pay.

What really happens in the economic process of production is this: Entrepreneurial-minded venturers put together production firms that actually manufacture goods and services on speculation. They make an educated guess at what the public will want at some date in the future, and they estimate how much the public might be willing to pay at that date. Then they set about organizing the various factors of production (land, labor and capital) in such a way that profitable production can take place. If their guess of product (or service) is correct, and if their estimation of price is accurate, then the public willingly exchanges money for the goods and services offered. Profit then appears as after-the-fact evidence that the producer-entrepreneurs have indeed engaged in worthwhile economic service to the community. In such a situation, that is, in a profitable one, employment will tend to expand. But if freely acting consumers refuse to validate the prior estimations and actions of those who have produced on speculation, then the risk-takers experience economic loss. The risk-takers then have no alternative but to disemploy the workers they had hired to engage in economic production.

Economics of the Employee-Employer Relationship

It is important to understand the economic relationship that exists between workers, firms and the public if we are to understand the overall workings of the economy as a whole. For the entire macroeconomy is composed of millions and millions of microeconomic units. Each and every participant in the voluntary association we call "business" has a unique and important economic role to play.

Investors supply the producing firm with needed risk capital—first to get the firm started, and then to expand it. They also appoint company directors who hire key managers. These in turn are charged with the responsibility of running the firm and making innumerable day-to-day decisions.

Managers have the responsibility of efficiently organizing and operating the business firm in response to consumer demands. The unique economic function of the business manager is to successfully anticipate and interpret consumer demands and then to communicate these demands to his workers so that profitable production can take place. In order to do this, a manager must gain the willing cooperation of his workers. Failure to successfully achieve any one of these crucial responsibilities will result in uneconomic production and monetary loss. The ensuing losses will threaten the continued existence of the firm as well as the continued employment of its workers.

The recent experience of major industries in these United States[1] (steel, auto, rubber and others) serves as a case in point. Company managements in these industries had allowed their input costs—primarily labor costs—to get out of line. For years they had succumbed to the pressures of strong labor unions which sought wage increases that outran gains in productivity. Rather than risk the possible cost and unpleasantness of long strikes, company managements opted for passing their increased costs on to consumers in the form of higher asking prices. Unrealistic government controls, high taxes and long-continued monetary inflation added to the increased costs consumers were asked to pay.

For many years consumers continued to validate management's pricing decisions by acquiescing to pay higher prices for automobiles and other union-made products. But the process of continually foisting higher prices on consumers could not go on forever. Finally, consumers turned to cheaper imports; and the net result was very high levels of unemployment in the affected industries. In 1980-1981, for instance, a number of large steel companies closed down many unprofitable steel mills. U.S. Steel Company, the largest domestic steel maker, closed down 14 plants. In 1982 the large auto firms and the United Auto Workers Union (UAW) were forced to renegotiate their labor contracts, before they expired, in a cooperative effort to reduce production costs with an eye toward lowering the price of autos to consumers.

---

[1] The term **"these** United States" is used instead of the more popular term **"the** United States." The author's reason for using this form is to focus the reader's attention on the fact that, from a constitutional standpoint, we are a democratic republic composed of 50 independent republics. The original 13 states compacted together, through the Constitution, to establish a federal government rather than a national government. Therefore, such usage emphasizes the historical fact that the U.S. Federal Government is a political creation of the states rather than the states being mere appendages of a centralized government.

Successful business firms have managers who are adept in each of these crucial responsibilities: anticipating consumer demands, interpreting consumers' demands and communicating them to workers and gaining the cooperation of workers. Managers usually earn relatively high pay because their skills are relatively scarce in the marketplace. Not only do expert managers serve as a built-in guarantee that investors will enjoy rising profits, but they also serve to guarantee, in the process, that workers' wages will trend upwards in the long run. The reason for this is that both rising profits and rising wages are based on rising productivity. We might summarize management's key responsibility as that of doing whatever is necessary to provide ever-rising levels of productivity of the firms they supervise.

Workers have what appears to be a rather unimportant role in the production process, but this is not the case. They have the very important task of co-operating with management in the ever-present need to adjust the firm's operation to the demands that consumers place on the business firm. One book on the economics of the employee-employer relationship classifies employees as the most important asset that an employer can have.[2] Willing cooperation between workers and managers invariably results in profitable production, expanding sales, rising levels of employment and an upward pressure on wage rates.

One way of summarizing the economic relationship that exists between employees, employers and consumers is this: Employees **wholesale** their labor services to their employer. He in turn **retails** his employees' services to customers in the form of the goods and services he sells.

The employer, in effect, serves as a middleman or as a go-between for employees and the public. He is the key factor in making it economically possible and mutually beneficial for workers and consumers to cooperate with each other. Each party in the production process gets what he wants because he places a lower value on what he gives than upon what he receives through the business process. The consumer values the good or service more than the money he spends. The worker values his wage more than the labor services he sells to his employer. And the employer, if he has planned accurately, ends up with a profit. The employer's key role in the cooperative business process is to discover what his customers want, even though they themselves may not be consciously aware of what they want; how much customers are willing to pay; and then to interpret his findings in a meaningful way to his employees so as to gain their willing cooperation.

It can be seen from the previous description of the business process that the employee-employer relationship is indeed an honorable one. Ideally, it is a relationship in which both parties should show great respect for the other's contribution because each party needs the other. In essence, each party ex-

---

[2] Tom Rose, *How to Succeed in Business* (Dallas: The Institute for Free Enterprise Education, 1975), p. 40.

ploits the other economically to the advantage of both. Both are really "part-ners in production" intent on serving the needs of consumers who ultimately employ them through their purchases. In a purely economic sense, the employee-employer relationship is thus a **cooperative** relationship rather than an antagonistic relationship. Mutually beneficial exploitation must take place for a wholesome employee-employer relationship to exist.

The Apostle Paul has some sound advice for employees and employers which, if followed, would eliminate much of the existing strife between work-ers and employers. His advice amounts to what might well be called a Chris-tian philosophy of labor-management relations:

Masters, give unto your servants [employees] that which is just and equal; knowing that ye also have a Master in heaven.

Colossians 4:1

Servants [employees], obey in all things your masters [employ-ers] according to the flesh; not with eyeservice, as menpleasers; but in singleness of heart, fearing God: And whatsoever ye do, do it heartily, as to the Lord, and not unto men. Knowing that of the Lord ye shall receive the reward of the inheritance: for ye serve the Lord Christ.

Colossians 3:22-24

Let nothing be done through strife or vainglory; but in lowliness of mind let each esteem other better than themselves. Look not every man on his own things, but every man also on the things of others. Let this mind be in you, which was also in Christ Jesus.

Philippians 2:3-5

The Development of Labor Unions in England and These United States

The modern-day labor union movement developed out of stresses that accom-panied the gradual shift in production from one-man producing units, to the larger master-journeymen shops of the pre-industrial age, and finally to the much larger factory system which began in the late eighteenth and early nine-teenth centuries in England, France and other Western European nations. As long as the individual craftsman ran his own shop and dealt with his own pub-lic, he, in effect, served as both employer and employee. When he met resis-tance from customers concerning price or quality, he readily adjusted to what, today, we would call the dictates of the consumer without any internal dissen-sion in his business. After all, he could only quarrel with himself in such an in-stance! Even though craftsmen in the intermediate master-journeymen shops were only one step removed from pressures exerted by the public, the close personal relationship that existed between the master-craftsman (the boss) and his journeymen-craftsmen (the workers) remained strong enough to prevent serious employee-employer squabbles over wages and working conditions. But the situation changed with the advent of larger manufacturing units. The more impersonal employment relationship which seems to be part and parcel of large factories, plus the complete exclusion of factory workers from direct contact with the buying public, created a fertile seedbed for labor-management misunderstandings. When the factory manager, for instance, is faced with the need to reduce prices in order to sell his output and keep his factory operating, he is virtually forced to reduce wages. The reason for this is that his labor costs constitute the largest production cost over which the manager has some degree of control. But since the workers in his factory are far removed from the price-resistance pressures exerted by the public, they are very likely to oppose any cut in wages. Part of the workers' opposition is the result of not understanding the economics of the business firm. Few workers recognize that the consumer is the ultimate employer who has the power of "hiring" or "firing" workers by the act of purchasing or refusing to purchase the firm's output.

The secret of mass production in factories is to reduce prices through the greater efficiency of large-scale production, thereby enabling lower income groups to purchase goods which had previously been priced beyond their means. This is what the early Industrial Revolution was all about. And this is what the continuing industrial revolution is all about; even in our day, the needed adjustment of industry to lower cost production is an ever on-going process. Low cost factory production made previously high-priced clothing and other items more readily available at lower prices to the mass of consumers, instead of high-priced custom-made goods to only the elite.

Part of workers' resistance to any drop in wages in the early industrial era was because they needed every cent earned to support their families. Wages and incomes were very low by today's standards because output per worker was very low. It is important to note, however, that the great reductions in consumer prices that resulted from the growth of factories came, not from wage reductions, but from cost-saving efficiencies generated by using more highly mechanized machinery. Strong general downward pressure on wages usually occurred only during depressions, such as the post-war depression in England after the Napoleonic Wars in the second decade of the nineteenth century and the depression of 1837. In general, workers in the developing factory system earned higher wages than non-factory workers during the Industrial Revolution.

In England and France labor union movements took a radical/anarchist direction which later gradually mellowed into a less radical communist/socialist direction. Even to this day, labor unions in England, France and other European countries are devoted to the Utopian goal of attempting to change the economic/political structure of their countries from free market capitalism to that of state-directed capitalism, that is, socialism. The English Fabian Society successfully gained control of the British Labour Party and used the finances of English labor unions to push its socialistic platforms to reconstruct society and the economy along socialistic lines.

In these United States some of the early labor unions were also strongly influenced by the anarchist/communist movement. (During the 1800s and up to the Bolshevik Revolution in Russia in 1917, the words **socialism** and **communism** were often used interchangeably.) Most American unions finally repudiated the drastic revolutionary tactics that were espoused by the anarchists and the communists in favor of a similar gradualistic socialism that was being followed in England, called Fabianism. Samuel Gompers, who served as president of the American Federation of Labor (AFL) from 1886 until 1924, led his unions to seek "bread and butter" economic gains (higher wages and improved working conditions) instead of trying to change the whole political/economic structure of these United States to socialism. In 1903, when the terms socialism and communism were still being used interchangeably, Samuel Gompers made this scathing denouncement against the radical socialist/communist elements in the AFL:

> . . . I want to tell you, Socialists, that I have studied your philosophy; read your works upon economics, and not the meanest of them; studied your standard works, both in English and German — have not only read them, but studied them. I have heard your orators and watched the work of your movement the world over. I have kept close watch upon your doctrines for thirty years; have been closely associated with many of you, and know how you think and what your propose. I know, too, what you have up your sleeve. And I want to say that I am entirely at variance with your philosophy. I declare to you, I am not only at variance with your doctrines, but with your philosophy. Economically, you are unsound; socially you are wrong; industrially, you are an impossibility.[3]

Many of the Marxian ideas and attitudes held by early labor union leaders, the very ideas Gompers opposed, have, of course, persisted in milder forms in modern-day labor unions. Most labor union leaders today, for instance, foster the Marxian concept of a class struggle between workers and their employers along with the idea of unfair exploitation.

A historical knowledge of what happened in England prior to and during the early part of the so-called Industrial Revolution will be helpful in developing an understanding of the anti-capitalist (pro-Marxian) mentality which is still so evident in many labor unions today.

In England there was a series of land enclosure movements which dispossessed many rural families from their land holdings. The enclosure movements

---

[3] Gerald Emanuel Stearn, ed., *Gompers* (Englewood Cliffs: Prentice-Hall, 1971), p. 52.

began about 1550 and continued until about 1800 or a bit later. Here is what happened:

During the sixteenth century an early type of factory system was developed in France to produce woolen cloth. This development created a demand for wool in England which the larger landowners desired to meet. Previous to this time, agriculture in England was largely of a subsistence type—that is, it was not primarily directed toward the production of money crops.

The larger landowners petitioned Parliament to pass "land enclosure acts." These enclosure acts divided up the commonly held pastureland into smaller privately held tracts. Up to this time few large towns existed in England. Each family in an agricultural community had an acre or two that it tilled plus the right to graze a few animals (cows, pigs and chickens) on the commonly owned land called "the commons."

The larger landowners, who were the more entrepreneurial minded, could not act to meet the developing overseas market for wool unless they could fence off or enclose the land on which they wanted to graze sheep. Their interest in enclosing land was to prevent their higher quality sheep from interbreeding with the lower quality, less-wool producing types owned by the yeomen farmers. The larger landowners were also desirous of improving their own pasturelands and keeping other animals from grazing on their land.

There is no doubt that the enclosure of fields made a more productive agriculture possible. But when Parliament passed the "enclosure acts," many smaller landowners, and this constituted the majority of the population, soon discovered that they could not produce enough food on the small allotments which they retained. Thus, they either abandoned their small plots or sold out at low prices to the larger landowners. In many instances, the cost of surveying small plots going to the small landowners was more than the value of the land. Also, many smaller landholders were unable to prove their ownership claims to the satisfaction of the courts; so they were dispossessed without payment.

The economic and social results of the land enclosure movement were both drastic and revolutionary. Large groups of idle masses were created almost overnight. They turned to begging, robbing and vagabonding for a living. Gradually these dispossessed masses tended to settle in the towns. The resulting squalor and unsanitary conditions have often been wrongly blamed on the Industrial Revolution which developed some years later.

From 1700 to 1750 Parliament passed 100 enclosure acts; from 1750 to 1800 it passed 1,500 enclosure acts. In the 100-year period from 1700 to 1800, some three million acres of open fields and more than one million acres of wasteland were enclosed. Farm production soared as agriculture became more efficient, but the social cost incurred was the creation of landless masses who roamed the highways and swelled the ranks of the unemployed in the towns. Many children were orphaned or abandoned because their parents could no longer feed them. Children roamed the streets and alleys searching for food in garbage heaps. Some fell prey to older vagabonds who employed them for immoral purposes.

Interestingly enough, the wages of farm workers **fell** even though farm productivity **rose** after the enclosure movements began. This would be in conformity with supply-demand theory, for the available supply of workers was forcibly and drastically increased by wrenching so many people from working their own plots. The increased supply of available labor more than offset the increased demand for farm workers. Professor James E. T. Rogers, in his book entitled *Six Centuries of Work and Wages — The History of English Labour,* reported that even by the time of King George's reign (1760-1820) common agricultural wages had fallen well below those paid in 1260 under King Henry III (1216-1272). At the earlier date the threshing of wheat was paid with one-eighteenth of the harvest, but at the latter date it brought one twenty-fourth. For oats it was one-fourteenth versus one-twentieth at the latter date. In 1860 in England the average woman's wage in agricultural districts was 4s2d per week, whereas in 1450, allowing for depreciated purchasing value of the monetary unit, it was between 12s to 24s per week.

In his book Professor Rogers writes:

> . . . But I am convinced that modern civilization will be judged, not by what it has done, but by what it has left undone; not by what it has remedied, but by what it has failed to heal, or at least to have relieved; not by its successes, but by its shortcomings. . . .
>
> . . . there is collected a population in our great towns which equals in amount the whole of those who lived in England and Wales six centuries ago; but whose condition is more destitute, whose homes are more squalid, whose means are more uncertain, whose prospects are more hopeless than those of the poorest serfs of the middle ages and the meanest drudges of the mediaeval cities. . . .[4]

It is upon this background — upon the background of a governmentally imposed enclosure movement which forcibly dispossessed untold thousands of people from their land — that the Industrial Revolution in England took place. The general condition of poverty and social squalor was not, as is commonly believed, brought about by "greedy industrialists" who engaged in the mistreatment of workers for the sake of profits. Indeed, a strong argument can be made that the growth of the factory system saved many persons from literal starvation. The newly developing factory system gave dispossessed men, women and children an opportunity to earn, what was for those times, relatively high wages. The mushrooming factories, based on newly developed steam power, cried for workers. Higher than average wages were offered to attract needed workers, even though wages were still low by modern standards

---

[4] James E. Thorold Rogers, *Six Centuries of Work and Wages; The History of English Labour,* with a new Preface by G. D. H. Cole (London: Allen & Unwin, 1884), p. 186.

because productivity was low.

Factory wages in England were relatively lower than in these United States, where the Industrial Revolution occurred somewhat later, in the mid- and later 1800s, because of one very important difference. In England, the land enclosure movement, through governmental acts, forcibly dispossessed large masses of people from the lands. This provided a surplus labor pool from which the emerging industrialists could draw. But in these United States, the long-continued availability of low-cost land drew labor away from the towns and factories, thereby creating a relative scarcity of labor. The land policy followed by the infant American Republic was friendly towards the workingman's interest. Our land policy made it easy for man to combine his labor with God's gift to man, the land. This gave the American workingman a viable alternative to selling his labor services in the towns. In contrast, the land policy followed by the English Parliament was unfriendly towards the workingman. The English land policy forcibly put the worker in a position where he had little choice but to sell his labor services in the emerging factory system. Ironically, the free market system has been blamed for the miserable living conditions and low wage rates which existed at the time of the Industrial Revolution. The free market system did not cause these problems, although it eventually served to cure them! Wrong governmental policies produced the surplus supply of labor in early industrial England as well as the squalid living conditions in the towns. It was the rising level of productivity in the factory system which eventually raised the English workingman's standard of living.

Karl Marx was one who wrongly attributed much of the poverty and squalor he observed in early industrial England to free market capitalism as a system. He and others who lived during the English Industrial Revolution did not realize to what extent the underlying social and economic conditions had been brought about by the politically induced land enclosure movement. They blamed the capitalistic system when the real perpetrator of the social evils they observed was the civil authority.

Actually, the English factories, even though the factory owners did not consciously plan it that way, kept many men, women and children from starving to death. Evidence of this fact can be seen from the rising population figures, which resulted from a steadily dropping death rate and which paralleled the rise of the factory system. If Marx had lived in these United States instead of in England during his writing years, it is doubtful that his writings would have been as revolutionary as they were. It is also doubtful that he would have developed his mistaken theories about private capitalism — mistaken theories which have been embraced by labor unions all over the world.

The following observations of other authors will give additional insights to the Industrial Revolution in England:

> The factory owners did not have the power to compel anybody
> to take a factory job. They could only hire people who were ready to

work for the wages offered to them. Low as these wages were, they were nonetheless much more than these paupers could earn in any other field open to them. It is a distortion of facts to say that the factories carried off the housewives from the nurseries and the kitchen and the children from their play. These women had nothing to cook with and to feed their children. These children were destitute and starving. Their only refuge was the factory. It saved them, in the strict sense of the term, from death by starvation.[5]

. . . In 1697, John Locke wrote a report for the Board of Trade on the problem of poverty and poor-relief. Locke estimated that a laboring man and his wife in good health could support no more than two children, and he recommended that **all children over three years of age** should be taught to earn their living at working schools for spinning and knitting, where they would be given food. "What they can have at home, from their parents," wrote Locke, "is seldom more than bread and water, and that very scantily too."[6]

Child labor was not ended by legislative fiat; child labor ended when it became economically unnecessary for children to earn wages in order to survive—when the income of their parents became sufficient to support them. The emancipators and benefactors of those children were not legislators or factory inspectors, but manufacturers and financiers. Their efforts and investments in machinery led to a rise in real wages, to a growing abundance of goods at lower prices, and to an incomparable improvement in the general standard of living.[7]

. . . The first child labor law in England (1788) regulated the hours and conditions of labor of the miserable children who worked as chimney sweeps—a dirty, dangerous job which long antedated the Industrial Revolution, and which was not connected with factories. The first Act which applied to factory children was passed to protect those who had been sent into virtual slavery by the parish authorities, **a government body:** they were deserted or orphaned pauper children who were legally under the custody of the poor-law officials in the parish. . . .[8]

The post-war depression of 1815 and the depression of 1837, which were largely monetary phenomena and not caused by inherent deficiencies in the

---

[5] Ludwig von Mises, *Human Action: A Treatise on Economics* (New Haven: Yale University Press, 1963), p. 620.

[6] Robert Hessen, "The Effects of the Industrial Revolution on Women and Children," in *Capitalism: the Unknown Ideal,* Ayn Rand (New York: New American Library, 1966), p. 105.

[7] Ibid., pp. 106-7.

[8] Ibid., p. 106.

private capitalistic system, produced much unemployment and misery among workers. It is understandable under such observed circumstances that Marx developed his theories of "labor exploitation" and "the reserve army of the unemployed," which labor unions later embraced. Marx's theory of labor exploitation holds that employers exploit workers unfairly at the point of production by failing to pay them the full value of their production. He held that **all** value is created by labor, and **none** by machine power. Thus, workers should receive 100 percent of the value of what is produced. No payment rightfully should go, according to this theory, for the use of tools (interest) or to the entrepreneur (profit).

Marx's theory of the reserve army of the unemployed holds that, given a free labor market, there always exists a large pool of unemployed workers who are eager to work. This reserve pool of unemployed workers will constantly force wages downward. This downward pressure on wages serves to increase the continuing misery of the working class. Finally, the plight of workers becomes unbearable. At this point the working masses (the proletariat) will rise up and forcibly overthrow the capitalistic owners (the bourgeoisie).

As stated previously, Marx failed to observe that the English factory system grew up in an atmosphere of mass unemployment because of the earlier land enclosure acts passed by Parliament. It was this **political** action that created the **economic** problem of unemployment and produced Marx's reserve army of the unemployed. It was not created by the free labor market. The labor market, as any economist might predict, simply adjusted to the politically induced situation that already existed. In these United States no such reserve army of the unemployed ever appeared because our national government followed a different land policy. But real wages in England, as in these United States, rose steadily as technology boosted industrial output. This made the workingman's economic situation better instead of worse, as Marx's theory had predicted.

The condition of the working class continued to improve during the Industrial Revolution hand-in-hand with rising industrial productivity. But Marx was too blinded by his hatred of free market capitalism to see the evidence that was readily apparent even in his day. The Marxian theories of the unfair exploitation of labor and of the reserve army of the unemployed, then, are some of the ideas that labor unions have inherited from Marx and his followers. The ideological tie between Marx and labor unions has long been recognized by critics of Marx and labor unions. But socialists/communists have also recognized the tie. The following quote is from a Russian who emigrated to these United States. He was long an avid follower of revolutionary Marxism before finally repudiating it:

> Marxian principles concern themselves with the welfare of the producer, with exploitation at the point of production. Labor unions also concern themselves with the welfare of the producer,

with exploitation at the point of production. These reasons alone ought to furnish sufficient basis for wedded bliss between labor unions and Socialists.[9]

A realization of where, why and how Marx's theories developed helps us to understand some of the existing views held by modern-day labor unions, and also helps us to view unions sympathetically even though we might not agree with them.

Unions and Labor Legislation in These United States

One of the earliest labor unions in these United States was formed in 1794 by the cordwainers (shoemakers) in Philadelphia, Pennsylvania. It was the first workingman's association to gain a formal contract with employers. It lasted until 1806.

The recurring cycle observed in the early labor union movement is this: Membership tended to increase during prosperous times when labor was relatively scarce, only to fall back sharply during periods of depression when labor was relatively plentiful.

The Pennsylvania Workingmen's Party, formed in 1828, was the first statewide labor organization in these United States. The International Ladies Garment Workers' Union was formed in New York in 1830 and continues in existence today. In 1831 the National Trades Union was formed in New York. It was America's first national labor organization. When the depression of 1837 occurred, however, union membership again plummeted.

In 1842 the Massachusetts Supreme Court heard what turned out to be a "landmark case," Commonwealth vs. Hunt. Prior to this date, the courts regarded unions, or workingmen's associations as they were called, as illegal conspiracies against trade because of their goal of attempting to raise wages by combining against employers. But in Commonwealth vs. Hunt, the Court ruled that unions were not illegal per se. Therefore, the mere existence of a union was stated as not being contrary to the public interest. Rather, the Massachusetts Court ruled that it is necessary to determine whether the specific actions of a union are illegal or not. Henceforth, the right of unions to exist was generally recognized by the courts in other states as long as their actions stayed within the law.

In 1869 the Knights of Labor, a very broad-based fellowship of workingmen, was formed under the leadership of Uriah Stephens, a Baptist preacher. The Knights welcomed people from all ranks of life into its membership (except bankers, lawyers, doctors and purveyors of liquor—all of whom were held in low esteem by the organization). Its membership grew very rapidly after

[9]Maurice William, *The Social Interpretation of History; A Refutation of the Marxian Economic Interpretation of History* (New York: Sotery Publishing Co., 1921), pp. 163-64.

1881, two years after Terence V. Powderly replaced Uriah Stephens as "Grand Master Workman." Powderly was popular because he had led a successful strike against the railroads. In 1881 membership in the Knights of Labor was around 200,000. By 1886 it had risen to 750,000, the high mark of its membership; but by 1890 membership had dropped to 100,000. By 1900 the Knights were an insignificant factor in the labor union movement. In 1917 the organization quietly passed out of existence.

A number of factors contributed to the demise of the Knights of Labor. One was that the organization tried to bring too many divergent interests into one fellowship. Another is that it wasted union resources in attempting to change the political/economic structure of these United States along socialistic lines instead of focusing on "bread and butter" issues such as wages and working conditions. Still another factor was the Knights' failure to use the strike effectively as a weapon against employers. The Knights of Labor did not believe in strikes, even though a successful strike was what gave its membership an initial thrust. Lastly, the Knights were not very adept at getting signed labor contracts which bound employers to maintain previously established wage levels even during periods of economic depression.

In 1881 six craft labor unions met in Pittsburgh, Pennsylvania, to form an organization called the Federation of Organized Trades and Labor Unions (FOTLU) under the leadership of Adolph Strasser, president of the International Cigar-Makers Union, and Samuel Gompers, a former political radical. The group was composed of carpenters, cigar-makers, glass-workers, iron- and steel-workers, molders and printers. In 1886 some strong national unions pulled out of the Knights of Labor because of dissatisfaction with Terence Powderly's policies. The six unions merged with the FOTLU and formed the American Federation of Labor (AFL). Samuel Gompers, who got his start in the cigar-makers union as a "reader,"[10] was elected president.

The AFL followed what is called a **craft** policy. Only skilled craftsmen and apprentices were allowed to join the federated unions. Membership was not open to semi-skilled or unskilled workers, who made up the majority of workingmen. Thus, union membership was limited to the highest earners among workingmen — skilled craftsmen. The AFL allowed only one union to a trade in order to exclude competition between unions and to eliminate jurisdictional disputes between them. Instead of trying to reform society as the Knights of Labor attempted to do, the AFL focused on narrow economic goals which benefitted members economically, such as higher wages, improved working conditions and a shorter work-week. Union resources were thus used to help union members directly by striving for such "bread and butter" gains.

When asked what the goals of the AFL were, Gompers' short and caustic reply was, "More! Now!"

---

[10] A "reader" was usually a young person who read books and other literature to the other cigar-makers as they worked at rolling cigars.

The AFL became quite adept at negotiating labor contracts which required employers to continue to pay the agreed-to wage even during times of depression. This was accomplished, of course, at the cost of increased unemployment among union members. In the absence of such a contract, an employer had the option of reducing wages across-the-board for all employees and thereby keeping more of his workers on the payroll. But unions have generally opted for freezing wage levels downward and settling for less employment rather than accepting flexible wage levels and continued high employment. Such a policy benefits those union members who remain on the payroll, but their gain is at the expense of younger workers and those with less seniority who are laid off during times of economic downturn.

By 1898 AFL membership reached 250,000. By 1904 it reached 1.7 million. In 1914 membership reached two million, and by 1918 membership had doubled to four million. At this time, the AFL included about 80 percent of all union members. Thus, we see that the American labor union movement continued to be mainly associations of skilled craftsmen rather than unskilled workmen. Union craftsmen were recognized as the elite of the working class.

All during the nineteenth century and the early part of the twentieth century, labor unions played a rather unimportant role in the overall American economy. This should be evident when we consider the very low percentage of workingmen who belonged to unions. Before the 1860s and the advent of the War Between the States, union membership never exceeded more than 2 percent of the total workforce. Even at the turn of the century, union membership was still under 3 percent of the total workforce. Unions did not become an important factor, percentage-wise, until Congress passed pro-union legislation in the 1930s.

In 1932 Congress passed the Norris-LaGuardia Act which prohibited employers from automatically getting a court injunction to prohibit strikes during labor disputes. This Act also prohibited so-called "yellow dog" contracts, which were agreements that some employers had workers sign as a condition of employment. In such a contract, a worker would agree not to join a labor union or work to have a union installed as long as he worked for the employer. If the worker subsequently did join or attempt to organize a union, his employer could then resort to legal action for breach of contract.

In 1935 Congress passed the Wagner Act, which is also known as the National Labor Relations Act. The effect was to spur union membership sharply upward.

Two contrasting views might be expressed here. One view, held by employers, holds that before 1935 unions and employers were on approximately an even footing relative to a balance of power and were thus able to compete effectively with each other.

The other view, ascribed to by union leaders, holds that, given a free labor market, the cards are stacked against workers (remember Marx's theories of labor exploitation and the reserve army of the unemployed?). Therefore, without special help from the government to "even up" the situation, workers will continue to be unfairly exploited by employers.

Congress apparently bought the pro-Marxian labor union view (there are more voters who are workers than who are employers). Congress passed the National Labor Relations Act (NLRA) which established the National Labor Relations Board (NLRB) to supervise elections for determining whether workers wanted a union to represent them. Congress also established a list of "unfair labor practices" that severely limited employers' freedom in communicating their side of the story to employees. The NLRA thus tilted the scales of power strongly in favor of unionization. In addition, employers were forced by law to recognize a union as representing **all** employees in a bargaining unit if the union won a majority vote. Previous to this, an employer could refuse to recognize a union at all, and workers who did not want to be represented by a union were not forced to allow the union to speak for them. The NLRA changed this historic policy of democratic freedom in the labor market.

Table 1:1

Labor Union Victories in NLRB Supervised Elections

1946	79.5%	1970	55.0%
1950	74.5	1975	48.2
1955	67.6	1979	45.0
1965	60.8		

Source: National Labor Relations Board.

The net effect of the NLRA was a sudden rise in unionized industrial plants and in total union membership; an increase in the number of labor-management disputes (see Table 1:2); and a rise in internal union corruption which later resulted in the Taft-Hartley Act of 1947 and the Landrum-Griffin Act of 1959.

Table 1:2

Time Lost in Strikes

Years	Annual Average Number of Strikes	Workers Included*	Percent of Working Time Lost
1935-39	2,862	1,130	.27
1940-44	3,754	1,386	.16
1945-50	4,210	2,940	.61
1951-55	4,540	2,510	.31
1956-60	3,602	1,620	.29
1961-65	3,560	1,365	.14
1966-70	4,567	2,375	.21

Source: U.S. Department of Labor.

*Thousands.

In 1938 Congress passed the so-called Fair Standards Labor Act which imposed a minimum wage and the legal requirement for most employers to pay "time-and-a-half" for time worked over 40 hours during one week or worked in excess of eight hours per day. The effect of minimum wage laws is discussed in the chapter on Labor Economics.

By 1947 Congress was receiving so many complaints about union abuses, and the country was threatened by so many strikes (See Table 1:2), that Congress passed the Taft-Hartley Act. This legislation allows the President of these United States to impose an 80-day injunction against strikes that threaten to disrupt the economy in order to provide a "cooling-off period." It also makes both secondary boycotts and the "closed shop" illegal. A secondary boycott occurs when union members picket an employer who is not directly part of the labor dispute — for instance, a retailer who sells a product manufactured by the firm against which the union is striking. According to English Common Law, which is the basis of American law, such a boycott is an illegal restraint of trade and is thereby detrimental to the public interest. A "closed shop" agreement is an agreement by which an employer promises to hire new workers only from the union. A "union shop" is one in which the employer is free to find workers who are not already members of the union; but newly hired workers must join the union within a certain period of time — usually 30 days — if they are to continue being employed. An "open shop" is a shop where a worker is free to join or not to join the union; but he must allow the union to bargain for him, and he is bound by the union agreement.

State legislatures are allowed to pass so-called "Right-to-Work Laws" by Section 14-B of the Taft-Hartley Act. Such a law makes it illegal to require a worker to join a union as a condition of employment. Thus, in Right-to-Work states, workers cannot be forced to join a union in order to continue to be employed; Section 14-B of the Taft-Hartley Act is the employer version of the section of the Norris-LaGuardia Act, which prohibits "yellow-dog" contracts and which was passed in 1932. The Norris-LaGuardia Act outlaws contracts which prohibit a worker from joining a union in order to get and hold a job, while the Taft-Hartley Act outlaws contracts which force a worker to join a union in order to keep his job. Unions generally favor doing away with agreements which prevent workers from joining unions as a condition of employment, but they strongly oppose Section 14-B of the Taft-Hartley Act which frees workers to decide whether or not they wish to join a union. Employers generally opposed the law of 1932 but favor the law of 1947.

In 1959 Congress, in a further attempt to reduce internal corruption in unions, passed the Landrum-Griffin Act (the Union Disclosure Act). This Act requires unions to disclose their finances publicly by filing annual reports with the federal government.

What has been the long-range effect of labor legislation in these United States?

An objective evaluation of the major bills passed in 1935, 1947 and 1959 indicates this: The NLRA of 1935 served to upset the existing "balance of power" between unions and employers. Lord Acton once stated that "Power tends to corrupt and absolute power corrupts absolutely."[11] The resulting imbalance of power generated by the NLRA tempted some union leaders to abuse their power in both labor relations externally and member relations internally. These abuses eventually caused a public outcry and, in turn, prompted further government intervention into labor-management affairs and the internal operation of unions.

If there is a lesson to be learned, it is this: Net power always flows to governmental authorities whenever the civil authority upsets existing power balances between parties in society. For, the civil authority is always the final arbiter between disputants in society. Therefore, a disputant should be very hesitant in seeking government-bestowed advantages against an antagonist. In practice, it seems that the first intervention by government creates a need for another, and another and yet another — in an unending series until both disputants lose the freedom to maneuver. For the "wronged" party always calls on the government to "even up" the balance.

There is little evidence that the resultant increase in government intervention has really helped labor-management relations in these United States. But there is much evidence that it has hindered the healthy development of negotiations. Now there is a noted tendency on both sides of the labor-management table to move away from free market bargaining in favor of arriving at solutions through government mandate or at least through "moral suasion" by government officials. The reason for this is obvious: One party or the other usually hopes that the expected mandated solution will favor its side. That such interventions usually favor unions is only natural in a society where union members outnumber employers at the ballot box. Thus, important decisions become more and more based on "political clout" instead of economic realities.

In this chapter, we have briefly reviewed the historical development of labor unions and labor legislation. The next chapter will analyze them economically.

Questions

1. State concisely the economic relationship that exists between the employee-employer and the customer. In what way can the customer be regarded as the employer of both?

2. What major responsibility does the employer have in the business firm relative to employees? What major responsibility does the employee have?

---

[11] John Emerich Edward Dalberg-Acton, Lord Acton, in a letter to Bishop Mandell Creighton, April 5, 1887, quoted in John Bartlett, *Familiar Quotations,* 14th ed. rev. and enl. (Boston: Little, Brown and Co., 1968), p. 750.

3. Is the economic relationship between employee and employer antagonistic or cooperative? Explain.

4. Paraphrase in your own words the apostle Paul's philosophy of labor-management relations.

5. How did the shift from one-man production units, to master-journeymen shops, to factories set the stage for the development of labor unions?

6. Who was Samuel Gompers? What was his view of the socialists/communists?

7. What was the "enclosure movement" in England? What impact did it have on wage levels and living conditions of working people?

8. Defend or counter this statement: "Low wage levels during the Industrial Revolution in England were caused by greedy businessmen who unfairly exploited the helpless masses."

9. If Karl Marx had lived in these United States during the last half of the nineteenth century, do you think he would have developed his theories of "labor exploitation" and "the reserve army of the unemployed"? Why or why not?

10. What impact did the Commonwealth vs. Hunt case have regarding labor unions?

11. Contrast the philosophy held by the Knights of Labor and the American Federation of Labor.

12. What percentage of the work force belonged to unions in 1900? What percentage today? Has the percentage increased or decreased during the last two decades?

13. What impact did the National Labor Relations Act have on union membership? Explain.

14. Explain the difference between closed shop, union shop and open shop.

15. The Norris-LaGuardia Act outlawed the "yellow dog" contract, and Section 14-B of the Taft-Hartley Act outlaws (in Right-to-Work states) forcing a worker to join a union as a condition of employment. Do you favor one, both or neither of these laws? Why or why not? Can a person logically be in favor of one and against the other? Explain.

16. What has been the net impact of government intervention into labor-management relations? Who has been the net recipient of power?

2

Labor Economics

. . . Go ye also into the vineyard, and whatsoever is right I will give you. . . .

Matthew 20:4

THE **goals** of labor unions are to do the following for union members:

(1) to raise wages (which includes reduced hours of work for the same pay),
(2) to gain improved working conditions and
(3) to gain more economic security.

Another important goal, which is usually not openly stated but which is nevertheless legitimate, is to secure "status" for workers who are members. One of the strongest psychological drives people feel is the need to be respected and appreciated as individuals—that is, to feel that they are "persons of worth." We all have such a need.

The impersonal atmosphere that generally exists in large factories and in large work groups fosters a deep psychological need to be respected as an individual. Belonging to a union that has "clout" with the employer is one means the unidentified worker can adopt to receive immediate "status" as a person with whom to be reckoned. This fourth goal is probably even more important than the first three combined; for wage levels, working conditions and economic security all tend to improve anyway over the long haul regardless of the existence of unions. They tend to improve right along with the general increase in productivity which results from increased capital investment and technological advances.

The **means** labor unions apply to attain their goals are:

(1) gaining monopoly control over employer's labor supplies and
(2) influencing the passage of legislation that unions deem favorable to their cause.

The **weapons** used by unions are the strike (primary boycott), picket lines, secondary boycotts and threats of illegal force. This last weapon, of course, is always applied "unofficially" so that individuals within the union, or even outsiders, are blamed rather than the union itself. There has been a noted tendency for law enforcement officials to "wink" at union excesses for which ordinary citizens would be arrested. Example: The use of force by pickets to stop persons from crossing a picket line. Example: Bombings of employers' facilities in Pennsylvania and West Virginia coal mining districts that hired non-union workers during the 1980 coal miners' strike.

An employee strikes or imposes a primary boycott when he withholds his labor services from his employer. Union members regard striking as different from quitting a job because they hope to return to the vacated job after the labor dispute is over. Thus they will often use force to keep other job seekers from accepting the jobs they have vacated. A striking worker, in effect, chooses not to work temporarily; but he does not want "his job" to be available to anyone else, lest his act of striking lose its economic clout on the employer, who is faced with meeting the continued expense of maintaining his plant. Workers whom an employer hires to replace striking employees, who from the employer's viewpoint have voluntarily quit, are colorfully referred to by union members as "scabs."

Picket lines are set up by unions during labor disputes to advertise the union's side of the dispute to the general public. The picket line helps gain a form of moral suasion, helps secure cooperation from other unions, and also helps to intimidate customers, suppliers and other employees from carrying on their usual business with the offending employer. Members of one union will not generally cross a picket line which has been set up by another union. This interunion cooperation serves to impose additional economic pressure on the employer by cutting off his supplies of raw materials and his outlets for finished goods. Hopefully, from the union's point of view, this will hasten the employer's submission to the union's demands.

An Economic Analysis of Labor Unions

The economic effect of unions on wage rates and employment is shown graphically in Graph 2:1. If a union can gain control over the supply of labor, it can restrict the supply available to an employer at any given price. Let curve D indicate the existing demand of the employer for the labor services of workers. Let curve S_1 indicate the supply of labor services which would be offered for sale to the employer in an unrestricted labor market. The intersection of the two curves at point A indicates the amount of labor services offered and purchased (Q_1) and the price paid (W_1). At wage W_1 everyone who is willing to work for that wage is employed.[1]

Now suppose a union successfully unionizes the employer's workers, thereby gaining some degree of monopoly control over the supply of labor. Since the union is generally interested in raising wages above the free market level — which it assumes, according to Marx, leads to unfair labor exploitation

---

[1]A more detailed explanation of supply-demand curve analysis is given in Tom Rose, *Economics: Principles and Policy* (Milford, Mich.: Mott Media, 1977), Chapter 9.

Graph 2:1

Restricted Labor Supply

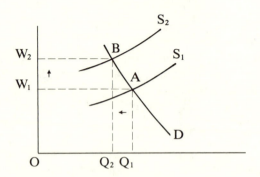

through depressed wages—the union will seek to restrict the supply of labor available to the employer in order to bring about a wage increase. Graphically the supply of labor will shift upwards or to the left from S_1 to S_2. The new point of equilibrium will move along the demand schedule (curve) D to point B. The resultant wage will be W_2, which is higher than the free market level. The quantity of labor services demanded by the employer at the higher wage will be Q_2, which is less than the free market full-employment level. Employees who are disemployed because the employer cannot use as many workers at the higher wage must then seek employment elsewhere or remain unemployed. In effect, the economic cost of the rise in wages gained by workers who continue to be employed is borne by those unfortunate workers who lose their jobs. The net effect on the individual firm and the effect on the general labor market is shown in Graphs 2:2 and 2:3.

Graph 2:2

Individual Firm

Graph 2:3

The General (non-Union) Labor Market

The number of workers who are disemployed by the company is equivalent to Q_1 minus Q_2. These workers now shift over to the general (non-unionized) labor market (Graph 2:3), thereby increasing the available supply of non-union workers from Q_1 to Q_2. The end result is to depress wage levels in the non-union labor market from W_1 to W_2.

Question: Does it pay to belong to a union if higher wages are gained at the expense of some workers being laid off?

Answer: It depends on who you are. Yes, it pays those union members who continue to work and who are thus able to enjoy the rise in wage levels. But the cost of the higher wages is borne by those union members who are forced to shift to non-union employment as well as workers in the non-union sector whose wages are depressed by the influx of ousted union workers. When we view the economy as a whole, it thus becomes evident that unions do not raise wage levels in general but rather that employed union members gain only at the expense of other workers — both union and non-union — who are either disemployed on a long-term basis or who are relegated to lower paying jobs.

Question: Are labor unions the only workingmen's associations that attempt to raise wages by restricting the supply of labor to a market?

Answer: No! Some professional associations have been very successful in doing the same as labor unions, even more succesful. Professional medical associations (doctors, dentists and others) have been very adept in getting the civil authorities to enact licensing laws and prescription laws which prohibit non-licensed persons from either practicing or having access to medicinal drugs. Also, lengthy periods of study and training have been required before a person can enter medical practice. The professional associations defend their efforts of gaining monopoly control to exclude would-be practitioners on a "We need to protect the public from quacks" basis.

The economic effect of licensing and the general critical viewpoint we present of it here was upheld by a medical doctor who recently gave the commencement address at a Texas school of medicine. In his address to graduating seniors the doctor asked for whose benefit licensing is promoted. Is licensing aimed at helping the public, or is it designed to help members of the licensed profession? His unequivocal answer was that state licensing laws help those in the profession by elevating their prestige and raising professional incomes. The doctor also raised a question concerning the validity of licensing, pointing out that the practice of licensing began about 200 years ago out of self-interest versus the interest of the public.

When the author wrote to the speaker to ask permission to quote him, he replied in a letter:

> I am, of course, flattered that you recall my remarks. First of all
> I would not have put the issue quite as you have done; secondly
> there are new aspects of the issue that have developed in the last five
> years. Let me make some points:

I was not speaking so much of physicians and dentists who have been universally licensed for more than a century, but of the newer health occupations that seek licensing and/or certification and/or hospital regulations as devices for 1) enhancing professional prestige, 2) restricting scope of practice. I suppose that, derivatively, these goals could tend to enhance income, but I don't believe that increased income is the conscious primary motivation. . . .

. . . A scenario that may be of interest to you is one being acted out here in the District of Columbia. A hospital licensure bill currently before the City Council would require hospitals to grant staff privileges to nurse midwives, psychologists, and several other categories of independent practitioners. It has sent the Medical Society into a tizzy. A compromise is being reached, but the outcome will be a clear erosion of exclusive physician control of diagnosis and management in the hospital setting.

. . . In summary, I would say that "licensure" is not the only mechanism that occupations use to "protect territory" and enhance prestige. While higher income is not usually the primary motivation, I won't deny that it often has that effect. I think your metaphor of the long lines in the physician's office is off the mark. Long lines today are only encountered in the ever fewer underserved areas where regulation and restriction is no issue at all. Those communities that are underserved are those where physicians do not choose to live or work. In the high priced urban markets, competition is such that lines are non-existent. . . . The fact is that the larger the number of physicians competing with each other, the fewer the patients each will see, and the higher the required fee for each service in order to maintain income. So much for conventional marketplace economics.

It is of interest to note that the doctor regards the **principle** of licensing as **good** when applied to medical doctors but as **not** good when applied to the newer health occupations who wish to enjoy the same benefits of protection as the doctors. Note that he does agree that higher incomes, though possibly not directly intended, is certainly a result of licensing.

The same "We need to eliminate quacks" argument can be used by electricians, plumbers, auto mechanics or any other industry group that favors laws which restrict legal practice to "duly licensed persons." But the net economic effect of licensing is always to substantially raise the wage levels in the protected industry by making it illegal for many would-be competitors to sell their skills in the marketplace. This also explains why the medical profession is almost unique in having its customers, that is, its patients, endure long waiting lines in their offices waiting for appointments. In short, licensed professions can more readily be centered on the convenience of the practitioners rather than on the convenience of the customers. The next time you face a long waiting period for an appointment, think of the economics behind your wait. The explanation is that the medical profession as a group of workingmen has been eminently more successful in restricting the supply of labor to the market than many other workingmen's associations. The licensed professions, in general, have been so successful in selling their program of restricting the supply of labor to the market that the public has accepted the illusion that such protection is in their own best interest! The public's acceptance has been so universal and people in general are so blind to the economics of licensing, that any move toward freer markets by eliminating licensing laws would be strongly resisted by the public—the very group who unknowingly bears the full brunt of the extra costs.

For a graphic example of what happens to the incomes of persons who work in a licensed profession, refer to Graph 2:1. The supply-demand curve analysis is exactly the same: The supply curve shifts to the left and intersects the demand curve at a higher point, indicating that the reduced supply of services causes prices to consumers and incomes of the practitioners to go up.

Wage Levels Set by Agreement or by Legislation

The effect of establishing wage levels above the free market level—either by contract with an employer or a group of employers, or through minimum wage legislation is shown in Graph 2:4. In a free labor market, the demand and supply for labor services will equilibrate at point A. The wage level will be W_1 and the quantity of labor services purchased will be Q_1. No unemployment will exist, for all who are willing to work at wage W_1 can find work. Those who are not willing to sell their labor services for wage W_1 voluntarily withdraw from the labor market, so they cannot be said to be unemployed in the sense that they are actively looking for work. These people are represented by the portion of the supply curve S from point A and upward to the right. When we say that no unemployment will exist, we are referring to long-term institutional unemployment. In any free labor market, a certain percentage of people will always be in the process of changing jobs. This is called "frictional unemployment" and is natural to a free society.

So far we see that point A represents the free market point of equilibrium where supply equals demand. But now suppose the legislature passes a bill mandating that employers cannot pay workers less than wage level W_2. What happens? Employers, whose demand schedule for labor services is depicted by curve D, find that the amount of labor services they can profitably use at the higher legally mandated wage is reduced. Thus, the quantity of labor services they can profitably use shifts along the demand curve from point A to point B. At wage level W_2 employers can only use the lesser amount of labor indicated at Q_2.

This move alone would be sufficient to create unemployment, but some-

Graph 2:4

*Wage Set Above the Free
Market Level — by Agreement
or by Legislation*

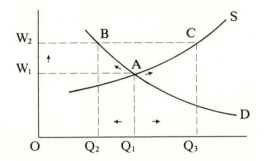

thing else also happens. Since the government authority has mandated a higher wage, some workers who were previously withholding their labor services at the lower W_1 level now rush into the market seeking the higher wage to which the government says that workers are entitled. These workers are depicted by the supply line segment A-C.

The end result of the government's intervention by mandating a higher-than-free-market level of wages is not only that **fewer** people are actually employed than before (a drop from Q_1 to Q_2), but also that **more** people want to work at the higher legally mandated wage (a rise in the number of unemployed workers from Q_1 to Q_3). In summary, the labor market moves from a condition of full employment equilibrium at point A to a chronic condition of unemployment in which the number of unemployed persons is depicted by a line drawn between points B and C (or between Q_2 and Q_3). Instead of helping workers by ordering a wage level higher than can be obtained through the free market, the governmental intervention actually hurts marginal workers by causing them to be disemployed and by inviting new workers into the market whose higher wage expectations cannot be met. Disappointment and frustration are increased in both directions.

This condition of chronic unemployment will remain as long as the legally mandated wage level effectively disemploys marginal workers whose productivity will not sustain the higher wage and as long as the higher mandated wage continues to attract new workers who cannot actually find a job at the higher legal wage. This explains the persistent high rate of unemployment among teenagers, the unskilled and minority groups. The sad effect of government-mandated wage laws has been to exclude large segments of our population from finding productive work because their productivity is not sufficient to justify the wage employers are required to pay by law. Thereby, such excluded workers are prevented from gaining needed skills to work their way up the employment ladder. Would it not be much more humane to let young people, the unskilled and minorities find work at whatever wage they can so that they could gain needed skills which would arm them with bargaining power to obtain higher paying jobs? Such workers could soon make worthwhile contributions to society economically, and their incomes would soon reflect this fact by higher take-home pay. The cost of government welfare payments would be reduced, and so would the size of the government bureaucracy which administers welfare programs. In addition, the opportunity for idle hands to seek criminal avenues to generate income would be reduced.

Labor unions have been strong agitators for increasing the legally mandated minimum wage under the belief that minimum wage laws serve to boost union members' wages. Their thinking is that most employers maintain wage differentials between entry workers and experienced workers. But such laws clearly reduce the number of job opportunities available to marginal workers. Such laws also, as mentioned previously, increase pressures on government to provide "busy work" or welfare payments to workers who are idled; and they also lead to pressures for the government to serve as an "employer of last resort." In short, the long-range effect of minimum wage laws is to encourage government-sponsored programs which result in the growth of a socialistic state which regards itself as a provider and caretaker of the people.

The Cleveland Trust Business Bulletin, October, 1977, reported that during the 22-year period from 1954 to 1976, adult unemployment averaged about 4 percent while teenage unemployment averaged about 15 percent. During this same 22-year period, the unemployment rate for Negroes and other minority groups averaged 26.8 percent versus 13.2 percent for white youths. Negro youth unemployment rose from 30.2 percent in 1973 to 35.9 percent in 1975. In 1976 unemployment for Negro youths averaged 37.1 percent and rose to an average of 38.6 percent in 1977. In the early 1980s the unemployment rate for minority youth rose to over 45 percent. Behind these cold statistics are many, many broken dreams and frustrated ambitions when large numbers of people find themselves more or less permanently excluded by legislative action from making worthwhile contributions to society.

A Further Look at the Minimum Wage

A minimum wage has been legally established in these United States since enactment of the so-called Fair Standards Labor Act of 1938. Economists have been debating the economic effects of the minimum wage law ever since. Some economists claim, as presented in the previous section, that young people and minority groups are unfairly priced out of the labor market by legally imposed restraints. Other economists claim that studies in the 1940s and 1950s of unemployment relative to rises in legally imposed minimums show that employment has even risen after higher limits have been imposed. Who is right?

Classical economic theory would agree with those economists who hold that legally mandated wage rates above the free market level will tend to disemploy marginal workers. One explanation of the lack of detrimental effects

Table 2:1

Minimum Wage Legislation, 1938-1981

Year	Legal Wage		Minimum Wage Related to Average Hourly Wage in Manufacturing
1938	$0.25	—	40.3%
1939	.30	39.8%	47.8
1945	.40	29.5	39.4
1950	.75	27.8	52.1
1956	1.00	38.5	51.2
1961	1.15	43.1	49.5
1963	1.25	46.7	50.8
1967	1.40	44.1	49.4
1968	1.60	46.5	53.1
1974	2.00	36.3	45.4
1975	2.10	42.3	44.5
1976	2.30	41.0	44.9
1978	2.65	43.0	48.0
1979	2.90	40.2	44.0
1980	3.10	41.7	44.1
1981	3.35	—	—

Source: *U.S. News & World Report,* September 14, 1981, p. 13.

Table 2:2

Unemployment

	1980*	1981**	1982**	1983**
All Workers	7.1%	7.6%	9.7%	10.4%
Minority Teenagers	38.5	41.4	48.0	45.4
All Teenagers	17.8	19.6	23.2	22.2
Negro	14.3	15.6	18.9	19.7
Hispanic	10.1	10.4	13.8	15.8
Women	6.4	6.8	8.3	8.9
Men	5.9	6.3	8.8	9.9

Source: *U.S. Department of Labor, Monthly Labor Review,* January 1983, p. 74; and **Ibid., April 1983, p. 55.

of minimum wage legislation during the 1940s and 1950s can be explained by the percentage of persons covered. In 1938 the minimum wage law covered only 43.4 percent of non-supervisory employees, but in 1977 the law covered 87.3 percent of such workers. Thus, the law is now harder to escape; it is more potent in its economic effect today than it was in earlier years. Table 2:1 shows rises in the minimum wage rate and Table 2:2 and Table 2:3 show recent levels of unemployment.

Table 2:3

Teenage Unemployment

Year	All	Negro
1976	19.0%	39.2%
1977	17.7	41.1
1978	16.3	38.6
1979	16.1	36.5
1980	17.7	38.6
1981	19.6	41.4
1982	23.2	48.0
1983	22.2	45.4

Source: Data for 1976-1981 from *U.S. News & World Report,* March 3, 1981, p. 81; and Data for 1982-1983 from U.S. Department of Labor, *Monthly Labor Review*, April 1983, p. 55.

The Question of Unemployment Benefits

One government program that has almost universal popular acceptance but which has very deleterious economic effects generally is unemployment compensation. Under this government-sponsored program employers pay approximately 3 percent of a worker's base wage into a government-administered fund. Workers who are disemployed through no fault of their own are then paid a certain amount per week for up to six months while they are supposed to look for other work. The idea is to provide workers with a minimal floor of income and thus to reduce the economic shock of having their flow of earned income terminated.

It is difficult to speak against a seemingly beneficial program designed to help the unfortunate, for to be opposed to putting a floor under unemployed workers' incomes would seem to classify the opponent as a callous or hard-hearted individual. But, in truth, while the receipt of unemployment benefits appears to help the **individual** worker when we view him in isolation, the program works out exactly the opposite when we view the impact of unemployment compensation of **all** workers as a whole. How can this be so?

It works out like this: The availability of a flow of unearned income will cause disemployed workers to take longer to return to work than otherwise. Some workers will use these unearned funds to keep testing the market while searching out the highest paying job available. But others will use the funds to unduly procrastinate—some will just loaf, some will take jobs that pay off-the-record income while continuing to accept unemployment compensation, while still others will pursue various interests such as hunting, fishing or working at their favorite hobbies. Almost everyone in our society knows at least a few persons who have received "rocking chair money" while not seriously looking for work. One long-term unemployed man who receives unemployment compensation payments looks for work every Wednesday morning; the rest of the week he devotes to off-the-record income-producing activities.

The existence of unemployment compensation benefits coupled with supplemental unemployment benefits (SUB) has been particularly harmful to the U.S. auto industry. These two programs—one a government program and the other a union-sponsored program—bring the take-home pay of laid-off auto workers up to 90 percent of their regular take-home pay. Is it any wonder, in such an instance, that workers have pulled seniority rank to be laid off first? Even workers who are laid off, perhaps against their wishes, have little economic incentive to seriously look for other above-board income-producing work until their benefits begin to run out; thus they tend to sit idly around waiting to be called back to work. There have been reports of United Auto Workers (UAW) union members who have held underground jobs while "waiting" to be rehired. These instances are repeated thousands upon thousands of times throughout the nation at any given time.

If we consider the macro effects of unemployment compensation programs, we see that the costs involved must be passed onto consumers in the form of higher prices; for employers, as we have pointed out before, must be able to recoup all their costs of production from consumers if they hope to stay in business. During the recession which started in 1979 and continued into 1983, the auto industry was particularly hard hit with sagging sales and high levels of unemployment. Other industries such as steel and rubber could also be cited. The combined cost of carrying large numbers of unemployed workers on unemployment and SUB adds considerably to the production costs that are built into American-made autos—costs which the auto manufacturers must ask the consumer to pay. This helps explain why the sale of American-made autos hit a 30-year low in 1982. Elimination of unemployment compensation and SUB would serve to immediately lower price tags to consumers, to quickly stimulate sales and to rapidly boost employment upwards. Another hidden aspect of eliminating such unemployment programs would be to give each unemployed worker an irresistible economic incentive to seek immediate re-employment after being laid off, even if it meant taking a lower paying job on a temporary basis. This would cause two things to happen: First, the increased supply of goods coming from the otherwise unemployed workers would cause prices to be lower. Secondly, the earned incomes of these workers would continue to stimulate demand for the services of other workers, thereby indirectly reducing unemployment elsewhere in the economy.

We are thus faced with a dilemma: Unemployment compensation programs, viewed from the individual worker's viewpoint in isolation, seems to be beneficial. But when their overall economic impact is weighed from a macro viewpoint, unemployment compensation programs can only be seen as counterproductive to the individual's welfare as both a worker and as a consumer.

Table 2:4

Detected Cases of Unemployment Compensation Cheating

1974	68,512	1978	126,636
1975	81,130	1979	142,726
1976	103,306	1980	175,722
1977	122,461		

Source: *U.S. News & World Report,* March 16, 1981, p. 63.

Union Influence

The relative influence of labor unions in the economy of these United States with regard to rising wage levels can be ascertained by noting the very small percentage of the civilian labor force that belonged to labor unions during most of our history (see Table 2:5). It must also be remembered that ordinary

Table 2:5

Union Membership

Year	Total*	Percentage of Labor Force
1800-1860	Less than 2% of labor force belonged to unions	
1860-1900	Less than 3% of labor force belonged to unions	
1900	.9	3.0
1910	2.1	5.6
1920	5.0	11.8
1930	3.4	6.8
1932	3.1	6.0
1934	3.1	5.9
1936	4.0	7.4
1938	8.0	14.6
1940	8.7	15.5
1942	10.4	17.2

Year	Total*	Percentage of Labor Force
1944	14.1	21.4
1946	14.4	23.6
1948	14.3	23.1
1950	14.3	22.3
1952	15.9	24.2
1954	17.0	25.4
1956	17.5	25.2
1958	17.0	24.2
1960	17.0	23.6
1962	16.6	22.6
1964	16.8	22.2
1966	17.9	22.7
1968	18.9	23.0
1970	19.4	22.6
1972	19.4	21.8
1974	20.2	21.8
1976	19.6	20.3
1978	20.2	19.7

Source: U.S. Bureau of Labor Statistics and U.S. Bureau of the Census.
*In millions.

factory workers and unskilled laborers had little opportunity to join labor unions until the advent of widespread industrialized unionism in the late 1930s, which was stimulated by passage of the National Labor Relations Act (Wagner Act) in 1935. Up until the early part of this century, the large majority of union members constituted a "labor elite" of highly skilled craftsmen who joined together in craft unions (carpenters, brick layers, stone masons, etc.). Thus, the large majority of unskilled workers who made up the bulk of the labor force was outside the labor union movement and little affected by it.

Understanding the Wage-Price Spiral

It is commonly believed by many people that labor unions are a major cause of inflation. (In popular terminology **inflation** is understood to mean rising prices. This is wrong. Inflation, correctly defined, means **an increase in the money supply** or **an injection of new money into the economy.** When the newly injected money is spent on the fixed amount of goods and services already existing in the economy, prices rise as a result. Thus, prior monetary inflation is the **cause** and a generally rising price level is the **result**.) But this is a problem for which labor unions cannot be held directly responsible. A persistent rise in the general price level is a **monetary** phenomenon. In these United States persistent rises in the general price level invariably occur because the federal government has created new money via deficit spending through the

Federal Reserve System. The Federal Reserve System is the avenue through which much new money is injected into the economy, which in turn causes prices to rise when recipients of the newly created money enter the marketplace to spend the dollars they have received. Therefore, neither labor unions nor employers can be held responsible for general rises in the price level.

It is not surprising that the public wrongly believes unions and business firms to be responsible for rising prices because government officials often point the finger of blame at them. The government officials know better, really, for their pointing the finger of blame at "wage-hungry unions" and "profit-greedy businessmen" is just a clever ruse practiced by demagogues to escape the blame which rightfully should fall on them. At worst, the only accomplishment that labor unions can point to by forcing wage rates above the free market level is unemployment.

In order to understand the so-called "wage-price spiral," study the much-simplified diagram and accompanying step-by-step sequence of events shown in Chart 2:1.

Chart 2:1

The Wage-Price Spiral

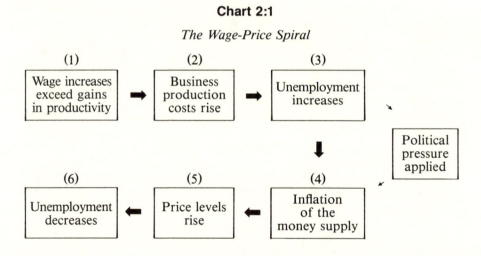

Step 1: Assume that labor unions succeed in forcing wage increases that exceed gains in productivity onto employers.

Step 2: The unearned rise in wages that union members receive causes the production costs of unionized business firms to rise. These employers will first attempt to pass their higher production costs on to consumers in the form of higher asking prices. This is the path of least resistance if it can be accomplished.

Step 3: When consumers balk at the higher prices businessmen attempt to get them to pay, the managers of these firms will be forced to cut costs internally. Since the cost of labor is the single largest cost factor over which businessmen have some degree of control, they will seek to reduce employment costs by laying off marginal workers and/or replacing high-cost labor with more productive machines by more highly automating their production processes. In either case, unemployment results because consumers refuse to adequately reimburse unionized employers for the higher labor costs their business firms have incurred.

Step 4: It is between steps 3 and 4 that an interesting phenomenon occurs. When the rate of unemployment rises above a certain point, the public becomes worried. And their worry is agitated by the cries of labor union leaders that "the government should do something about the high level of unemployment." Thus, an almost unbearable amount of political pressure is applied on Congress and the President. Being political creatures, the main concern of these elected officials is usually to do whatever is necessary to be reelected; so Congress and the President readily capitulate to the political pressures of the moment (for, who can be in favor of unemployment and remain popular with the masses of voters?!). Spending programs are hastily passed to "cure" the problem of unemployment through deficit government financing. When Congress passes deficit spending bills, new money is created through ready cooperation of the Federal Reserve Board. This newly created money is injected into the economy through massive government spending programs.

Step 5: The newly created money is received by individuals and business firms who are the recipients of government spending programs. These people quickly spend their funds. Because there has been no increase in the amount of goods and services in existence, there are relatively more dollars to spend on purchasing goods and services. Price levels start rising as people compete with each other to get the limited amount of goods and services that are available. Note that the phenomenon of generally rising price levels is the **result** of the prior monetary inflation, but this result is popularly misbranded as "inflation."

Step 6: As the government-induced monetary injections continue, prices continue to rise in response. When the price level reaches the point at which consumers balked in Step 3, consumers will begin to buy the higher priced goods they had previously refused because all other prices have risen in relation. As sales begin to pick up, business inventories start to fall; and business managers start to hire back the workers they had previously laid off. Unemployment gradually drops to the point at which it was before the unions had forced wage increases onto employers, and the whole process is ready to begin all over again.

It is important to note in this sequence of events that, in the absence of government deficit financing (between Steps 3 and 4), a high level of unemployment among union members would continue until the unions backed down on their demand to get wages in excess of what they had earned through increased productivity. Without the government's validating the unearned increase in wages, the unjustified wage increase would have to be rescinded, business costs would return to their earlier level and fuller employment would be restored.

Validation of the unearned wage increase through government deficit spending accomplishes the same purpose of restoring fuller employment, but with crucially important side effects. Fuller employment is restored for the union members who are re-employed; and the wage, in monetary terms, is also higher. So, the employed union members really do not suffer when conditions are restored. But — and this is a big **but** — because of the government deficit spending, the general price level has risen. This means that **everybody** is now paying higher prices, even workers who have not received increases in pay and persons who are living on fixed incomes — such as retired people. In short, in order to "bail out" militant labor unions from a situation which they have created and which they doggedly refuse to rescind, Congress and the President find it politically expedient to become parties to an insidious plan of secretly taxing the whole population through what is called the "secret tax of inflation." Not only is this bad economics, it is bad morality; for the process allows some parts of society to benefit while foisting the cost onto society as a whole.

If everyone's income rose equally through the monetary inflation process, there would be no problem; but this never happens. Some groups of workers are more successful in forcing wage levels upward than other groups are. As the spiralling process of forcing unearned wage increases onto employers and having them validated through government expansion of the money supply continues, it becomes a matter of plundering other segments of society before they plunder you. Society tends to break down into hostile camps which wage economic war on each other — society disintegrates into warring factions.

The whole process explained above poses a serious moral question: Is it morally defensible for the federal government to engage in monetary inflation to "bail out" one segment of society when the very act of doing so robs other persons and segments who have not caused the problem? Is such a validating process not equivalent to "legalized theft" even though it might be a very sophisticated form of thievery? Does the commandment "Thou shalt not steal" apply in this instance? This is, of course, a **normative** question; but the **positive** process of tracing cause-effect patterns in the wage-price spiral is what brings the normative issue in focus. Let us make an important point here. Most of the difficult economic problems we face in this world are the result of wrong **moral** choices we have made in the past. This is certainly true of the widespread problem of high levels of unemployment coupled with generally rising price levels which we have experienced during the last two decades.

Let us lean over backwards to be fair. Union spokesmen would disagree with the sequence shown in Chart 2:1. They would argue that Step 5 is the point at which to begin and that higher wages are required to bring union members' purchasing power back to normal. In other words, they would claim that prices rise **first** and that wages rise in **response** to union efforts to restore lost purchasing power through needed wage increases. The difficulty with this line of reasoning is that it does not explain what caused Congress and the President to inject new money into the economy through deficit spending. Also, the argument ignores the fact that Keynes and his followers have clearly admitted that their recommended solution for curing unemployment is to use the government as a means of inflating the economy. It is true that, once the wage-price spiral process starts, a person can begin his economic analysis at any of the previously described steps. But wherever one starts his analysis, the **key factor** in causing the spiral to go round and round is the government's act of

Graph 2:5

Productivity, Compensation, and Labor Costs

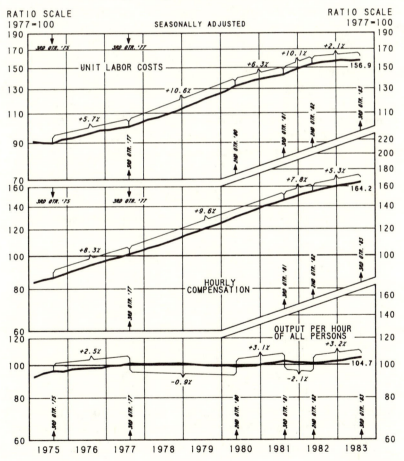

Source: Federal Reserve Bank of St. Louis, *National Economic Trends,* January 1984, p. 11.

creating new money and injecting it into the economy. Without this crucial factor there could be no long-continued wage-price spiral.

Is there any data which can be used to ascertain whether labor unions push for higher wages to compensate for prices which have **already** risen, or whether labor unions force higher wages onto employers which are then **later** validated through government inflation of the money supply and subsequent rises in the general price level?

The preceding set of graphs (Graph 2:5) correlates hourly compensation and productivity with resulting unit labor costs. The graphs show that hourly wage rates, which include both union and non-union workers, have generally outpaced rises in productivity. Accordingly, these data would tend to support the thesis that unearned increases in wage levels do indeed create higher labor costs to employers which, if not validated by inflationary increases in the money supply and subsequent rises in the general price level, would otherwise produce higher levels of unemployment. In the five-year period from April, 1976, to March, 1981, for instance, hourly wages rose 9.4 percent per year while productivity rose by only 0.6 percent per year. The rise in unit labor costs during the same period of time was 8.8 percent per year.[2] It is interesting to see what happened to wages, productivity and unit labor costs during the recession years of 1981 and 1982 with the rate of unemployment approaching 10 percent. From January, 1981, to December, 1982, wages rose 7.1 percent; productivity rose 0.8 percent; while unit labor costs rose 6.2 percent.[3] These

Table 2:6

Comparison of Hourly Compensation and Productivity

Year	Hourly Compensation	Productivity*
1976	8.3%	3.5%
1977	7.9	1.5
1978	8.6	0.5
1979	8.9	-1.1
1980	10.2	-1.4
1981	7.9	-0.7
1982	6.3	1.1
1983	4.4	4.3

Source: *U.S. News & World Report,* July 18, 1980, p. 58; and Federal Reserve Bank of St. Louis, *National Economic Trends,* January 1984, p. 10.

*Productivity figures are for hourly output among non-farm workers in private industry.

---

[2] Federal Reserve Bank of St. Louis, *National Economic Trends,* December 31, 1981, p. 10.
[3] Ibid., April 1983, p. 10.

relative shifts are a normal occurrence during a recession. Actually, it would take a greater drop in wages along with a greater increase in productivity to bring about a hoped-for decrease in unit labor costs in order to spur employment.

The year by year comparison of labor costs and productivity in Table 2:6 corresponds with the data shown in Graph 2:5.

Impact of Militant Unionism

The impact of militant unionism on an industry can be seen in the steel industry in these United States. Most large integrated steel mills are unionized. As a result of their aggressive tactics, unionized steelworkers have been successful in imposing higher wage costs on their employers. Table 2:7, which

Table 2:7

Average Hourly Earnings, 1961-1980

Year	All Manufacturing	Steel Industry	Spread in Favor of Steelworkers
1961	$2.32	$3.20	$0.88
1962	2.39	3.29	.90
1963	2.46	3.36	.90
1964	2.53	3.41	.88
1965	2.61	3.46	.85
1966	2.72	3.58	.86
1967	2.83	3.62	.79
1968	3.01	3.82	.81
1969	3.19	4.09	.90
1970	3.36	4.22	.86
1971	3.57	4.57	1.00
1972	3.81	5.15	1.34
1973	4.07	5.56	1.49
1974	4.40	6.38	1.98
1975	4.81	7.11	2.30
1976	5.19	7.86	2.67
1977	5.63	8.67	3.04
1978	6.17	9.70	3.53
1979	6.69	10.77	4.08
1980	7.27	11.84*	4.57

Source: American Iron and Steel Institute.

*The inclusion of fringe benefits raised the 1980 total wage to over $20.00 per hour.

does not include the cost of fringe benefits, shows how steelworkers have gradually overpriced themselves in the marketplace.

The hourly wage rate of $11.84 for the steel industry in 1980 compares with $9.89 per hour earned by members of the United Auto Workers Union (neither wage rate includes the cost of fringe benefits). According to the objective signals registered in the marketplace — that is, by the high level of unemployment experienced by both steelworkers and auto workers during the early part of the 1980s — both groups have tended to price themselves out of the market.

The average wage of steelworkers in 1980 was 64 percent greater than the average wage of workers in all manufacturing ($11.84 ÷ $7.27 = $1.63). It would take an extremely high level of technology and capitalization (i.e., investment) to make workers who are paid 64 percent above the average to be competitive price-wise with other workers. But the truth is that the excessively high wages paid to steelworkers have hindered steel companies by draining income from them and reducing profit levels. Thus, the steel companies have not modernized their plants as they otherwise would have done. Instead, steel company managements have opted to run plants until they wear out and/or become obsolete before the companies close them down. U.S. Steel Company, the industry leader, for instance, closed down 14 plants in 1981. Other large steel companies have done the same, closing down their highest cost, most inefficient plants. In some instances, the plant closings were announced tentatively, giving the concerned unionized workers the option of keeping the plants open if the workers would accept cuts in pay.

We see in Table 2:8 how foreign steel imports have grown hand-in-hand with the excessive rise in steelworkers' wages.

Table 2:8

Steel Imports as a Percentage of Domestic Consumption

Year	Imports	Year	Imports	Year	Imports
1961	4.7%	1968	16.7%	1975	13.5%
1962	5.6	1969	13.7	1976	14.1
1963	6.9	1970	13.8	1977	17.8
1964	7.3	1971	17.9	1978	18.1
1965	10.3	1972	16.6	1979	15.2
1966	10.9	1973	12.4	1980	16.3
1967	12.2	1974	13.4	1981	19.1

Source: American Iron and Steel Institute.

For years, the steel companies as well as the steelworkers' union have petitioned the U.S. government for help, claiming that the surge in foreign imports is unfairly subsidized by foreign governments. There is no doubt that much foreign steel sold in our country is priced somwhat below its full cost of production in the foreign country as a result of certain foreign governments' policies to keep their plants operating. But to the extent that such subsidies are given, the subsidies amount to a gift from foreigners to the people of these United States because they are selling to us below their total cost of production.

The real question to ask is: How should this competition be met? Should it be met politically by government fiat to exclude foreign steel? This would only end up by allowing steel firms and steelworkers in the U.S. to push their higher production costs and higher wages onto American consumers through higher prices. Instead of foreign steel producers voluntarily subsidizing American consumers, the government protection route would result in American consumers being forced to subsidize the high wages of domestic union workers and to pay the penalty of steel company managements' failure to take a firm stance against unwarranted wage demands.

At the time of this writing, the free market process is well under way **without** government interference. Both the steelworkers' union and the steel company managements have been, however unwillingly, forced to face the rigors of the competitive marketplace. Unemployment among unionized steelworkers has remained very high, and company profits have been either very low or negative. Market forces have forced managements to close down even more plants, and the threat of more closings in the future has softened the previously militant attitude of the unionized workers. As a result, a healthier atmosphere of worker-management cooperation is developing. How long it will last no one knows. However, progress in raising productivity has been made. The previously uncontrolled spiral in wage rates has definitely slowed, workers have been willing to make some helpful concessions in work rules and practices which allow increased output and company stockholders are now finding it more attractive to invest the needed capital into modernizing their plants and equipment. The net effect of this "new look" is that the break-even point of capacity in the steel industry has been lowered dramatically. In the late 1970s the break-even point was about 82 percent of capacity, but today is around 70 percent and heading lower. As new technology continues to be introduced, and if the unions remain cooperative, the profitability level of the American steel industry may drop toward 60 percent of operating capacity. At this level of efficiency, it would be impossible for foreign steelmakers to undercut American steel companies; for the American firms and their employees would be just as efficient in producing steel as their competitive counterparts overseas. Thus, though the present situation may not be a pleasant one for steelworkers' unions and steel companies to endure, the future—assuming needed self-disciplinary measures continue to be taken by the unions and company managements to correct the evils they brought upon themselves—looks much brighter.

Would Free Market Unionism Work?

Labor union leaders hold strongly to the position that they should be able to negotiate contracts with employers which **require** workers to become members of a union as a condition of employment. They believe that enough workers will not voluntarily join unions and that union strength will thereby decrease unless this form of coercion is applied. The union view is that, if a union successfully negotiates a higher wage rate or better working conditions, the non-union workers should **not** be left in a position to enjoy union-produced benefits as "free riders." This argument is based on the presupposition that workers never receive increased pay or better working conditions outside of union efforts—a presupposition that is not borne out by the historical evidence of long-term rises in pay during periods in which union influence in the economy was neglible. Even today membership in labor unions is only about 20 percent of the total labor force—and this includes about three million persons in associations which are counted as unions, plus about four million public employees, many of whom have been just recently added to union rolls by legislative permit.

The union argument also overlooks the fact that the so-called "free riders" are **required by law** (the NLRA of 1935) to acquiesce to the terms of the union-negotiated contract even if they would prefer **not** to be included. In the absence of such a legal requirement, non-union members would be free to bargain with management separately and perhaps receive higher wages based on their own productivity.

Some observers feel that labor unions could indeed exist and prosper **without** using force to make unwilling workers join, but doing so would require a change in union philosophy in order to convince workers of the merits of joining. The following editorial column presents the idea of voluntary unionism.

Free Market Unionism

Is the idea of labor unions in direct conflict with the ideal of individual freedom and self-responsibility? Or is it possible that a labor union could be operated to the benefit of all concerned without impinging on anyone's liberties?

I contend that the idea of collective bargaining via a labor union is not inherently in conflict with the free enterprise ideal, but a free enterprise-style union would certainly operate on a much different basis than unions do today.

Today (as well as in the past) unions operate on the basis of force, which is contrary to the ideal of freedom and self-responsibility. If 51 employees of a 100-employee group vote in favor of union and representation, then the 49 employees who voted against union representation are forced to allow the union to represent them, too. In effect, the 49 employees who do not want a union become unwilling participants to a contract they do not want. In "right-to-work" states, the 49 unwilling passengers on the union boat cannot be forced to join the union and pay dues. But in "union shop" states, the unwilling 49 can be forced to join and pay dues if they do not want to be forced to quit their jobs. Their choice is join or quit! This choice is forced upon them by the National Labor Relations Act (Wagner Act) of 1935, which has the net effect of putting unions in a strong monopoly position.

But how could a union operate on a strictly free enterprise basis?

I have sometimes dreamed of starting a truly revolutionary union movement which I believe would be welcomed by employers and the consuming public with open arms. It would work like this:

First, this free enterprise union would be strictly voluntary. No one would be forced to join it. In matter of fact, employees could join only upon invitation, and the union would represent only those employees who were members in good standing. All non-member employees would be left to negotiate separately with their employer. (Note: The NLRA of 1935 outlaws this kind of voluntary arrangement, so the law would have to be changed to allow the kind of voluntary unionism we are talking about.)

Why would employees want to join such a voluntary union? Because the union would conduct continuous training programs for its members to increase their productivity and thereby their worth to their employer. Since the wage each employee received would be based on productivity instead of the outmoded system of threatening to go out on strike, employees would be eager to join if the union's productivity engineers did a competent job. On the average, members of such a voluntary union would be more productive workers than non-members; so they could command a higher wage in the labor market.

But what if the employer refused to go along with the unions' opinion of how much its employees are worth? There would never be a need to use any form of coercion or threat to strike. The union would merely test the market. It would advise the employer, "We think our members' higher productivity warrants your paying such and such a wage. Since you do not agree, we will attempt to place them in higher paying jobs with competing employers. So please be expecting to receive a number of quit notices as we find jobs for member employees who are willing to leave your employ." If the union indeed overcalculated the worth of its members' productivity, then it would not be successful in finding higher paying jobs. But if, on the other hand, its productivity calculations were correct, then member employees would gradually shift out of the company's employ. As the loss of productive employees continued to grow, the employer would experience a peaceful economic pressure which would cause him to change his mind and agree to a higher wage to prevent further losses. In short, wages would rise naturally in response to market pressures without animosity on the part of anyone. Peace would have entered union-management relations for the first time in history.

Employers would even welcome such a union with open arms. Why? Because new employers would be approached on this basis: "If you would like our union to represent employees in your plant, we will limit our requests for wage increases to only a portion of the increases in productivity which we are certain will result when our expert engineers sit down with your own engineers and share our knowledge of how to gain increased productivity via improved production techniques, better employee training and more willing worker cooperation which results from a consistent free enterprise approach to union-management relations. Our approach will thereby allow increased profits to owners while also providing lower prices for consumers."

Now, does this kind of unionism not make sense? Is it not time we start trying it?[4]

The Sabbath

The science of economics focuses on producing goods and services efficiently. Since economics is production oriented, it may seem strange to discuss the need for periodic rest. But God Himself, who was certainly production oriented when He created the universe, states that He rested after His work of creation. And He admonishes man to rest from his labors also:

> *Remember the sabbath day, to keep it holy.*
> *Six days shalt thou labour, and do all thy work:*
> *But the seventh day is the sabbath of the Lord thy God: in it thou shalt not do any work, thou, nor thy son, nor thy daughter, thy manservant, nor thy maidservant, nor thy cattle, nor thy stranger that is within thy gates:*
> *For in six days the Lord made heaven and earth, the sea, and all that in them is, and rested the seventh day: wherefore the Lord blessed the sabbath day, and hallowed it.*
> *Exodus 20:8-11*

The Lord repeats His command concerning our honoring the sabbath in Deuteronomy, but in the second passage the emphasis is somewhat different:

> *And remember that thou wast a servant in the land of Egypt, and that the Lord thy God brought thee out thence through a mighty*

---

[4] *The Santa Ana* (Calif.) *Register*, 19 September 1976.

hand and by a stretched out arm: therefore the Lord thy God commanded thee to keep the sabbath day.
                                                    Deuteronomy 5:15

We see, then, that men are commanded to rest one day in seven as a memorial — first, as a memorial to God's work in creation; and, secondly, as a memorial to God's work in redeeming Israel. The prophet Ezekiel tells us that the sabbath is a sign between God and man, a sign of man's relationship to God (Ez. 20:12). Thus, we see that man is a religious being because of his spiritual relationship to his Creator. The fact that man is an economic being, a creature who chooses and acts rationally, is an outgrowth of his spiritual relationship to God.

A godly nation will observe the Lord's sabbath commandment, while those which fail to do so give outward evidence of their rebellion against God. The growing practice in our own country of "doing business as usual" on Sunday is an indication of our own growing apostasy. Our apostate practice carries with it the imminency of the social and economic curses which are visited upon a nation which refuses to live according to God's commands. "The wicked shall be turned into hell, and all the nations that forget God" (Ps. 9:17).

God's command to observe the sabbath is not only a religious requirement, for it deals with the economic and social aspect of man as well. First, let it be noted that man is an indivisible whole; he is, at the same time, both a religious and an economic being. All of man's activities are to be religious in that everything he thinks, says and does is to be worshipful of God and respectful of God's instituted law-order. While primarily a religious being, man also acts economically. Cessation of work one day in seven requires that man be economically productive and frugal in the six days which are allotted to him for working. The Bible also requires a sabbath year and a year of jubilee once every 50 years, that is, after seven sets of seven-year periods, or 49 years. During a 50-year period, man is to rest every seventh day, every seventh year and another whole year after seven sabbath years. In our modern age this may seem to men who are not guided by God's law as too much time off from economically productive activities. But God promises economic as well as spiritual blessings for those nations who obey His word:

> *If thou turn away thy foot from the sabbath, from doing thy pleasure on my holy day; and call the sabbath a delight, the holy of the Lord, honourable; and shalt honour him, not doing thine own ways, nor finding thine own pleasure, nor speaking thine own words:*
> *Then shalt thou delight thyself in the Lord; and I will cause thee to ride upon the high places of the earth, and feed thee with the heritage of Jacob thy father: for the mouth of the Lord hath spoken it.*
>   *Isaiah 58:13-14*

How can we summarize God's teaching about the sabbath? It seems evident, from a study of Scripture, that the nature of the sabbath is both ceremonial and moral. While it is true that Christ came to fulfill the ceremonial law, which is no longer incumbent upon us (Col. 2:13-17), the moral aspect of the sabbath still remains for man to observe. The moral aspect has not been removed by Christ's finished work on the cross, nor was it meant to be. Thus, the sabbath—while designed to be a day of refreshment and recuperation for man, for his animals and for his servants—is also to be a day of both rejoicing and resting in God's salvation. Apostate men will fail to see the spiritual and economic tie-in of which we speak. Man is to become spiritually refreshed while at the same time enjoying physical and mental rest from his economic pursuits. The sabbath is both spiritual and economic in its import because man is both a spiritual and an economic being.

God's word does not lay down minute details of how man is to honor the sabbath. Rather, God lays down broad principles for man's general guidance; for the sabbath is made for man and not man for the sabbath. We are admonished to turn away from seeking our own pleasure, and we are to delight in communing with the Lord. If we follow Jesus' example (Matt. 12:1-13; Mark 3:2-5), the sabbath is to be used for rest, for prayer, for fellowship, for doing works of mercy and for attending religious services.

An apostate world tends to overlook both the spiritual as well as the economic blessings which flow from observing the sabbath. On the one hand, apostate man places too much importance on the economic cost of allowing capital investments to lie idle and seemingly unproductive one day out of seven. On the other hand, apostate man gives too little significance to the promised social and economic blessings which flow from faithfully obeying God's word. We find Sunday work splitting up families, thereby denying them a special day of recreational fellowship. We also find overly industrious individuals working seven days out of seven until they finally succumb to stress-induced ill health and nervous breakdowns as the cost of "burning the candle at both ends."

Years ago farmers who relied on horsepower to do their work found out by experience that horses cannot stand up to a continuous regimen of working every day. They discovered that more total work was accomplished with better health to the animals by letting them rest one day out of seven. This is just a practical example that God's word applies as much to economic matters as to religious matters. Those who continually break the sabbath pursue a course that in the long run will be counter-productive economically.

Is There a Biblical View of Labor-Management Relations?

Any chapter dealing with employee-employer relations must delve into the antagonistic relationships which have developed in order to discuss the problems intelligently. In doing so, the reader is likely to get the idea that the relationship between workers and employers is naturally one of opposition. This is wrong because, as the author stated earlier, the employee-employer relation, viewed economically, is one of joint service to the consumer whose funds support both the employer and his workers. The antagonistic relationship which seems generally to exist is the result of ignorance (the failure of both employees and employers to recognize their mutuality of economic interest) and man's fallen nature (because of sin there is a tendency for each party to take advantage of the other if the opportunity should arise).

The biblical view of labor-management relations is that both parties are servants of the Lord in all that they do, including their mutual relationships, and that they should act honorably and kindly as a testimony to the other party. Serious Christians can gain policy direction in employee-employer affairs from the verses quoted earlier as well as those which immediately follow.

Servants [employees], be obedient to them that are your masters [employers] according to the flesh, with fear and trembling, in singleness of your heart, as unto Christ;

Not with eyeservice, as menpleasers; but as the servants of Christ, doing the will of God from the heart;

With good will doing service, as to the Lord, and not to men:

Knowing that whatsoever good thing any man doeth, the same shall he receive of the Lord, whether he be bond or free.

And, ye masters [employers], do the same things unto them, forbearing threatening: knowing that your Master also is in heaven; neither is there respect of persons with him.

Ephesians 6:5-9

Thou shalt not oppress an hired servant that is poor and needy, whether he be of thy brethren, or of thy strangers that are in thy land within thy gates:

At his day thou shalt give him his hire, neither shall the sun go down upon it; for he is poor, and setteth his heart upon it: lest he cry against thee unto the lord, and it be sin unto thee.

Deuteronomy 24:14-15

Thou shalt not defraud thy neighbor, neither rob him: the wages of him that is hired shall not abide with thee all night until the morning.

Leviticus 19:13

And I will come near to you to judgment; . . . and against those that oppress the hireling in his wages, . . . and fear not me, saith the Lord of hosts.

Malachi 3:5

Let as many servants as are under the yoke count their own masters worthy of all honour, that the name of God and his doctrine be not blasphemed.

I Timothy 6:1

Exhort servants to be obedient unto their own masters, and to please them well in all things; not answering again;

Not purloining, but showing all good fidelity; that they may adorn the doctrine of God our Saviour in all things.

For the grace of God that bringeth salvation hath appeared to all men.

Titus 2:9-11

Servants, be subject to your masters with all fear; not only to the good and gentle, but also to the froward.

I Peter 2:18

Questions

1. List the goals of labor unions and the means used to achieve these goals.
2. When an employee "strikes," is this the same as quitting his job? Explain.
3. Depict graphically the effect on wage levels and employment when a labor union can successfully restrict a company's labor supply. Also show graphically what happens to wage levels in the non-union labor market.
4. Does it pay to belong to a union? Explain.
5. What other groups besides labor unions attempt to restrict the supply of labor? What effect is there on wages?
6. Does the minimum wage law help or hurt teenagers, the unskilled and minority groups? How? Defend your answer.
7. If unemployment benefits are of help to the individual, how can it be that they are counter-productive when the economy is regarded as a whole?
8. What causes wages to rise? What effect have labor unions had on wage rates?
9. Recapitulate the wage-price spiral depicted in this chapter and explain it step-by-step. What key factor is necessary for the spiral to continue?
10. What moral problem is involved when Congress engages in deficit spending to alleviate unemployment?
11. Could free market unionism work? Explain why or why not.
12. Summarize your understanding of God's sabbath requirements and the economic and social blessings or curses which follow from obedience or disobedience.

13. Summarize as best you can your concept of the biblical philosophy of employee-employer relations. (See Romans 12:1-21; Ephesians 6:5-9; Colossians 3:22-4:6).

14. Does the civil government have a responsibility to maintain full employment (i.e., to see that people have an opportunity to work)? Defend your view from a biblical viewpoint. If government arrogates such a responsibility to itself, what are the implications concerning:

    (a) the role of the Church and of individual Christians to take care of the needy?
    (b) who will become the "employer of last resort?"
    (c) who is to control the economy?
    (d) the practice of freedom and self-responsibility?

3

Taxes and Public Revenue

. . . Render therefore unto Caesar the things which are Caesar's; and unto God the things that are God's.

Matthew 22:21

CIVIL governments exist on the power to tax. They secure their life's blood by imposing burdens upon the populace — burdens which the people are forced to pay by law. The inherently coercive nature of taxation may be ignored or overlooked by a people who are not jealous of their God-given freedom and right to property. But such lack of awareness does not in the least change the fact that a tax is an **involuntary** levy and that it will be collected by force if the person taxed refuses to pay.

Civil government, by its very nature, is a **coercive** agency of society. Its very *raison d'être* is that men, at heart, are sinful — that men have a fallen nature and therefore do unjust acts. In *The Federalist Papers*, Alexander Hamilton (1755-1804) wrote:

> Government implies the power of making laws. It is essential to the idea of a law, that it be attended with a sanction; or, in other words, a penalty or punishment for disobedience. . . .
> . . . Why has government been instituted at all? Because the passions of men will not conform to the dictates of reason and justice, without constraint. . . .[1]

What Is a Tax?

The word **tax** is derived from Latin *taxare*, which means "to touch sharply." It also carries the meanings "to censure, to value or to estimate." The dictionary explains that a tax is a charge or a pecuniary burden imposed by authority. Specifically, a tax is a charge or burden laid upon persons or property for public purposes; it is a **forced contribution of wealth** to meet the public need of civil government. The word **pecuniary** derives from Latin *pecunia,* which means "money" or, originally, "property in cattle" (from *pecus,* meaning "cattle").

---

[1]Alexander Hamilton, "#15," in *The Federalist Papers,* with an introduction . . . by Clinton Rossiter (New York: New American Library, 1961), p. 110.

From the previous definition and root derivations, we can see that a tax is indeed an **involuntary** payment or impost that is laid upon the people by authority. People sometimes claim that they pay taxes voluntarily; but taxes, by definition, are **not** paid voluntarily. If not always paid under overt duress, taxes are always, at least, paid under the **covert** threat of having force applied in the event of refusal. It is by such income—that is, by coercively derived income—that civil governments exist. I know of no civil government in the world that exists on voluntary contributions, though such a practice is certainly within the realm of possibility and might even be advisable. If such were the case, we can be sure that citizens would never be burdened with more government than they were willing to pay for!

It is crucial that the student of economics thoroughly understands what a tax is and that the use of force always attends the word, for important policy considerations follow this recognition. For instance, when Chief Justice of the U.S. Supreme Court John Marshall (1755-1835) declared, ". . . the power to tax involves the power to destroy; . . ."[2] he implied a need to use such awesome power in a judicious and equitable manner. From a value-judgment standpoint we might further ask: Since the income of civil government is raised through coercive levies which are involuntarily paid, are there any limits or boundaries the poeple should place on **how** tax monies are spent?

This is a **normative** question since it involves the concepts of good and evil or equity and justice. In this chapter, we will investigate the **positive** (or scientific) aspects of taxation; but tax policy must ultimately be based on **normative** (value-laden) principles—and these principles will either agree or disagree with biblical precepts. There is probably not one nation in the whole world whose tax policies do not in one way or another go against clear biblical teaching. Therefore, the challenge faced by all rulers—whether they recognize the challenge or not—is to devise taxing and spending policies which are in conformity with biblical precepts.

> The counsel of the Lord standeth for ever, the thoughts of his heart to all generations.
> Blessed is the nation whose God is the Lord; . . .
>
> Psalm 33:11-12

The Basic Issue: Private vs. Public Control of the Spending Stream

Wealth and work generate streams of income and therefore streams of spending. The person who owns more wealth or has more valuable labor skills is able to generate more income and thereby has control over a larger spending stream than the person who owns less. It is very important to the economic

---

[2]Chief Justice John Marshall in decision of "McCulloch v. Maryland (1819)," in *The Living U. S. Constitution,* . . . Completely Rev. and Enl., Presented with Historical Notes by Saul K. Padover (New York: New American Library, 1968), p. 121.

and social welfare of a community as to **who** controls the income and spending streams because the persons in control are in a strategic position to decide priorities as to how productive resources will be allocated.

As long as citizens conduct their personal lives and social relations according to biblical precepts, the practical conduct of civil government will reflect this state of affairs. Power wielded by civil authorities will then be minimal. Individual freedom and self-responsibility and the private control of property will by maximized. The economy will be market directed. Control of economic production will be widely dispersed among the populace. Taxes will be minimal, of almost negligible impact. But as men individually, and governments collectively, become less Bible-centered and more humanistically[3] oriented, governmental authorities will gradually arrogate more and more power to themselves. Individual freedom, self-responsibility and the private control of property will decline. The economy will become centrally controlled by a humanistic government elite and taxes will become burdensome to the point of stifling personal initiative and productive creativity.

The essential point at issue between the biblical view versus the humanist view of man and its outworking in society thus becomes: Who shall have active control over the spending streams generated by the people's work and their private wealth? Will it be the people themselves as they freely go about ministering to each other's needs? Or will it be the elected politicians and their appointed bureaucrats who gain and hold control of people and property through a "legally wielded" power to tax? Whenever the civil authorities levy a new tax or raise an existing tax, income streams and the effective control of wealth (and thus the loss of individual responsibility to God as trustee for wealth) pass from private to public hands. The great Christian statesman Edmund Burke (1729-1797) recognized that the growth of tyranny in government begins in the hearts and minds of the people. In 1790 he made this observation about the French Revolution, ". . . Kings will be tyrants from policy, when subjects are rebels from principle."[4]

Who Pays Taxes?

Neo-Keynesian followers of the British economist John Maynard Keynes (1882-1946), who developed the thesis that governmental intervention in the

---

[3]A humanist is a person who dethrones God and His revelation (the Bible) and enthrones man's reason in God's place. A humanist views man as the highest development of a chance evolutionary process rather than as a precious, God-created person. Man, therefore, according to the humanist view is not essentially different than the lower animals from which he supposedly evolved, but is only more intelligent. There is, then no special reason why a supposedly more intelligent government elite should not direct and control the supposedly less intelligent masses.

[4]Edmund Burke, *Reflections on the French Revolution and other essays,* Everyman's Library, no. 460, with an Introduction by A. J. Grieve (London & Toronto: J. M. Dent & Sons [1910]) (New York: E. P. Dutton & Co., [1910]), p. 75.

economy is necessary to produce a state of "full employment," have devised a sophisticated economic model which shows something called the "balanced budget multiplier." The model, if one accepts the suppositions upon which it is based, purports to show how the government can tax and spend equal amounts, thus keeping its budget balanced and yet have a "multiplier effect" on the national income. For instance, levying a tax of five billion dollars and matching it with government spending of five billion dollars will supposedly **increase** national income by five billion dollars. This theoretically happens because each dollar of government spending is viewed as generating a full dollar of demand, while each dollar of taxation is viewed as not reducing demand by a full dollar. The supposition held by the neo-Keynesians is that an increase in taxes comes partly from people's savings which otherwise are **not** presumed to flow back into the economy through capital investment. We can readily see that **if** the supposition that people's savings do **not** re-enter the economy in the form of capital investment, and thus reconstitute the prior existing level of aggregate demand, the "magic multiplier" will indeed be envisioned. Believers in this neo-Keynesian model will thus naturally opt for **less** private activity and **more** government influence in the economy as a means of achieving full employment through government-mandated taxing and spending schemes. This, essentially, is what Harry Hopkins meant in the 1930s when he depicted Franklin D. Roosevelt's policy as ". . . tax and tax, spend and spend, elect and elect!"[5]

It is perhaps too elementary to point out that the civil authority is never a source of wealth in and of itself. Governments cannot **give** to the people anything they do not first **take** from them. There is no magic multiplier that somehow allows governing authorities to give the people a "free lunch" or to generate a higher level of national income through clever taxing and spending schemes than the people themselves will generate if left free to follow their own desires. The cost of every governmental activity is always, and must always, be paid for by someone. The only question to be answered is: Who will pay? Will the cost of government programs be paid for by those who use and benefit from them? Or will the cost be paid for by others on whom the burden is placed authoritatively by the rulers? For, ultimately, only people pay taxes.

Sources of Tax Revenue

Over the years, governmental authorities have been quite ingenious in devising new revenue-producing schemes. There are property taxes, land taxes, improvement taxes, sales taxes, income taxes, excise taxes, license fees, payroll taxes, use taxes, tariffs and others almost too numerous to recite. But regardless of what name a tax is called, all taxes, in the final analysis, can only

---

[5]Rose L. Martin, *Fabian Freeway* (Santa Monica, Calif.: Fidelis Publishers, Inc., 1968), p. 278.

be levied on one or more of these economic sources: labor, wealth or land.[6] Regardless of which economic source is taxed, only people pay the taxes.

One of the technical problems in collecting taxes is the administrative costs involved in collecting them. In many instances — such as sales, payroll and excise taxes — much of the financial cost and chore of actual tax collection is pushed onto the business community. Employers are required by law, for instance, to withhold social security and personal income taxes from the paychecks of workers who are in their employ. Such practices, while not eliminating the cost of collection as a process, does effectually shift the cost from the agency of government onto the private sector. Also, the development of sophisticated computer technology for use in business firms has helped to drastically reduce the cost of tax collection. Ironically, the superior cost-efficiency of business firms has thus contributed to the government's ability to squeeze out more taxes from the public; and it has thereby helped to effectively increase the role of government in society, often to the detriment of the firms who assist the government in its collections.

Federal Taxing and Spending

The estimated receipts and expenditures of the federal government during 1984 are indicated in Table 3:1.

The total sum of "transfer payments" in Table 3:1 is approximately 64 percent of the total budget of the federal government. Defense expenditures, on the other hand, approximate only 23 percent of the budget — about one-third of the transfer payment total. A so-called transfer payment is money that the government taxes away from some citizens and pays to other citizens. The money is not earned by the receiving party, nor can it be classified as a gift since a gift by definition is given voluntarily by the donor. In the case of a transfer payment, the money is forcibly wrested from the giver by the government's coercive power of taxation.

The practice of transferring income from some citizens to others raises a number of implications and questions. One obvious implication is that citizens have little, if any, control over how much money can be wrested from them for transfer payments. Another is that the individual citizen has even less control over who gets the transfer payments and what the money might be used for. A burning issue of the day for many Christians is the issue of government-

---

[6]Remember these economic definitions: **Wealth** is man-produced goods to which people impute value. If you produce something that no one values, it is classified as junk or garbage. Wealth may be further divided into consumer-wealth (consumption goods) or producer-wealth (capital). **Land** is defined as nature or natural resources as they are found before being altered by the hand of man. Land is God's gift to the children of men (Ps. 115:16). Improvements made on a land site are thus properly placed in the economic category called wealth — they are a capital improvement.

Table 3:1

Income	Billions	
Taxes on individual incomes	$295.6	
Social security taxes	210.6	
Taxes on corporate profits	51.8	
Excise Taxes	28.1	
Crude-oil excise taxes	12.3	
Unemployment insurance taxes	24.1	
Estate and gift taxes	5.9	
All other revenue	31.3	
Total income	$659.7	$659.7

Expenditures	Billions	
National defense	$245.3	
*Social security	178.2	
Interest on national debt	144.5	
*Medicare/health programs	90.6	
*Public aid/food stamps/etc.	45.8	
*Education/social services	25.3	
*Aid to veterans	25.7	
*Aid to transportation/business	25.1	
*Civil service retirement	22.2	
*Unemployment compensation	28.8	
*Foreign aid	13.3	
Energy	3.3	
*Community development	7.0	
*General revenue sharing	4.6	
*Rivers/dams/resources	5.8	
*Science/space/technology	8.3	
Pollution control	4.1	
*Aid to agriculture	12.2	
*Payment to Postal Service	0.4	
All other spending	-19.2	
Income from outer continental shelf	-11.9	
Interagency deductions listed as spending above	-10.9	
Total expenditures	$848.5	$848.5
Deficit		-$188.8

Source: U.S. Office of Management and Budget.

Note: Figures may not add because of rounding.
*Classified wholly or largely as "transfer payments."

funded abortions, which are largely funded through the transfer payment scheme. Some relevant questions which arise are:

(1) Does the government practice of forcibly transferring income and wealth from some citizens to others break the eighth commandment, "Thou shalt not steal"? If the income people earn through honest economic activity is not really theirs anyway but actually belongs to the governing authorities whom the people elect to office and is only held by the people at the sufferance of elected officials, then the commandment against stealing is not broken. But if people's earned income is really their property for which they are responsible to God for how they use it, then the scheme of transfer payments would indeed seem to be a sophisticated way of breaking the eighth commandment.

(2) To what extent, then, are Christians obliged to acquiesce in being shorn like sheep — especially when transferred funds are used for ungodly purposes?

(3) What is the proper role of civil government in society? Is it simply to maintain law and order and foster an atmosphere of peace so that the people can live freely and responsibly under God's law? Or is it to attempt to feed the hungry, clothe the poor, equalize wealth and in general to attempt to build a Utopia on earth?

(4) When and if government becomes destructive of its original purpose, to what extent do a free people still owe it allegiance? If the policies followed by such a government actually foster conditions and practices which are clearly against biblical precepts, do Christians sin positively by humbly acquiescing, or does duty to God demand what is called "loyal opposition"?

These are difficult questions to pose, and they are even more difficult to answer because the Bible teaches submissive obedience to lawful authority. Leaders of the Protestant Reformation wrestled with such questions when the civil authorities turned tyrannical in their day. Christians of today, it appears, must again take Bible in hand and restudy the problem and come up with some viable solutions. Christians are God's kingdom-builders, and one of the most challenging issues of our day is how to bring all man-made social institutions, including the God-appointed agency of civil government, into conformity with God's will.

Land as a Productive Resource

As an economic factor of production, land is inherently different from either labor services or capital. Land is fixed in total supply, and it is non-renewable. The creation of land did not cause disutility to anyone, so it is a "free good." The total amount of land existing today is exactly the same as when God created the earth. Remember that we define land as "nature" or as "natural resources." Man can change the form or the physical appearance of land-sites by applying human and mechanical energy to the sites, but it is impossible for him to create or to destroy the land itself.

The Bible teaches in a number of places that we should regard land differently than other factors of production.

In Psalm 115:16 we are told that the earth is God's gift to men: "The heaven, even the heavens, are the Lord's: but the earth hath he given to the children of men."

What does God mean when He instructs us that He has given the earth to the children of men? Could He mean, according to His divine plan for mankind, that all men should, as private individuals, have economic access to land in order to produce the food and other products men need to support their families? In chapter 47 of Genesis we find a historical record of what happened when the land was collectivized and control of it was put into the hands of the civil authority—the people were enslaved. In Leviticus 25:23-28 the Old Testament Israelites were admonished **not** to disenfranchise mankind from the land by allowing it to be sold permanently. In other passages they were admonished **not** to cheat others by removing their neighbor's landmarks (see Deut. 19:14, 27:17; Job 24:2; Prov. 22:28, 23:10; Hosea 5:10). Truly our Lord recognized the importance of individuals having private access to land in order to guarantee their economic and political independence.

Examples of countries which have denied masses of citizens economic access to the land are Russia, Red China, India, Mexico, Peru, Ecuador, Colombia, various African nations and even England after the land enclosure movement. In each instance, government land policy favors a relatively few large landowners who control more land than they can productively use, thus forcing the masses to live as serfs and peons instead of as small private landholders. The resulting social discontent creates a fertile field for communist agitators to promise "bread and land" to the masses of disenfranchised people—as the Bolsheviks did in Russia in 1917. Once in power, however, the promises are immediately forgotten as the new communist-controlled regime becomes the sole landowner. (See the supplement "The Land Problem in Mexico" at the end of this chapter.)

In countries where individuals own title to land and have private control over its use, men are free and are economically independent; thus market-oriented economic production is fostered, and the production and accumulation of wealth is maximized. Charles de Secondat, Baron de Montesquieu (1689-1755) recognized this truth when he wrote, "Countries are not cultivated in proportion to their fertility, but to their liberty; . . ."[7]

Countries that have masses of economically impotent people invariably have land policies which have disenfranchised the people from economic access to the land. All that is necessary for economic production to take place is

---

[7]Montesquieu, Charles Louis de Secondat, baron de la Brède et de, *The Spirit of Laws,* trans. from the French by Thomas Nugent, with a special introduction by Hon. Frederic R. Coudert, the World's Great Classics, Rev. ed., 2 vols. (New York: Colonial Press, 1900), vol. 1, Bk. XVIII, Chapter 3, p. 272.

to allow free men to have ready access to land, which is God's gift to the children of men (Ps. 115:16).

The Effects of Taxing Labor, Capital and Land

Since labor, capital and land fall into different economic categories by their very nature, it is not unreasonable to expect that imposing a tax on them will produce different economic results. This indeed is the case.

Labor and capital are **fixed** in supply at any one instant in time, but they are **variable** over the long run. Over a period of time, the amount of labor services and capital in existence and available for sale in the marketplace will vary in response to prices. Labor services can be increased almost immediately by offering workers special inducements to work longer hours. Over a somewhat longer period of time, workers can be trained through employer training programs or by attending schools, colleges and training institutes. The number and quality of productive tools and machinery, likewise, can be increased by raising people's incentive to save and invest. But the total amount of land in existence, both in the short run and in the long run, is absolutely fixed. There is no more land in America, for instance, than when Columbus first came to our shores in 1492; though settlers for hundreds of years, and people even today, have been cultivating and developing land **at the margin.**

Let us analyze, then, how the imposition of a tax on labor, capital and land will variously affect the quantity of goods and services offered for sale in the marketplace. Then let us make a judgment about which sources of revenue should or should not be taxed in order to maximize the well-being of the people.

Taxing Labor, Capital or Goods at the Point of Purchase: Since labor services and capital are **variable** in supply in the long run, imposing a tax on them will reduce the quantity of these factors offered for sale in the marketplace. Since a reduction in supply of any productive resource will serve to restrict total output, prices will then rise as a result. This chain of cause-and-effect is shown in Graph 3:1.

Graph 3:1

Taxing Labor or Capital

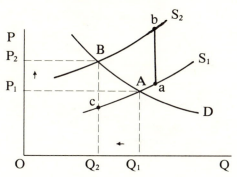

If S_1 equals the supply of either labor services or capital being offered for sale in the marketplace at any one time, and if D equals the demand for such factors, then general equilibrium is attained at point A. The quantity of labor services or of capital gainfully employed will be Q_1, and the price paid will be P_1.

But if the civil authority imposes a tax on the labor services of workers or on the capital provided by investors, the market will gradually adjust to the new situation. In the case of **workers,** the new tax will hasten early retirement of some older workers as well as serve to prevent the employment of younger and marginal workers. Some economists contend that, under certain conditions, a tax on labor services may even serve to increase the amount of labor offered to the market because workers will want to maintain their prior level of take-home pay. This could be the case in some instances.

In the case of a tax on **capital,** existing capital will become less profitable after the tax is levied; therefore, the incentive for people to save and for investors to incur risk by investing additional funds in business enterprises will be diminished. Thus, some existing capital will not be replaced when it wears out; and the available stock of capital will gradually diminish.

We see that, in both instances, a tax on a variable factor of production will serve to **reduce** the supply offered for sale and thereby cause prices to rise in the marketplace. Graphically, the supply curve will shift from S_1 to S_2. The new point of equilibrium will then be at point B. The quantity of either labor services or of capital offered for sale will drop from Q_1 to Q_2, and the price will rise from P_1 to P_2.

Note that the tax increase (indicated by line segment a-b, or by the vertical distance between S_1 and S_2) is **greater** than the rise in price from P_1 to P_2. What does this indicate? It means that consumers will bear the part of the tax cost indicated by the vertical distance between P_1 and P_2 (see line segment B-C); in other words, this is the amount that prices rise in the marketplace because of the new tax. (This is the amount of tax that is shifted forward to consumers through higher prices.) This, of course, leaves the remaining portion of the tax cost to be borne by producers — either employers alone, workers alone or probably to be shared jointly by both employers and workers. This portion of the tax is shown graphically by the line segment between P_1 and point C.

The **ratio** of how the cost of taxation is borne by producers versus consumers depends on the relative elasticity (indicated by the relative steepness of slant) of the supply and demand curves. If demand is **less** elastic than supply (i.e., if the demand curve has a steeper slope, which indicates that consumers are less price-conscious than suppliers are), then the greater portion of the tax will be borne by consumers. If, on the other hand, producers are less price-conscious than consumers, then the larger portion of the tax will be borne by producers. You may experiment graphically with this interesting phenomenon by redrawing the relative slopes of the demand and supply curves.

In summary, we note this observation: A tax on either labor services or capital will decrease the available supply of goods and services to the market and thereby increase the price to consumers, as well as decreasing the earnings of producers. In short, a tax on labor or on capital serves to reduce the overall welfare of the whole community by lessening production and raising prices. Clearly, if the public desires low prices and increased output, they should only reluctantly allow the civil authorities to impose a tax on either labor or capital.

This important point calls for an additional observation which runs contrary to popular misguided sentiment. It is this: Workers and capitalists (i.e., those who supply labor services and those who provide the tools and equipment that workers use to multiply their productivity) have a mutually supportive position regarding taxes. A tax on either labor or capital works to the detriment, not only of consumers (which includes workers and capitalists when they buy things in the marketplace), but also to the detriment of workers and capitalists as producers. This observation would cause Karl Marx to turn over in his grave, for its refutes the primary tenet of Marxism — the supposed undying conflict of economic interest between workers and capitalists!

Question: Does it make any difference whether the taxing authorities levy a tax on **producers** (workers or the owners of capital) or on **consumers** at the point of purchase?

Answer: Not one bit! The effect is the same. In both instances, the supply curve is raised (or shifted) from S_1 to S_2. The reason for this sameness in effect is that, since the seller collects the tax, the amount of the tax is simply added to the price offered to consumers. In the graphic example shown previously, consumers simply react by sliding up the demand curve from point A to point B. The tax does not change **demand** but only the **quantity** demanded.[8]

Taxing Land: What happens when a tax is imposed on land is shown in Graph 3:2.

Graph 3:2

Taxing Land

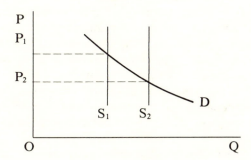

---

[8] Tom Rose, *Economics: Principles and Policy* (Milford, Mich.: Mott Media, 1977), pp. 237-239.

Let S_1 equal the amount of land offered for sale before the imposition of a tax. When a tax on land is imposed, the amount of land offered for sale will **increase**, thus shifting from S_1 to S_2. Because the amount offered for sale increases, the price will decrease from P_1 to P_2.

Note that the supply curves for land are **vertical** instead of sloping upward like the curves for labor services and capital. Why this difference? The reason is easily explained. The total amount of labor services or capital in existence at any one time are the result of some **cost** or **disutility** that individuals have experienced or undergone. This cost or disutility would be expressed by an upward-sloping supply curve. But land is costless because it is a gift from God. Man cannot by his own efforts either increase or decrease the amount of land in existence. This costless fact of life is expressed with a **vertical** supply curve.

Now let us continue our analysis. What effect will **lower** prices of land have on production cost and ultimately on consumer prices? When the price of land decreases, the cost of capitalizing land for producers falls. More land will be put to productive use; this will expand the supply of goods and services offered for sale to consumers, and consumer prices will drop in response.

Note again the interesting contrast in the effects of taxation:

A tax on either labor services or capital serves to restrict the amount of these resources used in production. The resultant decrease in production reduces the supply of goods and services offered in the marketplace for sale, thus causing consumer prices to **rise**.

A tax on land serves to increase the amount of land used in production. The resulting increase in production expands the supply of goods and services offered for sale in the marketplace, thus causing consumer prices to **fall**.

We might inquire again into this interesting contrast. Just why does a tax on land produce **opposite** effects on supply and consumer prices than does a tax on either labor services or capital?

The answer is simple and straightforward: It involves a combination of taxing policies on real estate and government spending programs, both of which under present taxing policies encourage individuals to hold land idle with the speculative hope that it can be sold for a higher price in the future.

To show what we mean, let us ask a question. In travelling about your community, have you ever noticed what appear to be valuable pieces of land that are just lying idle, such as vacant lots in downtown areas or open fields surrounded by homes or industrial or commercial buildings? Have you perhaps noticed land that is being put to much less productive use than surrounding land, such as one-level parking lots in expensive downtown commercial areas or slum areas in the center of town? The reason why such nonproductive or under productive use of land can occur is explained in the following paragraphs.

Real Estate Taxes: The tax that people pay on real estate[9] is really **two**

---

[9]Real estate is defined as **land** plus the **improvements** that are attached to it.

taxes in one because the tax is drawn from **two** different sources.[10] One tax is levied on the land **site** itself, and the other is levied on land improvements such as fences, ponds, barns, homes, manufacturing plants, hotels, retail store buildings, office buildings, etc.

It is common for the civil authorities to tax real estate in such a way as to **retard** constructive land development and to **foster** land speculation, that is, the holding of land in an idle state while waiting for land prices to rise.[11] How? In this way: Present tax laws in most communities cause taxes to go up when property owners erect larger buildings to renovate existing homes and buildings because the total amount of taxes paid is tied to the value of the **improvements.** This is a tax on **capital**, which, as we have seen, serves to restrict capital accumulation. The natural result of taxing improvements is that property owners become reluctant to build new structures or to renovate old ones because they know the tax assessor will soon visit them and re-evaluate their property and raise the amount of taxes they must pay. Thus, we see that taxing improvements produces a **negative** incentive rather than a positive one.

Because of this, landlords in central city areas have an unnatural incentive to allow their properties to fall into disrepair. For, if they do, their taxes will go down instead of up. This explains why slums tend to develop in many of our central cities. If land improvements were not taxed at all, or at a much lower rate, property owners would have a natural incentive to tear down older buildings and to erect better ones, or to renovate existing properties as a means of generating more income. The resulting boom in construction activity, real estate sales and related economic activity would do much to relieve any existing unemployment.

On the other hand, the total tax that owners must pay on unimproved land is relatively so low that the owners feel little pressure to use the land to its full economic potential. Low taxes on unimproved land allow landowners to hold their land idle while they wait for land values to rise as a result of increases in population and community growth, much of which is financed with tax expenditures. The general trend of land prices as civilization progresses is upward. There have been very few instances of widespread declines in land prices. These have generally been caused by prior declines in population, such as the "Black Death" of 1348-1350 in Europe which killed an estimated one-fourth of the population in many areas.

---

[10] The author is indebted to Noah D. Alper (a land economist who served for many years as President of the Public Revenue Education Council, St. Louis, Mo.), for teaching me the contrasting effects of taxing land vs. taxing labor services or capital. It is he who introduced me to the concept of taxes being only "pumps" that draw public revenue from one or more of the only **sources** available: land, labor or capital. The author is much indebted to Mr. Alper for making the economics of tax policy both interesting and easy to understand. He would patiently instruct and then inquire, "Now that's simple, isn't it?" And, finally, the basic truths he focused on **did** become easy to understand.

[11] In no way should the reader interpret this statement of fact as an indictment of individuals who engage in land speculation, for man is a profit-seeking creature. He was created by God that way. If tax policies create profit opportunities for observant individuals to benefit from, it is only natural to expect men to take advantage of them.

A higher tax on the **site** value of land would make it less profitable to hold unimproved land for speculative increases in land value. A rise in taxes on land sites produces a **disincentive** to hold land out of production because the higher tax serves to offset the expected future rise in land value which would accrue to the title holder. It is this impact on land speculation which causes a reverse effect on taxing land versus taxing labor services or capital. A higher tax on land motivates land speculators to sell their holdings, thus moving the supply curve from S_1 to S_2 (see Graph 3:2), with the resultant expansion of production and fall in consumer prices.

Even though the total amount of land in the world is fixed and has not varied from the time of creation, there are considerable acreages of land in every community being withheld from full productive use, thereby reducing the economic production of goods and services (and employment) and raising prices to consumers. To make note of this fact and to trace the economics of cause-and-effect is a **positive** scientific process. But deciding what to do about it and how to solve the problem is a normative question which will no doubt generate heated debate from all affected parties.

We still have an additional factor to consider. It is:

Government Spending: Current government spending programs clearly benefit persons who engage in land speculation at the expense of those who engage in economic production (workers, employers, industrialists, entrepreneurs, etc.).[12] How? In this way: Much of the tax money paid to the civil authority is taken from persons in their role as producers through taxes levied on labor and capital. A considerable portion of the tax monies so generated is expended on roads, highways, bridges, airports, hospitals, schools, libraries, museums, symphony halls, government buildings, water and sewer lines and in the maintenance of fire and police departments and other government services. Relatively little of such tax expenditures comes from the taxes levied on unimproved land, but the listed government expenditures serve to increase the value of unimproved land tremendously. These increased values are thereby publicly created values which accrue to the private gain of those who speculate in land by holding it off the market waiting for values to rise.

Again, let us make note that the facts as to who pays taxes and who receives the benefit of how taxes are spent is a **positive** aspect of economic science. This positive aspect of economics does not pass judgment as to whether something is moral or immoral; but it simply says, "This is the way it is." The step of deciding whether "what is" is morally good or morally bad brings the student into the **normative** area of economics which involves value judgments based on one's system of morals and ethics. Here, above all else, wisdom and guidance must be sought from the Bible so that we may properly

---

[12] The categories **economic producer** and **land speculator** can be separated by function, but not by person. Thus, a worker, an industrialist or any other person who purchases land on speculation of future price rises plays a dual role—he is both a producer and a speculator.

discern the mind of God and strive to make our thoughts to be in conformity with His thoughts (II Cor. 10:5).

Land Value Taxation

The constitution of Pennsylvania allows cities and boroughs and townships which have home rule charters to tax capital improvements at a lesser rate than land sites. The effect of such a policy is to shift taxes from capital onto land, with the resultant economic effects we discussed earlier. The Center for the Study of Economics at Indiana, Pennsylvania, which publishes a bulletin entitled *Incentive Taxation*, reports that five cities have recently adopted tax policies which shift taxes from capital to land with beneficial results. The equalized tax rates for the cities in 1982 are shown in Table 3:2.

Table 3:2

Equalized Tax Rates

	Land*	Buildings*
New Castle	4.0%	2.3%
Scranton	3.4	0.9
Pittsburgh	3.3	0.8
Harrisburg	3.3	1.1
McKeesport	2.3	0.5

Source: *Incentive Taxation,* Jan.-Feb. 1982, p. 4.

*Does not include school and county tax rates, which are levied equally on land and buildings.

Table 3:3

Number of Building Permits

Date	McKeesport	Clairton	Duquesne
1977	258	165	111
1978	422	178	83
1979	442	202	77
1980	525	174	131

Dollar Value of Permits

Date	McKeesport	Clairton	Duquesne
1977	$1,669,637	$ 622,157	$ 586,730
1978	1,863,985	1,072,499	1,195,670
1979	1,886,908	638,280	1,022,892
1980	3,583,911	435,593	1,043,476

Source: *Incentive Taxation*, May-June 1981, p. 1.

An interesting study of the economic effects of relatively up-taxing land and down-taxing capital was conducted with reference to McKeesport, which adopted land value taxation in 1980, and two nearby sister cities, Clairton and Duquesne, which have not. New construction and rehabilitation of older structures boomed in McKeesport while they declined or remained stable in the other towns. The data is shown in Table 3:3.

The overall economic impact of up-taxing land and down-taxing capital is greater than one would think at first. The doubling in building permits in McKeesport from 1979 to 1980, for instance, generated increased sales of building materials and supplies, which in itself generates additional employment; and this is in addition to the increased employment directly stimulated by building contractors.

The same result in increased building permits and expanding economic activity is reported by cities in Australia which have been following a land value taxation policy for a number of years. In the township of Kilmore Shire, Australia, which voted in 1971 to tax only land values and to untax buildings completely, new construction grew at the rate of 104 percent in the four years prior to the switch, as compared to 209 percent in the four years afterwards. Thus, economic activity doubled. By 1977 (the last year for which data are available), construction had grown by 508 percent in Kilmore, as compared to only 160 percent for the region as a whole. According to data shown in Table 3:4, it appears that shifting taxes from variable factors of economic production (labor and capital) to the fixed factor (land) has a universally beneficial effect.

Table 3:4

Value of All Building Permits

	Kilmore with LVT	Adjoining Area without LVT
1971	$ 570,000	$ 474,000
1972	925,000	509,000
1973	1,394,000	799,000
1974	1,830,000	1,450,000
1975	2,577,000	1,527,000
1976	2,658,000	1,598,000
1977	3,602,000	1,539,000

Source: *Incentive Taxation,* October 1981, p. 1; and Australian Bureau of Statistics, building permits reference number 7, 1978, Victorian Office.

. . . This right way of raising public revenues must accord with the moral law. . . .

It must not take from individuals what rightfully belongs to individuals.

It must not give some an advantage over others, as by increasing the prices of what some have to sell and others must buy.

It must not lead men into temptation, by requiring trivial oaths, by making it profitable to lie, to swear falsely, to bribe, or to take bribes.

It must not confuse the distinctions of right and wrong . . . , by creating crimes that are not sins, and punishing men for doing what in itself they have an undoubted right to do.

It must not repress industry. It must not check commerce. It must not punish thrift. It must offer no impediment to the largest production and the fairest division of wealth.[13]

The backbone of any real estate tax program is encouragement of improvements and discouragement of holding of vacant land for speculation. When vacant land is assessed at a small percentage of true value, it invites its owner to hold it from improvement and to speculate on its future high value. This drives people further from the center of municipalities, requiring expanded area services at a higher cost to the taxpayer.[14]

Government Ownership of Land

We have pointed out how land speculation tends to reduce the supply of land being used for economic production, thus lessening the potential supply of goods and thereby raising prices to consumers. We have also seen how a shifting of taxes from labor and capital onto land sites would tend to correct this situation. But there is another factor that serves to withhold vast acreages of land from useful economic production—this is government land policy.

During the nineteenth century, the U.S. government became owner of nearly two billion acres of land through various land acquisitions (the Louisians Purchase of 1803, the Oregon Compromise of 1846, the Mexican Cession of 1848, purchase of a part of Texas in 1850 and the Alaskan Purchase of 1867). Until the middle of the twentieth century, it was government policy to return public lands to the private sector; for in a democratic republic there is no valid reason why the agency of government should own any land other than the extremely small percentage that might be needed for such things as military installations or government offices. So far, over one billion acres of

---

[13]Henry George, *The Condition of Labour* (London: Land and Liberty Press, 1947), p. 8.
[14]Mayor John H. Poelker, St. Louis, Mo., in *Incentive Taxation*, October 1981, p. 4.

the previously mentioned acquired land have been sold or given back to the citizens (homesteading, grants to local and state governments, land grant colleges, railroads and timber companies).

Today the U.S. government still owns approximately 738 million acres of land, only a small part of which is made available to economic production through leases. The extent of federal land ownership, which goes as high as 60 to 86 percent of the land area of some states, is shown in Table 3:5.

Table 3:5

Land Ownership by the U.S. Federal Government

	Acres Owned*	% of Total		Acres Owned*	% of Total
AL	1.1	3.4	MO	2.2	5.0
AK	217.7	59.6	MT	27.7	29.7
AZ	32.0	44.0	NE	**	1.5
AR	3.4	10.0	NV	60.5	86.1
CA	46.7	46.6	NH	**	12.5
CO	23.6	35.5	NJ	**	3.1
CT	**	.3	NM	25.9	33.3
DE	**	3.2	NY	**	.8
DC	**	32.9	NC	2.1	6.5
FL	4.0	11.6	ND	2.4	5.4
GA	2.3	6.1	OH	**	1.3
HI	**	16.1	OK	1.6	3.6
ID	33.8	63.8	OR	32.3	52.5
IL	**	1.7	PA	**	2.5
IN	**	2.1	RI	**	1.2
IA	**	.6	SC	1.2	6.1
KS	**	1.4	SD	3.5	7.1
KY	1.4	5.5	TN	1.9	6.9
LA	1.1	3.8	TX	3.4	2.0
ME	**	.7	UT	33.5	63.6
MD	**	3.2	VT	**	5.0
MA	**	1.6	VA	2.4	9.5
MI	3.5	9.5	WA	12.5	29.2
MN	3.4	6.7	WV	1.1	7.1
MS	1.7	5.7	WI	1.9	5.3
			WY	30.3	48.7

Source: U.S. General Services Administration.

*In millions.

**Less than 100,000 acres.

Opinion regarding the ownership of federal lands divides into two basic camps. One camp feels that the federal government should continue holding vast acreages in order to preserve it in its primitive state for the benefit of wildlife and for the sake of retaining its untouched beauty. This camp's idea is to preserve these lands untouched for posterity. The other camp holds the view that private ownership is the better means of assuring a proper balance between man's needs today as well as the needs of posterity in the future. Members of this camp point out that there are untold quantities of oil, minerals, lumber and other resources which can be beneficially exploited from these publicly held lands for the benefit of mankind both today and in the future. Some of the resources — timber land is a good example — actually become **more** productive on a long-range basis by being actively managed for harvesting and replanting.

In 1964 Congress established a wilderness system of some 80 million acres. Some of the land was already owned by the federal government, but the act also used condemnation procedures to take over privately owned parcels of land, thus depriving the owners of their property.

How much land, if any, should continue to be owned by the government for the "benefit" of citizens living today, of those who might be living a century from now, or even for the benefit of wildlife today and in the future poses a volatile issue. The majority of the public still seems to favor a continuing policy of letting the federal government serve as caretaker and preserver of public lands. But a growing body of citizens, of which your author is one, contends that men's needs — both now and in the future — will be better met if public lands were sold off to private individuals as quickly as possible. Here are some of the reasons cited:

• The sale of public lands would generate multi-billions of dollars which could be used to pay off much, if not all, of the public debt, thus saving additional billions annually in interest payments.

• The existing government bureaucracy needed for overseeing the vast extent of federally owned lands would be sharply reduced, thus saving even more on an annual basis.

• The additional output from these lands would help expand supply, thus causing prices to consumers to be lower.

• The economic activity called into being to utilize these lands productively would help to reduce the level of unemployment that has been of such concern the last few years.

• Property is better preserved and replenished when it is owned by private individuals who stand to gain economically by giving it proper care. It was private persons, for instance, who took steps to preserve the American bison from complete extinction. Another example of private versus public care can be seen by comparing the neatness of private lawns and estates with public parks.

• When government bureaucrats manage publicly owned lands, the use to which they are put is too much influenced by partisan political pressures rather than by impersonal market forces. Thus, the desires of the public, which would otherwise be registered through the price mechanism of the market-place, are instead short-circuited by autocratic decisions which have the force of law.

• Every acre of publicly owned land reduces the overall tax base, thus increasing the burden of taxation for the remaining private landowners. This is an especially important point to consider in those states where federally owned lands constitute high percentages of the total land area.

• God's plan for economic production, if we use the Bible as our guide, calls for individual persons to have control over their own land sites. All that it takes for economic production to take place is to put man in touch with God's gift to man, land. This plan was followed in the Garden of Eden as well as in the Promised Land when the Israelites crossed the Jordan. Political freedom and economic freedom go hand-in-hand with private land ownership. The one biblical instance of widespread government ownership of land quickly devolved into government tyranny and the enslavement of the mass of citizens (see the historical account of Joseph and the Pharoah of Egypt).

The economics of the government land issue is clear cut. More economic activity would take place with an increase in private ownership. The level of employment would rise; the supply of goods and services would be increased, and price levels would trend downward if publicly owned lands were turned over to private use. From a free market standpoint, public demand would be better served because consumers and the entrepreneurs who serve the public could directly register their desires through the freely fluctuating price mechanism of the marketplace.

Principles of Taxation

There are a number of so-called principles or guidelines that taxing authorities generally attempt to consider in levying taxes. These are based on varying degrees of objective, subjective and pragmatic evaluations. As we list the principles, we indicate in parentheses what seems to be the major basis of each.

The Benefit Principle: (Objective) According to this guideline, the taxing authorities attempt to measure the cost of whatever service is being provided and then levy a charge on those people whom they deem are benefitting from it. Use charges—such as water and sewer taxes, garbage collection fees and a home owner's pro-rata share of municipal services—are examples of the "benefit principle" in action.

The Equity Principle: (Subjective) The idea applied in this principle is to keep the economic status of the citizen relatively the same after a tax is levied as before. "What is fair to everyone concerned?" is the focus of this question. A problem arises, though, because different people's concept of "fair" varies with their background, experience, status in the community and religious presuppositions. Therefore, what may seem equitable from one point of view may not seem so from another. When our nation was admittedly more Bible-based than it now is, there was more widespread agreement that the rules set up by the Bible could be used as normative guides. But our people and courts have tended to disregard the Bible as man's authoritative guide in every aspect of life.

Take, for instance, an issue that is of growing importance to the Christian community and which has increasingly been a matter of dispute between Christians and the secular state — the question of educating children and paying their costs of education. The Bible teaches that the education of children is a religious duty, a duty that properly falls on the **family** rather than on the state (Deut. 6:4-9, 20-21). Thus, biblically minded Christians generally feel that tax-supported education usurps both a **right** and a **responsibility** from the rightful sphere of the home. They ask, "Should not we as parents have full control over the education of our children? Are they not entrusted to us by God? Why should the state intrude into this, our private responsibility to God? Is it fair that we should pay the cost of educating our own children in private Christian schools and still be forced by law to pay to educate other people's children in tax-supported schools? And what if we don't agree with the educational philosophy promulgated by tax-supported schools?"

The parents who send their children to tax-supported schools would reply, "It is your own choice to send your children to private schools! You can send them to public schools if you desire, so you should pay anyway."

Elderly persons who have already educated their children sometimes complain, "Why should we pay to help educate your children when we have already paid to educate our own?" To them the answer is given, "Well-educated children make law-abiding citizens; and this makes our community a better place to live. So it is only equitable that you help pay the cost of educating our children, since you also benefit."[15] This same argument is used for single people and childless couples.

This single issue serves to show that each person's concept of "equity" can be strongly affected by his own special interest, ingenuity or suppleness of mind unless it is solidly based on unchanging biblical principles.

The Ability to Pay Principle: (Pragmatic) In applying this guideline, a person's income or wealth is measured (an objective procedure), then an estimation of his relative ability to pay is arrived at (a highly subjective procedure) and, finally, a politically expedient levy is applied to all persons who fall within pragmatically established categories.

The basic idea here is to "soak the rich" and "let the poor man off." This idea became popular in these United States in the latter part of the nineteenth century and culminated in the ratification of the sixteenth Amendment to the

---

[15]Is the statement that well-educated children make law-abiding citizens true? What if children are well educated in principles and precepts that conflict with the Bible?

U.S. Constitution in 1913. The Amendment made it legal to tax citizens on a non-proportional basis. Today the graduated income tax varies from a low of about 15 percent to a high of 50 percent after legally allowable deductions. During World War II, the maximum marginal rate of taxation was upped to 90 percent.

The practice of graduating taxes according to a person's ability to pay is both attacked and defended, depending upon the value judgments of the person concerned. The men who founded the Constitution held that the only equitable direct tax, that is, one that is levied directly on citizens, is a "head tax" which is proportionately levied on all citizens, rich and poor alike. In the Bible it is recorded that Moses was ordered by God to accept an offering of half a shekel from each person (note that this was an **offering** and not a tax; see Ex. 30:13-15). But God instructed him that "The rich shall not give more, and the poor shall not give less . . ." (Ex. 30:15). The point we learn here is that God did not believe in the so-called principle of "soaking the rich" by increasing their proportion of payment.

The "Goose" Principle: (Pragmatic) The general tendency in this sinful world is for the role of civil governments to grow and grow. Part of this tendency is the result of sin on the part of the people themselves—sinful man continually seeks to avoid responsibility by turning his rightful responsibilities over to the public authority to handle. Part of the tendency is the result of sin on the part of rulers—they continually seek to arrogate power to themselves because of a lust for power over the lives of others. Part of this is a blatant denial of God's sovereignty and His ability to direct the affairs of men according to His divine plan. Thus, secular rulers attempt to use the powers of the state to build an "earthly Utopia" rather than simply striving to maintain a system of workable justice. This is blatant humanism at work—it is the dethronement of God and His law-system and the substitution of man and his law-system.

The end result of these two sinful tendencies on the part of both the ruled and the rulers is for the appetite of civil government for tax revenues to become insatiable and to grow at an exponential rate. So, the taxing authorities always end up by looking for new means of taxing citizens in order to get the revenues governments need and want to fulfill their grandiose humanistic plans of Utopia building. As the role of the secular state grows and grows in society as a result of its never-ending efforts to be a "worldly savior" of the people, all other principles of taxation are thrown out the window; and taxes are finally levied on the basis of "plucking the goose that squawks the least." A practical outgrowth of this principle is the continuous search by taxing authorities to discover new hidden taxes which they hope can be laid on the people without their knowledge.

When the governing authorities are empowered (or arrogate power to themselves) to take wealth from some citizens for redistribution to others, the natural effect is for masses of citizens to coalesce into competing self-interest groups. Some of these groups apply political pressure to escape from paying more **into** the public treasury, while others band together in attempts to increase their share of the "take" **from** the public treasury. Frédéric Bastiat, a French economist and political observer who lived during the time that a series of political revolutions was rocking Europe, observed in a speech to the French National Assembly on December 12, 1849:

> . . . When the people are encouraged to turn to government to settle all of their problems for them—the basis for all revolutions ("perpetual revolutions") is thereby established. For then the people expect the government to provide them with all of the material things they want. And when those things are not forthcoming, they resort to violence to get them. And why not—since the government itself has told them that these responsibilities belong to government rather than to them? "I am convinced that a revolution would not be possible if the only relationship between government and the people was to guarantee them their liberty and security."[16]

Lining Up at the Public Trough

When people get used to the idea of looking to the civil authorities for their income, pressures soon arise from all sectors of society for ever-increasing handouts. men who are already in political office, or those who are striving to attain political office, come under almost unbearable pressures to protect the existing "take" of established self-interest groups and to approve new pay-out schemes for others. The end result is widespread demagoguery, which is the practice of gaining votes by dispensing political favors.

The extent to which our nation has succumbed to "feeding at the public trough" can be visualized by the following:

• An economic consultant in New York recently estimated that **half** of all Americans are either directly or indirectly dependent on civil government for wages, pensions, welfare aid or other forms of income. This includes state, local and federal governments. In 1960 the percentage of people thus dependent was 36.7 percent.[17]

• In 1980 the federal government transferred $318 billion from the pockets of some citizens to the pockets of other citizens through such transfer payment schemes as social security, Medicare, welfare, food stamps, business and farm subsidies. Since 1945 the amounts transferred have grown as shown in Table 3:6.

---

[16]Dean Russell, *Frédéric Bastiat: Ideas and Influence* (New York: Foundation for Economic Education, Inc., 1965), p. 117.

[17]*U.S. News & World Report,* 9 March 1981, p. 73.

Table 3:6

Government Transfer Payments

Date	Dollars in Billions
1945	$ 6.2
1950	15.2
1955	17.5
1960	28.9
1965	40.4
1970	80.1
1975	178.3
1980	318.2
1981	350.7
1982	397.2

Source: *Economic Report of the President,* 1983, p. 189.

• Some 5,500 persons are registered as lobbyists in Washington, DC; but it is believed that over 10,000 persons spend all or part of their time attempting to influence lawmakers. These lobbyists are estimated to spend about one billion dollars annually on their activities. Any attempt to cut government budgets brings immediate and vocal reactions from the many special-interest groups that might be affected.

The point to keep in mind concerning the previous information is this: Every dollar taxed away from the people and redirected by political decision is a dollar forcibly wrenched from the free market sector of the economy. In short, if we view the free market as accurately reflecting the freely expressed desires of consumers through their "dollar votes," then any government interference with this free flow can only produce a misallocation of economic resources as viewed from the public's interest as consumers. How much misdirection an economy can withstand without suffering from economic stagnation is not known. America's historic year by year increases in productivity have turned negative in recent years when measured in real terms (i.e., when measured on a deflated basis). This may well be a signal that too much economic misallocation has already taken place. Stagnated markets occur when consumers refuse to validate existing cost structures and entrepreneurial decisions that have been made in the recent past. The symptoms are sagging sales, over-full inventories, high levels of unemployment and a general slowdown in business. When the symptoms become **general**, this is almost a sure sign that wrong governmental policies are the root of the cause. Other nations have followed similar policy routes as these United States only to suffer the same problem of stagnated markets that we have. In the 20-year period from 1960-1980 there was a general tendency for many nations to increase the percentage of taxation relative to GNP (see Table 3:7).

Table 3:7

Tax Revenue as a Percentage of Total Output of Goods and Services

	1960	1979
Sweden	25.5%	52.9%
Netherlands	30.1	47.2
Norway	31.2	46.7
Denmark	25.4	45.0
Belgium	26.5	44.5
Austria	30.5	41.2
France	33.0	41.0
W. Germany	31.2	37.2
Finland	28.1	35.1
Great Britain	28.5	33.8
Ireland	22.0	33.3
Italy	34.4	32.7
Switzerland	21.2	31.5
New Zealand	32.1	31.4
United States	26.6	31.3
Canada	24.2	31.2
Australia	23.5	28.8*
Portugal	16.3	25.9
Japan	18.2	24.1*
Spain	16.0	22.8

Source: *U.S. News & World Report,* 2 March 1981, p. 61.

*Data for 1978.

Supplement

The Land Problem in Mexico

When Luis Echeverría, the retiring President of Mexico, unexpectedly awarded multi-thousands of acres of privately held land to thousands of landless camp-esinos in 1976 just a few days before his term of office expired, he generated shock waves which were felt even in our own country.

Free enterprisers and conservatives in both Mexico and in these United States castigated Echeverría for once again cooperating with the socialists and communists. His impudent act of expropriating privately held land without just compensation was widely criticized as just another radical attempt to push Mexico further into the jaws of communism.

Indeed, Echeverría's term as President of Mexico was tragic for our friends south of the border. His consistent anti-capitalistic policies almost succeeded in bankrupting Mexico and in pushing that country to the brink of revolution.

Because private investors feared Echeverría's socialist policies, capital investment plummeted. Foreign investors feared to enter, and Mexican investors sent what capital they could out of their country for safe-keeping. Unemployment rose and prices soared upward as the Mexican government went on a money-making binge in useless attempts to stimulate a faltering economy. Government creation of new paper money just could not make up for the people's loss of confidence that was brought on by ever-increasing government meddling. Mexico lost so much foreign exchange that it was forced to devalue the peso drastically.

It might well seem that Echeverría's last official act of confiscating privately held land was indeed a final desperate move by a dedicated socialist to "socialize" his country.

But let us be careful that we not react blindly to Echeverría's action, thereby overlooking the crucially important economic issue which underlies the problem between the campesinos and the landholders. It would be a mistake for free enterprisers and conservatives, just because they uphold the principle of private property, to automatically line up against those who desire to unseat the large landholders in Mexico.

In reality, this part of the trouble in Mexico runs deeper than just another socialist attack against what is regarded as private property. This trouble stems from what can be called the land problem—from cutting off large masses of people from economic access to the land, thereby sabotaging their ability to maintain their economic independence.

It may well be true that Echeverría is a socialist—or perhaps even a communist—but this does not necessarily mean that his view of the land problem is wrong. In fact, he may see Mexico's land problem more clearly than many so-called free enterprisers and conservatives.

The burning economic evil in Mexico, as in most Latin American countries, is that the Spanish conquest has left a legacy of two distinct peoples. On the one hand is a landed gentry that controls vast acres of land, which gives them political power to pass laws favorable to themselves and which gives them the economic power to live off the fruit of other people's labor as rentiers. On the other hand is a people who have been disenfranchised from God's gift to man, the land (Ps. 115:16), and who can only subsist as hired workers who must pay part of their labor effort to the landed gentry as a tax for their privilege to work the land.

We who are free enterprisers can be easily misled by the actions of socialists and communists if we allow ourselves to be blinded by what they are, instead of carefully considering the economic issue their actions are aimed at correcting.

For instance, it is common knowledge that the peasants in Russia were largely disenfranchised from the land. Their landless state, which caused them to work as serfs, provided a handhold for communist agitation for generations — an agitation that was severely stomped out by the tsars.

Leo Tolstoy (1828-1910), a Russian novelist, recognized the land problem in Russia; and he recommended a policy of land distribution among the peasants. The Tsar refused to take his advice, and this gave the communist agitators a continuing opportunity to stir the people up against the ruling government. The revolution which unseated the Tsar and the landed gentry in Russia was actually a peasants' revolt designed to give people economic access to land. After the Tsar was overthrown, it was not much of a chore for the communist conspirators to stage a second revolution, which in short order again disenfranchised the people.

The point we must not overlook is that the communists used a **real** economic issue to make false promises in order to gain control. The communists in Mexico are following the same procedure.[18]

Questions

1. Define what a tax is. Can a tax be voluntary? Explain.

2. Based on your answer to question #1, what limits, if any, would you place on how tax monies should or should not be spent?

3. What is the essential point at issue between the biblical view of man versus the humanist view concerning control over income and wealth?

4. What is a humanist? Explain his view of man. Does it conflict with the biblical view of man? Explain.

5. Why do neo-Keynesians believe that an increase in taxes, matched by an equal increase in government spending, will produce a stimulating effect on the economy, thus raising national income?

6. In 1980 what source of income provided the federal government with its largest share of tax monies? Its second largest? On what were the largest six expenditures made?

7. Define transfer payments. How much did transfer payments amount to in 1980?

8. Attack or define the practice of government transfer payments from these viewpoints: (a) legal, (b) moral, (c) economic and (d) social effects.

---

[18]*Santa Ana* (Calif.) *Register*, 16 January 1977.

9. Show graphically what happens to the price and quantity of labor services or of capital in the marketplace when the civil authorities levy a tax on either.

10. When labor services or capital is taxed, who bears the cost? Explain.

11. A friend makes this statement: "There is a natural conflict of economic interest between the working man and the capitalist. Therefore, the more heavily capitalists are taxed, the better for us who are workers." Support or refute his statement.

12. If a tax on capital serves to restrict the amount of capital used in production and thereby to lower employment and to raise prices, can the taxing authorities escape this effect by imposing a sales tax on consumers instead? Explain.

13. We have stated that land is inherently different in its economic nature than either labor or capital. How is this so? Explain.

14. What do you understand as the meaning of Psalm 115:16 regarding man and land?

15. Read the following Bible verses, and others which you select on your own, and write a short paragraph explaining what you think is a Bible-based economic view of man and land. Compare your statement with those of other class members and discuss.

Genesis 47	Psalm 115:16
Leviticus 25:23-28	Proverbs 22:28
Deuteronomy 19:14, 27:17	Proverbs 23:10
Job 24:2	Hosea 5:10

16. Why are some countries plagued with masses of unemployed and economically impotent people? Can you cite some examples from your own knowledge or experience?

17. In late 1976, agricultural workers moved onto the estates of large landholders in Mexico and demanded that the vast estates be broken up and given to them to farm. They were aided and abetted by communist agitators. Discuss the pros and cons of this issue from both an economic and a political viewpoint.

18. Show graphically what happens to the supply of land in productive use when a tax is levied on it. What happens to the price of land? Why? What happens to consumer prices? Why?

19. Why is an upward-sloping supply curve used when depicting labor services and capital but a vertical supply curve is used to depict land?

20. Explain why a tax on land produces opposite effects on supply and prices in the marketplace than does a tax on either labor services or capital.

21. In what way do present tax policies serve to:

    (a) restrict capital and investment?
    (b) reduce the level of economic activity and employment?
    (c) create slums?
    (d) foster land speculation?

22. How does government spending help to increase the value of unimproved land? Who pays for the increase in value? Who benefits? Explain.

23. How much land is owned by the U.S. government? Should this land be sold for private use? List your arguments for or against. Which of your arguments are based on economics? Which are based on ideology?

24. What four principles of taxation do the taxing authorities use as guides? Evaluate them from a biblical perspective.

4

Taxes and Tax Policy

And he will take your fields, and your vineyards, and your olive yards, even the best of them, and give them to his servants.

I Samuel 8:14

I T is important to remember that taxes are nothing more than "pumps" which draw resources from one or more of the basic factors of production. Therefore, the only sources available for public revenue are land, labor and capital. Regardless of what name is given to a certain tax, it must fall on one or more of these basic sources of economic production. If we remember this basic fact, much of the seeming complexity concerning taxation quickly disappears.

Methods of Levying Taxes

In the following paragraphs, we list the various types of taxes, we identify the economic **source** the tax draws upon; and then we comment on its economic and political **effect**.

   1. Real Estate Tax: As we pointed out previously, this tax is really two taxes in one — a **site tax** on the value of the land itself and a **capital tax** on the capital improvements made on the land site.

   As you remember, a tax on land sites serves to expand employment, to stimulate capital investment, to expand the output of goods and services and to lower prices to consumers. On the other hand, a tax on capital serves to reduce employment, to retard capital investment, to restrict the output of goods and services and to raise consumer prices. These are the economic effects.

   Politically, it is very difficult to shift taxes from capital improvements onto land because the general public is ignorant of the contrasting effects of taxing land versus capital and vested interests have already solidified according to long-existing tax policies now being followed. It is, therefore, quite difficult to change from the status quo. Some communities have approached this issue by considering the possibility of gradually shifting taxes from capital onto land over a period of years — at 2 percent per year, for example — so as not to suddenly disrupt existing economic relationships or to unfairly penalize persons who may have recently made purchases or who may have made investments based on existing tax policies.

Representative Tom Curtis, who served for a number of years as a highly respected member of the House Ways and Means Committee of the U.S. Congress, said the following at a Tax Institute of America Symposium held in Chicago, November 3, 1966:

> . . . It [the payroll tax] certainly impedes the growth of its base — namely employment, from which it derives its income. . . .
>
> It [the property tax] requires an understanding that idle land — raw land — should be taxed at a somewhat higher rate than improvements on the land, so that there will be an encouragement to put land to its most productive use. . . .[1]

2. Sales and Excise Taxes: Both sales and excise taxes are levies on capital. They serve to retard investment and employment and thereby to raise consumer prices. A sales tax is an **overt** tax since it is out in the open for all to see. However, many excise taxes are **hidden** so that the public has little awareness of them. This does not mean, however, that the economic effects of reduced capital investment, reduced employment and higher prices to consumers are avoided; for the effects are not escaped just because a tax is hidden.

A cleverly concealed excise tax — such as the one that used to be put on new automobiles and which was included in the price — is a politically expedient tax because it generates relatively little resistance from the public. But such a deceptive technique of levying taxes only dupes the public by hiding reality from them, and this may have two adverse effects. First, hiding reality from the public keeps them from being able to make intelligent choices of how taxes, if they **must** be levied, **should** be levied. Secondly, in their ignorance of the existence of such a tax, the public will complain about the resulting high prices and will likely put the blame for high prices on employers or on labor unions. Thus, needless dissension is caused in society and unwarranted antagonisms result when the real blame should be placed on the taxing authorities. Wise economic or political decisions are not likely to be made in such situations.

3. Corporate Taxes: The corporate income tax is a very popular tax among the general public because it creates the illusion that others (i.e., the supposedly rich owners of corporations) are paying for benefits that the general public enjoys. But this is a clever subterfuge because, in the long run, corporations must collect from the public every penny of taxes they pay. While the corporate income tax is classified as a tax on profits, it is only partially so because of the way the tax laws are written. A tax on **pure economic profit** would fall on the owners of a corporation, in the short run, by lowering dividends received and by depressing the price of stock traded on the stock exchange. But in the

---

[1] Thomas B. Curtis, *The Property Tax: Problems and Potentials* (Princeton: Tax Institute of America, 1967), pp. 384-385.

long run, the effect of a tax on pure profits would be to lower the amount of capital being invested in the taxed business firms. The already-familiar chain of cause-and-effect would be induced. Productivity and output would fall, supply would decrease and consumer prices would rise. The major portion of the corporate income tax is really a tax on capital; thus it clearly serves to reduce capital investment, to lower the level of employment and to raise prices to consumers. Representative Curtis, at the same meeting mentioned above, discussed this fact:

> There is only one ultimate source of taxes, the individual human being. Federal, state, or local tax systems are only different methods of extracting tax money from the individual person. He can be taxed on the basis of his wealth, on the basis of his economic activities, as a consumer, as a transactor, as an investor, and, as has been recently developed, as a wage earner. I interpose, for emphasis, that a corporation is not an individual person. It is an artificial creature and, therefore, is not really a taxpayer. A corporation, just like a political government, is simply a mechanism for collecting taxes from the individual person. It must include in the price it gets for its goods and services from the consumers all taxes it pays, if it is to remain in existence. Only in the death throes of a corporation do the investors pay part of the corporate taxes.[2]

There is a side effect of imposing corporate income taxes that is generally overlooked by the public, and this side effect has serious economic and political implications. The corporate income tax makes it necessary for business firms to go to much additional expense in setting up special tax accounting procedures so that taxes will not be either overpaid or underpaid. Corporations are thereby sometimes forced to keep two sets of accounting books — one from which they make **economic** decisions in their continuing attempt to maximize productive efficiency, and the other set from which they make **tax** decisions in order to minimize the taxes they pay.

Business decisions which should be made to minimize the payment of taxes very often conflict with decisions that would enhance productive efficiency. To the extent that tax decisions outweigh economic decisions to improve efficiency, output declines and prices rise. This puts an additional, though a hidden, burden on consumers.

Finally, by the time additional accountants, tax specialists, bookkeepers, files, housing space and other involved costs are counted, the corporate income tax probably raises consumer prices by at least 15 to 20 percent.

Another effect of the corporate income tax is the political effect. The threat of audits can be used by government officials to bludgeon business firms to

---

[2]Ibid., p. 377.

support policies which, in the short run, are detrimental to business interests and the publics they serve, and which are detrimental to the free market economy in the long run. Another political effect is to present business firms with an economic incentive to lobby in the legislative halls and to bribe or "influence" lawmakers and administrators. We noted earlier that some 10,000 lobbyists are active in Washington, D.C., alone trying to influence legislation for special interest groups. Many of these lobbyists are on the payroll of business firms as well as unions and other special interest groups. But lobbying does not stop at the federal level; each of our 50 states have legislatures that are busily passing tax bills and other legislation which affects business interests and ultimately the consumers that business firms serve. Thus the billion-dollar annual lobbying cost cited for Washington, D.C., can be multiplied two or three times nationwide.

Most workers, if asked, would probably be against eliminating the corporate income tax because they operate under the illusion that it does not cost them anything. We have already pointed out that the corporate tax does indeed cost them something **as consumers** because corporations must eventually pass their costs on to consumers in the form of higher prices. But there is still another cost aspect to consider. As we have already pointed out, a corporate tax serves to reduce the rate of capital formation, which in turn serves to reduce the overall level of employment. That is, a reduction in capital formation decreases employers' demand for new workers. Therefore, the stimulus for employers to bid against each other for the services of workers is diminished, and wage rates fall in response—or at least they do not rise as fast as they otherwise would have risen. It becomes apparent that the corporate income tax is against the best interest of workers as a group. This result is in exact conformity with the model which depicts the economic effect of taxing either labor or capital (see Graph 3:2).

Another adverse effect on workers regarding the corporate income tax is its effect on their retirement incomes. Most workers' pension funds are big holders of corporate stock. Corporate income is taxed twice, however. The corporation is taxed on its earnings **before** dividends are paid; then the stockholder is taxed once again **after** he receives the corporate dividend. Recent attempts to eliminate this double taxation of corporate dividends have been vociferously opposed as a sop to the rich. This claim might have been true 60 years ago when the ordinary workingman had little ownership interest in corporations, but it certainly is not true today when union and other pension funds hold multi-million dollars' worth of corporate stock in their investment portfolios. Elimination of the corporate income tax, or at least elimination of the double taxation of corporate dividends, would substantially increase the net worth and incomes of pension holders upon retirements.

4. Payroll Taxes: Civil authorities have found it convenient to increase the overall level of taxation by taking numerous smaller bites off people's income rather than one big bite. One means of doing this is by levying a tax on payrolls. At present, both the personal income tax and the so-called social security tax are levied in this way.

5. The Personal Income Tax: The personal income tax was for many years foreign to the democratic spirit of American self-government. The American concept of limited government kept the need for funding rather modest, but this concept began a slow process of changing with the centralization of power that began rather rapidly during and after the War Between the States and has continued to present times. For the first century and a quarter of the American Republic, tariffs on imports were very adequate for needed funding of the federal government. But more ambitious government requires more ambitious funding, and the American people became saddled with the graduated personal income tax in 1913.

An immediate effect, both politically and economically, of an income tax is to make the taxing authority a "partner" in the financial transactions of the populace. This invites the tyranny of a host of snooping investigators, auditors and tax collectors, which pries into even the most personal affairs of citizens. The *London Times* had this to say in 1816 concerning the levying of an income tax in England:

> . . . Arbitrary power marches at a cautious pace. The despotic spirit of this inquisitorial impost, with its brood of petty tyrants in every village through the land, is the true and vital objection to our admitting it as a permanent branch of our financial system. A single root of arbitrary power will insensibly throw out shoots and suckers on all sides — so a government, exercising inquisitorial prerogatives in the collection of a single tax, will easily build upon this precedent of tyranny, and the subject, used to submit in one case, tolerates his degradation in many more; the first surrender of liberty, as of conscience, is ever the most painful sacrifice.[3]

How prophetic the writer was! The power of government in England gradually expanded under the influence of the Fabian socialists in the latter 1800s. Finally, England nationalized its key industries in 1946, thus openly embracing socialism. It has been economically stagnant ever since.

The English income tax law of 1799 taxed all income over £60 per year; the tax was one shilling per pound for all incomes over £200. The American income tax of 1913 taxed incomes of over $5,000 per year; the maximum rate was 2 percent. One senator who wanted to add a constitutional amendment to limit the income tax to 10 percent was laughed off the floor of the Senate. Those who laughed feared that mentioning a limit of 10 percent would spur Congress to raise it to that amount! The pay-as-you-go provision of withholding income taxes from American citizens by deducting money from each

---

[3]Letter to the Editor, *The London Times,* 15 February 1816.

paycheck or payroll envelope was begun during World War II in order to make the total "tax bite" on citizens less noticeable. The American people would never have accepted the pay-as-you-go provision when the income tax amendment was ratified in 1913. It is doubtful whether the American public would have acquiesced even later except for the fact that Congress passed the withholding bill during a war period when national patriotism was at an all-time high. Once adopted as a "wartime necessity," the withholding provision has become an accepted public policy. Its net effect, of course, is to make citizens less aware of just how much of their incomes government is taxing away. The net control that citizens have over their earned incomes is lowered as the total tax-take increases and as the relative influence of civil government over the lives of citizens correspondingly increases. The economic result is that citizens are thereby able to exert **less** control over their lives and their accumulated wealth. The import of this effect on the spiritual dominion of Christians in society is, of course, crucial.

The mushrooming growth of spending by the federal government on a per capita basis is shown in Table 4:1. Note the big jump between 1911 and 1920 (the income tax amendment was ratified in 1913), its subsequent drop during the 1920s, its rise again during the depression years of the 1930s and the steep and continued rise during and after World War II (when the payroll withholding method of taxation was imposed).

Table 4:1

	Government Spending (Billions)	Population (Millions)	Government Spending Per Capita
1901	$ 0.5	76.0	$ 7.11
1911	.7	92.0	7.60
1920	6.4	105.7	61.00
1930	3.3	122.8	27.00
1940	9.5	131.7	72.00
1950	42.6	150.7	283.00
1960	92.2	179.3	514.00
1970	196.6	202.3	968.00
1975	326.1	215.0	1,517.00
1980	579.6	220.0	2,635.00
1982	728.4	231.0	3,153.00
1984*	853.8	236.4	3,611.00

Source: Bureau of the Census; U.S. Office of Management & Budget; U.S. Dept. of Commerce and The President's 1984 Budget.

*Estimated.

6. "Social Security" Tax: The social security program was "sold" to the American people in the 1930s as a form of a government-sponsored forced savings plan through which workers were to build up a savings account to be held by the federal government. The people were later to draw upon their "account" during retirement years. But this fiction has finally been dropped, and even the Social Security Administration now admits social security to be what it really is in fact — that is, simply a tax on labor with no savings fund being accumulated for the benefit of individual workers. As a tax on labor, social security serves to restrict the amount of labor services offered for sale in the marketplace, to reduce the supply of goods and services in the market and thereby to raise consumer prices. The fact that the employer is legally required to match the amount withheld from workers' paychecks does not mean that he pays any of the cost. Since the social security tax is a cost of production that practically all employers are forced to pay, the employees' portion of the social security tax can be easily shifted forward to the consumer through higher prices and/or back onto the workers in the form of lower wages than would be paid in the absence of such a tax. The exact portions borne by consumers and by workers in each employment situation depend upon the relative elasticity of the employer's supply curve for product inputs, including labor, versus the elasticity for the employer's demand curve for the goods and services he sells.

The entire social security program is highly political and extremely sensitive because it affects close to 40 million persons and because the general public has been led to believe many false illusions about the program. But gradually the public's understanding of the economics of the social security program is improving. When people's understanding is raised to a high enough level to become concerned about the immorality and inherently bad economics of the system, we can predict that the social security program will either be terminated or drastically changed. At present, it benefits retired persons at the expense of those who are still working. During recent years, social security tax rates have been increased; and the taxable wage base has been increased repeatedly in vain attempts to keep the program fiscally sound. It was never actuarially sound on an insurance basis. But the political pressure to raise benefit payments has been so strong that the total benefits paid have far outstripped the tax payments going into the fund. Therefore, a fund on which to earn investment income was never accumulated; nor was the accumulation of such a fund ever seriously contemplated. Such an investment fund, to be actuarially sound, would have to be so tremendous as to drain off practically all available capital in the economy. In the fiscal year 1982, for instance, a total of about $160 billion in social security benefits was paid. At even 5 percent interest, such a level of payments would require an investment fund of over 3,000 billion dollars ($3 trillion). Such a sum is too staggering to really contemplate unless we put it into perspective. There are about 56,000 family units in these United States. In order to accumulate a $3.2 trillion investment fund that would pay out $160 billion annually, each family would have to accumulate a bit more than $57,000. In 1982 the median family income was between $19,000 and $20,000; so this means that the average family would have to put away three whole years of total earnings before taxes to accumulate such a fund.

One economic factor compounding the social security dilemma is that the number of people receiving benefits has risen drastically relative to the number who are forced by law to pay into it. (Federal lawmakers have been careful to protect their own interests by **not** including themselves and other federal employees under the social security program. They are under a separate federal retirement program). In 1950 the ratio of taxpayers to income receivers was 16:1. By 1970 the ratio had dropped to 4:1. In 1982 it was 3:1, and by the year 2025 the ratio is predicted to be 2:1 according to present population trends. The program will become economically insolvent, even on a pay-as-you-go basis, long before that date because it is very doubtful that younger working people will find it acceptable to shoulder such a heavy burden that calls for every two workers to support one retiree. The main economic responsibility of any family is to raise and prepare their own young to meet the challenges of the world, so we can safely predict that social security as people know it today is already on the way out. It is just a matter of time until the hard economic facts begin to dawn on enough people to influence political action.

> The requirement that the employer match his employee's OASDHI tax payments may have the result that many taxpayers are unaware of how large their tax bill actually is. Since the employer portion remains largely hidden, taxpayers may complacently believe the tax-benefit arrangement represents a splendid bargain.[4]

For a critical view of social security and its detrimental effect on the economy, see the supplement at the end of this chapter entitled "Social Security — America's Sacred Cow."

> . . . for the children ought not to lay up for the parents, but the parents for the children.
>
> *II Cor. 12:14.*

7. **Deficit Spending:** Even though taxes have been spurred on by easy access to workers' paychecks and have been rising steadily during the last 50 years, they have not kept up with the growth of federal spending. In effect, the growth of government and its influence in our society has grown faster than the people's willingness to pay for it. The accumulated deficits of each president since Franklin D. Roosevelt are shown in Table 4:2.

---

[4] *Economic Aspects of the Social Security Tax* (New York: The Tax Foundation, 1966), p. 57.

Table 4:2

		Total Deficit Accumulated in Each Administration*
Franklin D. Roosevelt	(1934-45)	$197.0
Harry S. Truman	(1946-53)	4.4
Dwight D. Eisenhower	(1954-61)	15.8
John F. Kennedy	(1962-63)	11.9
Lyndon B. Johnson	(1964-69)	42.0
Richard M. Nixon	(1970-74)	68.7
Gerald R. Ford	('975-76)	124.5
Jimmy Carter	(1977-80)	181.0
Ronald W. Reagan	(1981-85)	728.0**

Source: U.S. Office of Management & Budget.

*In billions; **Estimated.

Government deficits like those above can be financed in these ways: (1) The government can borrow money from the people. This is **non**-inflationary because the dollars borrowed have already been earned. That is, the money borrowed is already represented by goods and services in the marketplace. (2) The government can borrow money from commercial banks or from the Federal Reserve Bank. (3) The needed money can be printed.

The last two methods of financing deficits **are** inflationary because the net result is to increase the money supply either through the banking system or by the direct issuance of money. In both instances, new money is created; and the newly created money is used to purchase the already-existing supply of goods and services. It is this resulting imbalance of money relative to the fixed supply of goods and services that forces price levels upward as consumers and producers compete for limited resources.

In Table 4:3 we attempt to put government spending, the growth of government's role in the economy and the resulting rise in public debt into perspective.

Table 4:3

	1939	1984	Increase
Federal spending per capita	$ 68	$3,611	53.1x
Federal spending as % of GNP	10	24	2.4x
Federal debt per capita	$325	$6,768	20.8x
Total federal debt	$ 0.9*	$1,600*	1,778x
Interest on national debt	$ 0.9*	$149.5*	166x

Source: U.S. Office of Management & Budget; U.S. Dept. of Treasury and U.S. Dept. of Commerce.

*In billions.

Table 4:4

Recipients of Federal Monies*
1983 Budget

Social Security	36.9
Medicaid	22.9
Food Stamps	20.0
Medicare	30.2
School Lunches	24.6
Aid to Dependent Children	10.4
Unemployment Compensation	2.8
Military Personnel	2.2
Military Retirees	1.5
Aid to Aged, Blind, Disabled	3.7
Government Workers	2.8
Veterans Pension Survivors	4.1

Source: U.S. Office of Management & Budget; U.S. Dept. of Treasury and Dept. of Commerce.

*Million persons.

We show the data in Table 4:4 to indicate the relative growth of humanistic influence in our society and government. With or without the express approval of the individuals who comprise society, the civil authority tends to take on the humanistic role of attempting to build an earthly Utopia. Not being limited to its biblical role of simply maintaining peace and order, the civil government's appetite for income becomes so insatiable that citizens will no longer be either willing or able to finance its growing activities. As more and more citizens line up at the public trough for their "free handout," an ever increasing debt will be incurred until the process is either stopped through political pressure (which is not likely to happen) or until the whole structure comes tumbling down in a massive economic collapse (which is the more likely expectation). This is the difficult economic choice faced by the generation of the 1980s. The choice poses unpleasant economic alternatives, but the issue at heart is theological. The basic issue is: Will men willingly acquiesce to live in accordance with God's laws, which require a fine balance of personal freedom coupled with personal responsibility before God; or will men become enslaved to a tyrannical humanistic civil authority which regards itself as both the source of law and the saviour of mankind?

8. Use Taxes: As explained previously, use taxes are specific levies imposed on citizens who use certain government-provided services. The example given earlier was water and sewer taxes. Other examples are parking meter fees and landing fee charges which are added to airline tickets. These serve somewhat to retard unrestricted use of the governmental services concerned.

9. Capital Gains Taxes: A capital gains tax is levied on the net profit realized from the purchase and subsequent sale of assets. If you, for instance, buy a home or 100 shares of stock and sell them at a profit at a later date, a tax on your net profit would be called a capital gains tax. Thus, such a tax is a levy on entrepreneurial or speculative activity; and we would expect it to lessen such activity.

By law capital gains are defined as "short-term" or "long-term," depending on how many months an asset has been held. Profit realized from the sale of an asset that has been held long enough to qualify as long-term is taxed at half the short-term rate. Whether such gains on capital assets should be taxed at all or at a reduced rate is also a highly political question which is determined by people's ideological views of property and the assumed class struggle between workers and the owners of capital that Marx promulgated.

One problem that affects all owners of wealth in an inflationary era is the nominal price effect that monetary inflation has on real wealth. As the governing authorities continue to inflate the money supply, price levels trend upward in response. When a person sells an asset whose price has risen because of monetary inflation, he incurs a "capital gains" tax when, in truth, there has been no real gain at all because the relative prices of other assets have also risen in price. There is an additional net transfer of wealth from private hands to the taxing authorities because taxpayers have had to pay a "gains tax" out of capital because their "gain" is not real but only illusory.

10. Death and Inheritance Taxes: When wealth is taxed at the death of a person or at the point at which wealth is bequeathed to survivors, the underlying, though unspoken, presupposition is that the civil authority is the **real** owner of wealth and that citizens only have the privilege of using it at the sufferance of the civil authority during their lifetime. Some consistent critics of taxation go so far as to claim that **any** tax is based on such an assumption. They claim that the levying of any tax really implies that ultimate ownership rests with the taxing authority. Thus, such critics claim that the power to tax is destructive of people's right of ownership and of freedom in the long run. They do make a logical point. We shall return to this later.

The fairness of death and inheritance taxes is attacked on the basis that, since taxes have already been paid by the person while he was accumulating the wealth that is taxed, it is not equitable to tax it again when he dies. After all, what if the deceased person had spent all of his money instead of saving it? Then there would have been nothing left to tax. Seen in light of this complaint, it is easy to see that death and inheritance taxes penalize frugality.

Because of death and inheritance taxes, many tax-exempt foundations have been established as a means of legally avoiding the payment of taxes. Some of these foundations have served to keep the control of wealth in private hands which would have otherwise passed over to government control. But there is a growing sense of alarm among the public that some tax-exempt foundations, especially the very large ones, may have fallen under control of persons who are more interested in the benefits which accrue to the foundation controllers than in the welfare of the public. Their argument is that everyone should be taxed equally and that no one in society should be given the benefit of a special tax shelter which protects them from the same kind of rigors that all other citizens must face.

One expected result of high levels of taxation is the growth of political action to create special tax shelters. The beneficiaries of such tax shelters then feel an economic necessity to engage in political maneuvering in order to maintain present privileges and even to gain additional privileges. Drastic reductions in tax levels would not only spur economic production, but it would also lessen the economic incentive to create special tax shelters and the political maneuvering just mentioned.

11. Tariffs: A tariff is a tax imposed on the import or export of goods from one nation to another. The U.S. Constitution prohibits the federal government from levying export taxes. As we indicated earlier, until the personal income tax was passed in 1913, tariff revenue provided our national government with practically all of the revenues it needed for operation. However, this source of revenue is not nearly sufficient to finance the high levels of government spending and transfer payments that exist today.

The economic effect of a tariff is to raise consumer prices by establishing a government-created barrier to price competition from the producers of foreign goods. A tariff amounts to a government-imposed subsidy paid to domestic producers out of the pockets of domestic consumers.

The question of a suitable tariff policy has long been a bone of contention between various geographical areas of our country and between differing economic interests. Tariff policy was an important factor in the political strife which culminated in the tragic War Between the States in 1861. Manufacturers in the northeast had long favored a high tariff policy which protected northeastern manufacturers from foreign competition. Southern agriculturists, on the other hand, favored a "tariff for revenue only" policy. They correctly contended that protective tariffs subsidized domestic manufacturers at the expense of agriculturists and consumers by restricting supply, thereby causing prices to rise.

During the 1920s, higher tariff levels led to the loss of foreign markets because foreign buyers of our goods could not obtain claims to dollars unless sellers in their country were able to ship goods to us. Therefore, an increase in tariffs which effectively excludes foreign goods also effectively reduces the ability of foreigners to buy our goods. Strangely enough, the best way to stimulate exports is to freely welcome imports! When foreigners sell goods to us, they receive the needed purchasing power to buy our export goods. Those industries that are productive and which keep labor costs under control so as to be competitive find no problem in selling their output to foreigners. When productivity drops and unit labor costs rise, foreign markets are quickly lost. It is under such circumstances that political pressures for increased tariff protection arise. In the early 1980s, business firms and labor unions in the auto and steel industries sought special protection from foreign competition; but the real problem is not foreign competitors but inefficient domestic production. When the unions and managements begin to cooperate better in serving the needs of consumers, their productivity will rise, and their apparent problems with foreign competitors will vanish.

Having said this, it is not at all startling to find that some domestic manufacturers and the workers who are employed in their plants find a mutuality of interest in fostering protective tariff legislation. Labor unions have generally favored high tariff policies under the mistaken belief that the resultant barrier to foreign goods spurs domestic employment for their members and thus union membership. During the last two decades, United States aircraft producers and other high technology firms — many of which are unionized — have developed strong overseas markets. This may cause the involved union leaders to see that a free trade policy rather than protective tariffs is really to the advantage of the workingman.

As we have just indicated, in recent years the auto and steel industries have been particularly hard hit by an increasing flow of imports. The affected corporations and unions have joined forces in calling for import restrictions. To an unemployed auto worker or steelworker, the supposed cause of his unemployment seems clearly evident — too many foreign imports! But, in reality, too many imports is not the **cause** but the **effect** of the problem. The real problem can be traced to both company managements and union leadership. The union leadership has for decades propagandized rank-and-file members to believe that the corporations, given a free market wage level, would unfairly exploit workers. Thus, the rank-and-file membership has developed an antagonistic and militant attitude which has been translated into excessively high wage levels and unproductive work rules.

The wrong attitude and lack of economic understanding by the rank-and-file union members is the fault of the union leaders who have led them astray. But the corporate managers are not to be held blameless. It was they who found it easier to succumb to the militant demands of the unions by accepting unrealistically high wage demands and then passing the resulting cost increase on to consumers. (Corporate managers, with some justification, can claim that pro-union legislation such as the National Labor Relations Act has made it exceedingly difficult to effectively oppose the demands of militant labor unions). This worked fine as long as consumers were willing to pay ever-increasing prices for the union-produced goods. But, finally, the consumer turned to foreign-made goods that gave more value for the money. In 1981, for instance, the chairman of General Motors (GM) pointed out that labor costs in the Japanese auto industry were $12 per hour versus $20 per hour in these United States. It was this cost differential that was causing American consumers to buy foreign imports. He proposed that GM and the United Auto Workers (UAW) terminate their existing labor contract and renegotiate one that would put GM on a competitive footing with foreign auto producers. For a while it looked as if the UAW members might agree, for unemployment among auto workers was the highest since the Great Depression; but the proposal fell by the wayside. Why? For this reason: In spite of the fact that the UAW leadership finally realized that they had priced their members out of the market, they were unsuccessful in selling the idea of renegotiating the contract to rank-and-file members. For too many years union members had been conditioned by the militant attitudes of their leaders, and the ordinary worker was not capable of discerning the real cause of his and his union's problem. Thus, workers in the auto industry still can be heard speaking about the "need" for government protection from foreign imports.

What is needed in the auto and steel industries is a soundly based program in basic economics for the benefit of union members. Such a program would help members to learn just how far they can go in demanding wage increases which do not exceed gains in productivity. This would lessen the demand for government tariff protection.

12. Inflation: Inflation, correctly defined, is **an increase in the money supply.** Increases in the money supply are brought about by governmental authorities who have control over the monetary system through the Federal Reserve System. The persistent increases generate subsequent rises in the general price level. Inflation has been called "the cruelest tax of all" because debauchment of the monetary unit occurs quietly and insidiously. It thereby catches the public unaware; the value of their money quietly dissolves before they discover what has happened.

Governmental authorities invariably turn to inflating a country's money supply when the civil government changes from the limited biblical role of simply serving as a guarantor of law, order and justice to the anti-Christian and humanistic role of attempting to be the people's "secular saviour" by building an earthly Utopia. In its biblical role, civil government's need for revenue is minimal because the civil authority limits itself, and is constitutionally limited by a Bible-believing electorate, to playing a solely **protective** role in society. It requires only a very small percentage of national income, or income per capita, to finance the expenses of biblically based limited government. Many of the activities now carried on by governments would be carried on by the private sector—by individuals, by voluntary organizations and by the Church. A biblical view of civil government produced the American concept of limited civil government which is to provide protection against outside aggressors and to maintain police and court systems for punishing law breakers.

But when the civil authorities take it upon themselves (or when the people ask for "a king like other nations," I Sam. 8:5) to remake society according to non-biblical principles, then the government's appetite for revenue to fund expanding programs becomes insatiable. Very soon the point is reached where the people will stand for no additional taxation, but their hunger for additional government services and handouts continues to grow. Then a series of events occurs. First, the taxing authorities devise various means of hidden taxation. When these devious forms of taxation fail to produce the desired amount of revenue, the authorities turn to debauching the currency, that is, to inflating the money supply.

The kings of Europe engaged in the practice of calling in coins of gold and silver, remelting them and mixing the precious metal with baser metals and then reissuing the adulterated coins at face value. Prices would invariably rise when the people realized what had happened and also because of the increased amount of currency in circulation. But today's "kings" use a very sophisticated method of debauching the currency through central banks (our Federal Reserve System is a central bank) which cooperate with the ruling authorities by issuing "checkbook money." The average person cannot understand the intricacies of modern fractional-reserve banking, so it is almost impossible for the deceived public to control such government money manipulation. An axiom we will present to you in the chapter on money and banking is "People cannot control what they do not understand."

The people's **real** level of taxation can be measured by adding together all forms of direct taxation, hidden taxation and the annual loss of purchasing power of the monetary unit. Twenty years ago, the annual loss of purchasing power of the U.S. dollar averaged about 2 percent. During the 1970s, the loss averaged between 5 and 14 percent; in 1981 the annual loss in purchasing power was about 10 percent. No people of any nation have been able to preserve their economic and political freedom for more than one or, at the most, two generations once the governing authorities turn to persistently debauching the currency. Thus, it can be seen that honesty in monetary affairs has a direct relation to the degree of economic and political freedom the people of a nation enjoy. A people who allows its government to follow a persistent policy of monetary inflation is, in essence, asking to be enslaved.

Taxation: Some Practical Considerations

There is a tendency on the part of taxing authorities to focus on pragmatic questions such as:

• How will this tax affect economic growth? Will it help or hinder employment, capital investment and economic stability?

• Will this tax help or hinder the allocation of resources according to consumer choice?

• Is this tax **proportional** (i.e., does it bear equally on everyone)? Is it **progressive** (i.e., does it bear more heavily on the rich)? Or is it **regressive** (i.e., does it bear more heavily on the poor)?

• Will the people rebel against this new tax? Will they seek to avoid it legally and, if so, how? Or will they seek to evade it illegally?

• How much will the new tax provide in income versus the cost and trouble of collecting it?

• Is there any way we can hide the tax so the people will pay it without knowing?

It seems that the people of these United States are beginning to react adversely, from the tax imposers' viewpoint, against rising levels of taxation. A few years ago, the people in California passed Proposition 13, which established a constitutional limit on real estate taxes. A grass roots taxpayers' rebellion is presently sweeping the country. Some concerned citizens have suggested that a tax-limiting amendment be added to the U.S. Constitution. Others have suggested the elimination of the personal income tax altogether.

There is a group of Americans who are concerned with the growth of big government and the loss of freedom which has resulted from imposition of the graduated income tax. This group is promoting the "Liberty Amendment," which would direct Congress, over a three-year period, to sell to the public some 1,700 corporations owned by the U.S. Federal Government. They point out that the sale of the many government-owned business firms (such as TVA), most of which lose millions of dollars each year, would do three things: (1) It would generate enough funds to pay off the national debt and eliminate interest payments of around $100 billion per year. (2) It would eliminate the continued need for multi-billion dollar subsidies every year. (3) It would switch these firms from the public sector to the private sector where the need to compete with other privately owned firms would make them more efficient and thereby become net producers of taxes instead of net consumers of tax revenues.

What Tax Policy?

Perhaps we should ask some questions at this point. Is there any such thing as a "beneficial" tax? If so (or if not), what tax policy should civil authorities follow? Or, more appropriately, what kind of tax, if any, should the people allow the governing authorities to impose on them?

As we have already seen, the word **tax**, by its very meaning, implies the idea of being "touched sharply." That is, the very idea of taxation is inherently burdensome and repugnant to the payer. But, then, so is the taking of medicine by a sick person. If we may use this analogy, we can liken sinful man and the sin-burdened society in which he lives as "sick." Our sick patient needs a policeman or a "carrier of the sword" (Rom. 13:4) to maintain law and order so that men can go about their business of serving each other's mutual economic interests in peace and in safety. This analogy, if it is accurate (and the author thinks it is), implies the need for a very limited and restricted government. Such a civil government would not at all be burdensome on the incomes or wealth of the people who support it. Ideally, such a light burden might even be carried through the payment of **voluntary** contributions. This is the idea the author would prefer — at least with a voluntarily supported civil authority we would never have more civil government than the citizens were willing to pay for. Do not laugh! There are many worthwhile social services that are wholly financed through voluntary contributions (volunteer fire departments, medical services such as hospitals and clinics, private schools, etc.). It is only a matter of whether the people decide to live by the rule of voluntarism or by the practice of governmentally imposed coercive levies to support such services.

But we do not live in an ideal world, and our present system is already set up on the basis of supporting civil government through the imposition of forced levies, that is, through the imposition of taxes. Accepting the status quo, then the question arises: What kind of tax is least harmful or most beneficial?

Let us approach this question through the process of elimination. Probably the most harmful tax of all is the income tax — both the personal income tax and the corporate income tax — for the following reasons: It allows and fosters the growth of an extremely burdensome civil government cost-wise by levying a pay-as-you-go tax. Citizens end up with much more government than they really want or would be willing to pay for on a lump-sum basis. The income tax is essentially tyrannical in nature because it carries with it a host of government tax snoopers. A citizen's personal affairs can no longer be private with an income tax; for he must bare himself, literally undress himself financially, before the tax collectors at least once each year. There is no part of his life that the tax snoopers cannot delve into if they wish. Also, all of the taxpayer's personal records can be called out for minute inspection if the tax department bureaucrats even suspect, or claim to suspect, less than full disclosure on the part of the citizen. No people who value personal liberty would ever allow themselves to be put into such an exposed and defenseless position. The personal income tax also breeds a host of tax specialists and tax accountants to advise individuals and business firms in tax planning, to help maintain necessary records and to make the required tax filings. Elimination of the income tax would free hundreds of thousands of these people from unproductive busy-work and would allow them to devote their time and efforts to producing more highly desired goods and services for the market. Overall production would be positively stimulated by such an employment switch, and the elimination of the present cost burden to corporations would serve to lower the price of goods and services that consumers now pay.

Another unwholesome effect of levying an income tax is how it affects people morally and economically with regard to tax evasion. Citizens will pay a nominal tax, even if grudgingly, if the cost of payment does not outweigh the benefits of tax evasion. But, as humanistic civil governments impose higher and higher taxes, people will gradually develop feelings of alienation and will then resort to various methods of tax evasion. In these United States, the so-called "underground economy," in which people barter and exchange goods and services without generating taxable records, is already estimated to account for as much as 15-20 percent of Gross National Product (GNP). The underground economy is growing by leaps and bounds. This poses serious moral problems for honest tax-burdened citizens to wrestle with, especially if the citizen feels that the government is using his tax payments for purposes he does not condone or may even feel are immoral.

Other countries with high levels of income tax are also experiencing the rapid growth of underground economies. In Italy it is called *l'econmia somersa* — "the submerged economy." A social affairs organization in Italy, *Censis,* estimates that its underground economy boosts Italy's GNP by 15-20 percent and that it involves about 27 percent of Italy's total labor force.

In West Germany the name given the underground economy is *schwarzarbeit* — "black labor." It involves an estimated 3.3 million moonlighters who produce approximately $25 billion in goods and services which go untaxed. In Britain the term used is the "black economy," and it produced about $32 billion of untaxed goods and services in 1980. In France the term used is *travail noir* — "black labor." French officials estimate it produces enough total output which, if taxed, would generate some $16 billion in taxes. Other countries in Europe, South America and Asia are also plagued with similar tax evasion problems.[5]

In summary, such widespread evidence of worldwide tax evasion provides almost inescapable evidence that civil governments which rely on the income tax are following a wrong policy too far. Not only is the income tax inherently bad, but civil governments have increased levies to the point where the gains of evasion far outweigh the potential cost of getting caught.

Is there any other viable alternative? The answer is yes, and the solution involves some drastic changes. First, people all over the world need to answer the question "What is the proper role of civil government in society?" If they come up with a biblical answer (see the next section), which is a civil government of very limited powers and very limited services, then the need for generating income to support the civil authority will be greatly reduced. The income tax could then be easily eliminated. But if the citizens of each nation continue their ungodly way of turning their civil governments into secular idols and caretakers of the people, then the appetite of the civil government will continue to be voracious; and God's curse of burdensome taxation will continue (see I Sam. 8:5-18).

We have already seen that a tax on variable factors of production (i.e., on either labor or capital) will serve to lower production, to lessen the supply of goods and services sold in the marketplace and thereby to raise consumer prices. This would seem to call for a shift of taxes from labor and capital onto land sites. This would, as we have seen, serve to increase the production of goods and services, to increase overall supply and thereby to lower prices to consumers. Another advantage of shifting taxes from labor and capital onto land would be to put all taxation out in the open for all to see. The tax imposed on each land site would be a matter of public record. Such open disclo-

---

[5]"Tax Dodging — It's a World-wide Phenomenon," *U.S. News & World Report,* 3 August 1982, pp. 37-39.

sure would do much to promote honesty by wholly eliminating illegal tax evasion schemes which plague the present practice of taxing incomes or sales, both of which require self-disclosure by taxpayers. From a freedom standpoint, shifting taxes from labor and capital onto land would eliminate the tyranny of having the civil authorities snooping into every citizen's private affairs by investigating his personal income each year.

But a word of caution is needed. Remember that civil rulers are just ordinary sinful men raised to positions of power. They will, therefore, attempt to pervert and abuse **any** system of taxation on which they lay their hands. While we have shown that the economic effects of a tax on land is beneficial when compared to a tax on either labor or capital, there is no doubt that even an open policy of taxing land could be perverted by sinful rulers. A site tax on land could, for instance, be raised so high as to discourage production by forcing land out of use. Such a policy, if followed, would be counter-productive economically — but so are many present tax policies, so we cannot count on civil rulers to be guided by sound economic thinking.

One tax we have not yet discussed in great detail is the "head tax," a lump-sum payment that each person — rich or poor — would be required to pay. This is probably the most biblical tax of all, in that it would be similar to the half shekel offering that Moses was ordered by God to receive from each man aged 20 and older (Ex. 30:12-16). (This half shekel payment was **not** really a tax because it was not a forcible levy but rather a voluntary payment.) Of all taxes to be imposed, a head tax would be the least objectional from the standpoint of being a burden; and it would lead to the absolutely lowest level of involvement by the civil authorities in society. This would be especially appealing to lovers of freedom, as it would be equally appalling to pseudo-liberals who condone higher levels of government involvement in the affairs of men.

Let us finally take up the question: "Is there either a beneficial or an ideal tax?" In answering, we must keep in mind that the Bible admonishes us to pay legitimately imposed taxes (Rom. 13), on the one hand, and that taxes are a curse an apostate people bring upon themselves (I Sam. 8).

This author can only conclude, finally, that any tax is a burden and is therefore less than ideal. If given a real choice between a tax of any kind or no tax at all, a truly freedom-loving, self-responsible people will choose to pay no tax at all. On a relative basis, some taxes are less harmful or more beneficial than others — as we have pointed out regarding a tax on land sites as compared to a tax on labor or on capital. But all taxes constitute a "bite" out of people's produced incomes or accumulated wealth; and once power is given to the civil authority to levy taxes, the door is then open to increasing the level of taxation until the people will no longer bear more.

But if we accept the status quo and grant the civil authority the power to tax, then the ranking of my choice would be thus: (1) The head tax is the least harmful, for it severely limits the amount of money the civil authority can wrench out of the people, thereby limiting the potential tyrannical growth of civil government; and it does not require a host of tax snoopers. (2) A tax on land sites is the second least harmful — much less so than a tax on either capital or labor — for it serves to increase supply and to lower prices in the market-place. (3) The most harmful tax of all is any tax which requires a host of government tax collectors, for such a tax is inherently tyrannical in nature and destructive of the people's freedom.

The question of how to tax or if to tax at all is not one that is easily solved. If the answer is to be found at all, it will be found only by seeking light from the word of God.

Taxation: A Biblical Perspective

One thing that distinguishes Christians from other members of society is that they have God's word, the Bible, as a guide to use in every aspect of life and as a benchmark to use in constructing God-oriented social institutions, including the agency we call civil government. The psalmist prayed, "Give me understanding, and I shall keep thy law; yea, I shall observe it with my whole heart" (Ps. 119:34). And Moses, in his farewell address to the Israelites before they crossed the Jordan River into the Promised Land, admonished them to live according to God's word. He listed a number of blessings, many of them economic in nature, if they did so, and a number of curses, both economic and political, if they failed to do so (see Deut. 11:13-29, 28:1-68). There is no doubt that Christians are to use the Bible in judging all of man's social institutions as well as their own daily walk in life.

The Christian community in modern America has taken a rather acquiescent view towards civil government based on a misunderstanding of certain new Testament passages (Matt. 22:15-22; Luke 20: 19-26; Rom. 13:1-7; I Peter 2:13-17). A popular interpretation of some of the cited verses has led many evangelical Christians to accept the idea that almost any ruling that comes from the civil authority should be quietly obeyed and that any level of taxation imposed should be acquiescently submitted to. This acquiescent view of the civil authority has perhaps been fostered by the fact that American civil government has historically not been oppressive and that, at least up to recent times, it has been in general harmony with widely recognized biblical principles. God recognized that sinful rulers would tend to enslave their people, so He provided a safeguard. The ruler was continually to refer to God's revealed word so that he would not become tyrannical but would rule the people in the fear of the Lord (Deut. 17:14-20).

As American civil government has become less biblical, more anti-Christian and more humanistically oriented, many observant Christians have begun taking Bible in hand to seek God's guidance in re-evaluating the proper role of civil government in society. Some questions being asked are:

• Is it a proper role of civil government to educate the young or is this a religious duty which properly falls on parents?

• Is it moral for the civil government to use its taxing power to "help" the poor, or businessmen or farmers, through transfer programs which transfer wealth from some citizens to others through the legal force of taxation? Should the care of the poor and needy be solely a responsibility of the Church and other private institutions?

• Does the civil government have rightful authority to impose such programs as social security and medical care on citizens.

Some Christians are even beginning to ask whether the civil authority should have power to tax at all. If such power is granted, they ask, should it not be carefully limited to protect the people's control over their incomes and thus their responsibility to God for how they spend their incomes.

The matter of taxation is an area where economics, politics and religious views coalesce. Can the Bible provide any light?

It appears that the civil government in Old Testament Israel did **not** have power to tax until the people asked for a king such as the Gentile nations had (I Sam. 8). Remember that the word **tax,** by definition, implies a coercive levy which the authorities will extort from the individual if he does not pay willingly. Nowhere in the Old Testament before the era of the kings do we find even a hint that the tithe or half shekel offerings were forcibly levied. The Israelites were admonished by God's word to pay a tithe of their income, but payment of the tithe was **voluntary.** Sufficient revenue was thereby generated for public needs.

We are told in the last verse of the book of Judges that "In those days there was no king in Israel: every man did that which was right in his own eyes" (Judges 21:25). This would have been fine and would have produced a low level of government activity and a zero level of taxation if every member of society had walked in perfect communion with God. The psalmist said, "Thy word is a lamp unto my feet, and a light unto my path" (Ps. 119:105). But man's heart is inclined to do evil, and he refuses to be governed **internally** by God's law. Thus, **external** government must be applied to prevent robbery, murder, rape and other anti-social acts of sin. External government is forceful rather than voluntary.

We believe that the rise of all-powerful civil governments ". . . like all the nations [have]" (I Sam. 8:5) and the oppressive levels of taxation which are eventually imposed on the people by secular governments (I Sam. 8:11-18) are evidences of God's judgment on an apostate people who failed to govern themselves voluntarily according to biblical precepts. The rise of powerful, centralized civil government and oppressive levels of taxation can be regarded as God's judgment on a rebellious people. In contrast, a civil government that is carefully limited in power and which imposes only a light or negligible level of taxation simply to support the law enforcement of keeping the peace can be regarded as God's blessing on a people who are careful to walk in His way and to build godly social institutions. This is not to play the mystic or to be the least unscientific in our approach to economics by making such a statement, for we truly believe that God's word speaks authoritatively to every aspect of life. Those who recognize this truth can more easily see the chain of causation between personal and public morality and the emergence of widespread social and economic problems.

If this view of civil government correctly interprets the biblical view — and we hold that it does: That oppressive government and oppressive levels of taxation are a curse on the people for not following biblical precepts — then we can see that the illusory goal of a near-zero level of taxation is not an absolute impossibility. All that is needed is a people who consistently and faithfully live every aspect of their lives in absolute conformity to God's will. This ideal goal, of course, is not attainable is this sinful world before our Lord and Master comes again. It does at least point the direction towards which a Bible-believing people should strive in reducing the role of civil government to a minimum in society and, in doing so, to drastically reduce the level of taxation now being imposed. "Blessed is the nation whose God is the Lord; and the people whom he hath chosen for his own inheritance" (Ps. 33:12). But "The wicked shall be turned into hell, and all the nations that forget God" (Ps. 9:17). Christians are admonished to "Trust in the Lord with all thine heart; and lean not unto thine own understanding. In all thy ways acknowledge him, and he shall direct thy paths" (Prov. 3:5-6).

Certainly Christians are called upon to recognize the fact that secular, humanistically oriented civil governments may be opposed to God (Ps. 2:2-3) and, if so, must be staunchly resisted where they are wrong (Acts 5:20). The presupposition given by the Bible is that all governments, even secular ones, should rule for good (Rom. 13:4) and that all rulers are to bow the knee before Christ. It is in this light that Christians should regard the civil authority and its power of taxation — always recognizing that the powers that be are of God, but always judging the secular powers according to God's unchanging benchmark, the Bible.

Supplement

America's Sacred Cow

Most Americans have a hard time understanding the backward people of India.

In that underdeveloped country, millions of poor people suffer almost constant pangs of hunger and at times even starvation. Yet hundreds of thousands of sacred cows roam about, freely breeding and eating scarce grain which might otherwise be used to feed India's hungry and emaciated children.

"Cows ain't sacred," opine common-sense Americans. "Why don't the Indians get smart and barbeque some of those animals? Can't those people see how all those ill-bred cows are impoverishing their country?"

American reaction to India's false religion certainly makes economic sense, does it not? India's standard of living could be substantially raised overnight if the people could be made to see the harmful effects wrought by their sacred cows. But, alas, for India as for many other underdeveloped countries, economic abundance must await spiritual enlightenment—a job for Christian missionaries.

Yet, ironically enough, some astute Indians could well point to a sacred cow that is presently impoverishing America.

America's sacred cow is **Social Security**.

And America's sacred cow—this socialist system of financing old-age payments, this unique system of legalized theft—is most certainly impoverishing America.

Let me make myself clear: I am not intimating that 36 million fellow citizens who receive social security checks each month are immoral thieves. Some of my dearest friends and closest relatives are numbered among the 36 million. It is the **system** that is bad, not the people who are caught up in it. The large majority of these 36 million are no doubt loyal citizens and staunch patriots. But good people cannot make an immoral system produce moral results.

It is a sad fact that most Americans have never been challenged to consider the pros and cons of America's great sacred cow. Thus, they tend to register shock when someone is audacious enough to swim against the tide of public opinion and label social security as "legalized theft" or as "socialist insecurity" par excellence.

If this series of editorials causes at least a few observant people to re-evaluate America's social security program, it will have served a worthwhile purpose.

Social security has been based on a big lie from its very inception. Back in the 1930s, believing citizens were told that the program would work just like a private insurance plan. They were told that money would be deducted from workers' paychecks and that these "premiums" would accumulate at interest in the social security retirement fund. Then workers would draw down their funds when they retired. Trusting Americans believed this fiction. They were propagandized into believing that they were building a retirement account similar to the ones accumulated through private life insurance companies.

The truth is that social security is **not** like the retirement insurance plan it was purported to be.

First, there are not enough reserves in the social security fund, relative to its vast liabilities, for it to qualify as insurance. If any **private** insurance company were to attempt to operate with as thin a margin of reserves as does the social security system, it would immediately be shut down as insolvent by the appropriate state insurance commissioners.

Social security is an out-and-out tax. It operates on a revolving fund basis.

It pays money out to 36 million retirees and other beneficiaries just about as fast as the money is taxed away from some 90 million employed workers.

Retirees who receive social security checks each month do not, as many people think, draw on a fund of assets which the retirees have gradually accumulated during their working years. Rather, they receive checks which represent the product of present effort — checks which are drawn on the sweat of their children's brows. Social security is nothing more than a disguised socialist attempt to transfer earnings from those who work to those who do not. For good or bad, social security is simply a government-administered coercive plan to let the older generation live at the expense of the younger generation.

Note what the Bible says about proper economic relations between the older and younger generation: "For the children ought not to lay up for the parents, but the parents for the children" (II Cor. 12:14).

There is yet another reason why social security is not like a private retirement insurance plan, as it was purported to be.

Private life insurance companies issue written contracts which are legally binding upon the company. These contracts provide policyholders with written guarantees which can be enforced in our courts of law. A holder of a private insurance contract can choose from a number of retirement options, most of which will repay him or his heirs more than he has paid into the company.

This is not so with social security. It contains no written policy guarantees. A person can find his social security "contract" suddenly changed whenever Congress takes a whim to do so. The citizen, as "policyholder," has nothing to say as an individual about how his social security "contract" can be changed. It is a one-way street.

In contrast, a private insurance company **cannot** change any of its contracts without securing the voluntary agreement of **each** insured person.

It is true that most changes made so far in the social security "contract" have been made at the expense of working persons in order to benefit retirees. But this one-direction change process need not always take place. It is a matter of relative political pull. So far, social security retirees and beneficiaries have been a very powerful and vocal pressure group. Congress and the presidents have bowed to them in order to garner their votes. But as the tax bite on working people's paychecks continues to rise, more and more working people will get stiff backs when it comes to increasing social security benefits. In short, the political pressure that has in the past exerted an upward bias on social security benefits may soon be ready to do an about-face.

One factor in the probable about-face is the voice of youth. The reduction of the voting age to 18 increased the political importance of young people tremendously. I, as a college professor, find most young people sadly misled when it comes to understanding principles of freedom, sound economics and American republicanism; but this is an **effect** of the mis-education imposed on them by their mixed-up elders. Young people today are smart and quick to learn. Once the socialist mentality that they picked up through years of socialist exposure in 12 years of sitting in classrooms is cracked, real light begins to flow in and is quickly assimilated. It does not take long for the average young person, once awakened, to see for himself that the odds in social security are loaded against him.

Then there is the deeper question of personal freedom and individual responsibility. A few years ago, it was difficult to get young people to consider the question "What is the proper role of civil government in a free society?" Now young people are eager to wrestle with this question. One answer they usually do **not** come up with is that it is a proper role of civil government to force them to save for their own retirement, much less for millions of strangers.

Today many young people, thanks to the educational advantages provided them by their parents, start out earning high incomes. Thus, they quickly feel the social security tax "bite" when Congress raises the taxable wage base as it has been doing during the last few years.

In matter of fact, recent increases in social security benefits have been financed by increasing the "bite" on the paychecks of higher income workers. In 1973 the taxable wage base was $10,800. In 1974 it was $13,200. In 1980 it went up to $25,900; and by 1985 it is scheduled to rise to $42,900.[6] While this procedure is right in step with the age-old socialist tactic of taxing the productive middle class in order to pay for the "goodies" that politicians so freely pass around to win votes, many younger wage earners will, for the first time in their lives, be able to see the painful effects of socialism where it hurts most — in their own paychecks. There is little doubt that they will not like what they see. From there it is but a short step to political activism. Sooner or later the tide of "socialist security" will be turned around. All of the necessary elements are already in existence. All that is needed is a catalyst.

We are fast reaching the point where it will be more difficult, both economically and politically, to finance future increases in social security benefits by across-the-board increases in payroll taxes. According to data released by the Commerce Department, three-fourths of American families earn less than $25,000 per year (this included multiple wage earners). Because many $25,000-plus families have more than one breadwinner, this means that substantially fewer than one-fourth of employed people have incomes that are larger than the social security tax base now in existence.

In short, most of the cream has already been skimmed from workers' paychecks to pay for the existing level of social security benefits. Could it be that America's sacred cow has been just about milked dry?

I previously made the charge that the social security program serves to impoverish America. Let us investigate this charge:

The Social Security Administration itself imposes quite a drain on our country's resources. There are now 636 district social security offices, with 384

---

[6]The figures in the article have been brought up to date.

branches and 129 metropolitan branch offices, located throughout our nation. Administrative expenses for the Administration's network of offices have risen from a modest $27 million in 1940-41 to over $1 billion per year currently. The majority of employees in the Health, Education and Welfare Department work for the Social Security Administration. If participation in the social security program were made voluntary (happy thought!), or if the whole program were abolished (better yet!), think how many federal employees could be released to find productive employment in private industry, not to speak of the office space that could be vacated to more productive enterprises.

It is true that private insurance companies would have to expand employment if they were to take over the present role filled by the Social Security Administration, but the intense competition and great efficiencies that exist in that industry would assure greater overall savings in operation than government agencies have ever been able to offer.

One thing to keep in mind is this: The cost of operating the Social Security Administration does **not** come out of the social security taxes paid by workers, but costs of operating private insurance companies **do** come out of the premiums paid by policyholders. Yet, in spite of this, as I will show later, private insurance companies give policyholders more in retirement benefits per invested dollar than does social security.

It would be difficult to calculate the net drain on resources that the combination of higher operating costs and lower benefits add up to, but the drain is certainly there—and continues year after year. The drain on resources will increase as the sheer size of the social security program continues to mushroom. To give you some idea, let me give you the historical record of social security contributions and estimates of future benefits (which approximate contributions):

1950	$ 3.1 billion	1975	$ 63.0 billion
1960	12.3	1980	136.5
1965	19.4	1984*	210.6
1970	36.9		

*Estimated figure.

It is difficult to visualize just how big the $136.5 billion is that the social security program diverted in 1980, but this amounts to about one-fifth of the total assets owned by all the life insurance companies in these United States.

Let us now consider how social security compares with private methods of saving towards retirement.

We will take a person at random from among the 230 million citizens of America. He just happens to be 25 years of age. Let us call him Mr. John Q. Public.

At age 25, Mr. Public has 40 years to work before retiring at age 65. During this 40-year period, let us suppose that social security taxes and benefits remain stable. This is not a realistic assumption, of course; but it is necessary so we can evaluate its relative worth. Finally, let us further suppose that Mr. Public's taxable wage base under social security will average the $25,900 maximum that was in effect in 1980 and that it will remain at this figure for the whole 40 years of his working life. These assumptions will come very close to the situation in which many young men find themselves at age 25.

In 40 years, Mr. Public will **directly** pay $25,900 × 6.15% × 40 years = $63,714 into social security. He will also pay a like amount **indirectly** through his employer. This latter amount is the fictional "matching contribution" that the social security law requires employers to pay on behalf of each employee. Since the employer's matching contribution is an employment cost, any so-called employer contribution represents a real loss in wages that the employee would have received in absence of the matching contribution requirement. This provision is one of the lies upon which the whole social security program has been based from the very beginning. It was a false "sweetener" designed to marshall the support of workers for the social security idea back in the 1930s. Few workers would have gotten excited about any retirement program that was financed entirely with their own money, so the fiction of a matching contribution was created. Even today, few workers realize that their employer's "contribution" to social security really comes out of their own pocket!

In reality, then, we see that Mr. Public can expect to pay a total of **twice** the $1,593 that is withheld annually by his employer. In short, counting the so-called matching amount his employer pays, Mr. Public will pay a total of $127,428 into social security during his working life.

Now this is a substantial sum of money. Whether Mr. Public might be better off to spend his $3,186 per year in other ways (such as for more education for himself while still young in order to raise his long-term level of income; for college funds for his children; for a better home for his wife and children; for purchase of stocks or other investments; or even for beer and booze), we cannot tell. Only he can. But it is an academic question because the social security law imposes a **tax** on Mr. Public's paycheck. Since a tax is an **involuntary** payment, he has no other option.

For his $127,428 forced "investment" in social security, Mr. Public can hope to receive a rather complicated package of benefits which includes disability and medical payments in addition to a monthly retirement income. Let us exclude the disability and medical payments because these are only minor aspects of the program's monthly retirement income. For this simplification, we will reduce the cost of Mr. Public's forced investment by 20 percent; that is, we will reduce it from $127,428 to $101,960. What we are interested in doing is to compare the relative worth of social security as a pension income, and this healthy 20 percent reduction in cost will prevent the Social Security Administration from claiming that we have made an unfair comparison. If anything, the advantage will now lie with social security.

Remember, now, that we have reduced Mr. Public's forced investment in social security from $3,186 to $2,549 per year (i.e., $101,960 for a 40-year period). At the 1980 benefit rate, Mr. Public and his wife (if married and if they both live to retirement age) would receive a maximum of $981 per month, or $11,772 per year, in retirement benefits. Note that Mr. Public does **not** have an option of drawing a lump-sum cash payment. Also, if Mrs. Public should die, his monthly income as a widower would drop to $654 per month, or $7,848 per year. If Mr. Public should die, his widow would receive the same reduced income. But, if Mrs. Public should remarry, she would forfeit claim to the retirement income that Mr. Public had paid into for 40 years.

If we assume that both Mr. and Mrs. Public live for 15 years (to age 80), they would receive a total retirement income of $176,580 for the forced investment of $101,960. This is a robust assumption which heavily weights the social security program so it will appear in its most favorable light. For, if either married partner dies, or both, or if the widow should remarry, as often happens, they could easily fall far short of recouping even their original investment.

Now is the time to point out a gross inequity in the social security program. In the previous calculations we have assumed that Mrs. Public never worked, and thus never paid anything into social security herself. If she indeed did work, as most wives do, her forced investment in social security would be lost if she draws benefits as a survivor. If she worked for as little as ten years during her lifetime and earned only half as much as Mr. Public, she would lose about $12,500 plus interest (the amount she paid into social security). If she worked 15 years, she would lose $18,750 plus interest. This is equivalent to a husband and wife both taking out a retirement policy with a private insurance company, and the company saying, "Let us tear up your wife's policy, and let the company keep the premiums you paid!" In short, Mr. and Mrs. Public's **real** forced investment in social security will most certainly be much **greater** than the $101,960 pay-in we have conservatively estimated.

What if Mr. Public had put his money into a savings account instead of into social security?

If Mr. Public had saved $2,549 per year and invested it at 6 percent interest, he would accumulate $394,483 by the time he was 65. Note: This is for funds compounded annually. If interest were compounded quarterly, as many private institutions compound in order to be competitive, the effective interest rate would be 6.14 percent, and the savings total at age 65 would be correspondingly greater. There are many investment opportunities that pay more than 6 percent. Each year $2,549 saved and invested at 7 percent would produce $508,857 in 40 years. At 8 percent, the total would be $660,344.

With a sum of $394,483 invested at 6 percent, Mr. and Mrs. Public could draw $1,972 monthly, or $23,664 per year. Compare this with the **maximum** monthly payment of $981 that the Publics could receive under social security.

Now it is important to take note of another important difference under this private savings plan versus social security. The $1,972 per month under the private plan is an **interest** payment. Thus, it does **not** eat into the principal that the Publics have accumulated. They can go on drawing interest at this rate (six percent) until they die. And then they can pass the principal on to their heirs or to their favorite charities. In other words, their claim on their savings is not socialized away from them as it is under social security. They can leave it at interest for as long as they need it and then pass it on to those who are dear to them. But death or remarriage of the wife immediately stops future retirement income under social security.

Regardless of which spouse preceded the other in death under the private retirement plan, interest payments to the remaining partner would **not** be reduced; and Mrs. Public would not have to worry about losing her income if her husband should die first and she remarried.

At this point, people who condone socialist attempts to establish retirement programs will say, "Ahah! It is all well and good to talk about the wonders of compound interest. We know that private retirement plans will outstrip social security. But that is not the point; the real point is that the common man just will not save his money unless he is forced to do so. He will save for a while, but then he will spend it when some real or imagined emergency comes up. And when he gets too old to work, he will not have anything saved and will have to go on the welfare rolls."

This is wrong thinking. There is ample proof to the contrary. I happen to own a retirement policy with the oldest life insurance company in these United States, formed in 1717 and chartered in 1759. The 250-plus years of existence of this company—most of the multi-billion dollar life insurance companies are over 100 years old—publicly extoll the fact that people have been inclined to save money willingly for many generations. Down one socialist cliché! The billions of dollars paid out each year by life insurance and savings institutions stand as irrefutable evidence that many people have been consistent savers.

The **real** question about old-age pensions does not revolve around the mechanics of implementation because most knowledgeable observers agree that private plans are better than socialized ones, but the question revolves around ideology. Is man a self-responsible being who is capable of taking care of himself and of his own? Or is man a simpleton who needs a caretaker? The caretaker route which America has followed under social security has produced a plan that is devoid of accumulated savings because it is a "tax-as-you-go" plan.

But suppose Mr. Public should choose, if he could, to invest his social security tax of $2,549 per year in a life insurance policy? One leading life insurance company offers this policy to a 25-year old man: A yearly premium of $2,549 will buy a $130,000 Life-Paid-Up at 65 policy (including waiver of premium, which would pay out the policy for him in case he became disabled).

Mr. Public's guaranteed cash value and dividends at age 65 would amount to $223,357. If he bought some additional term insurance for extra protection while his children were young, the amount would be slightly reduced.

Upon retirement, Mr. Public could choose from a number of options:

• He could take cash. At 6 percent, this would produce a monthly income of $1,117 or $13,404 per year. At 7 percent the income would be $1,303 per month or $15,636 per year. This option would not consume any principal, so the $223,357 could be passed on to heirs or to charities.

• He could take a guaranteed monthly life income of $1,246, which would be raised to $1,732 including dividends. Or if he wanted an income guaranteed for as long as either he or his wife lived, the monthly income would be reduced to about $997, plus dividends. Compare this with the **maximum** of $981 monthly under social security for both husband and wife, and $654 for a single retiree. The important difference between this private insurance plan and social security is that real insurance is, as stated earlier, a **legally binding** contract. The guaranteed monthly payments **cannot** be lowered as they can be under social security if political pressures should shift, as well they might.

Also, under a pension plan provided by a private insurance company, the Publics would have what is called a vested interest in their account. Their account is their property. They can borrow on it if a need arises because of some unforeseen emergency or if common sense dictates. Many people, for instance, borrow accumulated cash values from their insurance company at 5 or 6 percent interest to purchase automobiles and repay the loan on an installment basis. This is better than paying 10 to 18 percent to the bank or finance company. Thus it represents a hidden savings that does not appear in the above comparison. During periods of high interest rates, the life insurance industry reports that many of their policyholders borrow cash values at 5 or 6 percent interest and invest the funds in government securities and high-grade industrials and utility bonds that pay 8 to 10 percent or more. Again, this represents hidden income that would tip the scales in favor of life insurance over social security.

Once the Publics start drawing a guaranteed monthly income, they still have a vested property ownership in it even in case of death. They can choose to have payments guaranteed for at least ten to twenty years, for instance. This means they are guaranteed the income for life; but in the event they both should die before the guaranteed period expires, the residual monthly income would be paid out to whomsoever the Publics designate. Add up another plus for private insurance!

Social security, of course, has no option. Because it holds a protected monopoly position (i.e., because people are **forced** to pay into it), there have been no competitive pressures to cause it to offer the attractive options that people can get under private insurance plans.

Why not make social security optional so people will have a choice?

We have been comparing **involuntary** social security with **voluntary** private retirement plans. We have seen that private plans are better from a number of viewpoints. First, they are non-coercive. This is important to people who still believe in the American ideal of freedom. Secondly, they accumulate more total assets for the participants. Thirdly, the people individually retain important property rights and ownership control over their accumulating funds. Lastly, private plans provide attractive options which retirees can select from, depending on their needs at retirement. This provides a flexibility that is absent from social security.

We have seen that the old socialist bromide, "People just will not save unless they are forced to!" does not hold water. The almost 2,000 private life insurance companies, 485 mutual savings banks, 6,000 savings and loan associations, 24,000 credit unions, 20,000 non-insured private pension plans, 250 mutual funds and 33 million persons who own shares in U.S. corporations all stand as a grand and eloquent testimony to the saving propensities of the American public. No, there is little doubt that the American people both **can** and **will** provide for their own old-age income if they are left free to do so!

This brings us to a fatal aspect of social security which has a very detrimental impact on the American economy. It is the aspect which tends toward the impoverishment of society. With every private retirement plan there is a long period of delay between the time that a participant starts contributing his money and finally begins to withdraw it. All during this delayed period, the accumulating investment fund gradually adds to the total fund of real capital in our country. That is, private savings plans provide growing quantities of new tools and equipment for industry to use in expanding the flow of goods and services to society.

A larger base of productive tools quickly increases the output of consumption goods, which means a higher standard of living for everyone in society. Historically, private savings institutions have been important sources of new capital for America to grow on.

This important process of tool accumulation tends to be short-circuited by social security, which is a tax-and-spend-as-you-go plan. The money that social security wrests from workers does **not** go towards the creation of new capital tools and equipment. Rather, it is paid out in benefits almost as soon as it is taxed from workers. Therefore, it helps foster consumption at the expense of investment.

Now, if we were talking in terms of only a few million dollars, social security would not be a significant factor in the overall economy because the American economy is so large. But each year social security will collect and redistribute over $200 billion. That is a vast amount of money. It is about one-fifth of the total assets of all the private life insurance companies in these United States! For 1985 the redistribution is estimated at $236 billion. This immense diversion of funds from potential investment to consumption cannot help but impoverish our country.

Let us put this in perspective. Private retirement plans are like a wise and far-seeing farmer who carefully saves his seed corn and plants it. Then after the growing season, at harvest time, he is free to eat from his increase; but saving had to come first.

Social security, on the other hand, is like a short-sighted and improvident

Social Security Legislation

	Taxable Wage Base	Combined Employee/ Employer Tax Rate	Maximum Combined Tax
1955	$ 4,200	4.0%	$ 168
1956	4,200	4.0	168
1957	4,200	4.5	190
1958	4,200	4.5	190
1959	4,800	5.0	240
1960	4,800	6.0	288
1961	4,800	6.0	288
1962	4,800	6.25	300
1963	4,800	7.25	348
1964	4,800	7.25	348
1965	4,800	7.25	348
1966	6,600	8.4	554
1967	6,600	8.8	580
1968	7,800	8.8	684
1969	7,800	9.6	748
1970	7,800	9.6	748
1971	7,800	10.4	812
1972	9,000	10.4	936
1973	10,800	11.7	1,264
1974	13,200	11.7	1,444
1975	14,100	11.7	1,650
1976	15,300	11.7	1,790
1977	16,500	11.7	1,930
1978	17,700	12.1	2,142
1979	22,900	12.26	2,808
1980	25,900	12.26	3,176
1981	29,700	13.3	3,950
1982	32,400	13.4	4,342
1983	35,700	13.4	4,784
1984	39,600	13.4	5,306
1985	43,500	14.1	6,134
1986	47,700	14.3	6,822
1987	51,900	14.3	7,422
1988	56,400	14.3	8,066
1989	61,500	14.3	8,794
1990	66,900	15.3	10,236

Source: *1980 Statistical Abstract* and *The Budget of the U.S. Government,* 1981.

farmer who eats most of his seed corn right away. Because he has eaten the largest part of his capital for immediate consumption, he will have less to eat in the long run. This is what social security is doing to America! Truly America's sacred cow is impoverishing the people of our country!

What is the obvious solution? Can a scrambled egg be unscrambled?

One obvious answer is to make participation in the social security program optional. This would allow those who object to social security on moral, ideological or economic grounds to check out of the system. Many people who are now captive riders of an involuntary system would gladly check out of this massive experiment in socialism, even if it meant forfeiting all past involuntary "contributions!"

What, after all, is wrong with that old American ideal of voluntarism?

Is social security such a bad deal that it would fall apart if people were not forced to participate in it? If so, then it is not worthy of the American people's support. If not, then there is no need to worry.

Anything that is truly worthwhile should be able to stand the test of voluntarism. Let each person be free to decide whether social security is good for himself and his family. Let us be confident that the way of freedom is the best way in the long run. Only in this way can we find out if America's sacred cow is truly sacred or whether it is just a false idol.[7]

Questions

1. What nine techniques of levying taxes are listed? Comment critically or favorably on each based on: (a) economic cause-and-effect, (b) political implications and (c) biblical principles. If you were asked to develop a tax policy, what techniques of taxing would you recommend? Why? Which would you not recommend? Why?

2. What effect does the corporate tax have on:
   (a) wages of corporate employees?
   (b) consumer prices?
   (c) pensions of retired workers?

3. By what percentage has per capita federal spending grown from 1900 to the present?

4. Defend or attack this statement: "The personal income tax necessarily makes the government a 'partner' in every financial transaction that a citizen engages in."

5. Do you favor or disfavor the payroll withholding method of taxing? Explain your view.

---

[7] *Santa Ana* (Calif.) *Register,* 14-20 January 1974.

6. Is social security a government-supervised "forced savings and retirement program," or is it a tax? What long-range effect is the social security program having on economic growth and people's standard of living in America? Explain.

7. Defend or attack the social security program from a biblical perspective.

8. What three methods of financing debt does the federal government have?

9. Why do civil governments eventually turn to inflation as a means of taxing? Evaluate this technique of taxation from a biblical viewpoint, citing appropriate Bible passages.

10. How much has federal spending increased since 1939? What significance do you see in this trend?

11. How should a people's real level of taxation be measured to get an accurate reading?

12. How many people are recipients of federal monies? Do you see any dangers or problems politically or economically? Explain.

13. What presupposition does the author say underlies death and inheritance taxes? Defend or attack his statement.

14. Trace the economic effect of a tariff on:
    (a) employment and wages in the protected industry,
    (b) employment and wages in export industries,
    (c) the prices that consumers will pay after a tariff is imposed and
    (d) the general level of demand that foreigners will have for the goods our country exports.

15. Define inflation. Why has it been called the "cruelest tax"?

16. What is a lobbyist? Is the need for lobbyists greater or smaller with limited government?

17. What do we mean when we say that a tax on real estate is really two taxes in one?

18. Explain this statement: "A tax is only a pump." What three sources of revenue might a tax-pump draw from?

19. Analyze the supplement on social security entitled "America's Sacred Cow." Do you agree or disagree that social security is impoverishing America? Explain.

20. How much has: (a) the social security tax base grown since 1955? (b) the total maximum tax increased since 1955? Do you predict they will continue to increase or decrease in the future? Explain your reasoning.

21. If social security were optional, would you opt in or out? Explain.

22. You have been appointed by the President to head a commission to terminate social security because of the growing political pressures coming from young people. Write a short memo to him explaining the essence of your plan for termination that would be fair to all concerned (young people just entering, middle-aged people who have paid in for years and still have some years to go before retirement and present retirees who are dependent on social security).

5

The "Isms"

. . . Cursed be the man that trusteth in man, and maketh flesh his arm, and whose heart departeth from the Lord.
Blessed is the man that trusteth in the Lord, and whose hope the Lord is.

Jeremiah 17:5 & 7

IDEAS are the controlling forces of society; they give both men and nations the directive orientation which impels them dynamically along certain philosophical and ideological courses. The ideas to which a people collectively adhere destine each country to develop economically, politically and socially in a unique manner.

It is not by chance that these United States of America have historically been recognized as the land of political freedom and economic opportunity — a country where the worth and dignity of the individual are held in high regard. Nor is it by chance that Communist Russia, Communist China and Communist Cuba have come to be recognized as lands of political oppression and economic slavery — countries where the individual is regarded as being of little value and thereby expendable. In each instance, the idea of man — what he is, his source and his destiny — controls the development of each nation. Truly ideas have consequences! And the consequences are predetermined according to whether or not the ideas that are held reflect the mind of God. Ideas that do reflect the mind of God are in harmony with reality. Such ideas do not conflict with the objective world as God has created and sustains it.

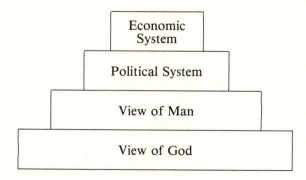

> *Through faith we understand that the worlds were framed by the word of God, so that things which are seen were not made of things which do appear.*
>
> *Hebrews 11:3*

Thus, it is important to the student of economics to understand the different ideas and world-and-life views which underlie the various politico-economic systems of the world and to evaluate these ideas and world-and-life views from a biblical perspective. Economic systems are directly and causally related to the political, philosophical and theological views that people hold.[1]

Humanism vs. Christianity

There are two basic and contrasting views or ideas about man—the secular humanist view and the Christian view.

The secular or modern humanist view of man holds that man is the chance development of a naturalistic evolutionary process. We might note, also, that there is nothing scientific about this view; for any view concerning man's source deals with faith rather than science. Although the humanists have tried to use science as a screen to "prove" their faith-held presupposition, true science cannot be used to prove origins. What man believes about his origin is simply and purely a matter of faith—either faith in God and what God's word says or faith in man and what ideas man has had the ingenuity to concoct.

The humanist view sees man as standing at the top of a long evolutionary ladder and sees him as reigning supreme over the world solely through his ability to engage in rational thought. It recognizes no God or "higher law" that unconditionally binds man to unchanging moral codes of conduct or behavior. But it does recognize the existence of certain immutable physical laws as well as a "nature of man" to which man must adjust. An implication follows: Since there is no higher law to restrict the implementation of man's fancies and imaginations, there is nothing that man may not do if he can do it physically. Any rules the humanist does happen to follow are recognized as originating in man himself by reason rather than from God or some "higher power."

The modern humanist view, such as the earlier classical humanist view of man held by many people in the last century, sees man as self-perfectible. Evil is nothing but the expression or outworking of man's present state of ignorance. So, to improve man's social performance, all that is necessary is to **educate** him. As man's knowledge increases, so the humanist thinks, so will his economic, political and social well-being improve because he will be better enabled to adjust to his environment or to change his environment to suit himself.

Robert V. Andelson treats this and related issues in a book entitled *Imputed Rights*.[2] He sees three broad traditions of human rights: (1) the Radical

---

[1] Tom Rose, *Economics: Principles and Policy* (Milford, Mich.: Mott Media, 1977), pp. 61-86.

[2] Robert V. Andelson, *Imputed Rights; an essay in Christian social theory* (Athens: University of Georgia Press, 1971).

Humanist, (2) the Utilitarian and (3) the Metaphysical, which includes two sub-categories: (a) Classical Humanism and (b) the Christian View of Man.

The radical humanist assumes that human rights are an end in themselves, and he holds that they come from venerating man as man. The radical humanist sees man as inherently good and perfectible. He views the end goal of man as that of being free, and the regulating principle is assumed to be equality—let all men be equal. Andelson correctly criticizes this view of human rights by pointing out that freedom is not an end in itself, that freedom is meaningless unless it is harnessed to the service of some further purpose (see Ex. 8:1) and that a radical humanist-based freedom will result in either collectivism or in anarchy.

The utilitarian, on the other hand, assumes that the most important goal in life is "the greatest good for the greatest number." He holds that so-called "rights" are nothing but pragmatic fictions based on the regulating principle of expediency. The utilitarian takes a hedonistic view of man, whose end goal he says is that of maximizing pleasure or "happiness." This view of human rights, says Andelson, does not work either because in practice its regulating principle devolves into rule by the majority. He correctly points out that the happiness of individuals cannot be summed up into a collective "greatest good." The reason, of course, is that some people achieve their happiness by sacrificing that of others. More importantly, though, happiness is a **subjective** state; thus it is unique to each individual. A subjective feeling of one person cannot be summed up with the feeling of any other individual.

The metaphysical view of human rights assumes that man is a created being and that his rights come from man's established place in a purposive order. Man is viewed as being related to something higher than himself. Man's end is to be found in a higher cosmic purpose, which is also the source of his regulating principle.

At this point the metaphysical view divides into two streams: (1) the **classical** view of humanism, which involves various theories that man is perfectible, and (2) the **Christian** view of human rights, which sees man's rights as a necessary means of fulfilling his destiny in God's purposive universe. The goal of man from the classical humanist view is that of maximizing his own personal fulfillment, while the Christian end of man is seen as fulfilling the authoritative will of God to His honor and glory (see Deut. 10:12; Eccles. 12:13; Micah 6:8).

The previous section may at first seem somewhat unrelated to the study of economics, but let me assure the student that the ideas people hold certainly **do** have implications economically. The humanist view of man, for instance, can logically lead in two different directions—anarchism or state totalitarianism.

Anarchism

Anarchism is the belief and practice of the total absence of civil government. The humanist who believes in anarchy holds strongly to the idea that man is inherently good and that man can be perfected through education. Man does not require outside restraint to keep him from harming his fellowmen, and he can achieve the ideal of self-centered freedom through education. The idea is that man, through appropriate study, can learn that the imposition of one man's will on another is counter-productive economically and socially. Therefore, society will gradually move toward the ideal of perfect freedom when each man learns to live in harmony with all other men. The occasional anti-social individual who **does** impose harm on his fellowmen will either be "frozen out" by the refusal of others to deal with him, and thus be brought into social conformity, or the other members of society will minimize the effect of his anti-social actions by individually taking non-violent safeguards to protect themselves. In either case, there is no need for a civil authority to punish or restrain anti-social persons through the use of force.

This is a beautifully logical system except for two points:

First, it fails to recognize that freedom is not a goal in and of itself. Secondly, it fails to recognize that man, because of his fallen sinful nature, has a built-in tendency toward doing evil. This view overlooks the hard facts of the real sin-burdened world that man must live in. It flees from reality because it is not in conformity with God's word. The need here is not for man to think his own thoughts but for man to search the mind of God so that he can bring into captivity every thought to the obedience of Christ (II Cor. 10:5). To do otherwise is to do nothing more than to build fairy castles in the sand instead of facing the world of economic reality.

Freedom simply for the sake of freedom produces a self-centered license from any higher law which might serve to restrain man from imposing violence on others, and this finally ends by allowing man to do anything he desires. In contrast, biblical freedom — that is, freedom that is in conformity with the law of God — produces a sense of godly fear and of one's responsibility to serve the living God (Deut. 5:29). A biblically based freedom combines one's personal freedom with one's self-responsibility to God. The view of freedom simply for the sake of freedom sees man's most important goal as maximizing his freedom from any restraint at all for the sake of maximizing his own pleasure; therefore, it removes all moral bounds in one's seeking self-satisfaction. The biblical view, on the other hand, sees man's most important goal and only duty in freedom as that of maximizing God's honor and glory through serving Him as a faithful trustee according to God's revealed will in the Bible. This view provides man with an **objective** guide for use in his personal and social affairs.

Man's tendency to do wrong — that is, his sinful nature — makes it impossible for him to live in society without at least a modicum of authority being imposed from outside his own person. This brings man face to face with a pressing choice. To the degree that men collectively — by individually submitting themselves to the authority of God's word — are able to achieve **internal** self-government, then **external** civil government can be allowed to wither away.

But to the extent that man rebels against God's law, the authoritative civil government must be imposed from the **outside**. This is the meaning of Thomas Jefferson's statement, ". . . In questions of power then let no more be heard of confidence in man, but bind him down from mischief by the chains of the Constitution."[3] Jefferson recognized that man, by his very nature, needs some outside restraint if freedom is to flourish in society. This is the whole idea of the American brand of constitutional government.

Totalitarianism

Totalitarianism is the practice of tyranny, and tyranny is the arbitrary or despotic exercise of power. It can occur in two ways: (1) In an anarchistic situation where there is no restraining governmental authority, one man can tyrannize another by imposing arbitrary rule over him by force or by the threat of force. (2) In a governmental situation, the rulers can use the force of law to autocratically impose their will on the masses. A tyrant can be a ruler who comes to power by **illegal means** or a **legally installed** ruler who arrogates unwarranted powers to himself.

It is this second version of tyranny that we observe most often in society. It springs from the same view of man that is common to anarchism, the view that man is self-perfectible. But in this instance, some individuals—that is, the government rulers—think they are wiser or more intelligent than the masses of ordinary citizens. They believe it is actually beneficial for the "less gifted masses" if the "more gifted and intelligent" (i.e., themselves) will accept the burden of directing and controlling the affairs of society. To the extent that the masses acquiesce, or can be made to submit by force, the controlling elite thinks it will be able to usher society into an earthly Utopia. All that is necessary, in the minds of such a ruling elite, is that they plan carefully and that the masses be willing to submit to the elite's superior direction of men's lives and social affairs.

> *Son of man, say unto the prince of Tyrus, Thus saith the Lord God; Because thine heart is lifted up, and thou hast said, I am a God, I sit in the seat of God, in the midst of the seas; yet thou art a man, and not God, though thou set thine heart as the heart of God:*
>
> *Behold, therefore I will bring strangers upon thee, the terrible of the nations: and they shall draw their swords against the beauty of thy wisdom, and they shall defile thy brightness.*
>
> *Ezekiel 28:2 & 7*

---

[3] "The Kentucky Resolution," written by Thomas Jefferson and passed by the Kentucky Legislature, November 10, 1798, in *We The States; and Anthology of Historical Documents and Commentaries thereon* . . . (Richmond: Virginia Commission on Constitutional Government and Wm. Byrd Press, 1964), p. 150.

The two great flaws in totalitarianism are: (1) Because of man's tendency to do wrong to his neighbor, it is **not safe** to entrust even the most gifted rulers with power over others, lest they despoil their fellowmen. (2) Even if man could withstand the temptation to take unfair advantage over others, he is still **finite**. Man does not have the infinite knowledge and wisdom that would be necessary to direct the affairs of even one other human being, much less masses of them. Therefore, as population increases and society becomes more complex, men need **more** rather than **less** individual freedom and self-direction. This truth runs contrary to popular opinion. He who attempts to direct the lives of other men thus arrogates to himself powers which can be safely entrusted only to God. The Bible is adamant that men are not to put their trust in princes (Ps. 118:8-9, 146:3), who are but ordinary men raised temporarily to high places. Rather, men are to put their trust only in God and His law-word (Ps. 7:1, 16:1, 31:1, 37:5, 62:8, 64:10, 125:1).

Totalitarianism in a governmental situation expresses itself in these forms, which we will discuss:

(1) Socialism
(2) Fascism
    (a) English Mercantilism
    (b) Italian Fascism
    (c) German Nazism
(3) Communism
(4) Welfare-Statism

Socialism: The dictionary defines socialism as a political and economic theory of social organization based on collective or government ownership and democratic management of the essential means for the production and distribution of goods. However, socialism can more accurately and succinctly be defined as government owernship and/or control of the means of production.

The problem with the former definition is that it excludes fascism (which is just a specific form of socialism) and that, in practice, socialism is never democratic. In socialism, control is **always** vested in a self-continuing elite which uses various strategems to maintain itself in power. About the closest socialism can come to being democratic in practice is that, in some countries, the government controllers are elected to office. But where this is so, the rulers gain and maintain popular support through the demagogic tactic of taxing and spending. In short, by promising the voting public a share of the state's largess, the rulers are able to "purchase" the votes they need to stay in power. They, in effect, prostitute themselves to maintain popular support; and they become the official dispensers of the "legal plunder" they confiscate from the public.

In practice, socialism amounts to the application of coercion by the few over the many. The power of the state is used to tax the people and/or to socialize the means of production. This is done without payment by enacting laws to nationalize industries. Thus, the control of money and real wealth flows into the hands of the state rulers. This economic control over resources is used, along with laws which impose political controls and economic regulations over the populace, to induce citizens to do the will of the state controllers. Citizens who acquiescently submit are duly rewarded by the state masters. Those who do not submit, as the English Fabian socialist George Bernard Shaw (1856-1950) so urbanely quipped, will "be mercifully put out of the way."

Socialism can be seen in various forms and in various stages, but it amounts to **control** — it amounts to effective control of the masses by a governing elite. Socialism is, in effect, the state's overruling of freely-arrived-at decisions made by millions and millions of individual citizens. Socialist planners assume that individuals, if left free to act in satisfying their own needs, will naturally act **contrary** to the state's interest and, thereby, develops the need to overrule them.[4] In its **milder** stages, socialism can be observed in the "welfare-statism" and state control that has been developing so rapidly in these United States over the last few generations. In its **more developed** stages, socialism can be seen in the state ownership and control which is currently being practiced in England, France, Belgium, Sweden and other countries. In its **forthrightly totalitarian** stages, socialism can be (or was) seen in the Soviet Union, Red China, Nazi Germany and Fascist Italy. Many of the countries in South and Central America, Africa and Asia practice socialism somewhere between the last two stages.

In all of these nations, the civil authority **owns** and/or **controls** the various means of production. The rulers of every socialist country regard it as their right and duty to direct the affairs of other men, much as a chess player moves his pawns on a chess board. The essence of their view is that men collectively exist as pawns for the benefit of the state. According to them, the state does not exist to protect the freedom of individual men who are personally accountable to God.

The underlying concept that is common to all these various expressions of socialism is that there is nothing morally wrong in state officials manipulating and controlling the populace in order to lead them into the blessings of an earthly Utopia — a Utopia, of course, that is envisioned by and directed by the "philosopher-king types" who are at the head of the state (on the idea of philosopher-kings as elite rulers, see Plato's [c. 427-347 B.C.] *Republic*).

It is important for the student of economics to take note that, in essence, **all** forms of state collectivism (socialism, fascism, Nazism, communism, welfare-statism and mercantilism) are but different expressions of socialism in action. Recognition of this fact will help us understand the "unity of sameness"

---

[4]This same governmental attitude was found in mercantilism, which was practiced in Europe from about 1500-1800.

to be found in all of these differently named systems which are the same in essence. Canned beans are still beans, regardless of the brand name one finds on the label!

Fascism: Fascism is what the author calls "college-level socialism." It is a form of socialism, but in practice it is a much more sophisticated and clever application of it. The **form** is different, but the **essence** is the same. It is socialism with just a different brand name on the package.

Under orthodox socialism, the state arrogates to itself outright ownership of the means of production. Accordingly, the state masters necessarily incur, along with the legal title of ownership, all the problems that accompany the ownership of wealth. They must maintain and replenish the wealth when it wears out. If we apply the concept of orthodox ownership to a horse, the state must feed, groom, maintain and care for the horse when it is sick. The state must also see that it is bred to produce its own replacement when it grows too old to work. Also, as any farm boy knows, the state must shovel out the manure! But the state is not a person, as such, so these chores will be delegated to a state employee. We can rest assured, however, that the top state officials, who will ride the horse when they wish, will never delegate to themselves the necessary work with the shovel! Even though the chores of ownership must be delegated, they still must be attended to. All of this simply to have use of a horse when the state officials want.

Let us ask: Is there a smarter way of handling the matter? Yes. How much smarter is the way of **fascism!** Under fascism, the state does not seek to become the **owner** of the horse. It only seeks to have control over the horse and to use the horse when desired. Thus, the legal title of ownership is left in the hands of the original owners; and the state simply enacts laws which, under the threat of punishment, tell the owners what to do with their own property, how to use it and even when they may use it. To follow our equine example, the real owners of the horse must feed, groom, breed and care for the animal through sickness and health; and, lastly, they must also shovel out the manure. The state officials, through the coercive powers they hold as rulers, can legally demand to use the horse whenever they wish. The state thus receives all the **benefits** of actual ownership, but it bypasses all the **tribulations** that legal title to property entails. The rulers can even enact laws to punish the owners if they do not properly take care of the property that they "own." "Ownership" in such a sitation is obviously just a fiction, for the very purpose of ownership is to guarantee the owner effective control over what he owns. But effective ownership is cleverly usurped under fascism.

This distinction between orthodox socialism and "college-level socialism" may seem like a joke because of the example used, but no joke is intended. The distinction is both **real** and **important** to an understanding of the different varieties of socialism. In these United States, orthodox socialism is seen in such things as government ownership of the Tennessee Valley Authority (TVA), the Hoover Dam and the U.S. Postal Service. Orthodox socialism is also seen in tax-supported schools and universities, city-owned utilities and municipally owned transportation systems. Still another aspect of orthodox socialism is the approximately 1,700 corporations owned by the U.S. Federal Government.

"College-level socialism" or fascism can be seen in the many government agencies which regulate and control privately owned business firms: the Interstate Commerce Commission (ICC), the Federal Trade Commission (FTC), the Federal Aviation Agency (FAA), the Civil Aeronautics Board (CAB), the Environmental Protection Agency (EPA), the Occupational Safety and Health Agency (OSHA), the Federal Reserve System (FRS) and many, many others. Each of these agencies of civil government is fascistic in that each imposes coercive control over the owners and operators of businesses so that they must do the state's bidding, but these agencies leave the legal title of ownership as well as the headaches of ownership in private hands. Thus, we see that effective control is achieved but that the many burdensome responsibilities of ownership are evaded. Many people complain that these United States are turning socialistic — this is true in a sense, but only in the sense that the **type** of socialism towards which our country is turning is **fascism.**

A perfect historical example of how fascism works in these United States can be seen in the railroad industry. The title of ownership has remained vested in the railroad corporations. The stockholders appoint a board of directors which, in turn, hires a team of managers to operate the railroad. But over the years, the railroad managements have been severely limited in what they can and cannot do. For almost 100 years, they have not been able to raise or lower rates in response to changing economic conditions without getting approval from the Interstate Commerce Commission (ICC). The ICC itself has recently eased up on this rule, so now railroads have more freedom in raising or lowering rates to meet competition from trucking and barge firms. Now they have freedom to change rates and subsequently seek approval.

Quite often in the past, the ICC has prohibited railroads from effectively meeting competition presented by over-the-road trucking firms. Though it is more efficient to haul bulky materials in large quantities in steel-wheeled cars that ride on smooth steel rails, the result of intervention by the ICC has been to foster the growth of trucking firms at the expense of the railroads. The increase in capital and labor drawn to the trucking industry and the decrease in capital and labor in the railroad industry has created a vast amount of misallocated resources that has cost consumers through higher prices.

Railroads have also been historically restrained from adding and deleting routes to meet changing patterns of traffic unless they received prior approval by the ICC. Formal ICC hearings had to be held, and every competitor or potential competitor was given an opportunity to file briefs explaining why the railroad should not be allowed to add or drop a line. Such formal hearings have dragged on, not only for years but for decades; and they have entailed millions and millions of dollars in expense for briefs, counterbriefs and high-priced legal counsel. Years ago, for instance, the public showed clearly through declining patronage that they did not value travelling on most railroad lines as passengers. The ICC, however, doggedly refused to let the railroads drop their unprofitable passenger service; nor would they allow the railroads to do much merging of services so as to lessen their passenger losses. Finally, the passenger-related losses became so huge that the railroads were desperate to divest themselves of the albatross that was hanging around their necks. Then a way out was proposed: Why not sell the passenger services of all railroads to the federal government and let the government serve the public?

The railroad managements jumped at the chance to unload their unwelcome albatrosses! Thus, the railroad passenger service in these United States was nationalized—AMTRAK was born. A change was made from "college-level socialism" (fascism) which exerted control without ownership, to orthodox or "high school-level socialism." Once the passenger service was nationalized, AMTRAK quickly did what the private railroads had been prohibited from doing for over 75 years by the ICC: superfluous and overlapping passenger services were eliminated, the most unprofitable routes were abandoned and some other more promising routes were added. In spite of these changes, the overall passenger service has generally proved to be unprofitable; and AMTRAK has chalked up losses year after year. The only difference is that now the losses no longer come out of the pockets of railroad stockholders but out of the pockets of taxpayers.

This historic example of fascism shows how burdensome government controls can lead to business firms' selling out or even giving part of their business to the civil rulers in order to avoid continued losses. Telephone companies and electric utilities in South and Central America have travelled this same route. Uneconomic controls became so unprofitable that the private firms sold out at low prices to the governments, and now countries in those areas have publicly owned telephone and electric utilities.

Fascism, in addition to developing in our own country, has also appeared historically in:

(1) England—Mercantilism
(2) Italy—Fascism under Mussolini
(3) Germany—Nazism under Hitler

English Mercantilism: Mercantilism was a popular form of state control in Europe for about 300 years—from about 1500 to 1800 England is perhaps the best example to use in explaining it; but Holland, France, Spain and Portugal also practiced mercantilism. Adam Smith's great work, *The Wealth of Nations,* published in 1776, was devoted to explaining why and how free market capitalism is superior to state control.

The basic idea underlying mercantilism was that it is right and proper for the state, that is, the king and his agents, to manipulate and control the economy in order to achieve state-established goals. Like the day in which we live now, it was a period of long-continued military confrontation between the leading European nations. The state established goals were to increase political and military power, to get more gold and silver (bullion), to stimulate full employment and to promote economic growth as a nation relative to competing foreign nations. If these 300-year old state goals sound surprisingly modern, do not be surprised. The ambitions of secularly minded rulers do not change. The similarity between mercantilism 300 years ago and state control in modern America results from accepting similar presuppositions, which in turn produce similar thought patterns. "For as he thinketh in his heart, so is he: . . ." (Prov. 23:7).

The kings did not come right out and claim they **owned** the people and the wealth of the people, but their actions indicated that they **thought** they did. Mercantile thinkers assumed that the people, if left to themselves and allowed to follow their own economic interests, would engage in activities which would conflict with state-established goals. Therefore, the king and his agents minutely controlled the economy through a massive and intricate system of rules, regulations, taxes, tariffs, bounties and subsidies. Adam Smith's great contribution was that he showed that there was a "guiding hand" which — through the free actions and mutual self-interest of millions of individuals — would automatically work to increase the wealth of the individuals. Thus, the wealth of the nation as a whole would also be increased if men were left free to act in their own self-interest.

Italian Fascism: The fascist movement in Italy grew out of the frustrations that the people felt after World War I. The word **fascist** is derived from the Latin *fasces,* which is a bundle of sticks. The meaning is that "in unity there is strength." Sticks can easily be broken one by one, but a bundle of sticks is very difficult to snap.

Politically, the Fascist Party viewed Italy as a corporate state which was a "living organism." Fascists viewed the state as having a separate existence apart from the people. The state had a greater existence which continued on and one, and the people were to serve it faithfully. The fasicsts were socialists/communists (there was little distinction between the terms then), but they broke with the international socialist movement in order to build socialism in one country. Benito Mussolini, the dynamic organizer of the Fascist Party, used the *fasces* as a national symbol. He organized a group of thugs called the Black Shirts. These became the State Police and were used to intimidate the people Mussolini could not win over to his side.

Mussolini used both democratic means and duplicity to achieve power. Once in power, he used outright force and terror wherever it was needed to remain in power. The Fascist Party immediately took control of education in order to train youth to be "useful" citizens. Youth groups were also started outside the schools for additional indoctrination purposes and to set the children against their parents.

The Fascists won the support of the Catholic Church because church leaders felt, at least during the early stages of development, that the Fascists stood for law and order and seemed to have a beneficial program for the people.

The fact that the Fascist Party considered the communists as their deadly enemies does not mean that the ideologies held by these two groups were opposed in basic principle. Their beliefs were quite similar. It only means that the two factions were engaged in a deadly struggle to see which group of revolutionaires would gain control of the state. Pitched battles between the two groups often occurred in the streets while both were vying for control. Many Fascist Party members — Mussolini being perhaps the best example — had devoted years of faithful service to the communist cause. Many one-time communists rushed into the Fascist Party ranks once it became clear that the fascists rather than the communists had won the upper hand in Italy.

Economically, the whole country was divided, according to industry, into government-controlled cartels. The ownership of productive facilities was generally left in the hands of private owners as long as they remained properly "cooperative." Effective control over productive wealth was shifted to state-directed boards called syndicates, which were made up of workers and employers. Only one syndicate was officially recognized in each branch of business or industry, and all officials of each syndicate were either Fascist Party members or persons of unquestioned loyalty to the fascist regime. Each syndicate was thus nothing but a closely controlled instrument of state power. Labor unions, in their real sense, disappeared. Where they continued to exist, they existed only to serve the state. Prices, wages, production, transportation and communications — in short, all forms of productive activity — were directed and controlled by the state. Italy became one great corporate state with a breathing, pulsating life of its own in the view of its admirers.

The people were continually propagandized to accept, serve and live for the "living state." Psychologically, the people tended to lose their individual identities by merging their identities into the more grandiose plans of the state. The people became appendages to the state which became the people's secular god and saviour. In addition to all of this, an interesting phenomenon which has been an item of study among political scientists appeared. A sado-masochist relationship developed between the rulers and the people. Psychologically, there seems to be a need for totalitarian rulers to impose pain on the people and for the people in totalitarian countries to seek pain. This phenomenon seems to be common to all totalitarian systems, regardless of the name given to a specific type.

Economic stagnation, of course, gradually occurred in the Italian Fascist State, as it does in all closely regulated economies. This is understandable, for the net effect of all government regulation is to overrule what would otherwise be the free market decisions of the populace. As the government controls spread further and further throughout the economy, the individual desires of more and more persons become frustrated. As evidences of stagnation gradually appeared, the state rulers diverted the people's attention to imagined foreign enemies whom they blamed for waging economic war on the state. Thus, the element of war is invariably closely tied to state-controlled economies. Hitler and Stalin also used the same "foreign enemy" tactic to maintain popular support of the people. Without a common enemy to hate and fear, the people might well come to recognize the economic deficiencies that are inherent in socialism. It is fair to say that totalitarian states have a built-in tendency to be warmongers as a means of controlling their own populations.

German Nazism: The fascist movement in Germany likewise developed out of the deep frustrations that existed in the country after World War I. The post-war inflation of 1921-1923 left the country in a shambles both economically and politically. This gave various socialist/communist groups opportunity to agitate for popular support of their "solutions." The fascists, under the leadership of Adolph Hitler, gradually gained precedence. The name taken by Hitler's group was the National Socialist Party. It used the acronym NAZI and a swastica as a national symbol.

The Nazis contested ferociously with the Communist Party, even to the point of pitched battles in the streets between the thugs of both groups. They battled in Germany just as the communists and the fascists battled in Italy some years earlier. The heated controversy, again, was **not** over ideology; for in that the opposing camps were agreed. Both groups adhered to the idea of a centrally controlled socialist economy. The contest was simply a matter of **who** would rule — the Nazis or the communists? Hitler, the dynamic force behind the Nazis, organized the German Workers Party and also set about organizing all the people into one mass movement. Like his predecessor in Italy, Hitler used the demagogic tactic of capitalizing on the people's frustrations and won their support through grandiose plans and promises of national greatness. He promised to build the German people into a super-race that would reign for a thousand years. He, too, like Mussolini, broke with the international socialists in order to build socialism in one country, thus the term National Socialist Party.

The Nazis were not able, as the fascists in Italy, to gain widespread church support. Church leaders were strangely silent as Hitler systematically built his atheistic state and as he set about systematically destroying orthodox religious beliefs. The Nazis, like the fascists in Italy, quickly took over the schools to "educate" German youth into being faithful servants of the state. " 'Tis education forms the common mind: Just as the twig is bent, the tree's inclined."[5]

In Germany, the state was not viewed as a "living organism" as it was in Italy. Instead, the Nazi State was viewed as the "voice of the people." The "voice," of course, was imagined to be most clearly and faithfully spoken only by the Führer (Adolf Hitler), who supposedly had some mysterious power of knowing the mind of the German *volk* — even if the people did not agree. It is amazing that intelligent people embraced this ideology. It shows the blindness

---

[5]Alexander Pope, *Moral Essays,* Epistle 1, line 149 in John Bartlett, *Familiar Quotations . . . ,* 14th ed., rev. and enl. (Boston: Little, Brown & Co., 1968), p. 406b.

of man's sinful heart (Eph. 4:17-19) and the social and economic outworkings which occur as a result.

Hitler also organized a tightly knit band of thugs, the Brown Shirts, around him. Those relatively few individuals who could not be bamboozled into cooperation were beaten into submission. Hilter used democratic means to gain initial popular support. Interestingly enough, the business community did not oppose Hitler, as is sometimes incorrectly reported. They liked the illusion of economic stability and resurgence that Hitler promised. The business community thus overlooked the totalitarianism that is inherent in national socialism; they did not stand on the side of freedom.

Economically, the entire German economy was controlled from the central seat of the government. In the early years, a tight non-inflationary policy was pursued; and prices were kept from rising. In addition, tight government control over wages contributed to an expanding foreign trade by keeping domestic production costs low. This allowed Hitler to obtain needed foreign currency to purchase war materials for expanding military power. In Germany, just as in Italy, the imagined threat of foreign enemies was used to rally continuing popular support and to keep the people's attention diverted. Productive wealth was also left in private hands, as it was in Italy, so long as the industrialists cooperated with the state and obeyed the regulatory laws and edicts. As indicated above, the large industrialists generally supported Hitler's program because it stimulated their businesses.

The basic idea underlying the Nazi State was that the people were to serve the state according to the dictates of their wiser and more far-seeing rulers. In this respect, **all** forms of state control—both of the outright totalitarian as well as the milder state-welfare types—are identical. When the President of these United States, for instance, imposes wage and price controls to control "inflation" or when the Federal Reserve Board meets to implement monetary policy, they are practicing **in essence** the very same idea which underlaid the Nazi State in Germany and the Fascist State in Italy. The only difference is that the forms of control are somewhat muted here in these United States so that the people do not yet recognize the frightful face of outright totalitarianism. The rulers here are still wearing velvet gloves, so to speak. But the mailed fist of brute totalitarianism is always under the velvet glove when the civil authorities exert economic controls, and it can quickly be uncovered if necessary. The ideal way for the civil authorities to control a people economically and socially, though, is **not** by the means of outright force. It is much more efficient to condition the people mentally and psychologically through state-directed education for young people, through careful control of broadcasting and the news media and through the establishment of state propaganda bureaus. The pattern is similar for all nations that move toward totalitarianism. Some observers fear that these United States could move toward totalitarianism if a biblically based understanding of individual freedom and self-responsibility before God is not inculcated in each new generation.

Communism: Communism developed by accident in Russia. (It is not technically correct to say that communism exists in Russia. We should rather say that the communists **took over** Russia and instituted **socialism,** from which some day they expect the ideal communist state to miraculously appear. More about this as you read on.) It grew out of the chaotic aftermath of the Russian defeat in World War I. The Russian people overthrew the Tsarist regime (actually the Tsar stepped down peacefully), and they established a democratic socialist government under the leadership of Alexander Kerensky. The peaceful revolution occurred in March, 1917. But Vladimir Ilyich Lenin (1870-1924) and a small group of his revolutionary followers forcefully overthrew the people's democratic government in November, 1917, and initiated the dictatorship of the proletariat under the Communist Party. From that moment on, Russia has been ruled by one of the most tyrannical regimes in history. Since 1917, it is estimated that the Communist Party in Russia has intentionally murdered and purposely liquidated some 60 million persons.

Marxian theory envisioned that communism would rise automatically out of the ruins of the highly industrialized capitalistic nations. According to Karl Marx (1818-1883), communism could **not** become established and develop in a predominantly agricultural nation like Russia. His theory of historical materialism dictated otherwise. The theoretical steps that historical materialism was to follow were for a nation to go from feudalism to capitalism, from capitalism to socialism and, finally, from socialism to the ideal of communism; but Marx was wrong in this theory, as in other theories that he held.

Marx, in his theory of the progressive misery of the working class, predicted that free market capitalism would mercilessly grind down the oppressed working class. Finally, unable to be ground down any further, the intolerable burden of their abject misery and oppression would cause workers to rise up spontaneously in rebellion and overthrow their bourgeois masters. The proletariat workers would murder the bourgeoisie and immediately establish a dictatorship of the proletariat under the rule of the Communist Party. While this dictatorship "temporarily" ruled, economic socialism would be practiced.

During this stage of economic development, each worker was to be paid according to his productivity (**not** according to his need as many people wrongly believe). The supposed inherent efficiency of the socialist system of production was expected to be so great that soon there would be a super abundance of wealth produced for all to enjoy. When this time in the future is reached, a most remarkable change is supposed to occur in human nature. At the present time, man is stingy and selfish because there is a scarcity of goods produced under free market capitalism; but when the socialist system of economic production flowers to produce a superabundance of wealth, there will be plenty to go around, so everyone can have all he wants. Thus man will lose his selfish nature. Accordingly, there will no longer be a need for the state to maintain law and order and to protect property, for no one will want another man's wealth. The state which is now controlled by the Communist Party (the dictatorship of the proletariat) will just "wither away." The long-awaited and hoped-for Utopia condition of pure communism will have arrived.

Each person will eagerly produce according to his ability, and each will consume according to his need. In this pleasant and happy state of affairs, man will be so satisfied with his social and economic condition that he will work and produce wealth for others to enjoy simply for the joy he receives from doing so. In short, the essence of this idea is what is called "economic determinism." This is the idea that man's economic situation is what determines how man thinks and acts; it determines what man is. If you want to change man's nature, all you have to do is put him in a different economic environment. Man is nasty and niggardly today, according to communist thought, because he lives under private capitalism where there is economic scarcity. Under the budding flower of socialism, the ideal state of perfect communism will finally come into full bloom; and man will change miraculously into a loving, considerate being.

That, in a capsule, is the dream of communism! Marx did not spend much time describing this ideal state of affairs because he theorized that the inexorable forces of history would necessarily and automatically bring it to pass at the proper time. Marx devoted most of his energies to criticizing free market capitalism and predicting how its demise would come about. The fallacy of Marxian theory is evident from both the historical record and the revelation of God's word. The Berlin Wall and the carefully guarded borders of the Soviet Union provide inescapable evidence which shouts to the world that communism in practice is a failure. For without armed guards to keep the people in Russia and its captive satellite nations, millions would flee to freedom in the West. The Bible clearly teaches that it is not man's environment which pollutes his heart but that it is the outworking of man's sinful heart which pollutes his environment (Matt. 15:18-19). Therefore, man can only be changed from the inside, which will then produce a beneficial outworking socially. Man's heart will never change simply by changing his economic or social environment. The hard evidence of history proves the Marxian dream of a communist Utopia to have been a failure, and God's word guarantees that it will ever continue to fail.

Behind the Iron Curtain: All is not well behind the Iron Curtain which the Soviet Union keeps tightly drawn between the Soviet bloc nations and the West. It has not been well since the Bolsheviks forcefully overthrew the Kerensky people's government in 1917.[6] This fact is generally not realized by large masses of the public in Western nations, but information which cannot be ignored keeps leaking out — especially in recent years as communications have

---

[6]Anthony Sutton has written a number of very revealing books on the Soviet Union, published by the Hoover Institute in California. Mr. Sutton exhaustively points out how aid and subsidized trade from these United States has time-and-time-again bailed the communist regime out of certain collapse. Without this aid and Western technology, provided over a period of more than 65 years, the people now living behind the Iron Curtain might well be free today.

improved with advancing technology. The following quotes will give the student a good understanding of what life and health care behind the Iron Curtain are like today.

As a recent immigrant from Russia, I would like to add one point to "Making It in America: 4 Immigrant Odysseys" (August 17):

If Americans knew what it is like to search for a piece of meat and never find it; how it is not to be able to buy a refrigerator unless you stay on a waiting list for 10 years; what it is like by mandatory registration to be committed forever to one living place; how easily people are put in jail just for complaining about it; what it is like to live in constant fear and to struggle for survival every day in a country where courts are designed to protect the government and justice is formulated in one simple concept of guilty unless you can prove otherwise; if they knew all this, they would become law-abiding citizens, never go on strike, not demand more freedom and never insult their government. But with amazement, delight and deserved pride, they would whisper as I do: "God bless this land and its people."[7]

Health Care in the Soviet Union: The September 4, 1981, edition of *Science,* published by the American Association for the Advancement of Science, presents a realistic view of health care in the Soviet Union.[8] The article was based on two sources: A book entitled *Inside Russian Medicine,*[9] by William Knaus, co-director of the intensive care unit at George Washington University, who spent a year (1973-1974) in the Soviet Union; and an analysis of hard-to-get Soviet statistics by Murray Feshbach of the Georgetown Center for Population Research, Washington, DC, and by Christopher Davis of the Center for Russian and East European Studies at the Universtiy of Birmingham, England. The analysis by Feshbach and Davis is contained in a statistical report entitled *Rising Infant Mortality in the U.S.S.R. in the 1970s.*[10]
The following quotes are from the *Science* article mentioned above:

. . . The report documents the alarming rise of infant mortality, perhaps the most significant single indicator of a nation's health,

---

[7]David Edelman, "Making It in America," *U. S. News & World Report,* 14 September 1981, p. 5.
[8]Our thanks to Dr. Fred Schwarz for calling our attention to this information through his monthly newsletter, *Christian Anti-Communism Crusade.*
[9]William Knaus, *Inside Russian Medicine* (New York: Everest House, 1981).
[10]Murray Feshbach and Christopher Davis, *Rising Infant Mortality in the U.S.S.R. in the 1970s* (Washington, D.C.: U.S. Dept of Commerce, Bureau of the Census, 1980).

since the mid-1960s. It is now more than double the U.S. rate, having gone from 22.9 deaths per 1000 live births in 1971 to 31.1 in 1976, the last year for which such statistics are available. And when adjusted to match U.S. criteria—the Soviets don't count deaths that occur within the first week after birth—the figure goes to 35.6 (the rate in the U.S. and Western Europe is currently under 13).

. . . they find the most likely causes to be repeated abortions (the average Soviet woman has six during her reproductive span); environmental pollution, which may cause genetic defects and miscarriages; poor management of childhood influenza (linked to malnutrition), which often turns to fatal pneumonia; and alcoholism, which has become increasingly rampant among women as well as men.

Higher mortality rates are not confined to infants; over-all mortality has risen from 6.9 per 1,000 in 1964 to an estimated 9.5 in 1979. This reflects a rise in death rates among men, for whom life expectancy has fallen to 63—which many observers attribute to alcoholism. . . .

. . . Not only is much of it [Soviet health care] shockingly inadequate by American standards, both in quality of care and the availability of supplies and equipment, but, he [Knaus] says, a large portion of what would in America be regarded as routine services are obtainable only through *blat,* or the connections, favors, and bribes that pervade transactions in the U.S.S.R. and that are necessary to get almost anything done well, on time, or indeed at all. He [Knaus] claims, for example, that hospitalized patients often have to pay nurses for such things as bedpans, fresh sheets, prompt injections, and other rudiments of care. . . .

. . . Equipment is old and faulty; the health minister himself, Boris Petrovsky, has said that 75 percent of x-ray film is of too poor quality to be useful; and diagnostic capabilities are thin. The result is that the average Soviet patient going into the hospital for surgery is not checked for most of the things an American would be checked for. . . . There are persistent shortages of drugs and of such minor items as thermometers. Wheelchairs are not available, says Knaus, an observation confirmed by an émigré physician who says they are not manufactured in the U.S.S.R. . . .

. . . it [alcoholism] is known as the 'third disease' after the two major killers, heart disease and cancer, and is a logical suspect in stomach cancer, the most prevalent cancer in the Soviet Union. . . .

The toll, socially, economically, and in terms of health, is staggering. According to Powell, [David Powell of Boston University's Russian Research Center] the economic cost of abuse is greater than the amount of revenue brought in by the state monopoly on vodka production—which in turn exceeds the amount they say they spend on defense (the real defense figures, of course, are larger). . . .

. . . In the U.S.S.R., as in the West, the population is aging. There are few nursing homes; housing is always in short supply; and increased burdens on already crowded hospitals can be expected. The steady increase in alcohol consumption shows no signs of abating. The nutrition picture is not improving. Rickets, commonly associated with underdeveloped countries, is showing up in the countryside, according to the Davis and Feshbach report. The incidence of lung cancer is rising, correlated with the continued increase in cigarette smoking. Health problems associated with pollution are likely to increase. . . .

. . . at this point it would appear the Soviet system offers little to envy.[11]

The Great Economic Failure of Communism: Instead of the superabundance that Karl Marx predicted, communism has produced low standards of living and long lines. Everywhere an observer goes in the Soviet Union or in the captive Soviet-bloc nations, one sees people queueing up. They spend hours upon hours every day waiting to get a chance to buy the barest necessities. In Russia the state stores are either bare—representing the fact that the state has not been able to produce enough to adequately supply the people's needs at the state-imposed prices—or the state stores are overflowing with high-priced shoddy goods, representing the fact that the centrally controlled state plan has inefficiently produced things people do not want. In short, the existence of either shortages or surpluses is a sure indication that the centralized state plan does not allow markets to clear through a flexible price mechanism. The Gosplan, the Soviet Union's central planning group, sets wages and consumer prices. It also establishes production goals and allocates what the planners think will be the resources needed by each plant. Many problems of misallocation occur because of mistakes in planning, for how can a small group of individuals have the minutely detailed knowledge that is needed to run a vast and complex economy? In addition to misallocations based on man's finiteness and lack of omniscience, other problems of misallocation occur because resources are allocated more on a political than on an economic basis. Instead of resources going to the highest bidder, as in these United States —where high price indicates the ability to use the resource most efficiently— resources in the Soviet Union go to those factory managers who have the most political "pull."

It is not surprising, then, that productivity in the Soviet system is abysmally low. The average Russian worker produces only about half of what his American counterpart produces. Outmoded equipment that is kept in poor working condition is partly responsible for the low overall level of productivity. The central planners allocate the newest and best equipment and technology to

---

[11]*Science*, 4 September 1981, pp. 1090-1092.

the vast military-equipment-producing sector of the economy because it has a high political priority. Thus the consumer-producing sector is starved. But a large part of the responsibility for the low productivity is because of the absence of economic incentives that are found in the freer Western economies. The ordinary worker or manager has no real incentive to work hard. Workers are hardly ever fired for inefficiency or rewarded for being efficient. The same is true of the managers who run the state-owned plants. In recent years, the increase in total national product has been averaging about 1.2 percent per year. A Moscow correspondent for the *U.S. News & World Report* recently wrote:

> The fact that the Soviet economy is an economy of scarcity is underlined by long lines at stores, black marketeering, bribe giving and bribe taking—and the government's new harsh campaign to stamp out speculation and corruption.[12]

Soviet agriculture continues year after year in not being able to feed the Soviet people, even though farm workers make up 24 percent of the work force in the Soviet Union versus only 3 percent in these United States. Soviet leaders keep putting the blame for bad crops on poor weather conditions, but the truth of the matter is that Soviet weather is no more unpredictable or harsh than in our own country. The difference is this: In these United States, harsh weather is overcome by private farmers who are motivated to produce and successfully harvest their crops through the hope of private gain. But in Russia who cares? Why should Soviet workers on vast state-owned farms exert themselves to produce and harvest crops for their state masters? The workers will eat no better or worse whether or not crops are harvested. Waste is rife with such a lack of economic incentive. Crops mature and stay in the fields until they waste away, or the crops are harvested and then left in piles to rot. Often a good portion of what is produced is loaded onto trucks but is secretly dumped along roads and later picked up and sold in the black markets that are found everywhere. In Moscow a joke is often passed around which depicts Soviet agriculture: **Question:** "What are the four enemies of Soviet agriculture?" **Answer:** "Spring, Summer, Fall and Winter."

The only continuing bright spot in Soviet agriculture is the small private garden plots each family is allowed to have for its own use. These small private plots amount to about 1.5 percent of total Soviet farmland, but they have long produced about one-third of the total vegetables and meat consumed in the nation. The percentage of food produced on these private plots for 1980, as reported by the Soviet publication *Ekonomicheskaya Gazeta,* are: meat, 31 percent; milk, 30 percent; eggs, 32 percent; vegetables, 35 percent; potatoes, 64 percent, and fruit and berries, 58 percent.[13]

[12]"Communism: The Great Economic Failure," *U.S. News & World Report,* 1 March 1982, p. 33.
[13]"It Takes Stealth and Bribery to Get By in Russia," *U.S. News & World Report*, 9 November 1981, p. 41.

The Soviet Union has not been able to feed itself since the communists took over in 1917. On the other hand, pre-communist Russia under the Tsars was a net grain-exporting nation from the mid-1860s until World War I. In 1981 the Soviet regime was compelled to sell 224 tons of gold in exchange for food imports.

One factor that compounds the shortage of consumer goods in Russia is their heavy cost of building the strongest military force in history. The military-producing sector gets first call on the best of everything: raw materials, scientists, engineers, equipment and manufacturing plants. The production of military goods requires about 12 percent of gross national product in the Soviet Union versus about 6 percent in these United States.

Theft and bribery are rampant all over the Soviet Union, according to Soviet newspaper reports. A letter from a Soviet citizen to the newspaper *Sovietskaya Rossiya* recently said:

> There is a crying need to put a stop once and for all to all the filching at such enterprises in our city as the meatpacking combine, the bakery, the dairy plant. Every day, each shift of workers at these plants leaves with bagfuls of food. They carry away meat, sausage, whole bundles of baked food, cream, cottage cheese, butter, cheese curds.[14]

Another newspaper, *Trud,* reported that wheeler-dealers in the south use their official powers to direct truck loads of watermelons, tomatoes and other vegetables north to Moscow and other cities where the produce is unloaded and sold in the black markets at high prices. One citizen in Moscow says, "The state is supposed to be working for the good of the people. The state is rich. So why not take?"[15]

The newspaper *Bakinsky Rabochii* recently reported that three men were executed because they were convicted of conspiring to turn the #3 knitwear shop in Baku into an underground factory to make private profits. Their scheme was to put on an extra work shift to increase production, and then to sell off the extra production through the black market. They earned more than two million rubles a year doing this.[16]

The diversion of state property into private channels happens daily all over the Soviet Union. Women service station attendants give free gas tank fill-ups for pairs of panty hose and cigarettes. Cement and asphalt is secretly dumped off trucks and sold for private use. Such deals are called *na levo,* which literally means "on the left." Without such deals, life in the Soviet Union would be even more bleak than it already is. The absence of private property breeds a

---

[14]Ibid., p. 43.
[15]Ibid., p. 43.
[16]Ibid., p. 43.

contempt for the moral concept of property. No one's property is safe in such a social climate, especially the state's.

The kind of social atmosphere explained above largely explains the growing problem of alcoholism in the Soviet Union. People have been taught that there is no God. There are no internally felt moral restraints; there are only external restraints imposed by the authorities.

It is appropriate at this time to recall what Dr. Fred Schwarz, President of the Christian Anti-Communist Crusade, calls the Roots of Communism and a few of the False Predictions of Marx.

The Roots of Communism:
(1) There is no God.
(2) All individuals are evolutionary animals, without soul, spirit or continuing life, and are completely describable within the categories of chemistry and physics.
(3) Intellectual and moral character are created by the experiences of the economic environment.[17]

The False Predictions of Marx:
(1) Industrial development would inevitably produce a communist revolution.
(2) Industrial development would lead to increasing poverty for the workers.
(3) Industrial development would lead to an increase in the length of the working week.
(4) Industrial development would abolish national patriotism among the workers.
(5) Industrial development would abolish the family among the workers.
(6) The abolition of Capitalism would abolish war. . . .[18]

Dr. Schwarz accurately points out that, since all of the above predictions have proven to be obviously wrong, Marxism is discredited as a science, even though the communists claim it is a science.

Welfare-Statism: Welfare-statism of the kind that has been developing in Western countries, including these United States, is no different in essence than the more tyrannical forms of socialism we have been discussing. Italian Fascism, German Nazism and Russian Communism all use varying degrees of orthodox socialism (state ownership) combined with "college-level socialism" (state control). We have already mentioned some of the numerous U.S. Federal Government control agencies which have the power to determine how

---

[17]*Christian Anti-Communism Crusade Newsletter*, vol. 21, no. 16 (15 August 1981), p. 7.
[18]*Christian Anti-Communism Crusade Newsletter*, vol. 20, no. 3 (1 February 1980), p. 4.

productive resources are to be used in our country but which escape the many problems of ownership. In truth, these United States are now more fascistic than orthodox socialist; but the result is the same. The government rulers impose their will on the people through various economic controls which bear the force of law.

The fact that the American government has not yet turned outrightly totalitarian does not mean that, under certain conditions, it could not. The advent of modern sophisticated electronic and computer technology now makes it possible for rulers to minutely monitor broad segments of the economy to secure needed information for imposing regulative controls without using the brute force that totalitarian rulers of earlier years were wont to use. Thus, a tyrant today can wear a "gloved fist" and thereby appear to use much softer methods and still get his way. The method of oppression appears to be so different as to be misleading, but the tyranny is there nevertheless. It is just much more sophisticated and pervasive; therefore, it is even more difficult to escape.

Already the hearts and minds of many Americans have been psychologically and attitudinally conditioned by some three generations of statist, humanistic education. It is difficult, if not actually impossible, for the biblical principles and values which underlie the free market system to be consistently taught in schools and universities which are owned, controlled and operated by the state. Such schools are naturally oriented along humanistic lines, so it is only natural to expect the present trend toward welfare-statism to continue and even to develop into a more overt form of totalitarian "ism." The Christian student should ever keep in mind that ideas **do** have consequences and that economic and political systems are but the practical outworking of the ripened fruit of long-watered and long-cultivated ideas. Thus, it is crucially important to use the Christian's "benchmark," the Bible, in evaluating practices, ideas and presuppositions; for these are what orientate man's actions.

The extent to which the ideas promulgated by Marx and other socialists/communists have been applied in these United States is not generally realized. In his work of 1848, *The Communist Manifesto,* Marx wrote:

We have seen above, that the first step in the revolution by the working class, is to raise the proletariat to the position of ruling class, to win the battle of democracy.

The proletariat will use its political supremacy, to wrest, by degrees, all capital from the bourgeoisie, to centralize all instruments of production in the hands of the State, i.e., of the proletariat organized as the ruling class; and to increase the total of productive forces as rapidly as possible.

Of course, in the beginning, this cannot be effected except by means of despotic inroads on the rights of property, and on the conditions of bourgeoise production, by means of measures, therefore, which appear economically insufficient and untenable, but which, in the course of the movement, outstrip themselves, necessitate further inroads upon the old social order, and are unavoidable as a means of entirely revolutionizing the mode of production.

These measures will, of course, be different in different countries.

Nevertheless, in the most advanced countries, the following will be pretty generally applicable:

(1) Abolition of property in land and application of all rents of land to public purposes.
(2) A heavy progressive or graduated income tax.
(3) Abolition of all right of inheritance.
(4) Confiscation of the property of all emigrants and rebels.
(5) Centralization of credit in the hands of the State, by means of a national bank with State capital and an exclusive monopoly.
(6) Centralization of the means of communication and transport in the hands of the State.
(7) Extension of factories and instruments of production owned by the State, the bringing into cultivation of waste lands, and the improvement of the soil generally in accordance with a common plan.
(8) Equal liability of all to labor. Establishment of industrial armies, especially for agriculture.
(9) Combination of agriculture with manufacturing industries; gradual abolition of the distinction between town and country, by a more equable distribution of population over the country.
(10) Free education for all children in public schools. Abolition of children's factory labor in its present form. . . .[19]

The Doctrine of Imperialism

Free market capitalism, contrary to Marx's expectations, steadily raised the real incomes of workers wherever the principles of private ownership were allowed to flourish. Lenin noticed this discrepancy between communist theory and real world experience and explained it by developing his theory of imperialism. This theory states that capitalist nations are temporarily deferring the extreme misery of workers in industrial nations by feeding off the misery of workers in underdeveloped nations.

Contrary to Lenin's theory of imperialism, the masses of people in less-developed nations are now benefitting from rising incomes and improved living standards as those countries benefit from Western institutions and technol-

[19]Karl Marx, *Communist Manifesto* with an Introduction by Stefan T. Possony (Chicago: H. Regnery Co., 1954), pp. 54-56.

ogy. Again, a serious discrepancy between communist theory and historic developments in the real world appears. During the 1970s, a new Marxist movement called "Liberation Theology" developed in South America and Central America, which built upon Lenin's theory of imperialism. It broadly teaches that man can achieve salvation, not by a personal saving knowledge of Christ and His finished redemptive work on the cross but by rebelling against capitalist oppressors and instituting a socialistic order to equalize wealth and to bring on a new social order.

In the development of each of the totalitarian systems we have just reviewed—Italian Fascism, German Nazism and Russian Communism—the way was prepared in advance by one or two generations of socialist propagandizing which psychologically prepared the people to relinquish freedom and to accept the chains of slavery. Richard Vetterli and William Fort explain that the intellectual community in each of these countries prepared the minds and hearts of the people for dictatorship.[20] In each instance, the rise of economic and political dictatorship was preceded by some years of spreading anti-Christian, pro-humanistic thought which served to undermine orthodox Christian beliefs. In each example we see that ideas certainly do have consequences.

> *Because that, when they knew God, they glorified him not as God, neither were thankful; but became vain in their imaginations, and their foolish heart was darkened.*
> *Professing themselves to be wise, they became fools.*
> *Romans 1:21-22*

Wilhelm Röpke in his *Umgang Mit Dem Bolschewsmus* emphasizes the fact that the real issue with communism is intellectual and moral rather than economic and political:

> The ultimate source of all mistakes in our dealings with communism is intellectual and moral. In fact, it is our inability or unwillingness to comprehend the full substance and nature of this conflict between communism and the free world, its tremendous implacability and deeply moral and intellectual implications [which has made the continuing advance of communism possible]. Again and again, we fall into the error of conceiving this conflict to be an old-fashioned diplomatic power struggle. In reality it is a collision of two irreconcilable systems that are intellectually and morally diametrically opposed. Communism, where it has already come to power, has destroyed the bases for the intellectual and moral exist-

[20]Richard Vetterli and William Fort, Jr., *The Socialist Revolution* (Los Angeles: Clute International, 1968).

ence of man, and now it threatens to complete this destruction for the whole world.[21]

The same statement also applies to any other branch of practicing socialism. Orthodox socialism, fascism (i.e., "college-level socialism") and communism are all based on an anti-Christian, humanistic view of man. They are all based on a world-and-life view that is in conflict with the biblical view of man, God and the world. Each denies the fundamental fact that man is created in the very image and likeness of God. Man, therefore, according to the biblical view, has not only a **right** to be free; he has a **duty** to preserve his freedom so that he can maintain his personal responsibility before God.

For over six decades, the Communist Party has tyrannically ruled the U.S.S.R. as the dictatorship of the proletariat. If one can believe the estimate made by the Russian author Aleksandr Solzhenitsyn, who fled that communist "paradise," more than 66 million people have been intentionally murdered by the Soviet rulers during this "temporary" socialist stage of communism. The long-dreamed-of communist Utopia is no nearer today than it was when the Bolsheviks forcibly gained power in 1917. Totalitarian regimes have no "chains of the Constitution" to deter them from doing anything that they deem necessary to retain power. Is it, we might ask, in the nature of sinful man to ever relinquish power once it is grasped? Both the failure of the communist regime in Russia to usher in the dreamed-of communist Utopia and the long-continued bloody rule of the "temporary" dictatorship of the proletariat demonstrate how the **theory** of communism and its **practice** continue to diverge.

The War of Ideas

On November 10, 1981, Maurice Tugwell[22] delivered an address to the National Strategy Forum in Washington, D.C. Some of his remarks are pertinent to our study of the various "isms."

> One of the great contests of history is being fought now, in the psychological arena. . . .
> . . . In the battle for men's minds, the Soviets are walking all over us. . . .
> . . . The Soviet empire is held together by an ideology that hardly anyone believes, and by a complex, sophisticated apparatus of control which causes nearly everyone to participate in a giant pretense of believing. Lip service to the dogma is at once a meal

---

[21]Wilhelm Röpke, *Umgang Mit Dem Bolschewsmus*, trans. Hans Sennholz, "How to Deal With the Communists," in Intercollegiate Society of Individualists, Inc., *The Individualist,* vol. 2, no. 1, January-February 1963.

[22]Mr. Tugwell is Director of the Centre for Conflict Studies, University of New Brunswick, Fredericton, N.B., Canada.

ticket and a proof of loyalty. All public actions are measured against it and all proposals justified by it. It is the stick with which one man beats another. The dichotomy between the truth which can never be spoken and the lies that can never remain unspoken, and the moral decay and intellectual despair that it causes, provides a fertile ground for psychological action. . . .

All revolutionary propaganda is founded upon three basic themes—the justice of the cause, hatred of the opposition, and the inevitability of victory. . . .

. . . In the Soviet countries, hatred is vital to the maintenance and justification of revolutionary zeal, and it also underpins the legitimacy of Party rule. Only through a shared perception of a malevolent external threat can the massive burden of arms production, the continuation of the draft, and the commitment to overseas interventionalist policies be explained. Only by the constant reiteration of spy scares, Western invasion plots or sabotage, can the Soviets justify the whole oppressive apparatus by which they maintain the Party in unchallenged power—the KGB, MVD, suppression of ethnic nationalism, total isolation from outside news, views or ideas, and their claim to unquestioning obedience. Hatred is as seminal to Marxist-Leninism as Love is to Christianity.

. . . Lenin's brightest idea was to steal Marx's theory of historical determinism and use it as a pseudo-scientific prop for this ubiquitous revolutionary theme. Thus, while the party replaces God as the proper focus of man's allegiance, the theory that the world is inevitably moving towards socialism, that the smart guys had better jump onto the bandwagon, and that resistance is futile, is projected as the Word of God. . . .

. . . Often in the past we have been guilty of accepting the CPSU's [Communist Party Soviet Union] claims to legitimacy at their own fraudulent evaluation. When we do this, we become accomplices to Stalin's Terror, the Gulag, the Cambodian genocide and the crushing of all human values. One day, when the chains are broken, we are going to have to account for our behavior to all those millions who have suffered under Marxist-Leninism, and I would dread to be in some so-called liberal shoes when that day dawns.

. . . Historically, the United States has impeccable anti-colonial credentials. Soviet propagandists have to be congratulated for producing a climate of world opinion in which the words "America" and "imperialist" are synonymous. Their achievement is particularly remarkable when we remember that the last Third World region under European colonial rule is the Central Asian Republics of the USSR.[23]

---

[23]Maurice Tugwell, "Beating Moscow in the War of Ideas and Ideals," address to the National Strategy Forum, Washington, D.C., 10 November 1981, pp. 1-13.

One of the final points Mr. Tugwell made in his address concerning the psychological battle for men's minds is that the free nations of the West should focus on the optimizing strategy that calls only for the transfer of ideas and ideals rather than attempting to solve the problem of Third World suffering by accepting liability and giving charity, which strategy will certainly fail. ". . . we must always show how the individual and not the state, and certainly not a party, is what really matters," he stated.[24]

American Free Enterprise

The system of free enterprise that once characterized these United States is based on a biblical presupposition. This is not to state that most or even a large minority of American citizens in the late eighteenth and early nineteenth centuries were true born-again Christians who had a personal relationship with Christ as Saviour and Lord of their lives, though some of America's early leaders certainly did have such a relationship. It is to state, however, that the average American strongly believed in the biblical view of man—that man was created by God, that God gave him precious and unalienable rights, that man has a right to be free economically and that man has a right to determine his own form of representative self-government. That all of these solidly biblical concepts were generally held by early Americans is only too clear from the Declaration of Independence and the early state constitutions and laws which were firmly rooted in Christianity.

The extent to which the Bible influenced America and her political and economic institutions is corroborated by the following persons, the last two of whom were foreigners who spent some years in these United States as astute observers:

> The actual state of religion in any country must, of course, be an interesting object of investigation to every sober and intelligent man. To give you a correct view of this subject so far as New England is concerned, it will be necessary for me to go back to the war which commenced in 1755 and terminated in 1763. . . . From the first settlement of the country to the commencement of that war, the same reverence for God, the same justice, truth, and benevolence, the same opposition to inordinate indulgencies of passion and appetite prevailed without any material exceptions. An universal veneration for the Sabbath, a sacred respect for government, an undoubting belief in divine revelation, and an unconditional acknowledgment and performance of the common social duties constituted everywhere a prominent character. . . .[25]

Timothy Dwight, President of Yale University (1795-1814)

---

[24] Ibid., pp. 13-14.

[25] Timothy Dwight, *Travels in New England and New York,* edited by Barbara Miller Solomon . . . , John Harvard Library, 4 vols. (Cambridge: Belknap Press of Harvard Univ. Press, 1969), vol. 1, p. 258.

The Americans combine the notions of Christianity and of liberty so intimately in their minds that it is impossible to make them conceive the one without the other; and with them this conviction does not spring from that barren, traditionary faith which seems to vegetate rather than to live in the soul.[26]

Alexis de Tocqueville (1805-1859)

The matter may be summed up by saying that Christianity is in fact understood to be, though not the legally established religion, yet the national religion. So far from thinking their commonwealth godless, the Americans conceive that the religious character of a government consists in nothing but the religious belief of the individual citizens, and the conformity of their conduct to that belief. They deemed the general acceptance of Christianity to be one of the main sources of their national prosperity, and their nation a special object of the Divine favour.[27]

James Bryce (1838-1922)

Even though the average eighteenth- or nineteenth-century American might not have consciously recognized the specific biblical foundations of his nation, Americans **thought** and **acted** upon biblical presuppositions in establishing and developing their civil government, their whole structure and procedures of law and courts and their economic and social institutions. No fair and impartial observer can deny this historical fact. An individual was considered by early Americans to be precious in the eyes of the law. The state existed for the **person,** not the person for the state. He was regarded as innocent until proven guilty in a court of law decided, not by his superiors, but by his social peers. His right to property and his right to make private contracts was regarded as sacred, and his freedom to do with his own property as he saw fit went uncontested both in theory and in practice.

These principles — the principles of **personal freedom, private contract** and **private property** — when consistently applied in society, can produce only one kind of economy: a **free market economy.** These principles which are crucially essential in producing a free market economy are solidly based on the biblical world-and-life view of man and his individual relationship to a sovereign and loving God.

It is at this level that economics, politics and theology merge. Recognition of this necessary converging explains why deviant religious presuppositions —

---

[26]Alexis de Tocqueville, *Democracy in America,* The Henry Reeve Text as revised by Francis Bowen; now further corrected and edited with a historical essay, editorial notes, and bibliographies by Phillips Bradley, 2 vols. (New York: Vintage Books, 1945), vol. 1, p. 317.

[27]James Bryce, *The American Commonwealth,* Third edition, completely revised throughout with additional chapters (New York: Macmillan and Co., 1895), p. 702.

including the religion called atheism or secular humanism—must necessarily produce different political and economic systems. This again indicates why it is so important for the student of economics to search deeper than scientific "positive economics" when he studies and evaluates different economic systems. He must search for the presuppositional base from which people think and act in order to understand the underlying basis of any particular system.

America's economic system has deviated from a free to a controlled system to the extent that Americans have individually and collectively given up the biblical world-and-life view their forefathers once held. Americans today are not as freedom oriented as their forefathers were because they no longer see the basis of man's individual freedom and self-responsibility as theologically based. Instead of being theistically oriented, most modern Americans are humanistically oriented. They tend to more readily acquiesce to economic manipulation and control by the ever-growing, more-powerful secular state. They fail to see the growth of big government as the humanistic attack against God that it is, and they are insensitive to the threat that the growth of humanistic government presents to their freedom. In short, biblical Christianity once formed the philosophical base from which America's political and economic structures sprang. But gradually the presuppositional base has turned humanistic; and the rise of a secular, humanistic state with all of its accompanying political and economic structures has naturally evolved. The evolution has occurred so gradually that each succeeding generation has not become alarmed but has accepted the slowly changing status quo. The Christian student of economics should note the import of this observation and should devote deep thought concerning these matters. His or her very liberty is at stake.

Questions

1. Describe the modern humanist view of man. What does this view of man imply concerning moral boundaries politically, economically and socially?

2. What three broad views of human rights does Robert V. Andelson see in his book *Imputed Rights?* What world-and-life view is each based upon? What does each view imply concerning man's economic freedom relative to the state?

3. Using appropriate Bible references to substantiate your position, attack or defend the humanist idea that man is inherently good, and thus potentially perfectible through education. Explain what kind of politico-economic system you think such a humanist view implies. Compare your statement with what other class members think.

4. What is the difference between self-centered license and biblical freedom?

5. How much civil government (i.e., how much authority applied from the outside) is needed for man to live harmoniously with his fellowmen? Explain. What kind of politico-economic system does your answer imply?

6. Define socialism. On what presupposition concerning the individual's economic freedom and the state's interest does socialism rest?

7. Define fascism. Contrast it with orthodox socialism. Why is it called "college-level socialism"? If you were the head of state, would you prefer orthodox socialism or fascism if you had to choose between the two? Why?

8. Can you cite examples of orthodox socialism and/or fascism in these United States? Explain why you think they are what you say.

9. Describe mercantilism. What common presupposition do mercantilism and modern forms of socialism/fascism share?

10. Describe the Italian Fascist state. Why was it called a "living organism"?

11. Describe Nazism. What does the word Nazi stand for? How did the concept of the Nazi state differ from the concept of the corporate state in Italy?

12. What economic policy did Hitler follow in the early part of his regime to keep domestic prices low relative to prices in foreign countries?

13. Compare the similarities and differences between Nazi Germany and Fascist Italy. Do you see any of the same principles or underlying ideas in either of the following? If so, what are they?
    (a) Mercantilism.
    (b) Modern welfare-statism in these United States.

14. Is communism or socialism practiced in the Soviet Union? What difference, if any, is there between socialism and communism concerning one's ability to produce versus his need to consume?

15. What is the dictatorship of the proletariat? How long did Marx envision it to last? Has his prediction come to pass in the Soviet Union after more than six decades of communist rule? Explain.

16. Define Marx's theory of historical materialism. Did the theory work in Russia? Explain.

17. According to Marx, when is the ideal state of perfect communism to be ushered in? How? When do you think the state will "wither away" as Marx predicted?

18. What was Marx's theory of the progressive misery of the working class? Has Marx's prediction come to pass in any nation? Explain.

19. What obvious discrepancy does Lenin's theory of imperialism help to

explain? Do the incomes of workers in less-developed nations support or discredit Lenin's theory of imperialism? Explain.

20. What role did the intellectual community in Italy, Germany and Russia play in the advent of totalitarianism in those countries? Do you see any similarity between what happened in those countries and in the intellectual development and education in this country?

21. Defend or attack this statement: "Welfare-statism is no different in essence than Nazism, fascism or communism."

22. Do you think the principles and values which underlie the free market system of economics can be consistently taught in tax-supported schools and universities? Explain why or why not.

23. Study the ten planks of Karl Marx's and Frederich Engels' *Communist Manifesto*.
    (a) Which apply to these United States?
    (b) Which are good? bad? neutral? Explain.

24. What principles of the American politico-economic system are biblically based? What Bible references can you cite to support your statement?

25. If the majority of early Americans was not even Christian, as some critics claim, how can we still claim that the basis of American civil government and economic policy was Christian?

26. What has happened to America's presuppositional base with the passing of one generation after another? Recognizing this, what might you predict concerning future trends in our country politically and economically?

27. Briefly describe some of the problems in Soviet industry and agriculture.

28. Suppose you are a member of the Soviet Gosplan. What recommendations might you give to solve the problems mentioned in response to question #27? Remember that you may not, for ideological reasons, recommend anything that is contrary to their accepted dogma.

29. List the "Roots of Communism" and try to predict the kind of economic system they would tend to produce when put into practice.

30. List the six "False Predictions of Marx" and attempt to explain why they turned out to be wrong.

6

Money

But they that will be rich fall into temptation and a snare, and into many foolish and hurtful lusts, which drown men in destruction and perdition.
For the love of money is the root of all evil: . . .

I Timothy 6:9-10

THERE is no topic of discussion that generates more universal and more lasting interest than the subject of money. Tonight's supper, your Saturday night date, a visit from Grandma, a broken arm, the future education of a newborn infant, the imbalance of trade between nations and even a decision by the church elders to sponsor a vacation Bible school for youngsters next summer — all of these can, and must, be translated into monetary terms. For when men think and plan in a monetary economy, they weigh costs and benefits in monetary terms.

Truly, money — or the need for money — permeates every aspect of our personal and social lives. For this very reason it is important that we understand what money is, how it comes into being and how it functions in the economy.

You are already aware, from practical experience, that with an adequate supply of money one can enjoy the niceties of life as well as experience the heady feeling of moving about the highest strata of society, secure in the assurance of being well accepted by others. But with a dearth of money, the same person can be destined to a life of continual scrimping in order to enjoy even the barest necessities of life (Prov. 22:7). Is it any wonder that so many people find themselves devoting such a large portion of their waking hours in the pursuit of money? Early in life we learn that money bestows power and prestige on those who control how it is spent. A realization of the economic, political and social "clout" that accompanies the possession of money also helps us understand the apostle Paul's warning that "the love of money is the root of all evil" (I Tim. 6:10).[1] It is clear that most people do not want money simply for the sake of owning it. Rather, they want money for the utility it

---

[1] The phrase translated in our English Bible as "love of money" is the Greek word *philaguria*, which means "love of silver," from *philos* = love + *arguros* = silver. Thus, we can draw an interesting economic insight concerning what the people in those days used for currency; it was silver. This biblical information has been corroborated by archaeological findings of silver coins that were widely used during biblical times.

provides—for what it will buy, the enjoyment of goods and services, the feeling of power and prestige and a general sense of well-being. That is how most people regard money. In one respect they are correct. Money is nothing but a **means** to an end. And the **ends** sought are determined by the set of one's heart (Prov. 4:23). In short, money is nothing more than an efficient tool in helping men to achieve the ends they desire.

But if people do not want money for what money **is**, it must be a strange commodity. What is this thing we call money? We answer this practical question later, but first a slight digression. As we have already intimated above, there is a need to emphasize the importance of understanding money for a number of reasons. We want to know: (1) What money is. (2) How money is created. (3) How it can be manipulated. (4) How money can and has been used through the ages by the civil authorities to cheat and deceive the public in order to control and enslave them. This will be the underlying theme that runs through this and the next few chapters. The Christian should view money as an efficient tool that God, in His providence, has allowed man to develop. Accordingly, Christians should learn to use this tool, as well as the rest of God's created universe, in the service of building His Kingdom. In order to learn the proper use of money, it is important to understand how sinful man has perverted its proper use and how to defend against such actions (Eph. 6:12).

When teaching courses in Money and Banking, this author always starts out by presenting this maxim to students: **Man cannot control what he does not understand.** The monetary systems of the modern world appear to be so complicated that the average person has little hope of understanding how they work. In our day and age, the civil government of each country generally has monopolistic control over the country's money and banking system.

This monetary control allows the rulers to control the **people** instead of allowing the people to control their **rulers**. This has come about because government leaders understand money and how to manipulate it, but the people generally do not have this understanding.

A clear understanding of money—how it functions in the economy, how banks and government agencies can create and destroy it and how it can be manipulated to the advantage of those in power and to the detriment of the general public—will better equip the average person, and especially the Christian, to more effectively chart his way and to better protect his economic and political freedom. Some Christians have wrongly viewed the subject of money as "unspiritual." But money is of great importance to the Christian who properly views his temporary sojourn on earth as a period of dedicated service to his Lord and Master, Jesus Christ.

Today, with the rise of humanistically oriented and anti-Christian civil governments, a crucially important question is coming to the forefront. It is this: Will the Christian be free to control his own wealth and thus be able to practice self-responsibility before God for what the Christian does or does not do with the riches with which God has blessed him (Deut. 8:18)? Or will the Christian's wealth be controlled by the humanistic state which denies the only true God? A clear understanding of money and banking may well determine who controls whom. In short, the essential issue is: Will the state control the Christian? Or will the Christian control the state? We see that the subject of money has a very important **spiritual** aspect which many people tend to overlook. To be properly concerned with monetary matters is not, therefore, to be mercenary; it is to be concerned with using a tool efficiently so that men can most effectively pursue their ordained purposes in life, which is to serve God and to bring honor to His name (Micah 6:8).

What Is Money?

Economists define money from a **use** standpoint. Money is anything that is generally accepted by the public in exchange for goods and services. The definition is simple, yet it has some elements that are important to our understanding of **what** can function as money and **how** it functions. Note that anything can function as money as long as it is generally acceptable to the people. Contrary to what most people think, it is not civil governments that determine what money is. Rather, it is the people. If the people generally accept something in exchange for goods and services, their general acceptance constitutes it as money. When people stop generally accepting something as money, it ceases to be money. This has happened a number of times throughout history when the civil authorities have persisted in debauching their countries' currencies. When this happens, the people finally refuse to accept it anymore; thus they reject the currency as a medium of exchange.

Many different commodities have been used as money in the history of mankind. The earliest biblical reference to money is in Genesis 13:2: "And Abram was very rich in cattle, in silver, and in gold." The Hebrew word *keceph,* which is translated as "silver" in this verse, is translated as "money" in Genesis 17:12. Another word translated as "money" is the Hebrew word *qesiytah* in Genesis 33:19, where we are told that Jacob bought a parcel of a field for 100 pieces of money. The word *keceph* means "pale in color," but the word *qesiytah* means "ingot," being derived from a root word meaning "to weigh out" or something that has been definitely estimated and stamped for a coin.

We mention these biblical references for two reasons — to show that meaningful economic and historical insights can indeed be drawn from the Bible and to show that the use of full-bodied coins may possibly date back further in history than we realize. Abraham lived some 2,000 years before Christ (Gen. 13); and Jacob, his grandson, lived a hundred or so years later. We can determine from the biblical account that people in Abraham's day must have used silver and gold as money, probably on a weight basis. There is also a possibility, at least by the time of Jacob, that pieces of silver were stamped or marked in some way to indicate their ingot weight. We might not be accurate in classifying the stamped ingots used by Jacob as real coins, but they were perhaps an intermediate step in their development.

Archaeologists date the earliest use of stamped coins about 700 B.C. by the Ionian Greeks in the small kingdom of Lydia, which was located on the west coast of Asia Minor (Turkey). These were crude pieces of a metal called *electrum,* which was a natural mixture of gold and silver. They were cut into small lumps of standard weight and then stamped with official marks to indicate their value. Another silver coin dated about 413 B.C. was minted in Syracuse (Sicily). The *tetradrachma* was minted about 350 B.C. in Ephesus (Greece). No money was minted in Israel until after the Babylonian exile. It is assumed that the Jews became acquainted with Babylonian and Persian coins during their 70-year captivity. The earliest Jewish coin, the *shekel,* is dated approximately 140 B.C. It was minted during the Maccabeean period (175-140 B.C.). The word *shekel* means "weight," which indicates that it was a full-bodied coin. A full-bodied coin is one whose value is determined by the amount of precious metal in it. Such a coin is not mixed with baser metals, except perhaps for a very small amount of copper or other metal to increase its hardness and durability.

The Roman *denarius,* which is mentioned in the New Testament, was minted from silver taken from government-owned mines located in various parts of the Roman Empire; two examples are the silver mines at Antioch and Ephesus. The *denarius* was long considered the equivalent to a day's pay for a worker or a soldier. New issues of this coin were minted every year or two as a means of widely disseminating information and propaganda on behalf of the emperor. The emperor's image and the message on these coins served to glorify his person and his deeds among the populace during an age when there were no newspapers, magazines or other means of public communication (see Matt. 22:20-21; Mark 12:15-17).

Besides silver, gold and cattle, many other things have been used as money. Remember that the only requirement for classifying something as money is that it be **generally accepted** by the people in exchange for goods and services:

(1) From the beginning of the Roman Republic until about 269 B.C., the Romans used copper coins as money. By this time, the Roman armies had conquered lands that contained silver mines, so production of the silver *denarius* began shortly after.

(2) Around the ninth century A.D. in Russia, marten skins served as money. A generic term for money is thus derived from the word for marten, *kung.* American and Canadian trappers also used furs as money during the eighteenth and nineteenth centuries.

(3) During the thirteenth century in China, the Kublai Khan used the inner bark of mulberry trees as a form of paper money. He prohibited the use of gold or silver and forced the people to exchange these metals for his "mulberry dollars," which they were forced to accept in payment for goods and services under pain of death. An interesting account of this is found in the book that

Marco Polo (1254-1324) wrote upon his return from the Orient:

How the Great Khan Causes the Bark of Trees,
Made Into Something Like Paper,
to Pass for Money Over All His Country

Now that I have told you in detail of the splendor of this city of the emperor's, I shall proceed to tell you of the mint which he has in the same city, in the which he has his money coined and struck, as I shall relate to you. And in doing so I shall make manifest to you how it is that the great lord may well be able to accomplish even much more than I have told you, or am going to tell you, in this book. For, tell it how I might, you never would be satisfied that I was keeping within truth and reason!

The emperor's mint then is in this same city of Cambaluc, and the way it is wrought is such that you might say he has the secret of alchemy in perfection, and you would be right! For he makes his money after this fashion.

He makes them take of the bark of a certain tree, in fact of the mulberry tree, the leaves of which are the food of the silkworms — these trees being so numerous that whole districts are full of them. What they take is a certain fine white bast or skin which lies between the wood of the tree and the thick outer bark, and this they make into something resembling sheets of paper, but black. When these sheets have been prepared they are cut up into pieces of different sizes. The smallest of these sizes is worth a half tornesel; the next, a little larger, one tornesel; one, a little larger still, is worth half a silver groat of Venice; another a whole groat; others yet two groats, five groats, and ten groats. There is also a kind worth one bezant of gold, and others of three bezants, and so up to ten. All these pieces of paper are issued with as much solemnity and authority as if they were of pure gold or silver; and on every piece a variety of officials, whose duty it is, have to write their names, and to put their seals. And when all is prepared duly, the chief officer deputed by the Khan smears the seal entrusted to him with vermilion, and impresses it on the paper, so that the form of the seal remains printed upon it in red; the money is then authentic. Anyone forging it would be punished with death. And the Khan causes every year to be made such a vast quantity of this money, which costs him nothing, that it must equal in amount all the treasure in the world.

With these pieces of paper, made as I have described, he causes all payments on his own account to be made; and he makes them to pass current universally over all his kingdoms and provinces and territories, and whithersoever his power and sovereignty extends. And nobody, however important he may think himself, dares to refuse them on pain of death. And indeed everybody takes them readily, for wheresoever a person may go throughout the great Khan's dominions he shall find these pieces of paper current, and shall be able to transact all sales and purchases of goods by means of them just as well as if they were coins of pure gold. And all the while they are so light that ten bezants' worth does not weigh one golden bezant.

Furthermore all merchants arriving from India or other countries, and bringing with them gold or silver or gems and pearls, are prohibited from selling to any one but the emperor. He has twelve experts chosen for this business, men of shrewdness and experience in such affairs; these appraise the articles, and the emperor then pays a liberal price for them in those pieces of paper. The merchants accept his price readily, for in the first place they would not get so good an one from anybody else, and secondly they are paid without any delay. And with this paper money they can buy what they like anywhere over the empire, while it is also vastly lighter to carry about on their journeys. And it is a truth that the merchants will several times in the year bring wares to the amount of four hundred thousand bezants, and the grand sire pays for all in that paper. So he buys such a quantity of those precious things every year that his treasure is endless, while all the time the money he pays away costs him nothing at all. Moreover, several times in the year proclamation is made through the city that any one who may have gold or silver or gems or pearls, by taking them to the mint shall get a handsome price for them. And the owners are glad to do this, because they would find no other purchaser give so large a price. Thus the quantity they bring in is marvelous, though those who do not choose to do so may let it alone. Still, in this way, nearly all the valuables in the country come into the Khan's possession.

When any of those pieces of paper are spoilt—not that they are so very flimsy neither—the owner carries them to the mint, and by paying three per cent on the value he gets new pieces in exchange. And if any baron, or any one else soever, hath need of gold or silver or gems or pearls, in order to make plate, or girdles, or the like, he goes to the mint and buys as much as he list, paying in this paper money.

Now you have heard the ways and means whereby the great Khan may have, and in fact **has**, more treasure than all the kings in the world; and you know all about it and the reason why. And now I will tell you of the great dignitaries which act in this city on behalf of the emperor.[2]

---

[2] *The Travels of Marco Polo* (New York: Library Publications, n.d.), pp. 137-140.

Marco Polo left Cathay too soon. For had he stayed, he would have seen that the Khan eventually flooded his country with the mulberry bark money until, finally, the people would no longer accept it, even under pain of death. European kings did not learn the trick of imposing paper money on their subjects until 1656. This was after the printing press was introduced into Europe from China.

(4) In colonial America, wampum,[3] deerskins, tobacco, cotton, rice, paper bills, salt and whiskey have all been used as money.

(5) South Sea islanders on the Island of Yap used a sparkling white rock called *fei* as money. The rock was cut into disks ranging in size from nine inches to twelve feet in diameter, the latter requiring the combined effort of many people to even move them.

(6) In the nineteenth century, American paper money in the form of banknotes (which were redeemable in gold on demand), "greenbacks" (non-gold-backed currency issued by the Union during the War Between the States) and checks (private promises to pay drawn by a depositor on his bank) were used as money. Today, checks or "checkbook money" constitute about 80 percent of the money in circulation in our country. At the banks, checkbook money is represented simply by numerical accounting entries which are transferred by the banks from person to person and from bank to bank. Checkbook money is really a privately developed form of money rather than a form of money developed by civil governments; therefore, checkbook money is a free market phenomenon.

The Functions of Money and Its Social Benefits

The **primary** function of money is to serve as a **generally accepted medium of exchange.** Again, let us remember that it is the willingness of people to accept it which determines whether something is to serve as money. If the people refuse to accept it, then it is not money. Money serves as a common vehicle for facilitating the exchange of goods and services in society. As such, money is a great saver of people's time because it eliminates the need to barter one specific good for another. Barter is a costly and time-consuming practice.

Consider, for instance, how many difficulties you would encounter in a money-less society if you wanted to exchange a horse for a number of things — such as a pair of shoes, a shirt, a set of books, a meal at a restaurant and an oil painting. Suppose that none of these items is worth a whole horse. And none of the people who have these items will want only a part of your horse in exchange! In matter of fact, it may possibly turn out that none of

---

[3] Wampum peage were beads made from the inner whorls of the *pirula carica* or *canaliculata* periwinkle shells that are common on the southern coast of New England. The Indians strung beads on hemp fibers or on tendon and then embroidered them on strips of deerskin about four inches wide. These belts were highly valued by settlers for their beauty, and therefore were generally accepted in exchange for goods and services.

them really wants a horse anyway. The chance of your finding one person who is a present owner of the entire list of items you want in exchange for your horse is very, very slim. Can you imagine the innumerable series of barter exchanges you would have to engage in to get rid of your horse and to end up with the selection of items you desire? It might take weeks of your time, during which your own productive efforts must either cease or be severely curtailed.

How much more efficient to sell your horse for a commonly accepted "go-between" commodity called money, and then to use it directly to purchase the things you desire! This is the great social and economic convenience that money provides as a medium of exchange. The use of money facilitates and speeds up the efficiency of multilateral exchanges between members of society. This allows each person to specialize in production and thereby to maximize his output for his own benefit and the benefit of others in society. Each person can devote his talents to the productive effort in which he is most efficient. The resulting specialization of each person's effort raises the total output of goods and services and, thereby, the general standard of living tremendously. In this respect, we can confidently state that the use of money as a common medium of exchange allows each person to maximize the unique gifts God has given him, not only for his own benefit but for the common benefit of his fellowmen (see: Rom. 12:3-8; I Cor. 12:4-31; and Eph. 4:4-16).

The **secondary** functions of money are to serve as a **standard of value** or a **unit of account**, a **standard of deferred payment** and a **store of value**.

If something is to serve as a generally accepted medium of exchange, then people will naturally come to use it as a means of valuing all other items. Thus, money also comes to serve as a "yardstick" for measuring other things in terms of money. It becomes a common standard of value or a common unit of account as a secondary function of its main use as a common medium of exchange. When you go into a store to purchase a dozen eggs, you do not think in terms of sweaters or shoes — that it takes so many dozen eggs to be of equal value to a sweater or a pair of shoes. Instead, you look at the price of eggs, and immediately you know the worth of eggs relative to the worth of a sweater or pair of shoes through monetary calculations. Calculating in terms of a common numerical denominator is much more efficient than having to think in terms of an infinite progression of interrelated commodity items, each different in nature from the other items.

Often when a person sells one item, he may not wish to purchase another immediately. This gives him the options of accepting a deferred payment in order to earn interest income, accepting cash and then lending the sum out at interest or accepting cash and holding it. In each instance, the seller considers two more functional aspects of money. The seller considers money in terms of a deferred payment and as a safe store of value.

If the seller lives in an economy where he expects the future value of money to be equal to or greater than its present value in purchasing power, then he may readily accept later payment or lend it out once it has been received. On the other hand, if he lives in an economy where the monetary unit is losing value, such as the situation in which Americans and people in many other countries presently find themselves, then the seller may well be reluctant to hold his money. He will spend his money immediately before prices rise any higher. The whole question of money serving as an efficient standard of deferred payment and as a safe store of value hinges on the long-term stability of the general price level.

In summary, money has four functions; the first is primary, and the rest are secondary.

Money serves as a:

(1) generally accepted medium of exchange,
(2) standard of value or standard unit of account,
(3) standard of deferred payment and
(4) store of value.

The extent to which money is able to serve efficiently in the previously mentioned functions is largely dependent on the morality and integrity of whoever has control over issuing the monetary unit in use. The outstanding historical example for stability of value is the gold *bezant* or *solidus* that was originally minted in Byzantium under Constantine the Great (288-337 A.D.). This beautiful coin was widely used throughout Europe and the Mid-East for nine centuries — from the sixth to the fifteenth century. For 700 years its gold content was not diminished. While the rulers of other nations made it a practice periodically to debauch[4] their currencies, the Byzantine rulers maintained the integrity of the *bezant* century after century. There seems to be a close parallel, in the rise and fall of nations, between the integrity of political rulers as expressed in preserving the worth of their country's currency and the policies they follow in other economic and political matters. (See the supplement at the end of this chapter entitled "All About Gold.")

In order for money to function effectively as a readily acceptable medium of exchange, it must have these additional characteristics: it must have a **high value relative to its weight** so people will not be burdened with the need to carry large quantities around with them; it must be **easily divisible** to facilitate small transactions; it must be **difficult to counterfeit**, lest dishonest persons flood the economy with false money which they have not earned by previously giving value for value received.

---

[4]To **debauch** means to corrupt or to vitiate in morals or purity of character. A debaucher is one who corrupts others or seduces others to lewdness or any dereliction of duty. Debauchery is any excess in eating or drinking; it is intemperance, drunkenness, gluttony or lewdness. To debauch a currency, then, means to issue it in excessive quantities after adulterating it with baser metals. A debaucher of money corrupts the monetary unit and seduces the public into accepting it at its earlier face value by deception.

Money—A Biblical View

We have seen that the development of a common medium of exchange, which we call money, is the natural outgrowth of free men exchanging goods and services. The appearance of money in society is an outworking of God's mandate to man to replenish and subdue the earth (Gen. 1:28). The use of money allows men to do away with costly barter and to specialize in production, thereby vastly increasing their productive capacity.

This resulting increase in output makes it possible for man to devote more material resources to building God's Kingdom on earth until His Son comes again. But there is a danger. Paul warns that "the love of money is the root of all evil" (I Tim. 6:10). While money, as an aid to improving efficiency, is a positive good, the Christian must always beware to keep this "tool" in proper perspective. Jesus never spoke against riches, as such. When He said, ". . . How hardly shall they that have riches enter into the Kingdom of God!" He went on to explain, when questioned by the apostles, ". . . Children, how hard is it for them that **trust** (emphasis added by the author) in riches to enter into the Kingdom of God!" (Mark 10:23-24).

Money prevades every aspect of modern society, thereby radically affecting the Christian's stewardship responsibility to God for the wealth he controls while sojourning on earth. This fact should motivate the earnest Christian to learn all he can about money and how it works in the modern economy. What the Christian does not understand he cannot master. Remember our earlier maxim: What man cannot understand, man cannot control. Rather, he will be mastered by it. Our trustee responsibility to God requires that we master the productive tool called money.

One additional point Christians should keep in mind is this: Paul warns that ". . . we wrestle not against flesh and blood, but against principalities, against powers, against the rulers of the darkness of this world, against spiritual wickedness in high places" (Eph. 6:12). We have pointed out that humanistically oriented civil rulers have tended to arrogate to themselves power over the monetary aspect of society. There is a built-in tendency for the governmental power to create, manipulate and destroy money in order to pursue its own humanistic goals. This is the great spiritual challenge for the dedicated Christian: To master the use of money as a productive tool in society—it is part of the Christian's kingdom-building mandate given him by God.

Supplement

All About Gold

Two generations of Americans have grown up in almost complete ignorance of gold. They neither appreciate gold as the precious and valuable metal it is, nor do they understand or appreciate gold's indispensable role in protecting the economic and political freedom of man in a highly organized society.

Because of the continuing unsettled conditions in the world's monetary markets, and since the overwhelming majority of schools do not convey critically needed information about gold to American youth, it appears timely to discuss the subject of gold and how it benefits mankind. Because of my special interest in the welfare of the ordinary family man who works for a living, I will show how the precious right to buy, own and sell this valuable property helps him to protect his own interests. Though many people regard gold as a rich man's commodity, it is my sincere belief that the legal right to own gold helps the hard-working family man, more than any other member of society, to safeguard his economic independence.

What Is Gold?

What is gold? It depends upon whom you ask. A chemist would explain that gold is a heavy metal that has an atomic weight of 197 and a density of 19.3 grams per cubic centimeter. Gold has a melting point of 1,063 degrees Centigrade; and it boils at 2,600 degrees Centigrade. Gold has been known to man since prehistoric times, and modern man has assigned it an atomic number of 79.

An economic historian, on the other hand, would give a completely different answer. Gold, he would explain, is a precious metal which men during all ages and in all parts of the world have valued more highly than any other metal. Because of its unique qualities, gold has served man since the dawn of history both as a dependable medium of exchange as well as a storehouse of value.

During the various periods of political and social unrest which have plagued the world throughout history, men have tended to look with suspicion on the doubtful value of money minted or printed by civil governments. But men have never lost faith in gold as a medium of exchange or as a storehouse of value. The poor man who has been prudent and foresighted enough to hoard a few gold coins in anticipation of the possible advent of evil days has consistently and invariably discovered that other people's insatiable desire for gold allows him to buy safety or food for himself and his loved ones.

Some people deride gold as a rich man's commodity. They think that the right to own gold benefits the rich man at the poor man's expense. But the lessons of history teach otherwise. Gold is man's great economic equalizer. Possession of gold allows the poor man to bargain as an equal with the rich man. Gold has been a faithful servant to all who have relied on it in time of need: king, merchant, craftsman, laborer, farmer, tenant or peasant. The man who had a few gold coins had economic security in time of stress because he had necessary bargaining power. The man who lacked gold was forced to rely on the fragile mercy of his fellowmen, which often breaks under the stress of adversity.

The biblical scholar would substantiate the testimony of the economic historian in favor of gold, but he would add a still richer dimension. Gold, he would say, is the first metal to be mentioned in the Bible (Gen. 2:11). It is the only metal mentioned before the fall of man, and the mention is favorable: "And the gold of that land is good . . . ," (Gen. 2:12).

Gold is next mentioned in Genesis 13:2, where we are told that Abram "became very rich in cattle, in silver, and in gold." This highly prized commodity is mentioned so often and so favorably in the Bible that the reader cannot help but gain a favorable impression of it. More than once, the kings of Israel used gold from the temple to buy military protection from surrounding kings. It is interesting to note that favorable mention of gold spans the entire Bible. Gold is mentioned in the second chapter of the first book of the Bible (Genesis 2), as well as the second-to-the-last chapter of the last book (Revelation 21), where we are told that the Holy City and its streets will be paved with gold transparent as glass.

Why Does Gold Have Value?

Some proponents of gold become over-zealous and make the mistake of claiming that gold has an intrinsic value. That is, they claim that gold has value in and of itself. This idea, of course, is erroneous, as modern psychologists will agree. Nothing has inherent value. Value, like beauty, exists only in the eye of the beholder. You cannot feel, touch or weigh value because it exists only in your mind. One man's prize is another man's burden.

Nothing can have an intrinsic value because all value is imputed. A person **imputes** value to an article or a good because he forms an opinion about its potential desirability or usefulness. This is true whether we speak about the food we eat, the wood we burn, the paintings we enjoy or the women we love.

Why Do People Impute Value to Gold?: People prize gold for the utility they can derive from it. We have already seen that gold provides the man who has it with a sure means of securing food, shelter and safety for his family — because people everywhere regard gold as a unique storehouse of value and as a universally acceptable medium of exchange. These functions provide gold's main social value.

But individuals also value gold for reasons other than its utility in social relations. These reasons are not difficult to deduce. Gold is scarce. It is warmly beautiful. It is durable almost to the point of being indestructible. Gold never rusts or dissolves. It lasts almost indefinitely — long after other metals have become corroded or oxidized. Of the common acids, only a mixture of concentrated nitric and hydrochloric acids (*agua regia)* will dissolve it. Even strong acids, when used alone, do not affect the chemical stability of gold. It always retains its beauty.

Gold is one of the most ductile and malleable metals known to man. It can be melted and shaped without harm. Gold can be hammered into exceedingly thin leaves — about 12,000 to the inch. When alloyed with other metals — such as silver, which is its natural alloy in nature — gold improves in hardness while still retaining its beauty.

Finally, the natural scarcity of gold assures that it will always have a prominent place in the comparative scale of man's esteem. For some psychological reason, man seems to impute a higher value to those things which are in scarce supply.

In short, if one believes in a providential and sovereign God (as this writer does), it would appear that gold is a unique and precious gift of the Almighty Creator unto man. Let me ask: Could it be that God gave gold the very physical properties that would cause man to value it **because** He knew such a commodity would be useful in preserving man's God-given freedom? Humanist skeptics who deny the existence of a Creator who purposively planned and sustains the universe moment by moment would, of course, scoff at such a view as being unscientific. But such thoughts are not unscientific; they merely go **beyond** the limited scope of science into the more important and basic fields of philosophy and theology.

The Spiritual Significance of Gold

A Christian might ask, "I am a Christian, so my eyes are on heaven and not on earth. Why should I, then, be concerned about a grossly material thing such as gold?"

To this question I would reply: While gold is a material or worldly thing, it has a great spiritual significance that many professed Christians have apparently overlooked. Let me explain: Christians believe in the doctrine of individual self-responsibility before God. That is what justification-by-faith and Christian good works are all about. Man is responsible before God, first for the choice he makes about Christ; and then, once saved, he is responsible as a Christian for everything he does thereafter. But self-responsibility presupposes the freedom to act; that is, the freedom to choose. Without freedom of choice, it is impossible for man to be self-responsible. Many libertarians recognize this truth.

But there is a deeper spiritual aspect of this truth to consider. **The mental act of choosing (an internal process) demands an outside economic guarantee of that action.** This is where the role of gold comes into play. Without economic freedom to validate his choices, man cannot be truly free; he cannot truly be a responsible trustee to God for the wealth he holds during his stay on this earth. Read the Parable of the Talents (Matt. 25:14-30). In short, how can man be morally responsible for the disposition of goods unless he has economic control over them? The spiritual significance of gold is that it helps guarantee the **outward** material base that man needs, by his very nature, to be spiritually free and self-responsible on the **inside**. That is, gold helps guarantee man's performance as a self-responsible being created in the image and likeness of his Maker.

Why Do Governments Not Want Citizens to Own Gold?

The important role of gold in preserving man's freedom from civil government is little understood in this age of mushrooming government bureaucracy. People today have come to regard civil government as a father-protector and supplier of their daily needs—a role which the Bible says belongs to God alone. Modern man has forgotten the most obvious lesson of history. More often than not, civil governments have tended eventually to enslave their own citizens under the guise of "caring for them." Some ancient examples are Egypt, Greece and Rome. Examples from the Mercantile Age are Spain, France and England. Some modern examples under the worldwide thrust of socialism are Italy (Mussolini), Germany (Hitler), Russia (Lenin and followers), England (Fabian Socialists) and, finally, these United States at present under our unique brand of state-welfarism.

Who Will Have Power Over the Purse?: A look at history reveals that rulers eventually strive with their own citizens over the "power of the purse." The important issue that citizens through the ages have had to face has been: **Who** is to have power over spending the incomes that free citizens produce through their own creative economic activity? Is it to be the **rulers?** Or is it to be the **people** themselves?

Rulers have answered this question by imposing taxes to the maximum that citizens will endure. When this point has been reached, they have generally turned to debauching the currency. In olden times kings clipped gold and silver coins or melted them down in order to recast them with a mixture of baser metals. The debased coins, by fiat of the king, were then to be accepted by citizens at their old face value.

In the thirteenth century, Marco Polo returned from China and reported in glowing terms how the great Kublai Khan financed an extensive program of public works and public welfare by forcing citizens to surrender gold and silver in exchange for paper currency made out of the inner bark of mulberry trees. Had Marco Polo remained in China a few years longer he would have personally observed the economic chaos that followed such monetary debauchery.

What is the point? Simply this: We learn from history that rulers have tended to enslave those they are committed to protect by forcibly relieving citizens of their rightful freedom to spend their own money as they wish. When citizens will no longer peacefully bear heavier tax burdens, rulers turn to the insidious method of stealing purchasing power from citizens by inflating the money supply. Each new unit of money created by the ruler competes in the open marketplace on an equal par with the money already held by citizens. Thus, wealth is stealthily but surely transferred from the private hands of citizens to the collective control of government bureaucrats. The faster the ruler creates more new money, the faster additional wealth is transferred to him from the control of private hands. Private wealth thereby becomes socialized. The result is that citizens lose economic control over their own destinies.

This is what is happening now on a grandiose scale in these United States. For instance, in 1932 — the year before U.S. citizens were denied the right to convert their money into gold by presidential order — our national debt was only $19.4 billion ($156 per person). But by 1970, only 38 years later, the national debt had soared to a monstrous $384 billion ($1,875 per person). By 1976 our debt had zoomed to over $620 billion ($2,895 per capita). Today, it is over a trillion dollars. Every indication is that even larger rises are coming in the future. Each succeeding president, with a pliant Congress, saddles the American public with billions of dollars of additional debt.

Economic Seduction Leads to Political Slavery: This constantly rising debt has been incurred through a highly sophisticated method of debauching the currency — the method used by modern government-sponsored central banks; in our case the Federal Reserve System. Every new dollar of this tremendous debt represents a new dollar of purchasing power that bureaucratic rulers have quietly and insidiously siphoned away from the control of private citizens. As this process continues, an ever-growing number of once-free-and-independent citizens are seduced into looking for sustenance to the very bureaucrats who steal from them. The end result of such economic seduction is political slavery.

I have given here the historical background of why civil governments do not want citizens to have the right to own gold. In summary, rulers do not want people to be free to convert government-decreed money into gold because the right to do so provides a haven of safety and economic independence for frugal wage earners and, thus, a strong bulwark against both political and economic enslavement.

When ordinary citizens have the legal right to take government money to their local bank and demand gold for it, they, in effect, have only the same option that any poker player has when the stakes get too high for his comfort — the option of "cashing in his chips" and sitting on the sidelines for a while. By cashing in their government-decreed money-chips for gold, citizens can indirectly, but surely, "veto" the grandiose spending plans of lawmakers and bureaucrats. But rulers — because they want to control rather than be controlled — find it exceedingly distasteful to allow this kind of economic power over their actions to reside in the hands of ordinary citizens.

Can Gold Protect?

"But," a person might ask, "can the right to own gold actually help citizens protect themselves from the tendency of rulers to enslave them?"

My answer: There are two kinds of control that citizens must maintain over political rulers if they hope to preserve a republican form of self-government. First, and most obvious, is **political control**. Citizens must have the power to replace elected officials whenever they become dissatisfied with their performance. Political control is assured by requiring elected representatives to stand for re-election at regular intervals. The powers of impeachment and recall help preserve at least a semblance of citizens' political control between elections.

There is a second kind of control which is less obvious but just as important for effective self-government. This is **economic control**. It is only natural for politicians to try to gain economic control over those who provide the tax monies for their support. Control over others, after all, is what the deadly game of politics is all about. Political power rests on economic power. So, if citizens are to have any hope of remaining independent from power-hungry individuals who from time to time find their way into office, they **must** preserve an "economic veto" over them.

Gold Provides Citizens With Needed "Veto Power": Without this day-to-day "veto power," it is only a matter of time until citizens lose effective political power over the politicians they elect. When citizens lack this power, politicians find it relatively easy to seduce citizens with their own tax money. Demagogic office holders do this by inflating the money supply and then "buying" the votes of unthinking citizens by spending the newly created money on vote-getting projects. It has become almost impossible today to unseat an incumbent American president who wants to be re-elected because he has billions of dollars of "stolen" inflation-dollars under his control.

This is exactly where the crucial role of gold comes into play.

When a country is on a gold standard, the amount of money in circulation is tied to the amount of gold held in reserve by the government treasury. When the government's gold reserve rises, the money supply can be inflated through the banking system. Prices will then tend to rise as a result. When the amount of gold held by the treasury falls, the opposite happens. The money supply will be restricted, and prices then tend to fall.

How does the right to own gold give citizens economic power over politicians under a gold standard? In this way: When politicians engage in deficit spending they must either **borrow** the money they want to spend, or they must **create** it by inflating the money supply. Since it is easier to inflate than to borrow, politicians usually choose to inflate. To the extent that they do this, they legally rob citizens of their hard-earned wealth.

Gold Allows Citizens to Act Individually: When some of the more astute citizens become aware of this robbery, they become worried and start cashing in their government-decreed money-chips (Federal Reserve notes) at banks and asking for gold in exchange. As banks pay out gold, they are forced to replenish their dwindling gold stock by withdrawing gold from the government treasury. This, in turn, causes what gold reserve is left in the treasury to be inadequate to sustain the existing money supply. Banks are then forced to call in loans and gradually to restrict the money supply until it again comes into balance with the smaller gold reserve held by the treasury.

This is the way that efforts of politicians to inflate through deficit spending can be effectively counteracted by the independent and straightforward actions of private citizens. The ensuing loss of public confidence in government leadership forces politicians to cancel their plans for further deficit spending. The economic power wielded by concerned citizens serves to maintain their political power over government officials. But when this crucial economic power is absent — as it is today and has been since 1933 — politicians are free to spend, spend and spend until they are able to enslave the populace. This is how gold serves as the protector of man's freedom. The current inability of citizens to individually draw down the central government's official gold reserve largely explains America's present flight into totalitarianism because their inability puts citizens irrevocably in the hands of the central bank money manipulators.

Goodbye Gold Standard!

Why did these United States go off the gold standard?

In order to understand why these United States went off the gold standard in 1933, we must understand the series of events that produced the pressures which made this crucial step possible. We must go back almost 20 years earlier and trace step by step the growing influence of the national government in our economy.

First, the background:

1913 — Congress voted to create the Federal Reserve System, allegedly to provide the business community with an "elastic" currency. The idea was to prevent financial panics like the one that occurred in 1907, which some economic historians attribute to business instability fostered by the trust busting vendetta of President Theodore Roosevelt.

In arguing against the bill which would create the Federal Reserve System, Senator Elihu Root (New York) warned, ". . . It provides an expansive currency, but not an elastic one. It provides a currency which may be increased, always increased, but not a currency for which the bill contains any provision compelling reduction."[5]

1914-1917 — During the early part of World War I, England and France purchased war materials from U.S. business firms on a cash basis. When their foreign exchange credits were all used up, our national government authorized continued selling to the Allies on credit. Much of the pressure for credit selling came from those business and labor interests that had an economic stake in the continued export of war material. The needed credit was created and sustained by monetary inflation engineered through the newly formed Federal Reserve System.

1917-1918 — Continued financial and material support of the Allies by these

---

[5]*Congressional Record,* 63rd Cong., 2d sess., vol. 51, pt. 1, 13 December 1913, p. 831a.

United States produced a growing strain with Germany which culminated in open warfare. A total of about two-thirds of the cost of World War I was financed by monetary inflation through the Federal Reserve System.

1919-1930 — Our inflated money supply caused prices to be higher than they otherwise would have been after the war. This produced two effects: First, a tendency for imports to rise, which was opposed by business firms, farmers and labor unions who faced foreign competition. This economic problem was handled politically by passing a series of higher tariff laws:

> *1921*: The Emergency Tariff Act, which placed higher duties on wool, sugar, wheat and other commodities.
>
> *1922:* The Fordney-McCumber Act, which established the highest tariff rates up to that time. This Act gave the president power to raise or lower tariff rates at his discretion. President Coolidge raised rates several times.
>
> *1929:* The Hawley-Smoot Tariff Act was introduced before the Crash, in April of 1929. During the presidential campaign of 1928, Herbert Hoover campaigned in favor of a higher tariff.

The net result of this series of protective tariffs was a decline in foreign trade — foreigners could not buy from us unless they were able to accumulate credits by selling to us.

This led to the second effect: In order to finance sales to foreigners, in the absence of allowing foreign goods to enter these United States, huge amounts of foreign loans and bonds were floated in our country by bankers and underwriters. This constituted a privately financed type of "foreign aid" similar to the post-World War II publicly financed foreign aid program. When Americans reduced their "investments" in these foreign bonds and notes in mid-1928, exports soon declined substantially. From the end of World War I to 1929, over nine billion dollars were lent overseas in an effort to shore up our sagging export markets.

Some Loose Threads: Now we must back-track to pick up some other threads:

1923 — This was the year that Federal Reserve officials accidently stumbled upon an interesting fact. They discovered that their purchases of government bonds in the open securities market tended to stimulate business activity by inflating the money supply. From this point on, the Federal Reserve started pursuing a **planned** policy of attempting to manipulate the level of business activity through what is now known as its Open Market Operation. In short, these United States moved another step towards the socialist ideal of a planned economy with this new discovery of manipulative money power.

1924-1927 — A series of manipulative efforts by Federal Reserve authorities produced a generally "easy money" policy.

> *1924*: The Federal Reserve increased the money supply in these

United States to help Britain re-establish a quasi-gold standard. England had abandoned the gold standard during World War I.

1927: The Federal Reserve again followed an "easy money" policy in order to help sustain British and other European currencies and to stimulate the sale of American commodities abroad.

1928 — By this time, it was clearly evident that much of the new money being created through the Federal Reserve and the banking system was finding its way into speculative activities. Both real estate prices and stock market prices were soaring.

FRS — Engine of Inflation: Federal Reserve officials belatedly found out that they could create new money but could not control where it might be spent. Thus, we see an evident truth. It was the **misguided policy established by federal officials** — and **not** private speculators — that was the root cause of the inflationary boom which preceded the 1929 Crash. Few people realize this important fact. Another fact that is not widely recognized is this: When monetary contractions occur in this age of monetary manipulation, the contractions are always initiated by the central banking authorities. The unsophisticated public — the small investor who has slender financial reserves — is the one who gets hurt. When banks call in loans, there is a net flow of wealth from the public to high-placed professional money managers.

1929 — By mid-year, Federal Reserve officials decided upon a deflationary step in order to dampen the rampant speculation that their "easy money" policy had produced. The Federal Reserve raised the discount rate to a high level. This forced banks to liquidate loans and thereby produced a sharp contraction in the money supply. The sharp drop in stock prices that started in October, 1929, was induced by this sudden deflation of the money supply, triggered by the Federal Reserve.

1929-1933 — During the next four years, the Federal Reserve followed its deflationary policy by perversely collecting on loans from financially shaky banks. These banks, in turn, put pressures on their own customers, who were forced to liquidate their investments, even if it meant selling at a loss. By mid-1933, the money supply had dropped by 30 percent; and these United States were in the depths of the Great Depression.

Stage Set for "Reflation": The stage was now set to abandon the gold standard in an effort to "reflate" the economy. And this "reflation" has continued almost without interruption ever since.

I do not mean to imply that the post-World War I economic intervention, the misguided attempt to "correct" the resulting economic maladjustments through inflation, the sudden deflation, the financial crash and the ensuing depression were **purposely** planned or masterminded by some evil force that was consciously intent on getting these United States off the gold standard. Such a conspiracy-view of history is, of course, certainly within the realm of possibility; and some knowledgeable historians hold this view. My personal view is that this is the chain of events which just naturally occurs when fallible man attempts to play God by intervening in the natural working of the competitive free market process.

The Culprit Plays Hero: Here are the conclusions I arrive at in my analysis:

First, the 1929 Crash and the ensuing depression were the direct results of earlier massive monetary and economic interventions by the federal government.

Secondly, when bad times finally came, the culprit attempted to play hero by even grosser interventions into the economy. The dislocations produced by earlier government mismanagement were wrongly blamed on free enterprise **as a system**. The terrible economic maladjustments that occurred as a result of government mismanagement were used as excuses for further federal interventions and controls by the national government, which controls have continued and grown more stringent up to the present time.

It is doubtful whether the degree of federal intervention that we have today could ever have been imposed on American citizens without first denying them their historic right to redeem dollars for gold. This, as I see it, is why the gold standard was intentionally abandoned by U.S. political leaders. **Elimination of the gold standard served to make citizens more dependent economically and more responsive politically to manipulation by politicians at the national level.**

How did these United States go off the gold standard?

The step by step process by which U.S. political leaders eliminated the gold standard provides a classical study of planned duplicity.

First, the background: Our country was in the very depths of its most severe depression. The severity of the depression had been brought about by the economic and political meddling of two persons — one a president and the other a president-elect.

In a vain attempt to "reflate" the economy after the 1929 Crash, President Herbert Hoover called industrial leaders to Washington and asked them to hold wages up, even in the face of falling prices. Many industrialists, to their later sorrow, cooperated. Those who did cooperate caused serious harm to the financial stability of the firms they headed. This served to reduce employment in the long run and thereby lengthened and deepened the downward trend of the economy. It practically guaranteed a Democratic victory in the election of 1932 because voters tend to blame any incumbent administration for existing woes.

The election of Franklin D. Roosevelt served to produce deeper economic and political instability because he refused to cooperate with the out-going administration. From November, 1932, (when he won the election), until March, 1933, (when he was officially inaugurated), Roosevelt refused to make any policy statements to alleviate the growing sense of alarm of the financial and business community. Roosevelt was interested only in making partisan political gains by thoroughly discrediting the Hoover Administration. The worse things got before inauguration, the better chance Roosevelt had of personally looking good when he came into power.

The Fateful Year—1933: Now we come to the historical record of what happened when Franklin D. Roosevelt took office as President:

March 6, 1933—Roosevelt, as one of his first official acts, closed all banks by executive order and forbade them to pay out specie (gold) for dollars.

March 10, 1933—Four days later, Roosevelt prohibited, again by executive order, the export of gold without a license from the Treasury Department. By removing free export, he effectively removed these United States from the full gold-coin monetary standard we had been on since 1879 (except for the war-time emergency between 1917-1919).

April, 1933—A month later, Roosevelt issued another executive order which nationalized the gold of citizens at the existing official price of $20.67 per ounce. Under penalty of law, citizens were forced to exchange their gold for paper dollars. On April 19, he stopped the free movement of gold. This gave formal recognition that these United States had departed from the gold standard.

These actions were taken because Professor George F. Warren of Cornell University had convinced the Administration that any attempt to "reflate" the economy would stimulate an **outward** flow of gold from the country **unless** the government imposed an embargo on it.

June 5, 1933—Congress, at the Administration's request, passed a joint resolution which voided any and all gold clauses in public and private debts.

October 25, 1933—President Roosevelt authorized the Reconstruction Finance Corporation to buy gold at prices to be determined by himself and the Secretary of the Treasury, Henry Morgenthau. They set the price at $31.36 per ounce to start—a price near the free world price—and gradually raised it over the next few months to $35.

January 30, 1934: Congress passed the Gold Reserve Act. This formalized President Roosevelt's earlier actions of nationalizing gold **without** legislative sanction and gave him legal power to devalue the dollar by raising the price of gold.

January 31, 1934: The next day Roosevelt issued another executive order. This order officially devalued the dollar by 41 percent by raising the price of gold to $35 per ounce. The price of gold was raised only **after** citizens had been forcibly relieved of their gold at the **lower** price of $20.67.

This act officially confirmed and completed the nationalization of citizens' gold. It had the ultimate effect of placing these United States on a fiat (paper) monetary standard domestically. Monetary control over U.S. politicians and their hired bureaucrats was thus effectively and legally wrested from the hands of citizens. Now federal officials would be free to manipulate and reflate the economy as they wished without having to worry about the threat of adverse reactions by independent-minded citizens. The way was now cleared for a more complete government-controlled economy.

Is Gold Impractical Today?

People sometimes ask, "Is it not impractical to think that these United States can ever return to the gold standard? It seems that there is not enough gold in the world to sustain the expanded volume of trade. And if there were, would not a return to the gold standard surely throw us into a depression?"

This question is based on two erroneous assumptions about gold that have been deliberately promoted by those who oppose the right of citizens to withdraw gold from the national government's official gold reserve.

First, gold is not used to sustain trade between nations. Rather it is used to compensate for imbalances in trade. For example, the total annual trade between these United States and foreign nations might be as low as $0.5 billion or as high as $50 billion. As long as exports and imports are in balance between each country, no gold will be exchanged. The only time a country gains or loses gold is when a sustained imbalance in trade occurs. Thus, there is no limit to the total volume of international trade that can be sustained by the official gold reserves held by central banks throughout the world. The problem is not the **amount** of gold in existence, but rather in keeping prices flexible so that trade will stay in balance.

Much nonsense about gold has been promulgated by economists and others who should know better. The "shortage of gold" myth is just one of the nonsensical claims made by those who make a fetish of deriding gold as a useless and outdated trinket.

Question: Why should so many otherwise knowledgeable experts so consistently and so volubly deride such an obviously useful metal as gold? If gold is so useless, why did the **entire** world output of gold in 1971 (40 ½ million fine ounces, worth about $1.4 billion at $35 per ounce) disappear into private hands? Someone—many someones, obviously—do not trust their own governments to hold this output for them!

People's distrust of civil governments and their preference to hold gold instead of paper dollars during times of political and economic uncertainty testify, not to their foolishness, but to their good sense! The long history of money teaches that civil governments are counterfeiters at heart and, therefore, cannot be trusted with the dangerous power to control money. If America's Founding Fathers made one mistake, it was certainly their decision to give the national government power to regulate the value of money.

The second erroneous assumption concerning the question about the practicality of returning to the gold standard can be shown by an interesting incident from American history. The Union had abandoned the gold standard during the War Between the States because political leaders chose to finance the war through inflation to the money supply instead of by imposing higher taxes on citizens. Pay-as-you-go plans for financing wars make citizens more reluctant to go to war. Monetary inflation, as usual, produced rising prices. After the war, a "hard money" administration decided to return to a sound currency by reinstituting gold redemption (i.e., by paying out gold specie to citizens who wanted to buy gold with paper dollars). Many wild statements had been made which predicted disaster if gold payments were reinstituted. But what really happened?

When these United States reinstituted gold payments on January 2, 1879, gold started flowing into the country and into the Treasury because people had regained their faith in the honesty of the government of our country. Shortly after, the so-called gold resumption business boom got underway. Thus ended the longest period of business contraction in United States history. Yearly imports of gold looked like this:

	Imports	*Exports*
1879	$ 5.6 million	$4.6 million
1880	80.8 million	3.6 million
1881	100.0 million	2.6 million

Why should not a return to sound money today produce the same beneficial results it did in the 1870s?

Here is how it could be done: The price of gold has been artificially controlled or manipulated for so many years by the U.S. government that no one has any accurate idea of what gold is really worth in a true free market situation. In January, 1974, our national government cut the tie between the dollar and gold internationally; and it also restored to U.S. citizens their precious right to buy and sell gold in the free market as they can do with any other commodity.

But this belatedly given right to buy and sell gold **still** does not give U.S. citizens the needed economic "veto power" over the grandiose spending plans of politicians and government bureaucrats. Why? Because citizens still have no way — with a non-gold-based dollar — to forcibly deflate our country's money supply. The U.S. Treasury — with a multi-billion dollar cache of gold that is not needed for official reserve purposes — has the awesome power to arbitrarily upset or destabilize the existing market for gold.

What should be done to get back on the gold standard is this: The U.S. government should refrain from buying or selling gold until its non-intervention establishes a true free market price. Once such a price is established — and it might be higher or lower than the existing price — it would be a painless and financially riskless step to re-establish the official redemption of gold for dollars at the objective price set in the free commodity market.

This simple process is all that is needed to put these United States back on a sound monetary basis. Then a fixed ratio between the total money supply and the U.S. government's official gold reserve would be established. Doing this would help to re-establish people's waning confidence in our national government. Such a step not only makes good sense economically, but it also makes good sense politically when viewed from the people's welfare. It would restore to citizens the important economic control over politicians and government bureaucrats which they lost under the Roosevelt Administration in 1933.

Who Will Control Whom?

Will enough liberty-loving citizens see the wisdom of how a return to the gold standard would help them regain control over their own civil government — not only for their **own** benefit but for the benefit of their sons and daughters? My head and experience warn me that the American public is likely to remain too apathetic to demand that our national government restore the precious "veto power" that was forcibly taken from them. But my heart keeps hoping and praying!

Let us never forget that money under a gold standard retains its integrity, while fiat money (paper money that cannot be redeemed) does not because civil rulers then have no restraint against inflating the money supply — thus insidiously robbing the very citizens who established the civil government in the first place.

Finally, let us remember the old French proverb, "We have gold because we cannot trust government." Also, let us not forget that nothing is better for the preservation of a republic than a healthy suspicion of civil government by economically independent citizens! A return to the gold standard will give citizens the economic independence they need to protect their rights and their duty to remain free and self-responsible before God.[6]

Questions

1. What importance does this maxim about money have? "Man cannot control what he does not understand."

2. What does an understanding of money have to do regarding Christian stewardship versus attempts of the humanistic state to control all things?

3. Define money. Who determines what is used as money?

4. What is the earliest mention of money in the Bible? What kind of money was it? According to archeological findings, when and where were the first stamped coins used?

5. Read Matthew 19:20-21 and Mark 12:15-17. How does knowledge of what was stamped on the *denarius* help you understand Jesus' reply?

6. Read the account of Kublai Khan's "Mulberry bark money." Would you recommend the practice? Why or why not?

7. What different things have been used for money? In these United States what is our most popular form of money?

8. What great economic and social benefit does money provide as a common medium of exchange?

---

[6]*Santa Ana* (Calif.) *Register,* 19, 26 March; 2, 9, 16, 23, 30 April; 7 May 1972.

9. What four functions does money serve?

10. What do morality and integrity have to do with how well money is able to serve in its four functions?

11. Defend or attack: Gold is preferable as money because it has intrinsic value.

12. Why do civil rulers not want citizens to own gold?

13. How does gold-backed money give citizens "veto-power" over the spending plans of civil rulers?

14. Briefly recite how these United States went off the gold standard.

15. How could these United States return to the gold standard today?

7

Money—Its Creation and Destruction

And Abram was very rich in cattle, in silver, and in gold.

Genesis 13:2

M ONEY can be classified according to various types:

(1) Precious metals
(2) Representative money
(3) Fiduciary money
(4) Deposit money
(5) Near money
(6) Fiat money

Precious Metals

When given an option, people have always preferred a precious metal as a monetary unit. The outstanding choices have been silver and gold—silver for smaller transactions and gold for larger transactions. Professor Elgin Groseclose, a highly respected monetary authority, has this to say concerning the utility of silver coinage:

> It is when we move abroad and especially among the millions of the world's population that live in Asia, Africa and Latin America that the significance and utility of silver coinage become apparent. At the levels of income on which they subsist, a silver coin, even if issued at much in excess of its metal value, represents tangible wealth.
>
> It is not commonly realized in the United States and Europe, where paper notes, check money and credit cards are a way of life, how important a single coin may be. Just as one reaches a million in accounting by adding one to one, and realizes that there can be no *million* quantity without a *one* quantity, so the accumulation of wealth proceeds by adding one dollar to another, or one rupee to another.
>
> Throughout these lands to which we have referred, with a few notable exceptions, government paper money has been unstable and

depreciating. The rate of depreciation is more rapid in some areas than in others, but the phenomenon is universal.

To the artisan who at the end of his day's labor has been able to set aside a portion of his earnings beyond his immediate needs, a piece of good silver money is strategic in his rise in the economic scale. Here is something durable that will not be eaten by termites, that will not rot nor mildew from the monsoons, nor burn if exposed to heat and the summer sun. Moreover, it is something that will retain its purchasing power from year to year, in contrast to government paper. Finally, if strung on a chain around his wife's neck or ankle, it is reasonably secure, at least as secure as the distant and unfamiliar savings bank. When he has acquired a sufficient number of these, he can rent a shop, if he has been an itinerant artisan, or purchase the tools of his trade, and he has taken the first step toward financial independence. This is the root of the capitalistic system.

Thus, good silver money can be in those lands a chief external mechanism for fostering an inner peace of mind, particularly a political contentment that makes for civic peace and stability.[1]

Most economists today "pooh-pooh" the idea of a precious metal-based monetary unit as being archaic and out of date. This attitude comes not from economic reasoning but from an unwarranted trust in man—from a trust that the civil authorities who have taken control over money and banking will be honest and will, therefore, maintain the integrity of the monetary unit. But hard lessons from the pages of history indicate that such a blind trust is unwarranted. Wherever civil governments have turned from a precious metal-based monetary unit to baser metals or to paper, money has soon lost its purchasing power through the insidious process of debauchment.

Precious metals such as gold and silver can be used in the form of:

(1) Bullion—pure metal in bulk form, usually in bars.
(2) Full-bodied or full-weight coins, stamped or unstamped.
(3) Less-than-full-weight coins—coins mixed with a baser metal.

Bullion is heavy and bulky to carry. Bars of bullion must, in order to prevent deception by secret adulteration, be assayed each time they change hands. This is both time consuming and costly. Also, because it is usually put up in fairly large and heavy bars, bullion is useful only for very large transactions or for storage. Therefore, it became a common practice to melt bullion bars down and to make them into small coins. When our country was on the gold standard, for instance, the U.S. Mint used to provide citizens with the service of minting gold and silver into coins. Because full-bodied coins are traded on a

[1]Elgin Groseclose, *Silver as Money; the Monetary Services of Silver,* Institute for Monetary Research, Monograph #2 (Washington, D.C.: Institute for Monetary Research, 1965), pp. 25-26.

weight basis, it soon became common practice in the early development of coins to stamp their faces and to mill their edges. Any attempt to adulterate or take away from their full weight would be readily noticeable.

There is a legitimate use for less-than-full-weight coins, that is, coins that have been mixed with baser metals such as copper, zinc or nickel. The addition of 10 percent of a baser metal serves to increase the hardness and durability of gold and silver. In their pure form, gold and silver are very soft and they wear away quickly.

There is even a legitimate reason for increasing the percentage of baser metals to more than 10 percent when the resultant coins are freely exchangeable for full-bodied coins. The cheaper coins will be used for less valuable transactions, and the people will naturally use them in their daily buying and selling activities. The public will hold onto the more valuable full-bodied coins and thereby conserve them from wearing out. However, an immediate danger appears in this practice of which citizens should be aware. Civil governments have been prone to use the issuance of less-than-full-weight coins as an intermediate step in weaning the people away from the use of full-bodied coins. Throughout history, governments have persisted in devious efforts to debauch the currency as a means of gaining spendable funds without having to levy additional taxes outrightly. The secret recasting of full-bodied coins into coins mixed with baser metals is one technique used.

Sir Thomas Gresham (1519-1579), founder of the Royal Exchange and Chancellor Exchequer under Queen Elizabeth I (1558-1603), prepared a paper for the Queen in 1559 on the circulation of debased coins. Henry VIII (1509-1547), had debased the coinage as a surreptitious means of raising needed revenues. Gresham noted that coins which are overvalued at the mint in terms of their value in the free market tended to drive the undervalued coins out of circulation. What does this mean practically? It means that people will bring debased or severely worn coins to the mint in exchange for better coins or that they will choose to pay taxes with such coins. Therefore, coins of **lesser** value (as judged by the market) tend either to accumulate at the treasury or to circulate in the economy, while coins of **greater** value (as judged by the market) are hoarded by the people. A popular way of stating "Gresham's Law" is: **Bad money chases good money out of circulation.** A more accurate statement is: **Coins seek their highest use value.** Debased and severely worn coins are more useful in trade, while high quality coins are preferable to retain. In 1560 Queen Elizabeth, following the advice of Sir Thomas Gresham, recalled thousands of debased silver coins and had them reminted into coins of standard value. Few civil rulers have had either the good sense or the integrity to reverse previous inflationary policies. One other such ruler was Napoleon Bonaparte, who replaced the fiat currency of the French Revolution, the paper *assignats,* with a silver *franc* and a gold *napoleon.*

One example of a lighter weight coin is the famous Pine Tree Shilling which was minted in Massachusetts Colony in 1652. It contained only 72 grains of silver in contrast with the 93-grain standard English shilling. The lighter shilling was produced in an effort to keep "hard money" within the Colony because full-weight coins tended to flow out to England in exchange for imported manufactures. The intended goal was not achieved because the price of imported goods simply rose in terms of the Pine Tree Shilling to offset its lesser weight of silver, and thus the currency outflow continued.

Representative Money

Representative money, as we can judge from the term, represents or "stands in" for more valuable money. This can be of two types: subsidiary coins and paper bills called **certificates**.

Subsidiary coins, if they are full-bodied as to composition, may or may not be equivalent to the corresponding weight-value of the money to which they are subsidiary. For instance, before the silver shortage that was brought about in the 1960s by our country's long-continued inflationary policies, the following coins circulated freely in these United States:

(1) The silver dollar — 371.25 grains of 90 percent silver, .999 fine.
(2) The silver half dollar or 50-cent piece — 173.6 grains of 90 percent silver, .999 fine.
(3) The silver quarter or 25-cent piece — 86.8 grains of 90 percent silver, .999 fine.
(4) The silver dime or 10-cent piece — 34.7 grains of 90 percent silver, .999 fine.
(5) The nickel or 5-cent piece made of nickel.
(6) The copper penny or 1-cent piece.

As you can calculate from the above-mentioned grain contents, two half dollars, four quarters or ten dimes did not quite amount to 371.25 grains of silver. The weight of these subsidiary coins totalled only 347 grains for a "dollar's worth" of change. Thus they were **representative** even though they were full-bodied at 90 percent silver, .999 fine. If a person wished to melt down silver coins for their bullion content, which is prohibited by law, it would be sensible to trade in subsidiary coins totalling 347 grains per "dollar's worth" in order to obtain silver dollars of 371 grains each.

When coins with a lesser content of precious metal are sold by the mint on a par with coins of greater content, or when a baser metal is used to replace silver or gold coins at the same face value (such as the cupronickel "sandwich" coins), a profit on the transaction is realized by the mint. The profit is the difference between the cost of producing the cheaper coins and the face value at which the mint sells them. This profit is called *seigniorage*. This same profit is realized when paper money is used to replace gold and silver coins. The profit realized from such operations explains the almost irresistable lure civil authorities have to replace gold and silver money with paper "fiat" money. The only barrier to government officials in replacing higher-valued money (gold and silver) with lower-valued money (copper, zinc, nickel and paper) is the unwillingness of the people to accept cheaper money. It is for this reason — to dispel an ignorance which can lead to their enslavement — that people should learn about money and the tendency of civil authorities to debauch the currency.

For many years, all of the above-listed coins, even the five-cent and one-cent pieces, were exchangeable at any bank or the U.S. Mint for a silver dollar because they officially represented the dollar as legally defined.

This changed in the 1960s. In 1965 Congress authorized the minting of cupronickel 25-cent and 10-cent pieces and the 50-cent piece in 1970, plus the minting of 40-percent silver Kennedy half dollars. For a while, these circulated side by side with the fast disappearing 90 percent silver coins. As long as they circulated and could be traded in to obtain silver dollars, they continued to be representative money. This effectively ended in 1967 when the Treasury started refusing requests to pay out silver dollars in exchange for subsidiary coins and silver certificates. Upon this action, the newly minted "sandwich" coins became what is known as **fiat** money. In other words, their officially designated face value resulted only from government fiat, from the federal government's decree that they were "worth" a certain amount.

This recent bit of history concerning how our government insidiously replaced silver coins with worthless paper and "sandwich" coins of very little value has escaped the observation of the mass of American citizens. Governments, obviously, do not advertise the steps they have taken to debauch the people's currency. In refusing to pay out silver dollars for silver certificates, the federal government actually repudiated its legal promise to pay **real** silver dollars for its representative paper dollars. In 1967, to cite a specific instance, this author took a number of silver certificates to the Federal Reserve Bank in St. Louis (as he had been doing since 1963), and requested silver dollars in exchange. The teller at the window refused and offered subsidiary silver coins instead. When the difference in silver content between silver dollars and a "dollar's worth" of silver change was explained, the teller at first denied this fact but finally admitted it. When this author insisted that the government had a **legal obligation** to stand behind its promise of redemption, the teller reluctantly showed him a letter from the Secretary of the Treasury, C. Douglas Dillon, which instructed that silver certificates would be honored for redemption **only** if they were physically presented at the U.S. Mint in San Francisco or at the Treasury in Washington, D.C. Since few citizens could afford to travel long distances to redeem a few silver certificates, this amounted to an unofficial repudiation. Congress later passed a bill in 1967 that officially repudiated redemption at a specified date in 1968. In the meantime, though, an interesting free market service sprang up to meet the needs of silver certificate holders, who had too few certificates to warrant a trip to either San Francisco or Washington, D.C. Entrepreneurial-minded persons in many parts of the country started running ads in newspapers and magazines offering to buy silver certificates for **more** than a dollar, usually for \$1.15 to \$1.20. Upon accumulating a goodly sum of silver certificates, these entrepreneurs would send them to their business associates located at the redemption cities who would then demand payment in silver. The free market presented a way for citizens to hold the civil authorities to their promise to redeem the certificates until the congressional bill took effect. This episode can be verified by checking newspapers and magazines for such ads during late 1967 and early 1968.

The representative paper money used by the U.S. Treasury were **gold certificates** and **silver certificates**. Each gold and silver certificate certified or promised to represent a stipulated amount of the precious metal that was supposed to be held on reserve at the Treasury. The promise to redeem for gold upon request was rescinded in 1933 when President Franklin D. Roosevelt issued an executive order which made it illegal for citizens to own gold or to use gold certificates for money. The promise to redeem silver, as already indicated, was rescinded in 1967 practically but legally in 1968. Upon repudiation, gold certificates actually became illegal to own except for numismatic purposes; and silver certificates changed from being **representative** money to **fiat** money.

Fiduciary Money

The word **fiduciary** means "holding or founded in trust." When the trust department of a bank holds stocks, bonds or money on behalf of another person, it stands in a fiducial relationship, or in a relationship of trust, to that person. The law recognizes that a fiduciary agent is in a strategic position to harm its client unfairly. Parents stand in a fiducial relationship to their children. Pastors, stockbrokers, doctors, attorneys and other professionals stand in a fiducial relationship to their clients. Governments and the issuers of private money, such as private commercial banks, put themselves in a fiducial relationship when they issue **more** money for circulation than they hold in reserve. For instance, if the government treasurer issues \$100 million in silver certificates based on \$100 million of silver bullion and stands ready to redeem the certificates for silver upon request, then the full \$100 million in certificates are truly **representative** money. Each certificate is fully backed by a dollar's worth of silver as legally defined. When the treasurer issues \$200 million of paper certificates based on only \$100 million of silver bullion, then there is no longer one dollar in the treasury for each dollar of certificates being circulated. The excess \$100 million is defined as **fiduciary** money. An obvious problem results: No one can tell which certificate is backed and which is not, for every certificate issued carries a promise to redeem upon demand. So each certificate in our example is, in actuality, backed by only 50 cents in silver.

You can easily see the great temptation that both civil governments and private issuers of money have to expand, expand and expand their fiduciary issues until it is impossible to redeem them at all. At such a time, the money becomes worthless in the eyes of the people—thereby ceasing to be money—because the people refuse to accept a debauched currency. The great danger of fiduciary money is that it often serves as a convenient "steppingstone" for rulers to change from a full-bodied precious metal coinage to fiat paper money. Citizens can easily be lulled into accepting fiduciary money because they trust their government and the monetary authorities. Then the civil government can surreptitiously overissue the fiduciary money and debauch it before the people realize what is going on. This has happened time and time again throughout recorded history.

Deposit Money

Another type of money is **deposit** money. It consists of two kinds: demand deposits, that is, checking account money and time deposits.

In the strictest sense of the term, **demand deposits** constitute true money, while **time deposits** do not. Demand deposits constitute "instant liquidity," that is, they can be spent at a moment's notice. Time deposits, on the other hand, are really what is called "near money." Banks and other financial institutions that accept time deposits may legally require 30 days' notice from the depositor before turning a time deposit into cash. Technically, time deposits are not really money. But they are so close that some economists consider them as money. Also, a recent development has moved time deposits closer to real money. This is the practice of making time deposits instantly transferrable from time to demand deposits, or directly transferrable from person to person through "negotiable orders of withdrawal," that is, NOW accounts. The net effect is to increase the liquidity of savings accounts and thereby to increase the effective supply of money in the economy.

Demand deposits are really privately created money because they are created by private commercial banks and not by government, though they are closely controlled by the government. Demand deposits are nothing more than numerical accounting entries on the ledger books of commercial banks. So popular is the convenience of demand deposits or checking accounts that they constitute approximately 80 percent of the country's money supply. The creation of demand deposits grew out of the practice of nineteenth century banks printing private bank notes which the issuing bank privately guaranteed. Both bank notes and demand deposits are a natural development in the process of free market banking. They both came into existence because they served a useful function in society, and private bankers were motivated by the profit incentive to provide services desired by the public.

Near Money

So-called **near money** is any evidence of wealth that is very liquid, that is, which can be changed into real money on short notice. This includes:

(1) Time deposits
(2) Short-term bonds and notes which do not fluctuate much in price
(3) Savings and loan deposits
(4) Cash value of life insurance policies
(5) Certificates of deposit
(6) Money market funds

The difference between near money and real money is this: **Real money** provides "instant liquidity," while **near money** is one step removed from being instantaneously liquid. Also, near money usually pays some kind of interest return. Both real money and near money are stated in fixed-dollar amounts. Thus stocks and long-term bonds, which tend to fluctuate widely in price, are not considered to have as much liquidity as near money does.

Fiat Money

The word **fiat** means an authoritative order or a formal decree. As we have already indicated, fiat money is recognized as money **only** because the civil authority legally declares it to be money.

A study of history shows that civil governments are the world's most dedicated and persistent debauchers of currency. To use more modern terms, we would say that civil governments are inflationists or legal counterfeiters. There is a well-noted tendency for civil rulers to want to spend more money than citizens are willing to pay in taxes. This occurs because citizens generally come to want more services from the civil authorities than the citizens are willing to be taxed for, and the politicians in office take steps to accomodate the people as a means of maintaining their political support. It is a common practice for rulers to engage in the easy habit of creating money by fiat. The Kublai Khan's "mulberry dollars" of the thirteenth century were fiat money. So were the "greenbacks" that were issued by the Lincoln Administration during the War Between the States. So are the Federal Reserve Notes which circulate in our country today. No Federal Reserve Note can be "cashed in" any longer for either gold or silver. They continue to be accepted as money solely because the federal government has decreed that they **are** money by legal fiat and because the people are still willing to accept them as such.

Government vs. Private Money-Makers

There is a common misunderstanding about money. In this day and age, people have become conditioned to thinking that the only proper kind of money is money that is either created or sponsored by civil governments. This is definitely a mistaken idea. While it is true that no country today has a national currency that is **not** government controlled, there is no inherent reason why money **must** be made a function of government. In matter of fact, a good case can be made for a strict separation of money from the grasping power of civil rulers. Since the matter of money is so very important to the welfare of the people in that it pervades every aspect of their personal and social lives, and since a study of history shows that civil rulers have been the world's most flagrant counterfeiters, does it not make more sense to entrust the money-making power to the **private** sector where competitive market forces will better ensure that the money-makers will remain honest? If private money-makers break their word or their guarantee, they can be hauled into court by the wronged parties. But if the civil government has a legal monopoly on the money-making power, to whom can a wronged people turn? This is a question that every liberty-loving person might well consider. Money can easily be turned into an instrument of enslavement by those who know how to manipulate it.

To the person who has a blind and misguided trust in the integrity of men in governmental positions of power, the previous point may seem too radical. This author admits that it is radical, but it is radical in the good sense in that it gets down to the root of the matter. Think on this: The worldwide tendency for the money-making function to be arrogated to civil authorities is simply an outward indication of the worldwide drive of humanistic civil rulers to gain manipulative power over citizens in their never-ending machinations to build their idea of an earthly Utopia, a modern Babel (see Ps. 2:2-12).[2]

Let us never forget this inescapable fact: It is the people, through their voluntary and general acceptance, who determine what is to be used as money. It is civil governments which then endorse the people's prior actions by declaring the people's choice to be "legal tender," thus superimposing government authority on what was originally a private matter.

To briefly review: The first creators of money were private individuals rather than civil authorities. At first, if we correctly interpret the biblical account and archaeological findings, private individuals used gold and silver bullion, cattle and other things as a common medium of exchange. Even as late as the nineteenth century in the western United States, prospectors and frontiersmen used bags of gold dust as money. After the use of bullion, full-bodied unstamped and stamped coins came into being. Many of the stamped coins were stamped by civil authorities. Subsidiary coins of lesser weight and of baser metals (representative money) were then introduced. Then came paper money (representative and fiduciary). Deposit money appeared last. In this very decade, as some watchful individuals have grown more and

---

[2]For more information on the developing trend of civil rulers to manipulate and control citizens by means of monetary and fiscal policy, as well as through the cooperation of international bankers, you might wish to research topics dealing with The Trilateral Commission and The Bilderberg Group. Both organizations are composed of persons who favor the development of so-called "international cooperation" between governments, international bankers and the heads of large business firms. For a sympathetic view of the movement, see *Tragedy and Hope*, by Carroll Quigley; for a critical view, see *The Naked Capitalist*, by. W. Cleon Skousen. Other sources of information are: *The Money Lenders*, by Anthony Sampson; *International Money*, by Charles P. Kindleberger; and *Money and Monetary Policy in Interdependent Nations*, by Ralph C. Bryant.

more concerned about the continued inflationary policies that have been followed by our national government and the effect of these policies on the purchasing power of the dollar, private mints in these United States and other
countries have begun to supply the people with privately produced full-bodied
coins of gold and silver.

All of the steps in monetary development up to this point can and have
been performed very adequately by private individuals and firms (goldsmiths,
money-changers and private banks). The medieval banks of Italy, of which
the Medici Bank (1397-1494) was a prime example, were private, non-
governmental institutions of high repute. They performed many sophisticated
monetary and banking transactions which were surprisingly similar to those
performed by modern banks. All this was done without government supervision. The early goldsmiths, moneylenders and bankers simply depended on
their personal reputations for integrity to gain the public's business. When
losses occurred, they were made good from the personal fortunes of the
bankers. At that time, there was no such thing as limited-liability corporations
that allowed risk-takers to legally avoid payment from their personal fortunes
by hiding behind what today is called the "corporate shield."

Records indicate that the early moneylenders and bankers were under constant pressure from civil rulers to make unsecured loans. These pressures grew
out of the monarchs' universal proclivity to spend more than they were able to
collect in taxes. It was largely this pressure from rulers which led to the formation of central banks and modern-day fractional reserve banking.

It is not until we get into the development of fiat money that we must necessarily turn from the private field of money and banking to the government.
Only the civil authorities are able to assume the power of declaring what
money is to be by legal fiat. Private money creators do not carry the "power of
the sword." They have no means of applying the coercion that is necessary to
enforce any declaration they might make.

Steps from Full-Bodied Money to Government Fiat Money

The historic procedure followed in the evolution of money (perhaps devolu-
tion would be a more accurate term to use) from a bullion-based or a full-
bodied currency to government fiat money is this:

Step 1: The people freely come to use, through voluntary choice and common acceptance, full-bodied gold and silver coins as a generally acceptable
medium of exchange. Thus, we see that the appearance of money in society is
a natural development of the free market process; the appearance of money in
society is voluntarism in action.

Step 2: The civil authority **declares** by legal fiat that the people's prior
choice is "legal tender." That is, the civil government declares that citizens are
now **forced** by law to accept for the payment of debts that which they have
been willing to accept voluntarily all along! The civil authority's legal fiat has

no practical effect immediately, for the government simply ratifies by law what the people were already doing in practice. This seems like a harmless step, but it will have a very practical impact later — practical but to the people's detriment.

Step 3: The civil authority next issues representative money (certificates) which it promises to redeem upon demand by guaranteeing to hold a specified amount of precious metal on reserve for each certificate issued. The government authorities find that they must do this in order to maintain the confidence of the people. The representative money is also declared to be "legal tender."

Step 4: The desire to expand government spending in excess of tax revenues occurs, so additional amounts of "representative" money are issued. This "representative" money is really **fiduciary** money because it is issued **in excess** of the amount of precious metal held on reserve for redemption. At this point, deception has already occurred since not all of the money can be redeemed; for no longer does the treasury hold enough precious metal on reserve to make full redemption. The people do not yet suspect that their money is being insidiously debauched, so they remain unconcerned.

Step 5: Finally, such vast amounts of so-called representative money (really fiduciary money) are issued that certain observant individuals become worried and start turning in the money they hold for redemption. Requests for redemption are honored for a while, but the government officials soon realize, as more and more people begin requesting redemption, that it will be impossible to continue honoring the government's promise to redeem all the money that has been issued. The cruel fact is that the vast majority of the supposedly representative money is not really represented by real precious metal held on reserve. The people's medium of exchange — their currency — has been insidiously debauched by the very authorities the people expected to protect it. The authorities have failed in their important fiducial relationship, but the people are powerless to take effective legal action. The legal promise of convertibility to precious metal on demand is finally repudiated. It is at this specific point that the civil government reneges on its word.

Since the civil government has officially declared the money as "legal tender," most people still are not too disturbed. Although prices have begun to climb in response to the increased supply of money in the economy, the people believe by now that the civil government's act of declaring money as "legal tender" is what gives value to it. Since the people continue generally to accept the money in exchange for goods and services, in an economic sense, the government fiat money still **is** money.

Step 6: The people's money is now nothing but **fiat** money. It is fiat money even though it still **looks** the same as money people have gotten accustomed to, first as representative money and then as fiduciary money. The ever-increasing flood of fiat money continues as the government is pressed by political pressures to increase spending beyond its revenues. Prices, which had begun creeping upward with each increase in the money supply, now begin to spiral higher and higher.

Step 7: Finally, a hyperinflation occurs. The quantity of fiat money is eventually expanded so rapidly that it loses practically all of its purchasing power. The German inflation of 1921-1923 is an excellent example of this stage of inflation during this century.

Step 8: The people finally refuse to accept the debauched currency any longer. They begin, by common choice and general acceptance, to make something else play the role of money. Thereby, a newly acceptable commodity becomes money by general consent, and the government fiat money ceases to function as money any longer. The new commodity may be a precious metal, chocolate candy, cigarettes, ladies hosiery or some other item of value. Finally, the people usually turn to gold or silver as a common medium of exchange because of the inherent characteristics these metals have. Order thus begins to grow out of chaos — a chaos caused by the civil government's debauching of the currency.

Step 9: The government authorities now step in again (as in Step 2) and once again declare the people's new choice of money to be "legal tender" by its fiat. The whole debauching process can thereby begin anew.

Practically every civil government in the history of mankind has, or is currently, engaged in the process of monetary debauchery. Why? Civil governments tend to be the world's greatest "legal counterfeiters" because, in their scramble to get more money to spend — that is, to put their hands on more money than the people are willing to pay in taxes — they break two crucial rules of sound money.

Rule 1: Money must be **earned** before it is spent. Government-created money does not and **cannot** represent values which have been produced and offered for sale in the marketplace. When the civil authority creates new money, the newly created money does not represent earning power. Rather, the newly created money **dilutes** the earning power of previously existing money. This, of course, constitutes a moral wrong; a breaking of the commandment "Thou shalt not steal" (Ex. 20:15).

Rule 2: There must be a **balance** between the amount of money in existence and the quantity of goods and services the money represents. When government authorities continue to expand the money supply, prices will most certainly rise in response, thus causing money to lose its purchasing power.

The Goldsmith-Bankers

The ability to create money — whether it is held by private or governmental entities — bestows a widespread and insidious power on the money creators. They can quietly channel unearned purchasing power to those who borrow the money they create. We will investigate the theory of money creation; we will then be in a position to arrive at value judgments concerning the ability to inflate and deflate a country's money supply.

The early goldsmiths and money-changers gradually evolved into the first bankers. Historical records lead us to believe that the development proceeded somewhat along these lines:

Precious metals are liable to theft and are risky for the average person to store as well as bulky to carry. Because craftsmen who worked with gold and silver already had safe places to store their own metals, they came to specialize in providing a safe place to store gold and silver for others. These individuals came to be known as goldsmiths. (See the account of the uproar by the silversmiths in Ephesus: Acts 19:23-41.)

The goldmsiths gave owners who stored their precious metal with them a **warehouse receipt**. When the owners of gold made purchases from other people in the community, they developed the habit of giving sellers their warehouse receipt for the goods received. This receipt allowed the seller of goods to redeem it for the gold or silver indicated on the receipt by going to the goldsmith and requesting redemption. Since it is much more convenient to carry paper warehouse receipts than bulky gold or silver, the practice of transferring these paper receipts from person to person for economic exchanges developed. At first the warehouse receipts were transferred by endorsement (this would be similar to endorsing a check today), but eventually **bearer receipts** were developed which simply entitled the bearer to claim a stated amount of gold or silver from the goldsmith on demand. These would be similar to the gold and silver certificates which used to circulate in this country.

Everyone in the community readily came to accept the warehouse receipts in place of real gold or silver, for they could exchange the receipts for gold or silver at any time upon presentation to the goldsmith. In short, general acceptance of these bearer receipts meant that they were true money. As we recall, the definition of money is anything that is generally accepted in society as a medium of exchange for goods and services. Two types of money naturally developed in the free market to serve the needs of people: full-bodied coins of gold and silver and representative money in the form of warehouse receipts.

It is important that we pause and take note of something that has already been called to your attention. At this point in the natural evolution of money and banking, every unit of circulating currency was either a **full-bodied coin** of precious metal, or it was a paper receipt which **represented** a full-bodied coin or bullion warehoused at the goldsmith's. As new gold and silver entered the community because of mining operations or from selling goods to foreigners, the new metal would either circulate directly as full-bodied coins; or it would be stored at the goldsmith's. In the latter case, additional warehouse receipts would circulate as representative money.

It is also important to note that, at this point, there is no monetary inflation—that is, there has been no creation of money which is not fully backed by gold or silver. Each unit of circulating media added to the community's money supply was earned by its owner and, therefore, was represented by actual goods or services which had been provided to some member in society. There was a stable balance between the amount of money in circulation relative to the quantity of goods and services offered for sale. The goldsmiths, who by this time might be called bankers, operated on a **100-percent reserve basis** because each circulating warehouse receipt represented, unit for unit, one unit of precious metal held at his place of business. The total money supply on such a reserve basis would be very stable, and so would the general price level. The price of specific commodities relative to others would, of course, fluctuate according to the market forces of supply and demand. But the general price level would remain quite stable. Private citizens would be motivated to work, save and invest because they would feel confident that money saved and invested would purchase as much or even more in the future as it did the day they saved it.

Actually, in such a non-inflationary monetary system, the purchasing power of money would tend to increase over a long period of time rather than remain stable. Why? Because as technology and productive efficiency improve year after year, the total quantity of goods and services supplied to the market would increase relative to the amount of money in circulation. In these United States, for instance, productivity has increased on the average of 2-3 percent per year over the last two centuries. Given a stable money supply, this would mean that prices would tend downward at about the same rate, thus raising real wages and people's standard of living. From about 1870 to 1900, for instance, the money supply was rather stable; prices did fall, and real wages doubled. During the last few decades, productivity has generally continued to rise, but the gains in output have been largely lost (especially in the 1970s and early 1980s) through a generally rising price level generated by government inflation of the money supply.

The Birth of Fractional Reserve Banking

Now we come to a change in policy followed by the goldsmith-bankers, who noticed that relatively few individuals ever turned in their warehouse receipts to actually claim the gold or silver held on deposit in their behalf. It seems that as long as people are confident that they can claim gold or silver on demand, they prefer the greater convenience of carrying the easier-to-handle paper receipts.

This stability in deposits created a money-making opportunity for the goldsmith-bankers, who were under continual pressure from other people in the community to lend them funds for business ventures and personal spending. "Why not," mused the goldsmith-banker, "lend out some additional (fictitious) warehouse receipts to willing borrowers and charge them interest? This seems like a safe scheme to increase my income as long as the additional warehouse receipts are returned and destroyed before other depositors come to claim their gold and silver. Even if some few individuals do come to claim their deposits, enough other people will not. Probably enough new deposits will come in anyway to cover such claims. As long as I do not create so many additional receipts (money) that depositors will begin to worry about the safety of their deposits, the idea should work to everyone's benefit."

Trial and error seemed to indicate that, in normal times, the goldsmith-bankers might safely lend out three unbacked receipts for each unit of precious metal on hand, for a total of four warehouse receipts per unit of metal held on deposit. The goldsmith-bankers could enjoy a larger income through the interest earned, and the people in the community who wanted funds could also have a means of acquiring needed capital goods. The goldsmith-bankers might even be able to pay interest on deposits in order to attract more depositors, thereby benefitting the general public. Hopefully, the borrowed warehouse receipts would be used to make wise business investments which would expand production and employment. If so, the resulting increase in goods and services would benefit society as a whole.

It is at this point that the community's monetary system changed from a 100-percent reserve basis to a **fractional reserve basis**. It is also at this point that duplicity entered the picture. Up to this time, each circulating warehouse receipt truly represented a specific unit of gold or silver held on deposit. But from now on, there might be as many as four receipts circulating for each unit of precious metal held in reserve by the goldsmith-bankers—one receipt being a truly **representative** form of money, with the other three being what might be called **fiduciary** money. All four receipts were identical in appearance and in function. Now, if there should ever be a "run" on the goldsmith-bankers by people in the community who wanted to redeem their outstanding receipts, three out of four receipt-holders would be disappointed; and this would force the goldsmith-bankers who could not meet their claims into bankruptcy.

The fatal temptation resulting from the above-described system of fractional banking is obvious. There is an almost irresistable tendency for the goldsmith-bankers (whom we will simply call bankers from now on) to overissue the number of fictitious receipts. Why? Because they want to maximize their interest income—for the more receipts issued, the more interest income bankers are able to collect on money they loan out.

The result of this kind of banking, that is, fractional reserve banking, has been a continuing series of boom-bust cycles coupled with the failure of banks that have overissued their notes (which are equivalent to warehouse receipts). Some people mistakenly believe that periodic boom-bust cycles (inflationary periods followed by deflationary periods) are characteristic of free market capitalism; but this is not correct. The boom-bust cycle is a monetary phenomenon that is brought about by the cyclical monetary inflations and deflations which are inherently characteristic of fractional reserve banking. Remember this point, for it is an important one in arguing against the socialists/Marxists, who claim that free market capitalism is inherently unstable.

Central Banking and Bank Regulations

There are two developments which have grown out of fractional reserve banking, and the student of economics should be aware of them. Both developments, in the long run, have served to increase the level of government intervention in the economy. They are: (1) the establishment of government-sponsored **central reserve banks** which serve as "lenders of last resort" to banks which periodically find themselves in a liquidity crisis as a result of overissuing money which they are later unable to redeem upon demand, and (2) the establishment of government control and regulation over the banking industry in order to prevent the overexpansion of bank notes.

With respect to the civil government's establishing a central bank and bank regulating agencies, it is appropriate to make the following point. We live in an era when economists, politicians and the general public take for granted that government control of banking is necessary to achieve economic stability. This situation was not always so, however. During medieval times, banks operated successfully in a "free banking" atmosphere; and the same can be said of banks in many countries up until the nineteenth century. Vera C. Smith has this to say:

> A central bank is not a natural product of banking development. It is imposed from outside or comes into being as the result of Government favours. This factor is responsible for marked effects on the whole currency and credit structure which brings it into sharp contrast with what would happen under a system of free banking from which Government protection was absent.[3]

> After 1875 the central banking systems of those countries which already had them were accepted without further discussion, and the practical choice of the one system in preference to the alternative [i.e., free banking without any government intervention] was never again questioned. Moreover, the declared superiority of central banking became nothing less than a dogma without any very clear understanding of the exact nature of the advantages, but there remained one among the chief commercial countries of the world which still lacked a central banking organization: this was the United States of America. . . .[4]

The point that Vera Smith makes in her book is that, strangely, once civil governments established central banks and regulating agencies, scholars ceased to consider banking without the guiding hand of government as a viable option.

---

[3]Vera C. Smith, *The Rationale of Central Banking,* Monetary Tract, no. 34 (Greenwich, Conn.: Committee for Monetary Research and Education, 1981), p. 2.

[4]Ibid., p. 29.

If we go back to medieval times, we find that private banks in northern Italy were quite large. They operated on a fractional reserve basis quite successfully for many years until they eventually went bankrupt because of overexpansion. They had no government supervision to "protect the public."

These banks were owned by individuals or by partners who **personally** guaranteed the payment of losses. The resulting degree of personal responsibility to draw upon their own wealth in case of loss served as a natural barrier against the tendency to recklessly overissue notes in an attempt to maximize bank earnings. Today banks are incorporated, and the owners are thereby legally protected by what is known as the "corporate shield." Bankers' personal assets are protected from the banks' creditors. Thus, in the absence of an interior restraint (the risk of losing one's personal fortune), an exterior restraint (government control and regulation) is used to inhibit the overexpansion of bank notes.

In the nineteenth century, bank stockholders, even though the bank they owned might have been incorporated, were subject to "double liability," which means that they stood to lose their investment in the bank plus an additional amount from their personal fortunes. This special safeguard on bank corporations did not do much good in protecting depositors, and it is no longer in practice. It is evident that the legal protection of one's personal wealth through the "corporate shield" produces a greater willingness for bankers to engage in risky undertakings in the hope of reaping greater profits. If these higher-risk ventures pay off, then both the risk-takers and the public benefit. But if they do not pay off, creditors (including bank depositors) end up paying the losses incurred while the risk-takers seek protection from loss behind the "corporate shield."

100-Percent Reserve vs. Fractional Reserve Banking

Economists have contrasting views on the issue of 100-percent reserve banking versus fractional reserve banking. One group holds that 100-percent reserve banking is the only system to use because (1) it is the only method that honestly holds a real unit of precious metal on reserve for each receipt (bank note) issued, and (2) it will not produce the economic boom-bust cycles which are wrongly blamed on free market capitalism as a system.

Proponents of the 100-percent reserve concept point out that any other warehouseman (a grain elevator operator, for instance) who issues receipts beyond those which truly represent the goods he holds on deposit would soon be arrested for fraudulent operations. They also point out the advantage of having a stable economy based on a stable money supply which cannot be arbitrarily inflated and deflated by bankers as they make loans and then destroy the fictitious receipts when the loans are repaid. This matter will be described in greater detail in the next chapter, but when bankers create additional (fictitious) receipts and lend them out, they **inflate** the money supply of the community; and prices tend upward as a result. When borrowers later repay their loans with receipts received in exchange for goods and services sold, the additional receipts are then destroyed by the bankers. The money supply is thereby **deflated,** and prices tend back to their prior level. In short, in a fractional reserve system, bankers **create** new money when they extend loans to customers and **destroy** existing money when loans are repaid. Proponents of the fractional reserve concept, on the other hand, hold that the long-range effect of fractional reserve banking is beneficial. First, they claim it is **not** inflationary in the long run. While the creation of additional purchasing media may cause prices to rise in the short run, the increased stream of goods and services which results from new capital investments inspired by loans will cause prices to fall. Why? Because entrepreneurs who borrow funds will use the newest and most productive technology and machinery in their new plants. Their lower costs of production will make it economically feasible to reduce prices in order to expand sales. The whole community will thereby benefit from an increased supply of goods at lower prices.

The second point proponents of fractional reserve banking make is this: While they admit an inherent danger of possibly overexpanding the money supply by issuing too many unbacked receipts, proponents believe that the tendency can be thwarted by imposing proper controls by the civil authorities. Besides, they claim, if the newly created money is loaned only on goods and services being produced for immediate sale, fractional reserve banking will not be inflationary because the new money is balanced off against the new goods and services that are enroute to market. If such a practice is followed, any new fractionally based money is only **temporary,** while the goods and services produced are longer lasting.

The idea of creating money through fractional reserve banking only to finance goods enroute to market is called the "commercial theory of banking" or "the real bills doctrine." In order for it to operate successfully, bankers must keep strict accounts so they will know what kind of money they are lending out. They must lend only fractionally based money on short-term, self-liquidating loans. But they may lend fully backed money on long-term loans if the fully backed money is deposited with them on a long-term basis which matches the length of time the banker used in extending loans. In short, the idea is simply this: Only money deposited for long terms can be lent for long terms; demand deposits, which are really short-term "call" deposits, can be lent only for very short periods.

English bankers seem to have had a better understanding of the difference between these two types of money, for their accounting procedures keep them advised as to how much of each type is loaned out. American bankers have never differentiated in practice between short-term and long-term deposits. Throughout history American bankers have had a tendency to accept short-term deposits and to extend long-term loans, a practice which tends to strain a bank's liquidity during periods of stress. The commercial theory of banking, or the real bills doctrine, though sound, is now held in disrepute. Current thinking is that it is a useless bother since the civil government has taken upon itself the responsibility of "protecting" the public by serving as a lender of last resort to banks.

The proponents of 100-percent reserve banking respond thus: (1) Even the temporary creation of additional unbacked money gives an economic advantage to those who borrow it. They can use the unearned newly created money, which is loaned at the banker's discretion, to acquire control over real wealth by purchasing it with the newly created money. This bestows a temporary advantage on those who have a special relation with the banking community in the acquisition of scarce capital goods. (2) Since the unbacked fiduciary money is identical in appearance with the truly representative money that is backed by precious metals, how can the lending banker effectively control the uses to which the additional money is applied? A borrower may say that he will use a loan for such and such a purpose, but he may not actually do so in practice. Instead of being used only for very short-term purposes, the newly created money may well be applied to long-term investments, which everyone

Table 7:1

Purchasing Power of the U.S. Dollar

	Value of the Dollar	CPI* 1940 = 100	CPI* 1967 = 100
1940	100.0	100.0	42.0
1945	77.8	128.3	53.9
1950	58.2	171.6	72.1
1955	52.3	190.9	80.2
1960	47.3	211.1	88.7
1965	44.4	225.0	94.5
1970	36.1	276.9	116.3
1971	34.6	288.8	121.3
1972	33.5	298.3	125.3
1973	31.6	316.9	133.1
1974	28.4	351.6	147.7
1975	26.1	383.8	161.2
1976	24.7	405.9	170.5
1977	23.1	432.1	181.5
1978	21.5	465.2	195.4
1979	19.3	517.6	217.4
1980	17.8	561.7	236.0
1981	15.9	625.9	263.0
1982	14.8	675.7	284.0
1983	14.3	699.3	294.0

Source: U.S. Department of Commerce.

*CPI = Consumer Price Index.

agrees is inflationary in the long run. (3) The Federal Reserve System, which was supposedly designed to **restrict** the inherent inflationary tendencies of fractional reserve banking, has in practice cooperated with the inflationary policies of the federal government by helping to monetize federal deficits. The "protecting agency" has not, in practice, served its purpose. Rather, it has served in the contrary direction as an "engine of inflation." Through the Federal Reserve System, the federal government's persistent deficits have been monetized, the country's money supply has been artificially increased and price levels have persistently risen in response. The exact process of how federal deficits are monetized, thereby inflating the money supply and generating a persistent upward bias on prices, is explained in the next chapter.

As we have already indicated, these United States have a fractional reserve banking system. This system is closely regulated and controlled by the Federal Reserve Board and other agencies of government with the stated objective of limiting the natural tendency of banks to issue too much money. The information in Table 7:1 provides historical data which will allow you to judge whether or not the Federal Reserve System has actually helped maintain a stable price level and thus protected the purchasing power of our money.

The Problem of Inflation

As we have already indicated, there is no country in which the civil authorities do not have control over the money-creating process and the banking system. While all civil governments pretend to protect the welfare of citizens by erecting elaborate systems of monetary control—supposedly to prevent the overexpansion of money by private banks—the net effect of such government control works in the **opposite** direction. How? It does so in this way:

Because of government controls, the banking system, which is not really complicated from a theoretical standpoint, **appears** to be very complicated. The ordinary citizen despairs of understanding how it operates, and **what people do not understand, they cannot control.** (Remember our maxim?) The long-range result is that citizens blindly put their confidence in government rulers whom they suppose to be more knowledgeable, and they thereby relegate all money and banking matters to the care of the civil authorities.

This, of course, is a very dangerous attitude for people to take; but it is exactly what the civil rulers want. Politicians and bureaucrats want to control the people rather than be controlled by them. Political rulers are intent on taxing citizens to the ultimate in their humanistic attempts to build an earthly Utopia instead of simply attempting to maintain a workable system of justice. Eventually the anti-biblically minded rulers, finding that the people resist paying higher taxes, turn to the secret means of taxation called **inflation**. Civil rulers are confirmed inflationists at heart. They create debts through deficit spending and then use the central back (our Federal Reserve Bank) to create enough money to "sop up" the deficit-created debt. In short, the governmentally imposed instrument of control is quietly turned into a tool of inflating the money supply. This enables the rulers to insidiously siphon off effective control of wealth from private hands to public hands.

The person who does not understand the process of monetary inflation and what its detrimental economic and political effects are does not really understand a most important aspect of the economic working of society. Nor does he have the knowledge that is needed to maintain and enhance his economic and political freedom.

Up to this point, we have discussed the basic theory and practice of monetary inflation in a simplified economy in which the money creators were goldsmith-bankers. In the next chapter, we will deal with the process of monetary inflation as it currently works in the American economy with a central reserve bank (the Federal Reserve System) in conjunction with banks that operate on a fractional reserve basis. We have also pointed out the humanistic bent of mind that impels civil rulers to be inflationists, and this is quite important for the Christian student of economics to understand. The problem of inflation is simply an outworking of the anti-biblical attitude of secular humanism. Once we recognize this fact, the advice from Proverbs 4:23 takes on additional meaning: "Keep thy heart with all diligence; for out of it are the issues of life." While we will investigate the actual **process** of inflation in the next chapter, it is timely at this point to list the **effects** of long-continued inflation so you will be able to recognize its symptoms and be enabled to diagnose the problem and recommend a cure.

Let us again define inflation. **Inflation** is the act of creating new money and adding it to the money supply of a country. In short, inflation amounts to an increase in the money supply through money creation. Most economics textbooks define inflation as "a period of generally rising price levels." This is a popular but incorrect definition, for it looks at the **subsequent effect** (rising prices) instead of the **prior cause** (an increase in the money supply). It is very important that we understand that the cause-effect pattern of inflation runs like this: (1) New money is created and added to a nation's money supply. (2) When the newly created money is used by citizens to purchase the existing limited supply of goods and services, prices rise as a result. As simple as this process is, many people seem unable to grasp it. They ignorantly believe political demagogues when the politicians blame rising prices on businessmen or labor unions, neither of which have the slightest capability of causing a general rise in the price level.

A correct understanding of what inflation is and what it causes would quickly dispel this widespread ignorance, and it would help people see that only the national government, which is the level of civil government that has primary control over money and banking, can possibly be responsible for a generally rising price level.

Ultimately, the problem of inflation must be seen from a theological as well as an economic perspective. Civil governments are inflationists because they deny the sovereignty of God; they do not think the world can progress without their guiding hand, so they attempt to remake the world according to their own humanistic ideas. They use monetary inflation as a means of arrogating money and the control of wealth to themselves. In fairness to civil rulers, it must be said that they are responding to the wishes of a people who are anxious to be relieved of their burdensome responsibilities. A people deserves the type of civil rulers they raise to positions of power.

With this introduction, here are the various effects of long-continued monetary inflation:

(1) The control of wealth is transferred from those who have worked to produce it to those who have control over spending the newly created money. Those who have control of the newly created money may be: (a) government agencies which spend the vast sums of new government money, (b) welfare recipients, (c) local or state governments that receive federal grants-in-aid, (d) foreign governments that have received foreign aid or (e) business firms that fill government contracts.

(2) When the newly created funds are used to purchase goods and services in the marketplace, entrepreneurs and producers adjust their economic activity to meet the new demand. Existing patterns of economic production are disrupted. In short, false monetary signals are sent to entrepreneurs and producers. Production thus comes to be more government-oriented and less consumer-oriented, for the effective demand is now coming from government sources.

(3) Prices begin to rise as the new money competes with existing money for the available supply of goods and services. Those who get their hands on the newly created money first are able to make purchases **before** prices begin to rise. They are enriched relative to those citizens who do not receive newly created money at all or who receive it only **after** prices have begun to rise. This poses a **moral** question, for government power is being used to enrich some members of society at the expense of others.

(4) Such government largess is always spent on a **political** basis, so citizens start to scramble and compete with each other to obtain "their share" of government spending. The incidence of demagoguery, graft and corruption rises; and an inevitable process of demoralization sets in. People start overlooking principle and start turning to expediency in their affairs because government policy pits one pressure group in society against another. People tend to lose their social graces because they subconsciously recognize that every citizen is now competing with all others in grasping for governmnent-distributed largess. The individuals in society gradually become dehumanized as they are pitted against each other.

(5) The increase in government spending serves to bolster the level of government control in the economy. Politicians and government bureaucrats impose certain social and political demands on those persons in society who

receive government monies. The leaders of business firms, schools and other organizations feel forced to acquiesce in whatever demands the government makes in order to receive government funds. As government spending balloons, government grows to be the single largest purchaser in the economy; so its impact in the marketplace also becomes very great. Business firms and other organizations tend to prostitute themselves in their search for profits or in their hope of receiving government handouts. A tendency for bribery and secret kickbacks begins to appear. Honest members of society are scandalized time and time again as new evidences of corruption are periodically discovered. Public attention is always focused on **specific happenings** rather than the **system** which generates such scandals. The general public is shocked at each new scandal because the people are not astute enough to realize that their system of government-by-law has been perverted into a system of government-by-men who use political power as a tool for serving special interest groups. The one point on which all opposing interest groups agree is that each wants more money from the government. An intense rivalry and competition to gain "political clout" begins and continues as people learn that political power is the surest avenue in getting more money.

(6) A new class of citizens rises to the top of society. Previously, when the economy was more consumer-oriented, market-directed entrepreneurs tended to accumulate and control productive wealth. But the successful acquisition of government funds calls for different gifts and skills; so people who are more politically adept start rising to the top of society. The control of productive wealth shifts to those individuals who are especially adept at political manipulation rather than economic production. Productivity thus begins to drop.

(7) Rising price levels cause lenders to be reluctant to lend money unless they are compensated through higher interest rates. So, interest rates rise. This squeezes many would-be home buyers out of the market, for they find that the combination of rising prices for homes plus higher interest rates causes their monthly mortgage payments to rise beyond their ability to pay. This reduces the level of home construction and thereby contributes to unemployment in the home-building sector of the economy. Disgruntled citizens who would like to own a home petition the civil authorities to "do something," and they are joined by home builders and workers in the construction industry to start new government programs to assist people to buy homes.

(8) Domestic prices begin to rise relative to foreign prices, so the public buys cheaper foreign imports. The level of imports rises, and domestic producers and unionized workers, who suffer unemployment, petition the government for protection from foreign competitors. The civil government raises tariffs and imposes import controls in response. This causes consumer prices to rise even higher, and the economy begins to stagnate as foreign markets for export goods are lost; for, foreigners cannot buy **from** us unless they get dollars by selling goods **to** us.

(9) Rising prices cause the need for government income to rise also. The

people do not want to pay higher taxes, but they still want more government services. The civil authorities turn to even greater deficits to make up for the gap between government tax income and government expenditures. The monetization of this additional debt causes prices to rise even faster. People become disenchanted with saving and investing, especially young people who have not yet developed habits of saving. The people turn to speculative activities instead of to productive investments. The real level of capital investment in productive tools and machinery begins to fall off because savings in real terms have dropped. This adversely affects the rate of real economic growth which begins to taper off until it finally becomes negative. The people's standard of living subsequently begins to fall. In the meantime, a widespread feeling of "buy-now-and-pay-later" develops because people want to spend their money before it loses its value.

(10) Public employees at the state and local levels who are not direct recipients of the newly created money begin to feel that their pay levels have not increased proportionately with price levels and the pay of other groups. Firemen, policemen, teachers and others go on strike or begin to agitate for higher wages.

(11) Elderly people who have retired on fixed incomes are systematically pauperized because their pension checks buy less and less as price levels rise. They find it in their interest to band together to seek help from the civil government to increase their pensions. Because this is a large and influential group, politicians turn to demagogic promises to gain their votes. Politicians find it almost impossible to be elected or re-elected to office unless they strongly cater to the elderly people's coordinated demands for higher benefits from the civil government.

(12) So much political pressure is applied to government leaders that they try all sorts of programs to alleviate unemployment, which strangely seems to coexist with rising price levels. Political forces arise to make civil government the employer of last resort. Government officials seek scapegoats on whom to blame the problems they themselves have created. They blame businessmen and labor unions for rising prices, and these two groups fight between themselves in attempting to place the blame on each other. The civil authorities, the very culprits who brought about inflation and rising price levels, impose wage and price controls as a "solution" to inflation and as a punishment on businessmen and labor unions. Gradually the entire economy becomes centrally controlled as the civil authorities intervene more and more, and the people lose their economic and political freedom.

When a government-run economy does not solve the many economic dislocations that have set in, the rulers may even turn to blaming their troubles on foreign nations. The resulting strain in international relations and the drop in international trade tend to create further misunderstandings. These create ideal circumstances for potential military hostility. A continuous state of international tension develops as hate and suspicion supplant the former peaceful exchange of trade between countries. This is what the totalitarian countries—Nazi Germany, Fascist Italy and Communist Russia—did, thus bringing about World War II. A more recent example of a centrally controlled country turning to military aggression in order to turn public attention from growing internal economic dislocations is Argentina and its aggressive move to reclaim the Falkland Islands from Great Britain in 1982. Observers from within the country reported that, rather than continuing to follow diplomatic channels in settling the Falkland Islands dispute, the military junta which controlled Argentina hoped to regain popular support by its military move.

The above-mentioned effects of monetary inflation do not all appear in every instance when the civil rulers follow inflationary policies, nor do the effects necessarily appear in the order listed. But they **all** are a subsequent result of prior monetary inflation which is long-continued. Acquaintance with these symptoms will enable the serious student of economics to correctly diagnose the underlying cause of seemingly unconnected surface problems in a troubled society. He will thereby be enabled to effect a cure: to reduce the size of civil government and to limit government spending so that deficits and long-term debt accumulation will not occur.

Money—A Biblical View

Is there a biblical view of money? We think there is. Money is a commonly accepted medium of exchange which serves as a standard of measuring the worth or value of all other items in society. We then can see that there is a **moral** requirement for the money creators—be they private or government—to maintain the integrity of the monetary unit. If they fail to do this, people will be cheated and duped out of their honestly gained wealth through a debauched currency. The prophet Isaiah spoke strongly against monetary debasement:

> *How is the faithful city become an harlot! it was full of judgment; righteousness lodged in it; but now murderers.*
> *Thy silver is become dross, thy wine mixed with water:*
> *Thy princes are rebellious, and companions of thieves: everyone loveth gifts, and followeth after rewards: they judge not the fatherless, neither doth the cause of the widow come unto them.*
> *Isaiah 1:21-23*

Other admonitions to use just weights and to deal justly are:

> *Ye shall do no unrighteousness in judgment, in meteyard, in weight, or in measure.*
> *Just balances, just weights, a just ephah, and a just hin, shall ye have: . . .*
> *Leviticus 19:35-36*

> *But thou shalt have a perfect and just weight, a perfect and just measure shalt thou have: that thy days may be lengthened in the land which the Lord thy God giveth thee.*
>
> *Deuteronomy 25:15*

> *A false balance is abomination to the Lord: but a just weight is his delight.*
>
> *Proverbs 11:1*

The above admonitions apply equally to either private or public money creators, though at the present time civil governments have arrogated to themselves all money-making powers—or at least control over it. The admonitions are all facets of the basic commandment "Thou shalt not steal" (Ex. 20:15), which government leaders sometimes appear to believe does not apply to them.

Government rulers stand, in effect, in a fiduciary relationship with citizens, especially when it comes to money matters. The immense majority of people remain ignorant and trusting when it comes to the seemingly difficult topic of how money functions in the economy. The temptation to dupe citizens by debauching the currency is great. True statemanship is required instead of demagoguery if civil rulers are not to transgress their fiduciary trust regarding money. A secret 5 or 10 percent tax one year through deficit government spending and monetization of the debt may not seem very great, but the question that must be asked from a moral standpoint is this: Is it honest? Next is the practical question of what such a practice, if long-continued, will produce in the economy. How the purchasing power of money can be eroded through monetary inflation is shown in Table 7:2.

Table 7:2

How Monetary Inflation Affects Purchasing Power

Year	5%*	7%*	8%*	10%*
Present	$100.00	$100.00	$100.00	$100.00
1	95.20	93.50	92.60	90.90
2	90.70	87.30	85.70	82.60
3	86.40	81.60	79.40	75.10
4	82.30	76.30	73.50	68.30
5	78.40	71.30	68.10	62.10
6	74.60	66.60	63.00	56.40
7	71.10	62.30	58.40	51.30
8	67.70	58.20	54.00	46.70
9	64.50	54.40	50.00	42.40
10	61.40	50.80	46.30	38.60

*Average price increase per year.

Questions

1. List the various types of money.

2. What is Gresham's Law?

3. Why was the Pine Tree Shilling minted in Massachusetts in 1652? Did it serve its intended purpose? Explain.

4. What is *seigniorage?*

5. Explain the difference between representative money and fiat money. What are Federal Reserve Notes?

6. What does the term fiduciary mean? How does it apply to money?

7. List the steps that generally occur in the transition of money from full-bodied coins of precious metal to fiat money. What safeguards would you recommend against this happening?

8. Why have civil rulers continually turned to debauching the currency throughout history? What civil government has the outstanding record for maintaining the integrity of its money?

9. What are two crucially important rules for maintaining the soundness of money?

10. Are demand deposits private or government money? Explain.

11. What is the difference between real money and near money?

12. Argue pro or con: Only the civil authority can safely be entrusted with control over the money-making function.

13. Why can private money creators not make fiat money?

14. During the goldsmith era, what two types of money evolved to meet the needs of the people?

15. In a non-inflationary economy, will real wages tend upward or downward? Explain.

16. At what stage in the development of money did the goldsmith-bankers change from a 100-percent reserve basis to a fractional reserve basis?

17. Discuss: Boom-bust cycles are an inherent phenomenon of free market capitalism.

18. What two important developments have grown out of fractional reserve banking?

19. Argue pro or con: These United States should change from a fractional to a 100-percent reserve banking system.

20. Commercial bankers create money when they lend money and destroy it when the loan is repaid. Is this statement true or false? Explain.

21. Discuss: Since the Federal Reserve System went into operation in

1914, it has served very effectively in preventing monetary inflation and thereby has served to preserve the value of the dollar.

22. Why must Christians view the problem of inflation from a theological perspective?

23. Explain the cause-effect pattern of inflation. Why is it important that the chain of causation be clearly recognized?

24. Review the list of effects brought on by long-continued inflationary policies. Which do you see in these United States? Compare your list of effects with those of other class members and discuss.

8

The History of Money and Banking
in These United States

Give instruction to a wise man, and he will be yet wiser: teach a just man, and he will increase in learning.

Proverbs 9:9

A N appreciation of the monetary problems our colonial forefathers faced and a historical familiarity with how early banking developed will help us better understand the banking system we now have in these United States. During the time our nation was being founded and developed economically — roughly the 300-year period from 1600 to 1900 — banking was a relatively new industry. The conduct of banking was a trial-and-error process of learning by doing. Practical men of business and commerce joined together — sometimes privately and at other times through the agency of civil government — to devise various means of supplying their communities with a readily acceptable means of common exchange.

The perennial problem, both during the colonial period as well as during much of the nineteenth century, was seen as a shortage of money. Therefore, most attempts to solve the problem followed along the line of striving to increase the supply of money. There is little doubt that our forefathers, especially during the early colonial era, did face times of real currency shortage. (By **currency** we mean specie, coins and paper money. **Specie** means gold or silver bullion or coins. **Paper money** has appeared in the form of bank notes, bills of credit, "greenbacks," gold and silver certificates, National Bank Notes and Federal Reserve Notes.)

In this respect, however, it is important for us to recognize a common human fraility. It is not at all unusual for people to diagnose their financial difficulties as a presumed scarcity of money. Whose financial situation would not be immediately improved by an increase of money in hand? Throughout American history we find that farmers and other small business entrepreneurs tended to regard an inflationary monetary policy as beneficial to their interests, for the resultant rise in land and commodity prices served to "bail them out" of debt which they found burdensome to pay off in money of stable value. In more modern times, the high ratio of indebtedness of large corporations, coupled with high levels of corporate income tax, has caused the managers of many large corporations to regard inflationary policies of government with some favor. One other point to note is that money, in order to fulfill its purpose as a general medium of exchange, **must** be relatively scarce lest it lose all value. Likewise, no other commodity that is in superabundance has value in the marketplace.

The Early Colonial Period

Wampum was widely used by the early New England settlers for many years. These beaded belts were accepted as "legal tender" in Massachusetts until 1661 and were used in New York as late as 1701. Maryland and Virginia used tobacco extensively as a medium of exchange. There is little doubt that the monetization of tobacco in these colonies stimulated its overproduction and thereby contributed to its depreciation in value. Other colonies designated such things as the following as "country pay" acceptable for taxes: hides, furs, tallow, corn, wheat, beans, cows, fish, pork, brandy, whiskey and even musket balls. Whatever the public treasury accepted, merchants would also accept. The East New Jersey law of 1668[1], for instance, stipulated that taxes be paid according to these valuations:

- Winter wheat at 5 shillings per bushel
- Indian corn at 3 shillings per bushel
- Rye at 4 shillings per bushel
- Beef at 2 pence, halfpenny a pound
- Pork at 3 pence, halfpenny a pound

Codfish were popular as money around Boston, beaver in New York and, later, rice in South Carolina. Some of these things were perishable, not very portable and they varied much in quality. They, therefore, did not perform perfectly as the ideal money, but their use as money did foster economic exchange and specialization of effort.

By the end of the seventeenth century, both specie and paper currencies were common in the seaboard cities. By the end of the eighteenth century, only communities on the western frontier still used commodities, particularly furs, as a common medium of exchange.

Specie: Gold and silver coins of all the major mercantile nations of Europe and their colonies in the Western Hemisphere circulated throughout the eastern American seaboard. English coins, of course, were important because of ties with the mother country. But even in greater supply, especially after 1700, were silver coins of the Spanish Realm. Most of these coins were minted in Mexico City, Mexico, and in Lima, Peru. They made their appearance because of the lively trade conducted with the Spanish colonies and because of piracy. Pirates tended to frequent those American ports where colonial cur-

---

[1] Aaron Leaming and Jacob Spicer, "Grants, Concessions and Original Constitutions of the Province of New Jersey, 1664-82," *New Jersey Law Journal*, 1752, p. 31.

rency was devalued so as to make pirate gold and silver worth more in terms of local currency. In matter of fact, the colonies actively competed with each other to attract pirate spending by competitively devaluing their currencies vis-à-vis Spanish coins; but local prices quickly rose in compensation.

The old Spanish *peso* or "piece of eight" was called a dollar by English-speaking people. It was first minted in Joachimthal, Bohemia, in 1517 and was later adopted by Austria and Spain. It circulated widely for some 300 years. The word **dollar** is presumed to have come from the German word *thaler,* which was about the same size. The Spanish coin was so popular in colonial America that it was eventually adopted as the basic monetary unit. The Spanish *peso* was often cut into eight fractional "pie slices" called the *real* or bit. Each bit was worth about 12.5 cents, thus the American terms: "two bits," "four bits" and "six bits" for 25 cents, 50 cents and 75 cents.

The "adverse terms of trade" with Britain caused an outflow of specie from the colonies in exchange for manufactured goods received. Massachusetts established its lighter Pine Tree Shilling in 1652, which contained 22.5 percent less silver than the English shilling, with the (unsuccessful) hope of its remaining in the colonies. This coin continued to be minted until 1683. Opposition by the British Crown prevented other colonial mints from being established. The Crown opposed the minting of coins in the American Colonies because, in its view, only a sovereign nation should have the power to mint. The existence of a mint in a dependent colony indicated an unwarrantable show of independence. British mercantile policy was to keep its colonies subservient appendages to the mother country.

Paper Money: The American colonies turned early to paper money for supplementing their meager supply of specie. **Promissory notes** of well-known individuals might be passed from person to person for several months before finally being turned in for specie. **Bills of exchange** drawn on English merchants also circulated freely as money.

In 1690 Massachusetts issued its first **bills of credit** as payment to soldiers who went on an unsuccessful expedition against the French in Quebec as part of that colony's role in the War of the League of Ausburg. Massachusetts did not have enough funds to pay the soldiers, so it issued £40,000 in bills of credit (treasury IOUs) which were supposed to be retired within a few years; but retirement was slower than promised. The colonial legislature had discovered what most governments eventually discover: that the issuance of paper IOUs is an easy alternative to the onerous chore of levying taxes but difficult to redeem. Five other colonies used bills of credit before 1711, and eventually the practice spread to all 13 colonies.

A second type of paper money, which was more like bank notes than treasury notes, also appeared between 1713 and 1739. These were called **land bank notes** when issued by private institutions and were called **loan office notes** when issued through the civil authorities. The first Loan Office Act of 1723 in New Jersey issued £40,000 in notes. These were borrowed by landowners who could secure half the value of their farms in these notes at 5 percent interest and were repayable in 12 years. The privately operated Massachusetts Land Bank System appeared in 1739. It put £50,000 into circulation. These land bank notes were repayable in 20 years at 3 percent interest per year. Governor Jonathan Belcher and his provincial council opposed the plan, and 150 merchants agreed not to accept the notes in trade. In 1741 the British Parliament ruled that the "Bubble Act of 1720," which had made such schemes illegal in England, also applied to the colonies. This gradually eradicated the practice of issuing land bank notes after a series of court cases which challenged the ruling.

The issuance of such paper bills and notes caused prices to rise in terms of paper money. In New Jersey, New York and Pennsylvania, paper currency depreciation was about 40 percent. In other words, it took about 40 percent more paper money to buy as much as specie would buy. In today's monetary unit, for instance, an item that cost $1 in silver currency was priced at $1.40 in terms of paper money. Connecticut, North Carolina, South Carolina and Massachusetts fared worse. The value of paper bills and notes dropped most in Rhode Island where relatively more were printed. In the Carolinas the value of paper money dropped to 10:1 versus sterling; in Rhode Island it dropped to 23:1. In 1702 in Massachusetts, £133 in paper bought £100 sterling; in 1713 the rate was 150:100; in 1740 it was 550:100; and in 1749 it was 1,100:100.

In 1720 a farmer wrote: "As to silver and gold, we never had much of it in the country; but we can very well remember that before we had paper money, there was a sufficiency of it current in the country and as the bills of credit came in and multiplied, the silver ceased and was gone; . . ."[2]

Parliament's Currency Act of 1751 prohibited New England colonies from issuing further bills of credit and from establishing new land banks; and the Currency Act of 1764, passed a year after the French and Indian War ended, extended the Act of 1751 to all American colonies. These monetary restrictions by Parliament helped acerbate the growing economic and political tensions between the colonies and Britain.

The Revolutionary Era

During the Revolutionary War, the colonies were in desperate need of money. Since the Continental Congress had no power to tax, money had to be sought in other ways. Nearly $8 million was borrowed from France, Spain and Holland, all of whom were mercantile nations opposed to Britain. Another $12 million was obtained through domestic borrowing; the rest was obtained by printing money.[3] By the end of 1779, the Continental Congress authorized

---

[2] Joseph B. Felt, *An Historical Account of Massachusetts Currency* (Boston: Perkins & Marvin, 1839), p. 74.

[3] There are three ways civil governments can obtain money to spend: (1) taxation, (2) borrowing and (3) money creation (i.e., inflation). The easiest method is the last; the most difficult, the first.

42 issues of Continental Currency amounting to $242 million. This was a great debt for a small group of independent states totalling only 3 million in population.

The individual states also issued paper money until 1777, when Congress urged them to stop. By 1780 the Continental paper currency had depreciated to the point where it took 100 Continental bills to buy one dollar in specie, thus the saying "not worth a Continental."

The Bank of Pennsylvania (Philadelphia) was founded by Robert Morris and some associates in 1781 with the purpose of helping to finance the revolution during the closing years of the war. The bank was granted a national charter as the Bank of North America in 1784 by the Continental Congress. It was founded on specie which was part of the $7.8 million borrowed from overseas. Two other specie-based commercial banks were also established in 1784: the Bank of New York (New York City) and the Massachusetts Bank (Boston). Another, the Bank of Maryland, was formed in 1790.

The discontinuance of wartime inflation led to an economic depression in 1785-1786. Farmers in western Massachusetts, who were pushed to the wall in paying overdue debts and taxes, rebelled under the leadership of Daniel Shay. (At this period of history, the American economy was based 90 percent on agriculture.) This is an early example of a monetarily induced boom-bust cycle — a cyclical phenomenon which has been wrongly blamed on private capitalism **as a system**.

The First Bank of the United States

One of the first acts of Congress under the new Constitution of 1787 was to establish the First Bank of the United States in 1791. President George Washington asked his cabinet for advice regarding the constitutionality of such a bank before signing the bill into law. Alexander Hamilton, Secretary of the Treasury, favored the bill under the so-called "implied powers" of Congress. Thomas Jefferson, Secretary of State, a strict constructionist regarding the Constitution, strongly opposed the bill as being unconstitutional. But President Washington followed Hamilton's advice and signed the bill into law.

The First Bank of the United States was established for a 20-year period (1791-1811). It was a huge institution for that day. Its $10 million capital was subscribed one-fifth by the federal government and four-fifths by private persons. It was based on specie, which means that it promised to redeem the notes it issued in gold and silver coins. One purpose of its formation was to serve as a financial agent for the federal government: to accept tax payments, to dispense funds spent by the government, to transfer funds from one part of the country to another and to act on behalf of the federal government in foreign exchange. By 1805 it had branches in Boston, New York City, Baltimore, Charleston, Washington, D.C., Savannah and New Orleans.

The great size of the bank and its favored position with the federal government generated both fear and hostility among the privately operated banks and the public. The sorest point was that the First Bank served to restrain the number of bank notes issued by state banks. (A state bank is a private bank whose charter to do business is issued by a state. This was before the era of **national banks** whose charters are issued by the U.S. Comptroller of Currency.) This restraint was accomplished when the First Bank of the United States presented state bank notes, which happened to be collected in the process of its own operations, to the various privately operated state banks for redemption in specie. (A bank note was simply a paper dollar issued by a commercial bank and which could be redeemed in specie upon demand by the public. Because three or four bank notes were issued per unit of specie held in reserve, bank notes were fiduciary money.) This constant threat of possibly having the Bank of the United States present bank notes for redemption in specie effectively served to restrain the tendency of state banks to overissue paper money and thereby inflate the money supply. The overall effect of the First Bank of the United States was, therefore, conservative in nature rather than inflationary. (Keep the conservative nature of the monetary influence of the First Bank, and also of the Second Bank, of the United States in mind when we come to the era of the Federal Reserve System. The influence of the Federal Reserve is inflationary in nature.)

The Coinage Act of 1792

The Coinage Act of 1792 adopted the dollar as the primary unit of money in these United States. The dollar was officially designated as 371.25 grains of pure silver or 24.7 grains of pure gold. Thus, the country was established on a bimetallic standard at the rate of 15 units of silver to one unit of gold. As the market price of silver and gold fluctuated above or below the 15:1 ratio, one or the other metal would be "chased" out of circulation. But this problem was eventually solved by our going on a *de facto* gold standard. Other coins authorized by the Coinage Act of 1792 were: the eagle, the half eagle and quarter eagle (all gold) worth respectively $10, $5 and $2.50; and the dollar, half dollar, quarter dollar and half dime (all silver); plus the copper cent and half-cent. The U.S. Mint offered free and unlimited coinage of silver and gold.

In 1811 the charter of the First Bank was not renewed because of widespread political and constitutional opposition. With the release of this conservative monetary restraint, the number of state banks quickly jumped from 88 in 1811 to 250 in 1816. The sudden monetary inflation caused by this rapid expansion of banks, plus the war of 1812, caused a boom-bust cycle that ended in the depression of 1814, when banks suspended the payment of specie. This financial crisis led to the formation of another Bank of the United States, called the Second Bank of the United States.

The Second Bank of the United States

The Second Bank of the United States was established in 1816 with a capital of $35 million, a tremendous concentration of money power for its day. Twenty percent of the capital was provided by the federal government; $7 million of the capital was in specie. It, too, served as fiscal agent of the federal government. The services and functions performed were to:

(1) receive and keep funds for the U.S. government.
(2) transfer funds to various parts of the country.
(3) make interest payments to government bond holders.
(4) provide a source of borrowing money for the U.S. government.
(5) serve as a "lender of last resort" to state banks.
(6) serve to prevent the overissue of state bank notes, which in turn served to minimize the discount at which overissued bank notes were accepted by other banks and the public.
(7) serve to facilitate domestic exchange by making privately issued bank notes more widely accepted.
(8) serve to facilitate foreign exchange.

In 1823 a man by the name of Nicholas Biddle became president of the Second Bank. He was a very able banker, but his steps to prevent the overissue of state bank notes — by buying them up and presenting them for redemption in specie to banks which he deemed were overissuing notes relative to the amount of specie held on reserve — caused widespread resentment. This resentment surfaced mainly in frontier areas in the western states beyond the Allegheny Mountains where bankers were more liberal in issuing bank notes. Also, the rise of a democratic-based free enterprise spirit which accompanied the Jacksonian revolution, led by President Andrew Jackson, caused people to fear the Second Bank of the United States as an institution of the eastern money monopoly. There was a real fear that the Second Bank, if it got into the wrong hands, could be used to create financial havoc and to oppress the people by its very size and influence.

The Second Bank of the United States became an election issue in 1832 when President Jackson ran for re-election. Jackson, a strict constitutionalist, viewed the Bank as decidedly unconstitutional.[4] When Jackson won re-election on this issue, he took steps to close the Bank. Nicholas Biddle retaliated to Jackson's action by having the Bank withdraw loans in frontier areas, thus causing financial stress. Biddle's perverse action served to substantiate the opposition's fear of the bank as too-powerful a financial institution if it happened to get into the wrong hands. After 1833 the Bank became practically inoperative, and its charter expired in 1836.

The loosening of outside restraints with the demise of the Second Bank led to another period of widespread monetary inflation as the number of state banks multiplied (the number of banks increased from 330 in 1830 to over 500

---

[4]See President Andrew Jackson's veto message to Congress on July 10, 1832.

in 1834) and their notes flooded the country; it culminated in the financial panic of 1837.

The rapid growth of state banks, shown in Table 8:1, indicates the dynamic expansion of business which occurred in the ante-bellum period.

Table 8:1

Number of State Banks 1790-1861

1790	4	1830	330
1800	28	1834	506
1811	88	1840	901
1816	250	1852	913
1820	307	1861	1,601

Source: *Historical Statistics of the U.S., Colonial Times to 1957.*

Both the First and Second Banks of the United States, as indicated earlier, served as conservative influences in restraining the inflationary tendencies of private state-chartered banks to increase the ratio of bank notes to the amount of specie held as reserve in their vaults. Whether or not this is a proper function of the federal government under the Constitution of these United States is a matter of debate. The First and Second Banks operated as bona fide central banks even though they were privately operated. The fact that they served as a conservative force in restraining monetary inflation is no doubt due to the period in which they operated. It was an era in which the philosophy of limited government held sway, thus the voracious appetite of civil rulers to tax and tax and to spend and spend had as yet little opportunity to develop. The advent of another central bank almost a century later (the Federal Reserve Bank) would find the political and social atmosphere radically different. As a central bank in the twentieth century, the Federal Reserve was destined to be quickly turned into a tool for liberally monetizing government debt, thus serving as an "engine of inflation" to fuel the most protracted general rise in price levels ever experienced by the American people. (From 1913 to the present day, the dollar has lost over 90 percent of its purchasing power.)

The Era of Free Banking

The era of "free banking," which some scholars refer to as the era of "wildcat banking," began in 1838 when the states of New York and Michigan passed "free banking" acts. These were soon followed by similar acts in other states. Up to this time, private citizens who wished to start a banking business had to make special application to their state legislature in order to get the special charters needed to enter the banking business. This requirement, of course, often involved bribery and political pay-offs. The idea developed that starting a bank should be no different than starting any other kind of business; it is a **right** to be enjoyed by **any** citizen as long as minimum requirements were met. Some states had "loose" banking laws which allowed questionable operations — such as Michigan, where some banks are reported to have kept their specie reserves at such out-of-the-way places in the frontier backwoods that only a wildcat could find them. A story is told how bankers in Michigan sent the same barrel of specie on ahead of a state inspector from bank to bank until the inspector finally came to recognize the same coins in the barrel! However, soundly operated banks were characteristic of the New England states, New York, Louisiana, Missouri, Ohio and South Carolina in particular. At this time, banking was still in its infancy; and what were good or bad banking practices had to be learned largely by trial and error.

By 1860 there were some 1,600 private banks operating throughout these United States. They issued, on the average, notes of six different denominations ($1, $5, $10, $20, etc.), each of which contained the unique imprint of the bank of issue. The size and shape of bills also varied. Thus, some 9,000 different types of privately issued bank notes were in circulation throughout the country.

Many economists point at this heterogeneity in bank notes as an example of gross monetary chaos, but this author disagrees. This diversity of issue was simply a **temporary** stage which, if the banking business had been left free of centralized control by the federal government, would have soon passed. It would have lasted only until cooperative arrangements were gradually developed among the bankers of different areas of the country in standardizing the type of notes issued. We must remember also that transportation in that era was, at best, still local and regional instead of nationwide. There was still adequate time for cooperative arrangements regarding a nationwide currency to develop on a voluntary basis. Most bank notes circulated very close to home, so the diversity of bank notes nationwide did not have too great an impact in any one locality.

One example of private cooperation was the development of private services such as the Bank Note Reporter and the Counterfeit Detector, which merchants and businessmen could subscribe to for determining whether distantly issued bank notes should be accepted at all or at a discount. Discounts for such "foreign" bank notes usually averaged only about 1 or 2 percent, but could go much higher depending on the rating that was given to the bank of issue by the rating service. We can see that the free market had already provided a privately operated means of meeting the people's and the banking industry's needs. This is the normal process of the market if it is left free to develop without government hindrances.

The Suffolk Banking System

Another example of beneficial voluntary cooperation among private bankers was the Suffolk Banking System, which operated from 1819 to 1858 in the

Boston area. It was a voluntary association of banks in the city of Boston that saw the inflationary danger posed when some "country" banks in western Massachusetts continued to indulge in issuing bank notes too freely. The increase in number caused the bank notes to depreciate in value; thus they could not be accepted at their face value by the city banks in Boston. A public relations problem was created between the Boston banks and Boston merchants, who wished to accept the famers' bank notes at full value as a means of inducing farmers to trade with them.

The Suffolk Bank of Boston took the initiative by arranging a cooperative system through which the country banks kept a reserve of specie at the Suffolk Bank. Then all Boston banks which were members of the Suffolk Banking System could accept the country bank notes at par and have them redeemed by the Suffolk Bank at 100 cents on the dollar. The accumulation of country bank notes at the Suffolk Bank were then taken periodically to the various country banks for redemption in order to rebuild the reserve of specie in Boston.

A $300,000 fund was established by six Boston banks in this cooperative venture. Its basic soundness is attested to by the fact that it successfully weathered the severe depression of 1837, when many other banks throughout the nation went bankrupt. The Suffolk Banking System finally passed out of existence in 1858 when a new system was started by competing banks. The Suffolk Banking System, however, stands as a shining testimony to the fact that **cooperative** and **voluntary** systems of decentralized monetary control can indeed function to the benefit of all concerned and that government controls are **not** necessary. The Suffolk Banking System provides an interesting, but almost forgotten, lesson in America's financial history.

The New York Safety Fund System

The first example of a government-operated "deposit insurance" program was the New York Safety Fund System, which was established by the New York Legislature in 1829. As each private bank charter came up for renewal, the bank was required to set aside a 3 percent reserve on its deposits to be held by the state. Out of this statewide fund, depositors were to be paid in the event their bank should go bankrupt.

The System seemed to be sound, but it collapsed in the financial panic of 1837 when so many banks went under that there was not enough money on reserve to meet all the depositors' claims for reimbursement. This early experiment in monetary socialism left the taxpayers of New York with a loss of $1 billion which they had to make good out of taxes collected—a tremendous sum of money at that time. The New York Safety Fund System was very much like the current Federal Deposit Insurance Corporation (FDIC) which is said to "insure" bank deposits today, but with this difference: In the event of a nationwide financial crisis today, the federal government, through the Federal Reserve Bank, has the ability to **create** any amount of money needed to adequately "insure" all accounts. No depositor would lose money **nominally,** but the resulting monetary inflation would produce a commensurate loss through depreciation of purchasing power of each dollar "insured." In short, the FDIC is an illusion which cannot stand the test of time. It will be unable to shield the people from real losses in a widespread disaster because it will pay off with "created" dollars which will have little value.

The Independent Treasury System

After the Second Bank of the United States ceased operations, Congress recognized the need for some agency to serve as the federal government's fiscal agent. The Independent Treasury System was established in 1846. It continued in operation, but not as Congress planned, until it was no longer needed because of passage of the Federal Reserve Act in 1913.

Under the Independent Treasury System, the U.S. Secretary of the Treasury was authorized to keep specie received in payment of taxes. The specie was to be held at the Treasury in Washington, D.C., and in various subtreasuries placed throughout the country. But a problem soon became evident. The seasonal monetary deflations that occurred when taxes were collected and the seasonal monetary inflations that occurred when Treasury specie was again injected into the economy via government spending produced an adverse pulsating impact on business activity. The law required that taxes had to be paid **only** in specie. If we remember that banks could issue multiple bank notes for each unit of specie held on reserve in their vaults, then we can see that the withdrawal of specie by depositors to pay their taxes had a multiple contracting (i.e., a deflationary) effect on the money supply of the country. This deflation or contraction would last until the Treasury subsequently released the specie through government spending, which would then cause a sudden reinflation of the money supply. This type of periodic monetary inflation and deflation is a natural occurence of fractional reserve banking systems as people deposit and withdraw from their checking and savings accounts at commercial banks.

To solve this seasonal deflation-inflation problem, each succeeding secretary of the Treasury — in defiance of the law — would immediately redeposit specie tax payments in commercial banks spread throughout the nation. In this manner, the seasonal monetary shocks were avoided.

The National Banking System

With the advent of the War Between the States in 1861, the Lincoln Administration was faced with the problem of how to finance the military invasion of the South in the North's attempt to force the seceded states back into the Union. It was not a popular war, for many people felt that each state was sovereign politically and thus had the right of self-determination — as the original 13 colonies had when they separated from Britain during the American Revolution. Because of this division of feeling even in the North, the Administration hesitated to impose additional taxes on the people. Import duties, which were at that time the main source of government income, had dropped drastically when the southern states seceded. When the first attempt to finance the war by floating a large bond issue did not yield all the funds needed to conduct military operations, some other means had to be sought. When taxing and borrowing fail, governments have only one other alternative — that is, to devise some means of taxing the people through monetary inflation.

Secretary of the Treasury Salmon P. Chase had long been convinced of the desirability of having a uniform national currency. Why not solve the North's financing problem and the currency problem at one stroke, he reasoned, by adopting a plan of organizing banks on a **national** basis through the federal government?

The plan Chase devised was one that required a uniform note issue backed by government bonds which were to be purchased by commercial banks. If the bonds used to secure the new note issue were U.S. government bonds, reasoned the Treasury officials, the demand for government securities would be stimulated; and the sorely needed funds to conduct the invasion of the South would be more easily obtained. An additional benefit would be that the many diverse state-chartered banks would be brought under federal control!

The system that today is known as the National Banking System grew out of the Lincoln Administration's determination to hold the Union together by force. The main purpose of devising the National Banking System was **not**, as many historians record, to provide the country with a uniform currency, which just happened to be one of the resulting effects. It was obvious to the Lincoln Administration that the war was **not** popular enough to be financed through either increased taxes or the sale of government bond issues: (It was not until **after** Lincoln issued his *Emancipation Proclamation* on January 1, 1863, that the "War of Northern Aggression," as it was called in the South, took on the air of a holy crusade to eliminate slavery and thus generated wider support in the North. Ironically, the Proclamation purported to free Negro slaves in the seceded states; but it did **not** declare any slave to be free who lived in states that remained in the Union. General Ulysses S. Grant, for example, remained a slave owner until after the war.)

Accordingly, Congress passed the Currency Act of 1863 which created the National Banking System. However, only 66 state banks joined; so it was necessary to pass a more comprehensive act the following year.

Congress passed the Banking Act of 1864 as a follow-up measure. This Act has left a permanent mark on the banking framework of these United States. Some economists feel that the Act also served to foster the concentration of industry into the very large industrial firms that characterized the American

Industrial Revolution which took place during and after the War Between the States.[5]

State-chartered banks, though, still showed a reluctance to change from state to federal charters; so Congress passed a bill in 1865 which imposed a prohibitive 10 percent tax on all state bank notes. Since this was a higher rate of interest than borrowers paid to use borrowed funds, state bank notes were quickly chased out of existence. Truly ". . . the power to tax is the power to destroy [!]"[6]

In 1863 only 66 state banks changed to national charters. In 1864 the number had risen only to 467. With the imposition of the 10 percent tax on state bank notes, the number of nationally chartered banks zoomed to 1,294 in 1865. The number of state banks, which had been 1,466 in 1861 dropped to 349 in 1865 and to a low of 272 in 1867.

The reason that all state-chartered banks were not chased out of existence is explained by a natural development in banking practices that took place in the free market: the gradual rise in popularity of demand deposits (checkbook money). By the mid-1850s, the amount of demand deposits being used as money finally surpassed the total quantity of bank notes being issued. It is much easier and less expensive for a bank lending officer to create new money by writing a number in a checkbook and giving the book to the borrower than to have bank notes printed up and counted out—especially for large loans, which would necessitate the issuance of many bank notes. A checkbook is also more convenient for the borrower to use in many instances because he can write a check for odd dollar-and-cent amounts.

It was because of the growing popularity of checkbook money that some larger state banks located in the larger metropolitan areas simply stopped issuing bank notes and switched entirely to issuing demand deposits instead.

After 1875 there was a steady increase in the number of state-chartered banks because of the continued rise in popularity of demand deposits. While national banks also issued demand deposits, the less strict regulatory rules that the states applied to banks prompted many national banks to again switch charters back to the states. By 1892 state banks again outnumbered national banks 3,773 to 3,759. By 1914, when the Federal Reserve System began operation, there were 7,518 national banks versus 17,498 state banks.

The National Banking Act required each national bank to purchase U.S. government bonds equal to one-third (later to one-fourth) of its dollar amount of capital stock up to $50,000 (more could be purchased if desired). Each bank

---

[5]Richard Sylla, "The United States, 1863-1913," in *Banking and Economic Development,* ed. Rondo Cameron (New York: Oxford Univ. Press, 1972), pp. 232-262.

[6]U.S. Supreme Court Chief Justice John Marshall in decision of McCulloch v. Maryland, 1819.

then deposited its bonds with the U.S. Treasury in exchange for standard engraved National Bank Notes to the amount of 90 percent of the bonds deposited. Millions and millions of dollars in specie flowed into the U.S. Treasury when the bonds were purchased; and 90 percent of these dollars were matched by new money—the National Bank Notes—which would be injected into the economy when people came into the national banks for loans. It is in this way that the Secretary of the Treasury, Salmon P. Chase, was able to monetize much of the war debt with, of course, a subsequent rise in the general level of prices. Originally, the required legal reserve was calculated on the basis of notes outstanding plus demand deposits. But after 1874, the reserve requirement was calculated on a percentage of demand deposits only.

It is interesting at this point to correlate the increase in money supply with the subsequent rise in price levels in both the North and the South during the war. The money supply, in the North, was expanded approximately 2.3 times, and price levels rose by a like amount. The South also resorted to monetary inflation to finance its military expenditures. There the money supply was expanded 11.6 times, and price levels rose about 28 times. The greater ratio of monetary depreciation in the South was influenced at the end of the war by impending defeat and the people's unwillingness to accept Confederate money.

"Greenbacks" (U.S. Notes)

When the War Between the States started, the tremendous cotton exports of the southern states no longer generated a corresponding flow of imports into northern ports from overseas. Tariff income, which had largely supported the federal government, quickly dried up. The Treasury filled this gap partly by issuing, what was for that time, a tremendous amount of printed money called "greenbacks" or U.S. Notes.

By 1863 three issues totalling $450 million had been authorized. This amounted to about 50 percent of the currency then in circulation, so it was a substantial injection of new money into the economy. This **fiat** money was declared "legal tender." It had the expected effect: The inflated supply of paper money quickly depreciated in value in terms of gold and silver. At one time during the war, greenbacks traded as low as 35 cents to the gold dollar. At the end of the war, they traded at about 80 cents to the gold dollar. It was not until a long post-war deflation, which was purposely brought about in order to get back officially onto the gold standard, that greenbacks again traded at par with gold and silver dollars. By this time, the number of greenbacks had been reduced to $347 million, which number is still outstanding today.

Private Coinage: The Alternative to Government Money[7]

We have pointed out that the sole determining factor of a commodity as being

---

[7]Information for this section is taken largely from Brian Summers, "Private Coinage in America," in *The Freeman*, July 1976 (Irvington-on-Hudson, N.Y.: Foundation for Economic Education), pp. 436-440.

money is whether the public is generally willing to accept it in exchange for goods and services. This practical requirement is apt to be overlooked today because the public has been weaned to the idea that money, in order to be valid, must be government money backed by "legal tender" laws which **force** the people to accept the government-designated currency as money.

Another point we have made is that people's needs can and will be adequately met through the operation of the free market if civil rulers do not preempt the market or prohibit would-be entrepreneurs from engaging in economic production to satisfy those needs. Such was the case regarding the need for a circulating currency in a dynamically expanding nation. For many years, the U.S. mints were unable to supply the volume of currency needed to support business activity; so, here and there throughout the country, private minters sprang up to fill the need.

John Higley, a blacksmith who lived in Granby, Connecticut, was one of the first minters of private coins. He issued high-quality copper coins between 1737 and 1739 and allowed the market to determine their value. He imprinted this slogan on one of his issues: "I Am Good Copper/Value Me As You Please." Edgar H. Adams, a numismatist of the early 1900s, had this to say about the quality of Higley's coins:

> In fact so pure was the metal contained in these pieces that they were much sought by goldsmiths of the period for the purposes of alloy, and the coins seem to have been in pretty general use until 1792, the time of the opening of the United States mint.[8]

In 1783 a man by the name of Chalmers, who lived in Annapolis, Maryland, minted silver shillings, sixpences and threepences that were "very creditable."[9]

The first privately minted gold coins were struck by Templeton Reid in 1830. Reid worked as an assayer at the gold mines located in Lumpkin County, Georgia. He issued coins in three denominations: $2.50, $5 and $10. Reid's private mint successfully competed with the Dahlonega federal mint located in the same county. His gold coins were of high quality. Many of them were later melted down because their worth as bullion exceeded their face value.[10]

From 1831 to 1847, an immigrant from the Grand Duchy of Baden, Christopher Bechtler of Rutherfordton, North Carolina, and his sons and nephew coined over $3 million in gold coins in three denominations: $1, $2.50 and $5. These privately struck coins circulated in competition with govern-

---

[8]Edgar H. Adams, "Higley Coppers 'Granby Coinage,' " *The Numismatist,* August 1908, p. 232.

[9]Henry Chapman, "The Colonial Coins Prior to July 4, 1776," *The Numismatist,* February 1948.

[10]Joseph Coffin, *The Complete Book of Coin Collecting* (New York: Coward, McCann & Geoghegan, 1973), p. 108.

ment coins produced by the federal mint which was established at Charlotte, North Carolina, in 1837. Clarence Griffin gives the following report on Bechtler's coins:

> Bechtler coins were accepted and passed at face value in all of western North Carolina, South Carolina, western Tennessee, Kentucky and portions of Virginia. One of the country's oldest citizens once told the writer that he was 16 years old before he ever saw any other coin than the Bechtlers. The coins filled a long-felt need for specie and continued to circulate long after the discontinuance of the mint in 1847. At the outbreak of the War Between the States, the new Confederacy began issuing currency, but did not put out any specie. Bechtler coins, especially in this locality, were carefully hoarded, and many contracts and agreements of the sixties specified Bechtler gold coins as a consideration rather than the Confederate States currency or the scant supply of Federal specie.
>
> Despite the fact that these coins bore no device emblematic of a national character, or any official guaranty of their purity, they were unhesitatingly accepted by all. In the proper sense of the word they were only "tokens" and when offered at the Government mints were worth less than the face value, as the Government deducted the seigniorage and assay fees for reminting. Yet these coins were passed over the counters of the stores, where they received the same consideration as if they were made by the United States Government. They were carried by traders into Kentucky and South Carolina, and many homeseekers going westward during the great immigration period of 1850-1860 carried their Bechtler coins with them. . . .[11]

A man who visited Bechtler in 1837 gave this account of his visit:

> Christopher Bechtler's maxim was that honesty was the best policy and that maxim appeared to govern his conduct. I was never so pleased with observing transactions of business as those I saw at his house during the time I was there. Several country people came with rough gold to be left for coinage. He weighed it before them and entered it in his book, where there was marginal room for noting the subsequent assay. To others he delivered the coin he had struck. The most perfect confidence prevailed between them, and the transactions were conducted with quite as much simplicity as those at a country grist mill, where the miller deducts the toll for the grist he has manufactured.[12]

---

[11]Clarence Griffin, "The Story of the Bechtler Gold Coinage," *The Numismatist,* September 1929, pp. 555-556.

[12]Ibid., p. 555.

At least 15 private mints produced gold coins in California from 1849 to 1855. The coins of Moffat & Co., Kellogg & Co. and Wass, Molitor & Co. were widely accepted by the public. An article in the January 8, 1852, issue of the *San Francisco Herald* commented on the $5 gold coins produced by Wass, Molitor & Company:

> The mechanical execution of the coin issued by these gentlemen certainly reflects the highest credit upon their skill. It is a beautiful specimen of art, far superior in finish to anything of the kind ever gotten up in California. . . .
>
> But the most important point to the public is its fineness and weight, as upon these two qualities combined must depend its value. In this particular it will be found highly satisfactory, and at once secure the confidence of the community. It has a uniform standard of .880, and contains no other alloy than that of silver, which is found naturally combined with gold. The weight of each of the $5 pieces, which are the only ones at present issued, is 131.9 grains.
>
> The standard fineness of the United States Five Dollar piece is .900 weight 127 grains. It is therefore 20/1000 finer than Wass, Molitor & Co.'s pieces, but this is more than counterbalanced by the latter's being 4.9 grains heavier, so that the new Five Dollar gold piece is in reality worth five dollars and four cents, a sufficient excess to pay the expense of recoinage at the United States Mint without cost to the depositor.
>
> The reason Messrs. Wass, Molitor & Co. have adopted the standard of .880 is because this is about the average fineness of California gold, and further because the cost of refining California gold to the United States standard is exceedingly heavy, and the necessary chemicals cannot be obtained in this country. But it will be remembered that the difference is more than made up by the increased weight of 4.9 grains, which every one can try for himself on a pair of scales.[13]

Between 1860 and 1862, Clark, Gruber & Co., minted over $3 million in gold coins in Denver, Colorado, to provide that area with a circulating medium. This mint was bought out by the federal government for $25,000 to eliminate it as a competitor to the federal mint located in Denver.[14]

In 1864 Congress passed an act which banned the private coinage of money, so the public has been dependent on government mints since that time.

---

[13]Edgar H. Adams, *Private Gold Coinage of California, 1849-55* (Brooklyn: Edgar H. Adams, 1913), pp. 79-80.

[14]Carl Watner, "California Gold: 1849-65," *Reason*, January 1976, pp. 27-28.

The Federal Reserve Era

The "Rich Man's Panic"[15] of 1907—which some economists attribute to the trust busting activities of President Theodore Roosevelt—convinced Congress that there was a need to create a central bank to serve as a "lender of last resort" to help banks that found themselves in an unexpected liquidity crisis. What was needed, said leading politicians and bankers, was an "elastic currency" which could expand and contract automatically with the needs of business. This so-called need for an "elastic currency" developed out of the correspondent bank relationships which had developed between small country banks and larger city banks on the one hand and between larger city banks and the very large New York City (NYC) banks on the other hand.

Correspondent bank relationships worked like this: Small country banks often found themselves with a surplus of investable funds during certain seasons of the year. These country banks would deposit their excess reserves with the larger banks in nearby cities with whom they had financial dealings. These two types of banks were then said to have a correspondent relationship. The city banks, in turn, had similar correspondent relationships with the very large banks located in New York City, which always seemed to have a place to lend money. Much of their money was loaned out for short-term speculative loans in the stock market.

As a result of these correspondent banking relationships, there was a decided tendency for excess reserves from banks all over these United States to concentrate in New York City on a seasonal basis. The concentration of these excess reserves in New York City was tremendous. At this time (1907-1914), six NYC banks—with two-thirds of the total resources held by national banks in that city—held three-fourths of all the reserve deposits of correspondent banks from other parts of the country. In the panic of 1907, the reserves of these six large banks dropped to 19 percent; the legal reserve ratio at that time was 25 percent.

The flow of money was reversed when country banks called for a return of their reserves in order to make loans to farmers for seed and machinery. Such seasonal flows could usually be scheduled and arranged for in an orderly manner because they were generally anticipated. Occasionally unforeseen emergencies appeared. These emergencies created sudden "credit crunches" that strained the liquidity of banks in New York City which had overextended themselves by making too many loans.

When banks throughout the country called for a return of their loaned reserves, the New York City banks would immediately call in the money they had loaned for speculative purposes. Because the money loaned for speculation could be called in by the lending bank at any time, it was known as "call money." The calling in of loans used to finance the purchase of stocks, in turn,

---

[15]See Elgin Groseclose, *America's Money Machine* (Westport, Conn.: Arlington House, 1980), pp. 22-30.

caused stock market prices to tumble as speculators were forced to sell securities to raise cash with which to repay their loans. In effect, the large New York City banks served the nation as a haven for putting excess reserves to work; and these large banks paid interest to their smaller correspondent banks for the temporary use of borrowed reserves. However, problems arose from time to time because the NYC banks could not always provide ready money when they were called upon to do so.

It was just such a credit crunch that occurred in 1907. Since the crisis affected mainly people in the key financial centers, it was called the "Rich Man's Panic."

The Federal Reserve Act was designed to provide a so-called elastic currency for the needs of business—it was to expand and contract automatically with the business cycle. We say "so-called" because the currency **was already** elastic. Like a rubber band, the money supply expanded and contracted very readily through the correspondent bank relationships explained previously; but proponents of the Act did not like the necessity for banks to hold idle reserves for the sake of safety in case of a potential bank run. Rather, the proponents of the Federal Reserve Act were looking for some form of government guarantee that would allow banks to stay **fully** invested at all times. That is, they wanted to be able to create as much money to lend out as the legal reserve requirement allowed, even if the legal limit was unsafe in practice. In effect, in their desire to maximize earnings by extending interest-earning loans, proponents of the Act wanted a rubber band that would stretch only in one direction. They wanted a money supply that would always expand, but not one that would contract.

In debating against the Federal Reserve Act, Senator Elihu Root attacked the proposed bill as both dangerous and inflationary:

> At present I observe that this is in no sense a provision for an elastic currency. It does not provide an elastic currency. It provides an expansive currency, but not an elastic one. It provides a currency which may be increased, always increased, but not a currency for which the bill contains any provision compelling reduction.
>
> . . . The universal experience, sir, is that the tendency of mankind is to keep on increasing the issue of currency. Unless there is some very positive and distinct influence tending toward the process of reduction, that tendency always has, in all the great commercial nations of the world, produced its natural results, and we may expect it to produce its natural result here, of continual, progressive increase.
>
> . . . I can see in this bill itself, in the discharge of our duty, no influence interposed by us against the occurrence of one of those periods of false and delusive prosperity which inevitably end in ruin and suffering. . . .[16]

---

[16]*Congressional Record*, 63d Cong., 2d sess., vol. 51, pt. 1, 13 December 1913, p. 831 a & b.

How the Federal Reserve System is structured and how it operates will be explained in the next chapter. But let us give a quick overview of its long-range effect on the American economy. This will help us judge whether or not Senator Root prophesied correctly.

The Federal Reserve System was sold to the American public on the basis that it would not be a central bank which would centralize the control of banking in the hands of the federal government. It was supposed to respond to the fluctuating needs of business more or less automatically by passively supplying an elastic currency during times of financial stress. But this is not how things worked out.

Shortly after the Federal Reserve was put into operation (1914), these United States found themselves involved in a European war, World War I. Immediately, the Federal Reserve was used as a handy vehicle for monetizing the war debt. Individuals could perform their "patriotic duty" by purchasing Liberty Bonds and taking them to their local bank, where the bonds were used as collateral for borrowing newly created money at the same rate of interest received on the bond. In short, the Liberty Bonds ended up as bank reserves on which new money could be created, thereby causing monetary inflation.

In 1923 Federal Reserve officials accidently discovered that their activity to earn interest by purchasing government bonds with newly created checkbook money had a short-term stimulating impact on economic activity. The purchase of government securites by the Federal Reserve served to **inflate** the money supply of the country, thereby stimulating business activity. In reverse, the sale of government bonds in the market would serve to **deflate** the money supply, thereby dampening business activity. From this point on, the temptation to influence the level of business activity by purchasing or selling government securities in the open market (this process is called "open market operations") became too great for the Federal Reserve officials to resist. The open market operation was destined to become the Federal Reserve Board's most important tool of monetary regulation in the humanistic attempt to "fine tune" the economy.[17]

Starting in 1924, the Federal Reserve Board purposely embarked on an inflationary policy designed to help Britain re-establish a quasi-gold standard. (See the supplement entitled "All About Gold" at the end of Chapter 7.) When this policy produced a stock market boom and a speculative land boom in the late 1920s, the Board implemented a sudden forced monetary contraction which culminated in the stock market crash of 1929. When the resultant credit crunch occurred, the Federal Reserve Board then followed a perverse policy by refusing to supply the elastic currency to the banking and business communities which it had been designed to supply.

Defenders of the Federal Reserve claim that the Board did not then fully understand how to apply its powers. Regardless of the reason, the Board's

---

[17]See Elgin Groseclose, *Fifty Years of Managed Money* (New York, Books, Inc., 1966).

policy worsened the financial situation by calling in existing loans which banks had rediscounted — banks which were in the midst of a serious liquidity crisis and which needed funds desperately. From 1929 to 1933, the country's money supply was forcibly contracted by approximately one-third, forcing many banks into bankruptcy and plunging the nation into the deepest depression of all time. Ironically, the public then turned to the federal government for help — to the very agency that was the source of the problem. The result was an unending series of government "make work" programs issued from Washington, D.C.

It was the advent of World War II in 1939, with the munitions orders from the Allies overseas, that pulled our nation out of a perplexing depression that no one seemd able to solve. Critics of governmental intervention claim that the persistent socialistic tinkering with the economy by the Roosevelt Administration in the 1930s only acerbated the uncertain economic conditions that the federal government and the Federal Reserve Board had caused in the first place. Defenders of government intervention take the position that conditions would have been worse without government programs and what was really needed was more deficit spending. Interestingly enough, the depression of 1921-1922 was of very short duration even though the federal government took no action to correct it.

The Federal Reserve System was again used in World War II as an "engine of inflation" to help monetize the war debt — this time a debt in excess of $200 billion. In 1946, with the passing of the Full Employment Act, Congress imposed on the Federal Reserve two contrasting policy goals — "full employment" coupled with a "stable price level." Invariably, public pressure has forced the federal government, and thus the Federal Reserve Board, to opt in favor of an inflationary policy in pursuit of high employment with the result of persistently rising price levels. The price index of 58.5 in 1946 rose, as a result of monetary inflation, to 300 in 1983, which means that the 1946 dollar has lost four-fifths of its purchasing value.

Critics of the Federal Reserve have pointed out that Board policy has not prevented boom-bust cycles and that there has been more economic and financial instability since the creation of the Federal Reserve System than before — the 1929 Crash and ensuing depression being the prime example. Proponents defend Federal Reserve Board policy by stating that cycles would be even more volatile without Federal Reserve monetary control. This is a continuing debate. (For a more detailed discussion, see the chapter on monetary and fiscal policy.)

Power Is Where the Gold Is

It is appropriate at this point to look back over the history of money and banking in our country in order to reflect a bit and see if we can discern a lesson concerning the people's freedom. If you recall, two broad changes occurred in the U.S. banking system which drastically altered where gold was held; and President Franklin D. Roosevelt's executive order of 1933 drastically altered who owned the gold of our country. Let us briefly review these and related happenings in order to gain an understanding of their impact:

(1) During the War Between the States, Congress passed the National Banking Act in order to help finance the Union's military campaigns against the Confederacy. The net result of the National Banking Act was to transfer the people's gold, which had been previously held in the vaults of hundreds of private banks throughout the nation, to the U.S. Treasury in Washington. Even after convertibility was restored in 1879, the gold reserve remained concentrated in our nations' capital. This might seem like an unimportant happening, but it was to be just the beginning of a series of steps which would result in nationalizing the people's gold and transferring control of it to the political rulers.

(2) With passage of the Federal Reserve Act in 1913, the ownership of gold passed insidiously yet effectively from the U.S. Treasury to the Federal Reserve. One effect of this Act was to increase the number of paper dollars that could be created upon the existing gold reserve.

(3) When President Roosevelt nationalized gold in 1933, U.S. citizens were emasculated of their gold; and the door was opened even wider for long-continued monetary inflation. No longer were the people in a position to deflate an overinflated banking system by turning in paper money and demanding gold in exchange. From this point in history, the American people were faced with the problem of being controlled by their government rather than being able to control the politicians and bureaucrats. The final steps of cutting all ties between the dollar and silver, domestically in 1968, and gold, internationally in 1971, were just a matter of time.

No careful observer of history will even try to deny that Americans have suffered severe losses of liberty during this century. This loss of freedom is often sloughed off as a necessary part of the growth of population and of the growing complexity of our social and economic framework. But this is a sadly deficient analysis. The ownership of and control over **real** economic resources is the bulwark of a people's economic and political freedom. Citizens who own and control substantial real assets cannot easily be dominated by politicians and bureaucrats, for the control of real wealth provides citizens with economic alternatives which lead to independence rather than dependence on the dictates of others.

It is in this light that we should regard the gradual draining of gold and silver from the pockets of citizens and the centralization of gold holdings under the control of political rulers. It is doubtful that Americans will ever again be able to exert effective control over their elected officials unless they demand the return of a gold- and silver-backed currency. The widely dispersed ownership of gold held in private bank vaults and in the homes of millions of citizens is a strong bulwark against the slow and eventual growth of totalitarianism. On the other hand, the centralization of gold holdings at the national level constitutes an invitation to tyranny that few political leaders have the character to resist.

A Biblical Perspective

Serious students of economics should investigate more deeply the issue of whether Federal Reserve policy has been perverse rather than beneficial in the long run. The real issue lies deeper than a pragmatic balancing of "goods" against "bads" from a historical viewpoint. The Christian should ask: Is there a biblical basis for the civil authorities to take upon themselves (or to accept a mandate from the people) the responsibility to attempt to control the level and direction of economic activity? Or is the seven-decade attempt to impose monetary control on the American people through the Federal Reserve System nothing more than a humanistic attempt of secular rulers to "play God" by attempting to build an earthly millenium?

These are **theologically based** questions, but the drive to control every facet of human activity by civil government is **also** theologically based. It is based on the secular religion called **humanism**, and it should be recognized as such. Monetary policy implemented by heads of government to control the level of economic activity is but one practical outworking of secular humanism in action. The continued existence — or, better, the **reclamation** — of free enterprise capitalism rests on how this question is answered. We must never overlook the interworking of theology, philosophy, politics and economics.

Questions

1. Who might favor an inflationary monetary policy? Why?

2. What commodities did the early American settlers use for money? Based on your understanding of the functions that money serves, were these ideal money substitutes? Explain.

3. What kinds of specie circulated in Colonial America?

4. List the kinds of paper money used by the colonists. Define each one. What effect did the issuance of paper money have on price levels? Give an example.

5. How was the Revolutionary War largely financed? What happened to the value of paper money?

6. Are boom-bust cycles an inherent part of private capitalism? Explain. What early example from western Massachusetts can be cited in support of your claim?

7. Read the powers granted to Congress by the Constitution of these

United States. Based on your understanding of the powers specifically granted, what would your advice have been to President George Washington concerning the constitutionality of the First Bank of the United States? Debate your advice with someone who holds a contrary view.

8. Why was the First Bank's charter not renewed? What monetary phenomenon soon resulted?

9. Why was the Second Bank of the United States chartered? What services did it provide? List and explain them.

10. Why was the Second Bank's charter not renewed? What effect did this have on the number of state banks and on the economy?

11. Were the First and Second Banks of the United States conservative or liberal forces in the economy? Explain.

12. Consider the various services provided by the First and Second Banks of the United States. Do you favor or oppose the existence of such government-connected central banks? Why? Debate your view with someone who holds a contrary position.

13. Read President Andrew Jackson's veto message of July 10, 1832. Do you agree or disagree? Why?

14. Argue pro or con: The monetary chaos that existed during the era of "free banking" would have continued to this day if the federal government had not nationalized the currency by establishing the National Banking System.

15. Contrast the Suffolk Banking System and the New York Safety Fund System — how they functioned and how they stood the test of time.

16. What government agency today is similar to the New York Safety Fund System? What happened to New York taxpayers as a result of the depression of 1837? How would massive losses be handled by federal officials today?

17. What happened to the money supply and business activity when taxes were paid in specie and the funds were accumulated at the various sub-treasuries of the Independent Treasury System? Explain the chain of cause-and-effect.

18. What was the motivating force behind establishing the National Banking System in the 1860s? Explain.

19. How did the federal government force state banks into the National Banking System? Why did a small number of state banks not join? Did the state banks that changed to national charters stay in the national system? Explain.

20. Explain how the National Banking System funneled money into the federal treasury to help pay for the War Between the States.

21. Defend or attack this statement: Only the civil authorities should be allowed to mint coins, for how else can the purity and value of currency be ensured?

22. Explain the correspondent relationship between country banks, city banks and New York City banks that developed in the latter part of the nineteenth century. What problems occurred during times of financial stress?

23. What is "call money"?

24. Explain the need for an "elastic currency" that was popularly voiced after the financial panic of 1907. Was there really a need for an elastic currency or was an elastic currency the problem? Explain.

25. What alternative was open to bankers instead of establishing a central bank to serve as "lender of last resort"? How would this alternative affect bank earnings?

26. Evaluate Senator Elihu Root's criticism of the Federal Reserve Act in light of the historical perspective we have today.

27. What was the purported function of the Federal Reserve System when it was originally established in 1913? Has it remained true to its original objective? Explain.

28. How was part of the war debt monetized during World War I, even though Liberty Bonds might be originally purchased by citizens with earned dollars?

29. What discovery did the Federal Reserve Board make in 1923? Explain how the discovery worked. What change in policy did this bring about in Federal Reserve objectives and its role in the economy?

30. What relationship was there between Britain's attempt to return to a quasi-gold standard in 1924 and the stock market crash in these United States in the fall of 1929?

31. When the 1929 Crash occurred, did the Federal Reserve System provide an "elastic currency" as it was designed to do? Explain.

32. What touched off the 1929-1939 depression? To whom did the people turn for help? Do you see an irony in this? Explain.

33. Comment on the twin policy objectives of "full employment" and a "stable price level." Have either or both been met? Explain.

34. How much did prices rise between 1946 and 1983? Translate this into purchasing power, assuming the 1946 dollar to be worth 100 cents.

35. Evaluate the idea of the civil authorities attempting to influence the level of economic activity through monetary control. Support or attack the idea from a biblical perspective, citing appropriate Bible passages.

36. Do you, or do you not, see the development of Federal Reserve monetary policy as a natural result of secular humanism? Explain. What position should a Christian take? Argue your viewpoint with someone who holds a contrary position.

9

The Banking System

Wherefore then gavest not thou my money into the bank, that at my coming I might have required mine own with usury?

Luke 19:23

VIEWED from a financial perspective, the numerous individuals who compose the amorphous group called society can be divided into two classes: savers and borrowers. Some persons, because of their willingness to defer consumption for the present, have a surplus of investable funds on which they hope to earn interest. Others, either because their desire for immediate consumption is especially intense or because they seek profit-making business opportunities, are willing to borrow funds on which they pay interest.

In a free market society, individuals and firms automatically appear to serve these contrasting needs. They serve as monetary "go-betweens" or, to use a more technical term, as **financial intermediaries** between savers and borrowers. In the chapter on money, we discussed the early money-changers and goldsmiths who used to provide this important service and who gradually developed into what today are called bankers.

Financial Intermediaries

Modern society is very complex in that many different kinds of institutions have been developed over the years to serve as financial go-betweens for money-seekers (borrowers) and money-providers (savers). If we keep in mind that the general purpose of all financial intermediaries is to provide efficient means to increase the liquidity of investments, then much of the seeming complexity disappears. To take a commonplace example: A person who lends money to another for building a home must expect to tie up his investment for as much as 20 to 30 years if he makes the loan directly to the homeowner. If he invests money in such a loan indirectly through a financial intermediary called a savings and loan company, however, his investment becomes much more liquid because other people are willing to buy savings and loan shares. In case of need, the original provider of money can, in effect, be "bought out" by new depositors in the savings and loan company. The owner of the home is not called upon to sell his home to generate the needed cash. The new depositors in the savings and loan company become the ones who are providing him with money.

The process of taking funds out of a financial intermediary such as a savings and loan company is called **disintermediation**. Until the late 1970s, there were enough new funds flowing into the savings and loan industry that depositors who wanted to withdraw their funds encountered no problems—that is, enough new depositors were found to "buy out" the earlier depositors. But serious problems developed after 1980.

The root of the problem was this: Interest rates remained fairly steady during the 1950s and into the late 1960s. But during the 1970s interest rates began to rise rapidly. The reason for the rise in interest rates was the long-continued inflation of the money supply, which was caused by continued deficits by the U.S. Federal Government. The inflation/interest rate sequence worked like this: When Congress voted to spend more money than it collected from citizens in taxes, government bonds were printed to make up for the budget deficit. Some of these government bonds were sold directly to the public, which process was not inflationary because the bonds were purchased with dollars that had already been earned—that is, the money paid for the bonds was matched dollar for dollar with goods and services that had been sold in the marketplace. Thus a one-to-one balance between money and economic produce still existed.

When the public did not purchase all the government bonds offered to it, the U.S. Treasury "monetized" the unsold bonds by selling them to the Federal Reserve or to commercial banks. In either instance the bonds are bought with newly created checkbook money, which thus monetizes this portion of the federal government's debt instruments, that is, the bonds. There is no limit, for instance, to the amount of new money that can be created by the Federal Reserve Bank, for it is just a matter of writing numbers in a checkbook.

As this newly created money was released into the economy during the last two decades, price levels started rising because more money was chasing the same amount of goods and services in the economy. As price levels tended upward, lenders realized that money loaned today would have less purchasing power a year later. If price levels rose by 10 percent a year, for instance, the person who loaned 100 dollars at 6 percent interest would only have 106 dollars with which to buy goods that were now priced at 110 dollars. So, intelligent savers started to seek higher rates of interest on money they invested or loaned out. With a 10 percent annual upward trend in price levels, the saver would require 10 percent plus 6 percent or a total of 16 percent interest, of which 10 percent is called an "inflation premium." This explains why interest rates soared to the 16-20 percent level in 1980 and 1981.

Various types of new investment media emerged during the late 1970s—one being the money market mutual fund which invests in very short-term liquid types of investments. These new investment media served the needs of savers; but, in doing so, they caused what is called "disintermediation" in the savings and loan industry. Savers withdrew their money from savings and loan firms in such a large volume that many of the savings and loan firms found themselves in a non-liquid condition caused by accepting money deposits on a short-term pay-back-on-demand basis while lending the money deposits out for perhaps 20 or 30 years. This is basically an unsound practice.

For many years the savings and loan industry existed in a government-protected environment which the officials of the industry rather liked. The federal government limited the amount of interest that savings and loan firms could pay on customers' deposits to 5 or 5 ¼ percent. The savings and loan industry thus had access to cheap money which stimulated the building of houses and the expansion of home ownership at the expense of the investing public who were legally deprived of higher earnings on their savings. Free market forces finally prevailed through the appearance of such new financial intermediaries as the money market funds which were willing and able to pay higher rates of interest.

As we have just indicated, a rapid disintermediation occurred in the savings and loan industry. That is an understatement. Money actually gushed out of the savings and loan industry into the newly emerged money market funds. In some respects, the money market fund is the poor man's solution to earning higher interest on his savings. Federal law limited interest paid on savings deposits to around 5 percent. Federal law also limited the amount of interest that could be paid on small time deposits or time certificates of deposits. But, federal law did not limit the amount of interest that could be paid on certificates of deposits of $100,000 or more. Thus the law clearly favored the well-to-do. The pooling of many small deposits through the new money market funds allowed small savers to enjoy the higher interest rates that previously were excluded by law.

Within a few years, the money market funds grew from zero to an almost 200 billion dollar industry. During 1981, many savings and loan firms were either forced into bankruptcy or were forced to merge with stronger firms. In 1981 fully two-thirds of the firms in the industry were in dire straits. The savings and loan industry reacted by seeking legislation which would limit the amount of interest that money market funds could pay, but strong political opposition was exhibited by millions of small savers who felt they should not be denied the market rate of interest they were finally able to enjoy. A compromise solution was arrived at when the federal regulators allowed the savings and loan firms to issue "All-Savers Certificates" which pay higher interest.

We have gone into this lengthy detail about the disintermediation which recently occurred in the savings and loan industry to emphasize the counterproductive effects of government controls. It took many years for this regulated industry to come upon hard times which were caused by the federal government's long-continued inflationary policy. The solution to providing small savers with higher interest rates was a free market development, not a government-provided development; and during all the years that the federal government legally held down the interest rates paid on savings, the small saver lost out.

Next we list some popular types of financial intermediaries. Keep in mind that the variety of such institutions is limited only by the diversity of the people who constitute society and the ingenuity of entrepreneurial-minded individuals whom the Lord raises up to serve those needs. Thus, at least theoretically, the potential variety of financial intermediaries is practically unlimited:

(1) Commercial Banks
(2) Savings Banks
(3) Savings and Loan Associations
(4) Life Insurance Companies
(5) Fire and Casualty Insurance Companies
(6) Credit Unions
(7) Finance (Small Loan) Companies
(8) Pawnbrokers
(9) Investment Funds and Trusts
(10) Pension Trusts
(11) Money Market Mutual Funds
(12) Government-Sponsored Credit Agencies

Government-sponsored credit agencies are not, of course, products of free market development. Rather, they are politically created institutions whose inception and continued existence depend on the coercive power of the civil authorities to supply them with capital funds through taxation. All other institutions listed above depend on voluntary efforts to attract necessary funds. Government-sponsored agencies include such institutions as: Banks for Cooperatives, Federal Intermediate Credit Banks, Federal Land Banks, Federal Home Loan Banks, Federal National Mortgage Association, U.S. Export-Import Bank and the Federal Reserve System. The Federal Financing Bank, created in 1974, was designed to lower the cost of borrowed funds and to eliminate the need for some governmental agencies to raise funds by borrowing directly from the public. By 1977 it had loaned $30.8 billion to various federal agencies including these direct loans (listed in billions): U.S. Postal Service ($2.2), TVA ($3.5), U.S. Export-Import Bank ($5.4) and U.S. Railway Association ($0.2). Critics of the Federal Financing Bank question the advisability of creating a special fund-raising agency such as the FFB because it insulates federal agencies from the marketplace even more and hides the impact of their financing from the scrutiny of Congress.

Types of Banks

There are two basic kinds of banks: **savings banks** and **commercial banks**. Since they operate on entirely different principles, it is important that we distinguish between them.

Savings Banks: In 1980 there were about 500 mutual savings banks and about 6,000 savings and loan associations in these United States. In 1981 and 1982 many savings and loan associations went out of business because of the disintermediation problem mentioned previously. Most merged with stronger survivors. The mutual savings banks operate almost exclusively in the New England states. Both types are called "thrift" institutions because their primary function is to serve as a financial intermediary between savers and borrowers. They can lend out only the amount of funds they have received in deposits minus a certain percentage set aside as reserves for safety purposes. In other words, savings banks and savings and loan associations operate on a 100-percent reserve basis. They are like the early goldsmith who did not create additional "fictitious" warehouse receipts but limited his issue of receipts to the actual amount of gold or silver deposited with him. They are unlike the goldsmith in these respects: (1) Their savings deposit receipts are **not** based on precious metal, for we operate on a **fiat** money basis today. (2) Their savings deposit receipts are **not** money, for they have to be changed into money in order to be spent. If you draw funds out of a savings bank or a savings and loan association, you are given a check drawn on the commercial bank at which your thrift institution holds its account; and this **is** money. At the present time, commercial banks have a government-bestowed monopoly on the power to create money. Unauthorized money creators who break in on this monopoly money-making power are called counterfeiters!

The development of the "NOW" (Negotiable Orders of Withdrawal) account, which some thrift institutions have been authorized to issue, has changed this situation. The "NOW" account received such an enthusiastic reception from the public that it was authorized for use in every state. It is simply an efficient vehicle for transferring savings deposits directly from one person to another. Since the use of negotiable orders of withdrawal has come into general practice, they actually constitute a new type of money. Historically, only cash and deposits that provided "instant liquidity" have been defined as money by economists. Time deposits and savings deposits were excluded because they first had to be converted into either cash or a demand deposit (checkbook money) before being spent. The development of "NOW" accounts, which can be directly transferred from one person to another, has changed this. Any institution that can offer "NOW" accounts is, in effect, in the banking business.

Commercial Banks: There are approximately 14,000 commercial banks in these United States. Their operations can be divided into two functions: (a) Savings Bank or Savings and Loan Association type operations and (b) Commercial Bank operations.

Whenever a commercial bank provides a savings account for a depositor, it simply performs the same function as a mutual savings bank or a savings and loan association. It serves as a thrift institution by acting as a financial intermediary between savers and borrowers. Since all commercial banks offer savings account deposits, we can state that they operate both as thrift institutions and as "banks of commerce." There is nothing more to be said about the former asepct of operations because it has already been covered.

It is from the latter function as "banks of commerce" that commercial banks get their name, and it is in this function that they provide their most valuable service to the public. In their function as true "banks of commerce," commercial banks provide depositors and borrowers with **demand deposits** (checking accounts). In the creation of demand deposits, a commercial banker is just like the goldsmith we discussed earlier; for the demand deposit or checking account he issues constitutes **real** money. Why? Because demand deposits can be transferred from person to person directly and demand deposits are generally acceptable in exchange for goods and services. Demand deposits fully qualify under our definition of money in the same way that the goldsmith's warehouse receipts and the nineteenth century banker's privately issued bank notes did.

There is still another feature of commercial banking which makes it unique among all other financial intermediaries. This is the fact that commercial banks are the only institutions that **create** deposits and do so on a **fractional reserve basis**. In this respect, modern commercial bankers are similar to the early goldsmith-bankers who created fictitious warehouse receipts and the nineteenth century bankers who issued their own private bank notes. Commercial bankers have the same power to inflate and deflate the money supply that early goldsmith-bankers and nineteenth century bankers had. Today, as we have already indicated, demand deposits are no longer based on gold or silver but are based completely on government fiat money.

Let us review: Remember that the goldsmith-bankers started operating on a fractional reserve basis when they began issuing more warehouse receipts than the value of gold and silver they held on deposit. New money was created and monetary inflation occurred when they extended loans by using these fictitious receipts. Likewise, money was destroyed and monetary deflation occurred when such loans were repaid. This same process, in principle, also occurs in modern commercial banking—although the process appears different and more complicated because of the existence of a central bank (Federal Reserve System) at which commercial banks hold their reserves.

It is crucially important to a correct understanding of commercial banking theory and practice to recognize the following facts: (1) Monetary inflation occurs when money is created and injected into the economy by commercial banks when they extend loans to borrowers. (2) Monetary deflation occurs when borrowers repay the loans and existing money is destroyed.

Sometimes a commercial banker is heard to say, "I cannot create money as the economists say I can. In matter of fact, I can lend out only 80 or 90 percent of what I receive on deposit because I am required to keep the rest on reserve at the Federal Reserve Bank. Therefore, my bank cannot multiply money by making loans; for we can only lend a fractional part of our deposits."

There is a reason why some bankers make such statements. Some bankers are good money practitioners but poor monetary theorists. From the individual banker's viewpoint, it indeed appears that commercial banks cannot create money. When all commercial banks are considered as a whole, however, the system can and does operate on a multiple expansion principle. If there were no central bank, the principle could be seen clearly — just as it could be seen with the early goldsmith-bankers and the bankers of the nineteenth century who held reserves in their own vaults. The introduction of a central bank for holding bank reserves works to cloud the issue, thereby making a simple principle seem mysterious. Remember our maxim: **People cannot control what they do not understand.** If the American people ever hope to control the money and banking system for their own benefit, instead of having political rulers manipulate and control them through the banking system, they must learn the "mystery" of how fractional reserve banking works in conjuction with a central bank (Federal Reserve System).

Fractional Reserve Banking

Commercial banks are private, profit-seeking institutions. Thus, just like any other private business, they will attempt to maximize income and minimize expenses. We will not bother to look at the cost side of banking, for in this respect commercial banks are not much different than many other businesses. Bank managers must continually search for ways of conducting operations more efficiently to remain profitable. We will look at the income side of this fascinating business.

In general, we can confidently state that commercial banks increase their earning potential and income when they increase their earning assets which are made up of loans extended and securities purchased. Loans constitute banks' preferred type of earning asset because loans generally pay a higher net return than securities. For example, the Bank of America — the largest commercial bank in these United States — had earning assets of $67 billion in 1978; $43.1 billion, or 64 percent, of these assets were in loans. We can see that, to the extent that safety will allow, commercial banks have a strong motivation to extend loans to the maximum extent possible. When loans are extended, new money is created.

But, we might ask, exactly **how** does this process of money creation and money destruction occur?

In order to get a clear picture of how our existing fractional reserve banking system functions, it is advisable to break our inquiry into two steps: (1) a one-bank system **without** a central bank and (2) a multi-bank system **with** a central bank. By doing this, we can more easily understand the principle of fractional reserve banking. Once we understand the principle, it will be easier to see how it applies to our present banking system in these United States where the Federal Reserve functions as a central bank or as a "lender of last resort."

A One-Bank System: A one-bank fractional reserve set-up functions much like the goldsmith-banker we described earlier and the nineteenth century banker — both of whom, in effect, created "warehouse recepits" on the gold and silver specie left on deposit with them.

Picture, if you will, an isolated island that has only **one** commercial bank. Suppose that the money supply is made up entirely of two kinds of money: silver coins and silver certificates. For simplicity purposes, let us designate each unit of money in terms of a dollar. Suppose also that our commercial banker limits himself to an expansion ratio of 4:1; that is, for every dollar of silver held on deposit at his bank, he can give the depositor a one-dollar silver certificate and lend out three additional fictitious certificates to other individuals. Finally, let us suppose that there are only 1,000 silver coins in existence, valued at one dollar each.

If we start out with the assumption that all of the one-dollar silver coins are held by the public and that the banker holds none on reserve, then the total money supply on the island is $1,000.

Next, suppose that some people deposit 100 silver coins with the banker in exchange for 100 silver certificates. The total money supply is now 900 silver coins plus 100 silver certificates for the same total of $1,000. We do not count reserves held by the banker as part of the money supply because reserves do not circulate as money. However, note that an important change has taken place! Even though we do not count the $100 in silver coins held by the banker as part of the money supply, these 100 coins can support a **potential** of three additional silver certificates each!

Suppose someone asks the banker for a loan of $300. The banker will simply print 300 extra silver certificates and hand them to the borrower; thus, the money supply has been instantly inflated by an additional $300. In short, the banker has **created** money — for the people on the island will regard each of these new silver certificates in exactly the same way they regard the first 100 certificates. The money supply has been expanded from $1,000 to $1,300 by simply transferring $100 from circulating **outside** the bank to being held on reserve **in** the bank and allowing the bank to issue $400 in paper money based on the $100 silver coins that the bank's customers deposited. The money supply outside the bank is now $900 in silver coins plus $400 in silver certificates.

This is the principle of fractional reserve banking. The principle allows commercial banks to **create a multiple of circulating media** based on funds held on reserve.

If we now suppose that the people bring the other 900 silver coins into the bank for deposit, the banker will issue 900 more silver certificates to the depositors; and he will still be able to lend out $2,700 to borrowers: $900 + 2,700 = $3,600 (plus the $400 in silver certificates already issued). In short, the original $1,000 money supply on the island can be expanded, through the practice of fractional reserve banking, to a maximum of $4,000. Whether the $4,000 maximum potential will be reached will depend on people's preference for holding real silver coins versus silver certificates for their financial transactions.

Now let us recapitulate: At this moment in time, the island has a total money supply of $4,000 — made up of $1,000 in real honest-to-goodness silver certificates issued to depositors of real silver coins, plus $3,000 fictitious silver certificates which have been loaned to borrowers.

What happens when the loans are repaid? The answer is that the fictitious certificates are destroyed when the borrowers come into the bank to repay their loans. When this happens the money supply is deflated. We can see this most easily by supposing that all those who borrowed the 3,000 fictitious silver certificates repay their loans at the same time. If this were to happen, the banker would accept their payments (we are ignoring interest for the sake of simplicity), cancel their IOUs and destroy the fictitious silver certificates he had previously loaned them. The money supply would drop from $4,000 to $1,000 again, and every depositor who still held silver certificates could have them fully redeemed. In practice, though, the extension and repayment of loans would be staggered; and there would be a tendency to make new loans as old ones were repaid. So the money supply would not tend to gyrate back and forth from $1,000 to $4,000 but would tend to have lesser fluctuations. The monetary fluctuations that did occur would happen in response to business conditions and the economic outlook (the desire of people to borrow money) and the judgment of the commercial banker as to whether or not it would be profitable to extend loans.

The essence of commercial banking, then, is this: Commercial banks, because they operate on a fractional reserve basis, have power to inflate and deflate the money supply by extending and cancelling loans. They operate in theory exactly the same way that the old time goldsmith-bankers operated when they issued fictitious certificates for precious metals they held on reserve.

Today in **practice** our money supply is not based on either silver or gold, but the **principle** is exactly the same. As we have already indicated, these United States have only **fiat** money. We now use Federal Reserve Notes instead of silver certificates. In addition, we have the option of using checkbook money (demand deposits) instead of Federal Reserve Notes. If we go back to our island example and start with $1,000 of fiat Federal Reserve Notes and allow the banker to issue $4 of checkbook money for every $1 of Federal Reserve Notes deposited with him, the fractional reserve banking system functions in exactly the same way. The only difference is that worthless paper is held on reserve instead of precious metals.

A Multi-Bank System With a Central Bank: Let us now go back to our island example and make some changes. The total money supply, to begin with, is still 1,000 one-dollar silver coins; but let us have **ten** commercial bankers instead of only one. Also, let us add a **central bank** which will hold the silver reserves. Finally, let us make a cosmetic change. Let us take away each individual banker's power to expand the money supply on a 4:1 ratio. Instead, let us require that each bank must keep on deposit at the central bank 25 cents for every dollar in silver certificates it issues.

In summary, this is our new situation:

(1) $1,000 in silver coins constitute the entire money supply.
(2) There are ten privately owned commercial banks instead of only one.
(3) There is a government-operated central bank which will hold the banks' reserves instead of allowing the banks to hold reserves in their own vaults.
(4) No longer can individual banks issue four dollars of silver certificates for each dollar received in silver coin as deposits from customers. Instead, each bank is required to deposit, in silver, at the central bank, 25 percent of all the silver deposits received. Then each bank is allowed to lend out the remaining 75 percent of silver to borrowers.

This new set-up **appears** to be much more conservative and safe, does it not? Instead of being able to create four silver certificates for every dollar in silver coin received as deposits, the banker is now limited to issuing only one silver certificate per dollar in coin deposited plus lending out only three-fourths of the silver received. He deposits the other one-fourth of the silver received at the central bank as reserves "to protect the public." In truth, however, the more conservative and safer appearance is only **cosmetic** — it is an illusion, for the new set-up produces the **very same** money-multiplying effect as before.

To see how the new fractional reserve banking system works in conjunction with a central bank, let us suppose that a resident of the island deposits $100 in silver coin at one of the ten commercial banks on the island. This is what happens: The banker will give the depositor $100 in silver certificates and deposit $25 in silver coin at the central bank as required. Then the banker will have $75 in silver to lend out to a potential borrower. Let us assume that the $75 in silver is borrowed by a man who wants to have his house painted and that this amount is paid to the painter.

Now we have this situation: (1) The original depositor still has the $100 in silver certificates which the banker issued to him. (2) The central bank has $25 in silver coin that it holds on reserve to support the $100 in silver certificates held by the depositor. (3) A painter has the remaining $75 in silver coins. The original $100 in silver coin that was deposited at the bank is now represented in the economy by $100 in silver certificates **plus** $75 in silver coins. In short, the money supply has been "mysteriously" expanded by an **additional** $75 under this more conservative-appearing arrangement! The $100 silver deposit now supports a total money supply of $175.

Suppose that the painter deposits his $75 in silver coin at another bank. He will receive $75 in silver certificates in exchange for his deposit. Banker #2 will place 25 percent, or $18.75, in silver on reserve at the central bank as required by law. He will then have 75 percent of $75, or $56.25, in silver coin to lend out to a potential borrower. When this $56.25 is loaned out, the money supply will again be expanded by that amount. The total money supply will then be: $175 + 56.25 = $231.25. (Stop at this point and compute these totals to make sure that you really follow the process.) The $231.25, of course, is **in addition** to the other $900 in silver coin that is circulating on the island, which we are ignoring for the moment.

Next, suppose that the $56.25 is spent on repairing a car and that the mechanic deposits it at bank #3. Finally, suppose that this multiplying process continues until the 25 percent reserve requirement causes this deplenishing amount of silver coin to be deposited at the central bank. The whole process is summarized in Chart 9:1.

Chart 9:1

How Fractional Reserve Banking Works

Bank	A	B	C	D	E
0	0	0	0	0	$100.00
1	$100.00	$25.00	$75.00	$100.00	175.00
2	75.00	18.75	56.25	75.00	231.25
3	56.25	14.06	42.19	56.25	273.44
4	42.19	10.55	31.64	42.19	305.08
5	31.64	7.91	23.73	31.64	328.81
6	23.73	5.93	17.80	23.73	246.61
7	17.80	4.45	13.35	17.80	359.96
8	13.35	3.34	10.01	13.35	369.97
9	10.01	2.50	7.51	10.01	377.48
10	7.51	1.88	5.63	7.51	383.11
∞	0	$100.00	0	$400.00	$400.00

A = amount of silver deposited; B = 25% required reserve; C = 75% silver available for loans; D = silver certificates issued; E = total money supply (added from column C).

Note: The $100 in column E is the $100 in silver coin with which we started. Gradually, the amount left for depositing dwindles to zero as shown in column A. In the process, all of the silver coin ends up as reserves at the central bank (column B). The total amount of silver certificates issued on the $100 reserve grows to $400 (column D), and this constitutes the total money supply (column E).

Note that the monetary expansion process — if continued until the starting amount of silver coin ($100) is deposited, loaned out, redeposited and reloaned until there is no more coin circulating — causes all the silver coins to gradually accumulate as reserves at the central bank.

As you can see, the existence of more banks plus a central bank in no way changes the **principle** of fractional reserve banking. The outward appearance has changed but **not** the principle. When banks are required to hold a 25 percent reserve at the central bank, this produces the **same** money multiplication as when individual banks are allowed to hold reserves in their own vaults and to create money on a 4:1 ratio. If the required reserve ratio to be kept at the central bank is 25 percent, the money-creation factor is 4:1. Thus, an easy way to determine the **potential** multiple expansion ratio in fractional reserve banking is to convert the percentage of required reserves into a fraction and then to invert: $25\% = \frac{1}{4} = \times 4$; $10\% = \frac{1}{10} = \times 10$; $16\frac{2}{3} = \frac{1}{6} = \times 6$; etc. In practice, the actual multiple always falls short of the theoretical potential because the public opts to hold a portion of their money in currency which they do **not** deposit in the bank. Currency held by the public does not enter the banking system.

There is a very **real** difference, however, when the civil government brings a central bank into the picture. It is this: Look at who holds the silver reserves! When there was no central reserve bank, the silver reserves were held in **private** hands (i.e., by the private bankers who were bound by the law of contract to pay silver out to depositors on demand). When a central bank is introduced, the silver reserves are gradually accumulated in larger and larger total amounts in the hands of the central bank which operates as a **governmental** function.

The very existence of a government-operated central bank poses a disguised threat to the economic and political freedom of a people. How? Because gold and silver reserves tend, imperceptibly but unerringly, to concentrate at the central bank. Thus, the political rulers of a country end up controlling the gold and silver, and the citizens end up holding either paper dollars or accounting entries called demand deposits (checkbook money). Even though the paper dollars or demand deposits are **supposed** to be redeemable into gold and silver by law, laws can be changed. Once the gold and silver reserves are centralized, it becomes a relatively simple matter for the rulers to pass an edict which nationalizes the precious metals held at a centralized location such as a central bank. This alarming event actually happened in these United States in 1933 when President Franklin D. Roosevelt issued a presidential order which nationalized the people's gold.

Once the tie between paper money and gold and silver has been cut, the ruling authorities become relatively free to expand at will the supply of money without limit. The monetary authorities, who outwardly claim to function as a protector of monetary integrity on behalf of the citizens, are in a position to debauch the people's money and thereby gain control of citizens' wealth by purchasing their wealth with worthless paper or demand deposits which the authorities can create without limit. When the rulers of a country gain control over an ever-increasing share of wealth, the citizens gradually become more and more dependent on the civil government economically. The stage is then set for tyranny. This important relationship between money and freedom must always be kept in mind: The economic and political freedom of citizens is directly dependent on where the gold and silver reserves for fractionally based money are kept.

Let us return to our island example: If we expand the $100 deposit example we have just used to the total island-wide money supply of the $1,000 in silver coin we started with, we can see that a 25 percent reserve ratio will produce a potential money supply of 4:1, or $4,000. In practice, as we have already indicated, the total money supply will not actually reach the upper potential because some people will choose to hold silver coins for making purchases instead of using the silver certificates which are issued by the banks. Each time a resident of the island makes a deposit or a withdrawal at a bank, he will increase or decrease the potential amount of money circulating in the economy by a multiple of four. If you doubt this, think through again what would happen if none of the $1,000 in silver coin had yet been deposited in a bank; and then imagine it being deposited all at once. Then take $100 of silver certificates into a bank for redemption back into silver. What would happen to the total supply of money in circulation? The answer is that withdrawal of the $100 in silver coin would necessitate reducing the supply of silver certificates by $300.

As we indicated in the chapter on money, central banks make their appearance as politically contrived institutions designed to "protect" the public from the tendency of private commercial banks to overexpand the money supply because the more money they create and lend out, the more interest they can earn. There would be no need for a central bank if commercial banks operated on a 100-percent reserve basis—like mutual savings banks and savings and loan associations do—rather than on a fractional reserve basis. This is why we pointed out earlier that the very existence of fractional reserve banking is unstable. This inherent instability produces political pressures for government regulation of banking and government creation of a central bank as lender of last resort.

The Federal Reserve System

Since no bank which operates on a fractional reserve basis and which promises to repay depositors on demand can immediately call in all of its loans at once in order to pay off depositors in case of a bank run, two alternatives appear: Bankers must hold at all times a sufficiently large reserve to handle emergency withdrawals which might occur during a widespread financial panic, or some "lender of last resort" must be created which can supply banks with an ample supply of funds to handle any liquidity crisis.

It is understandable that bankers do not like to hold idle cash reserves because they constitute the banks' inventory of unloaned money on which they could otherwise earn interest, that is, earn interest on the money they are able to create based on those reserves. Besides, who wants to run their business every day as if a potential emergency is always just around the corner?

Historically, this problem of fractional reserve banking was solved by banks' expanding their note issue on a multiple basis which was deemed adequate for "normal" times. Banks did not normally hold enough idle reserves to meet excessive withdrawals during times of severe financial crisis. When severe withdrawal crises would periodically occur, banks were allowed by the civil authorities to have a "bank holiday"—that is, banks were allowed to **refuse** to make good on their promise to convert their bank notes into specie upon demand. When the financial panic passed, banks that survived the crisis would then resume redemption. The "holiday" was designed to give banks that were temporarily illiquid, but not bankrupt, time to juggle their portfolio of assets in order to resume specie payments. In short, the "solution" was no solution at all. It was just a means of allowing banks to overexpand their note issue beyond the point of prudence in the event of an eventual crisis which everyone knew would someday appear but which everyone hoped would not come. Once the dreaded crisis did come, the "bank holiday" practice allowed bankers to legally evade their contractual responsibilities—something that other businessmen have not been allowed by law to do. The practice that developed was not consciously recognized by most people as an unprincipled way of doing banking business, but careful analysis shows that the whole concept and practice of allowing "bank holidays" lacked the integrity demanded by a high level of business responsibility. A few conservatively operated banks did generally hold what was considered to be excessive reserves for normal times in order to assure survival during any possible financial crisis, but their earnings potential—relative to other banks that expanded bank notes more freely—was hurt. Not many bankers were willing to make this sacrifice in profitability in order to survive a liquidity crisis they hoped would never come. Human nature being what it is, most bankers succumbed to the temptation to expand their note issue beyond the point of maximum safety because each newly created dollar loaned out would add to their total interest earnings; then they just hoped that any loans extended would be repaid before the always-possible-but-never-welcome financial crisis occurred.

Because of their reluctance to hold what they considered excessively large reserves for normal banking operations, the more attractive alternative was chosen. Bankers sought ways of establishing the desired lender of last resort which they could draw upon during financial emergencies.

The Aldrich-Vreeland Act of 1908 provided for a system of "national currency associations," each to be made up of no fewer than ten banks in sound financial condition. The purpose of the associations was to let associated member-banks issue emergency bank notes against the good, but illiquid, bonds and commercial paper[1] they were holding until the bonds and commer-

---

[1]Commercial paper are IOUs issued by companies who have goods enroute to the market. The IOUs are based on these soon-to-be marketed goods, and they promise repayment just as soon as

cial paper could be sold off without loss.

A second part of the Aldrich-Vreeland Act was to set up a National Monetary Commission designed to study the overall monetary problem. The Commission issued its report in 1912, and it focused on the presumed need for an "elastic currency." The Commission felt that banks' emergency needs for cash could not adequately be met by the banks' pooling money among themselves through small associations. It recommended that bank reserves should be pooled nationwide so as to make needed reserves available to all banks during periods of financial stress. The problem of individual illiquidity was to be miraculously solved by pooling the illiquid reserves of many banks on a national basis!

As we have already pointed out elsewhere, bank reserves were already pooled in New York City; and the money supply was very elastic. It was elastic in two directions: expansionary as well as contractionary. What bankers and political leaders actually sought was some vehicle to prevent the hated contractionary phase of elasticity. What was desired was a government-created central institution that would have the ability to create whatever amount of money was needed to guarantee bank liquidity. This is the "magic" of central banking: to provide banks with a lender of last resort so that each individual bank can operate continuously in an illiquid condition. Somehow, the pooling together of many illiquid parts was supposed to produce a financially liquid whole!

Since American public opinion was still against anything like a single central bank with the immense concentration of monetary power that such an institution would necessarily wield, and people still remembered and feared the power of the First and Second Banks of the United States, some other "reserve creating" agency had to be devised. A bill introduced by Senator Aldrich provided for a weak central bank with very little government participation in its operation. It would have established a National Reserve Association headquartered in Washington, D.C., with branches in the larger financial centers. Control would have been placed with the officers of large banks. The Association was to operate only during times of stress, and **no** commercial bank reserves were to be shifted to the central Association. Under the proposed plan, monetary control would have been exercised by private bankers instead of by government officials.

The Aldrich bill was not adopted. First, the public feared what they viewed as the private "money trust" and favored some form of government control. (This was the populist-progressive era of American history.) Secondly, the Democrats felt confident that they could elect a Democratic president in the

---

the goods are sold. Normally, commercial paper is issued for 30 to 60 days, but sometimes for as much as 90 days. The term "commercial" in commercial banks comes from the practice of extending loans on such commercial paper and this is done by money creation. When the goods are sold, the loans are repaid, the commercial paper is redeemed and destroyed and the money that was created to finance the loans is also destroyed.

election of 1912, and they wanted credit for establishing a central bank. The result was a very different plan with considerably more government control — the Federal Reserve Act — which President Woodrow Wilson signed into law on December 23, 1913.

In some respects, the resulting Federal Reserve System can be considered a subterfuge, for it is different in appearance than it is in function (see Prov. 14:15). Public opinion still would not tolerate a huge government-operated central bank, even though the existing populist-progressive sentiment apparently trusted big government more than big business. So, Congress gave the people a system which appeared to be widely dispersed into 12 Federal Reserve districts but which was eventually centrally controlled by a Federal Reserve Board located in Washington, D.C. Thus, the people were given the **illusion** of decentralization, but the **reality** was centralized government control.

It is important that this fact be kept in mind as we proceed to describe how the Federal Reserve System is set up functionally, for knowledge of this fact will help us see why such immense monetary powers have gradually become concentrated in the Federal Reserve Board. These United States, a republic constituted of politically sovereign and independent states, have come to have a central bank which is, in effect, just like the government-directed central banks that the unitary states of Europe have.[2] The object of a central bank, though this fact is seldom openly admitted by government officials who control such banks, is to exercise monetary control over the people to assist political leaders in more easily achieving the political and economic goals established at the national level.

Structure of the Federal Reserve System: These United States have been divided into 12 Federal Reserve districts, each with a district Federal Reserve Bank. There are also 23 Federal Reserve branch banks which serve particular areas within the districts. The Federal Reserve Banks are located in:

- Boston
- New York
- Philadelphia
- Cleveland
- Richmond
- Atlanta
- Chicago
- Minneapolis
- St. Louis
- Kansas City
- Dallas
- San Francisco

Each district Federal Reserve Bank is "owned" by the banks that compose its membership. (The word **owned** is enclosed in quotes because, while

---

[2]In a **republic**, primary political power rests with the states who create the republic and who then **delegate** certain limited powers to the national government. The states remain the creators, and the national government remains the creature. Thus, the states and their counties and cities are not creatures of the national government in a republic. In a nation with a **unitary** government, the national government is supreme, and all political power flows down from the national level. In a republic, political power flows upward to the national level. Unitary governments use centralized power; republics focus on local self-rule.

member banks technically "own" stock in their district Federal Reserve Bank, **real** ownership always connotes effective control over what is owned. In this case, the owners are controlled by what they "own." Member banks are controlled by the Federal Reserve Bank and not the other way around. Thus, when the statement is made that the Federal Reserve System is owned by its member banks, the statement is technically true but practically a subterfuge to hide the fact of government control. The Federal Reserve System is actually a fascistic form of government control over a privately owned banking system. [See Chapter 5 on "The Isms."])

Membership is compulsory for national banks, and state banks may join upon compliance with certain requirements. Upon joining, each member-bank must purchase capital stock in the district Federal Reserve Bank up to 3 percent of the member-bank's combined capital and surplus. Each member-bank receives 6 percent interest annually on its investment. Cash reserves, which previously had been held in the vaults of each commercial bank before the advent of the Federal Reserve System, are now transferred to the district Federal Reserve Bank to meet minimum legal reserve requirements established for Federal Reserve member-banks.

Each district Bank has nine directors—three "class A," three "class B" and three "class C." Member-banks elect class A and class B directors by ballot. Class A directors represent bank stockholders, and these are usually commercial bankers. Class B directors must be actively engaged in business (agriculture, industry or commerce); they may not be either bank officers, directors or employees. Class C directors are appointed by the Federal Reserve Board, and one of these is designated as chairman of the district Federal Reserve Bank.

The district Banks do not play an important role in monetary policy. They do establish the "discount rate" (explained later) for their specific Federal Reserve district, but this rate generally follows the market rate of interest instead of establishing it. They do elect 5 of the 12 district Federal Reserve Bank presidents who serve as members of the Federal Reserve Open Market Committee (explained later).

The real decision-making power of the Federal Reserve System rests with the Federal Reserve Board of Governors in Washington, D.C. This Board consists of seven members appointed by the President of these United States with the advice and consent of the Senate. Their terms of office are 14 years each, and they are not eligible for reappointment after having served for a full term. No two board members may come from the same Federal Reserve district. It is significant to remember that the district Federal Reserve Bank presidents originally called themselves "governors." Some of the early district Bank presidents insisted on using this title; apparently believing that **they** were the ones who should set policy, and they did actually wield much influence until they died. (Benjamin Strong, first President of the Federal Reserve Bank of New York, is a good example.)[3] The "battle of titles" was eventually won by the Federal Reserve Board. Only the members of the Federal Reserve Board now use the title "governor" with the head being called "Chairman of the Board."

The Board approves the salaries of all district Reserve Bank officers as well as their appointment. It also supervises the examination of each district Reserve Bank to ensure compliance with regulations. The Board's primary function is the formulation of monetary policy. This is interesting, for if we believe the public statements of those who created the Federal Reserve System in 1913, the System was not designed to exert **active** monetary policy. Rather, the Federal Reserve System was supposed to respond **passively** to the needs of business in providing the desired "elastic currency" during times of stress. The passage of time has seen more and more power being gradually concentrated in the Federal Reserve Board at Washington, D.C.

Tools of Policy Control: The Federal Reserve Board has three major tools of monetary control that it can wield:

(1) Changes in the rate of discount; implemented by Federal Reserve Banks;

(2) Changes in reserve requirements for member-banks; implemented by the Federal Reserve Board;

(3) Open market operations; implemented by the Federal Reserve Open Market Committee.

Changes in the Rate of Discount: The **discount rate** or **rediscount rate** is the rate of interest charged by a district Federal Reserve Bank to a member-bank when it borrows from the district Federal Reserve Bank. The process works like this: Suppose the commercial bank at which you do business is fully loaned-up, which means that it has no excess reserves on which it can create money to extend as a loan. Suppose you come in the bank seeking a loan. If you are a good customer, your banker will be hesitant to decline your request; but what other option does he have? He can take some collateral he is already holding to insure someone else's loan and discount this collateral at the district Reserve Bank.

Let us presume, for instance, that your banker is holding a $1,000 bond (though it could be a title to an automobile, a cash-value life insurance policy or any other evidence of wealth) that someone had used as collateral for his loan. Your banker can surrender this bond as collateral to the district Reserve Bank on a discounted basis. To **discount** means to lend a sum of money by deducting the amount of interest in advance. If the rate of discount is 5 percent and the bond has a face value of $1,000, your banker can borrow $950 from the district Reserve Bank by letting it hold the bond as collateral. As long as the rate of discount is **less** than the rate you pay, which difference must be

---

[3]See Ross M. Robertson, *History of the American Economy* (New York: Harcourt, Brace & World, 1964), pp. 498-501.

great enough to pay your banker's cost of doing business, your banker can earn a net profit on the money you wish to borrow. The discounting process shows the concept of a lender of last resort in action. In the event of a widespread financial panic, **all** collateral held by your banker can theoretically be discounted (or rediscounted, to use another term) at the district Federal Reserve Bank.

As originally conceived, the discount rate was envisioned as being the major monetary tool to be wielded by the Federal Reserve. By **raising** the rate of discount, the Federal Reserve Bank in each federal district could make it unprofitable for commercial bankers to come to the "discount window" to borrow additional reserves. (Going to the "discount window" is just a picturesque way of depicting the discounting process.) This would tend to **restrict** the total money supply by making commercial bankers unwilling to expand loans and even to refuse to renew existing loans. By **lowering** the discount rate and thereby making new reserves available at a lower cost, the district Federal Reserve Bank can entice commercial bankers to **expand** loans, thereby hopefully stimulating business activity.

Where does the district Federal Reserve Bank get the reserves it lends to commercial bankers through the discounting process? Simple. It just creates these reserves out of thin air! How? In exchange for collateral received, the district Reserve Bank simply enters a numerical figure on the reserve account ledger of the commercial bank. This bookkeeping entry at the district Federal Reserve Bank provides the local commercial bank with additional reserves, which, in turn, allow the commercial banker to write a number in your checkbook. Ergo, money has been created from nothing for you to spend!

As you remember from our earlier discussion of the goldsmith-bankers, the newly created money is snuffed out of existence when your loan is repaid. Only in this instance, bookkeeping entries instead of printed warehouse receipts are involved. This discounting process is the essence of a central bank serving as a lender of last resort. Theoretically, there is no limit to the amount of collateral that can be discounted at the district Federal Reserve Bank, for its power to write numbers on the reserve ledger accounts of member-banks is unlimited. The only limit is the "good sense limit" of the Federal Reserve Bank officials in not choosing to innundate the country with newly created checkbook money. We see that the populace must live by faith—they must trust in the Federal Reserve officials' good sense not to do the wrong thing (see Ps. 118:8-9, 146:3).

The potential misuse of such money-creating power is the reason why some economists (a minority to which this author belongs) favor the gold standard, which **limits** the amount of money that can be created to a certain multiple of the amount of gold held on reserve.

Misuse of their power to raise the discount rate led the Federal Reserve officials to precipitate the financial crash in 1929, but this tool is only used passively now because "open market operations" have superseded it in usefulness as a tool of monetary control.

Changes in Reserve Requirements: A second tool for implementing monetary policy is the Federal Reserve Board's power to change the level of legally required reserves that commercial banks must keep at district Federal Reserve Banks. By **lowering** the required reserve ratio from 16⅔ percent to 10 percent, for instance, the Board can stimulate an **increase** in the money supply. Why? Because commercial banks, since they are profit-seeking institutions, tend to lend up to the legal limit of their required reserve level. A legally required reserve level of 16⅔ percent means that one dollar of every six a bank has on deposit must be held on reserve at the Federal Reserve Bank, while a 10 percent reserve level requires only one dollar in ten to be held on reserve. A decrease in reserve requirements thus frees extra funds which the member-bank can loan out to increase its interest earnings. By **raising** the legally required level of reserves, the Federal Reserve Board can force banks to call in loans, thus serving to decrease the money supply. This tool of control is still actively used, but it is not utilized as frequently as in the past.

Open Market Operations: The third tool used for implementing monetary policy is by far the most important and the most used. It is the ability of the Federal Reserve Board to buy and sell government securities in the open market, thus the term "open market operations." Interestingly enough, this tool of monetary policy was not consciously planned by those who established the Federal Reserve System. Its potent effect as a policy tool was accidentally discovered in 1923, as we have already indicated, when the Federal Open Market Committee realized that its purchases of securities in the market had a short-term stimulating effect on business activity. Since that time, the open market operation (OMO) has become the primary tool of monetary control. While the Federal Open Market Committee limits itself to buying and selling U.S. government securities, this is a self-imposed limitation because they are easier to deal in. The same monetary effect can be gotten from buying and selling anything in the open market—wheat, cattle or even kitchen sinks if there were a market for them. U.S. government securities are ideal for the purpose because they have a wide market and can be easily cared for—thus, grains and cattle would not serve well as they are too bulky and require too much care.

Why has the open market operation become so important? Because on a daily basis the Open Market Committee can quietly and unobtrusively buy or sell an almost unlimited number of securities with the object of systematically inflating or deflating our country's money supply. Changes in monetary policy can even be changed from one moment to the next, if need be; though the manager of the open market "desk" usually receives broad policy orders which he follows on a two- or three-week basis. The manager is given a wide latitude of freedom to buy or sell securities in accordance with his instructions.

Remember that the Federal Reserve Board has unlimited power to create the checkbook money (demand deposits) it uses to purchase securities in the open market. The Federal Reserve Board did not always have such unlimited power. Why? Because the gold standard limited the amount of money in circulation to a multiple of the gold held on reserve by the Federal Reserve Bank. Gradually, the required gold reserve was lessened and finally eradicated entirely:

• In 1934 a 40 percent gold reserve was required on Federal Reserve Notes and 35 percent on demand deposits.

• In 1945 the required reserve was dropped to 25 percent on both Federal Reserve Notes and demand deposits.

• In 1965 the required reserve was dropped entirely for demand deposits.

• In 1968 the required reserve was dropped entirely for Federal Reserve Notes.

Since 1965 the Federal Reserve Board has had no restraints on its power to inflate the money supply via the creation of demand deposits, and since 1968 it has had no restraints on the amount of Federal Reserve Notes (paper money) that can be printed.

Theoretically, the Federal Reserve could create enough money to purchase the entire wealth of every person in these United States; but it could not do so, practically, because any attempt to do so would push prices sky high. In 1983 the amount of federal debt (U.S. government bonds or IOUs) owned by the Federal Reserve was approximately $155 billion.[4]

Power to influence the market rate of interest (this happens when buying and selling actions cause the price of bonds to rise or fall) as well as the power to increase or decrease the total supply of money in the economy (through the same open market operations) is an extremely powerful tool. It is a tool that can be used so quietly that the general public is not even aware of what is taking place when it happens. Federal Reserve data released a week or two later allows the public—the few who show an interest—to discover **after the fact** what monetary policy the Open Market Committee actually followed. A recent law requires the Federal Reserve Board to announce beforehand what monetary policy it intends to follow. This supposedly puts the people "on notice" of what to expect.

When securities are purchased in the open market, interest rates tend downward over the short run, and the money supply goes up. Why? Because the Federal Reserve open market manager's bid to buy bonds causes bond prices to rise. The rate of interest moves **inversely** with bond prices. Why is this so? Take an example: If a $1,000 bond pays 6 percent interest, it will generate $60 per year in interest. If the price is bid up to $1,500, the face amount printed on the bond remains the same; and so does the $60 paid in interest. The effective rate of interest on the market price of $1,500 falls to 4 percent. Selling bonds reverses the process. Bond prices fall and interest rates rise.

Just how does the purchase or sale of government securities raise and lower

---

[4]Federal Reserve Bank of St. Louis, *Monetary Trends,* December 1983, p. 13.

the money supply? It does so in this way: Suppose the Federal Open Market Committee purchases $1 million in U.S. government bonds. In exchange for the bonds received, the Federal Open Market Committee creates money by writing a check for $1 million and then gives it to the securities dealer who made the sale. The securities dealer then deposits this check at the commercial bank where he keeps his checking account. His commercial bank in turn deposits the check at its district Federal Reserve Bank, and the fractionally based money-creating process begins to work. The end result can be accurately envisioned. Imagine that the commercial bank deposits the entire $1 million as reserves at the district Reserve Bank. If the required reserve level allows an expansion of four, the purchase of $1 million of U.S. government securities by the Federal Reserve Bank's open market manager will increase the total money supply by four times, or a total of $4 million. This, indeed, is a powerful tool! Because the public chooses to hold about 20 percent of its money in currency, the average net expansion ratio is about 2.5 instead of 4.

Inflation and the Monetization of Government Debt

The average person has a difficult time understanding how deficit spending by the federal government brings about monetary inflation and thereby generates a persistent rise in the general price level. By now, we are equipped with the necessary knowledge to analyze this seemingly mysterious process.

In the third quarter of 1983, the total federal debt reached $1.4 trillion.[5] Those who held the debt on a given date are:

Government Agencies and Trusts	$232.9 billion
Private Investors	993.6 billion
Foreign Investors	163.7 billion
Federal Reserve Banks	154.6 billion

The government bonds held by the first three entities listed above are not inflationary. Why? Because the bonds purchased by these three entities were purchased with earned dollars and the bonds are held outside the banking system.[6] But the bonds held by the Federal Reserve Banks definitely are inflationary. Why? Because they were purchased with **created money**, and they are counted as official reserves which **provide a base for the multiple expansion of money** through the fractionally based banking system.

This is how the step by step process of inflating the money supply by monetizing government debt works:

---

[5]Ibid.

[6]This statement is almost true, but not absolutely. Why? Because it is possible that some government agencies used created dollars to purchase U.S. government bonds. Once new money has been injected into the economy, it is impossible to determine which dollars are "earned" and which are "created."

(1) Congress passes a bill to spend money the federal government does not have.

(2) When the bill becomes law, the Secretary of the Treasury is authorized to print U.S. government bonds to the extent of the deficit. Let us suppose this amount is $200 million.

(3) The Treasury will first attempt to sell the entire $200 million in the marketplace to private investors. If this can be done, no monetary inflation occurs from the transaction because the bonds are purchased with dollars the public has already earned. Let us suppose the Treasury sells only $100 million to savers and investors directly.

(4) The remaining $100 million of unsold bonds can be sold directly to the Federal Reserve Bank which purchases them with **unearned** money it simply creates by writing the figure "$100 million" in the Treasury's checking account. Up to this point, no monetary inflation has yet occurred as far as the economy is concerned.

(5) When the Treasury Department (or other agencies of the U.S. government to whom the Treasury Department has transferred some of the newly created money) starts spending money to purchase goods and services, the money is thereby **injected into the economy**. It is at this point that the first round of monetary inflation occurs – the money supply is increased by $100 million. The money does not have to be spent on goods or services. It may be given away as welfare payments, business and farm subsidies or other government spending programs. The important point is this: Various U.S. government agencies start writing checks on their Federal Reserve accounts and thereby inject the newly created money into the economy.

(6) Citizens who receive the new checkbook money either cash the checks or deposit part of them on their own checking accounts at private commercial banks. Generally, about 80 percent of the total money supply is held in checking accounts, as we have already indicated, with the remaining 20 percent being held as bills and coins.

(7) When commercial banks receive the newly created money as deposits, they in turn deposit the money on their checking account at their district Federal Reserve Bank.

(8) The process of money multiplication through the fractional reserve banking system, which we have already explained, begins.

(9) The resultant increase in the total money supply gives the people who are recipients of government spending more money with which to purchase the same amount of goods and services already in existence – which, naturally, do not increase just because more money has been created. These people start bidding prices up in their attempts to purchase what they desire.

(10) The general price level rises as a result.[7]

The problem is that the average citizen cannot understand this complicated and seemingly mysterious process, so he despairs of finding a solution. This leaves government officials free to inflate and spend and inflate and spend — always blaming the "problem of inflation" on others, usually on businessmen and unions.

A Biblical Perspective

The Federal Reserve Board has been instructed by Congress to achieve these incompatible goals:

(1) A stable price level
(2) Full employment
(3) A steady rate of economic growth
(4) A balance of international payments

From these goals, we can see that the Federal Reserve, in the more than seven decades of its existence, has changed from a passive service agency to the banking and business communities into an active agency of broad and powerful economic control.

As desirable as any one or all of the listed goals may be, the questions to be raised from a Christian viewpoint are these:

(1) Where in the Bible does God grant the agency of civil government such massive powers? This question is raised on the Bible's own claim that it is to be used as man's rule and guide to life in all aspects, including politics and economics (II Tim. 3:16-17). No aspect of our life, if the Bible is rightly understood, can escape this biblical scrutiny.
(2) Can such powers be safely entrusted to mere mortal rulers who also suffer from the bondage of sin (see I Chron. 21:1; Ps. 14:2-3; Ps. 58:3; Isa. 53:6; Rom. 3:10-12) and who do not have the infinite wisdom and knowledge that would be needed to effectively control the actions of others?
(3) Does the attempt by political rulers to minutely control the economy amount, in effect, to an indirect denial of the love and sovereignty of God in working out His plan for mankind and an attempt to build a humanistically based world order? (See Ps. 2:1-12; Ezek. 28:2-7.)

These are difficult, but very important, questions with which Christians must wrestle. How both Christian and non-Christian citizens answer them will

---

[7]The American Institute for Economic Research reports that bank failures in the Great Depression produced a total loss of $2.5 billion between 1929-1933, but that the loss in purchasing power of the dollar because of monetary inflation since World War II and up to about 1970 has produced a loss of $604 billion to the American public. Since 1970, the rate of monetary inflation has been increased even more rapidly because of huge deficits. See *What Would More Inflating Mean To You?* (Great Barrington, Mass.: AIER), p. 23.

have an important bearing on what role the civil authorities will or will not be allowed to play in manipulating and controlling the lives of God-responsible individuals. What must be remembered is that many so-called economic problems we see today may be nothing but judgments which God has laid on us for our failure to walk in His ways. That is, to put this principle in economic terms, current economic problems are nothing but effects brought about by a prior cause. The Christian economist must think in cause-effect patterns in order to uncover the earlier causes of effects discerned today. Then a normative judgment must be made in conjunction with biblical guidelines to discern how moral and ethical issues bear on the prior cause. More often than not, it will be seen that today's so-called economic problems are nothing more than the natural outworking of wrong moral and ethical decisions made in the past. We again come to the realization that we must take a holistic approach when studying economics — economics cannot be isolated from its underlying theological base. Remember this maxim: Good theology produces good moral and ethical decisions which in turn produce sound economics.

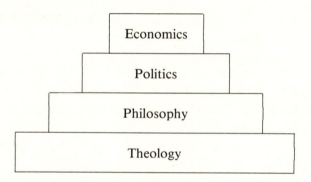

. . . O man, what is good; and what doth the Lord require of thee, but to do justly, and to love mercy, and to walk humbly with thy God?

Micah 6:8

But in the last days it shall come to pass, that the mountain of the house of the Lord shall be established in the top of the mountains, and it shall be exalted above the hills; and people shall flow unto it.

And many nations shall come, and say, Come, and let us go up to the mountain of the Lord, and to the house of the God of Jacob; and he will teach us of his ways, and we will walk in his paths: for the law shall go forth of Zion, and the word of the Lord from Jerusalem.

Micah 4:1-2

Questions

1. What is a financial intermediary? What is its primary function?

2. What two kinds of banks are there and how do they differ?

3. What is a "NOW" account? Is it money?

4. What is a demand deposit? Who can issue demand deposits?

5. What is meant by the terms "100-percent reserve basis" and "fractional reserve basis"? What institutions operate on each basis?

6. Can financial institutions create money? Explain.

7. What are commercial banks' preferred forms of earning assets? Why?

8. Explain how a fractional reserve system works in (a) a one-bank system and (b) a multi-bank system with a central bank.

9. What danger to economic and political freedom may arise when the civil authorities establish a central bank? Explain.

10. Assume a legal reserve ratio of 20 percent. What is the maximum potential expansion ratio of money relative to reserves held at the central bank? Is it likely that this maximum ratio will be reached in practice? Explain.

11. Why do civil governments establish central banks?

12. What two alternatives are available to bankers to ensure enough liquidity to pay off all depositors at all times? Which of the two alternatives is generally chosen? Why?

13. What is commercial paper?

14. How can a central bank help "solve" the problem of bank liquidity? What if all banks in the system are illiquid? Explain.

15. If bankers did not really want an "elastic currency" around the first decade of this century, what did they want? Explain.

16. Why did Americans of the 1900-1915 era not want a strong central bank? In what way is it accurate to say that the Federal Reserve System is a subterfuge, knowing what the people feared?

17. Distinguish between a republic and a unitary state. What is the source and direction of the flow of governmental power in each? Which system do you think is compatible/incompatible with having a central bank? Why?

18. In what respect is it correct/incorrect to say that member-banks own the Federal Reserve Bank in their Federal Reserve district? What does real ownership always connote?

19. Explain how discounting works at the Federal Reserve Bank.

20. How does Federal Reserve control over the rate of discount affect the money supply?

21. Where does the Federal Reserve Bank get the money it lends on collateral that member-banks give to it for discounting? Explain.

22. What limit is there to the Federal Reserve Board's power to create money through the discounting process?

23. Why do a minority of economists favor the gold standard?

24. Have Federal Reserve Board officials ever erred in judgment or misused their power to change the discount rate? If so, what were the results? Explain.

25. What monetary control tool has largely supplanted the use of changing the discount rate?

26. How can changes in the legal reserve requirement affect the total money supply?

27. Explain what the open market operation (OMO) is and how it is used to implement monetary policy.

28. When did the open market operation come into being? Why is it now the most important tool for implementing monetary policy?

29. Explain in detail what happens to interest rates, bond prices and the money supply when the open market operation buys/sells government securities in the marketplace.

30. Who owned the federal debt in 1983? What portion of it was/was not inflationary? Explain.

31. Explain in detail how government deficit spending leads to an increase in the money supply and thereby to a general increase in the level of prices.

32. Where does God grant the civil government authority to engage in monetary manipulation to achieve the four goals Congress instructed the Federal Reserve Board to attain?

33. What does the Bible have to say about entrusting power to fallible and sinful men? How much power are you willing, as a Christian, to have the Federal Reserve Board wield over you?

34. Discuss pro or con: The drive to implement monetary policy in order to "fine tune" the economy is an attack against God's sovereignty and His plan to allow men a wide degree of economic freedom in working out His plan.

10

Monetary and Fiscal Policy

*Then all the elders of Israel gathered themselves together, and
came to Samuel unto Ramah,*

*And said unto him . . . now make us a king to judge us like all
the nations.*

*. . . And the Lord said unto Samuel, Hearken unto the voice of
the people in all that they say unto thee: for they have not rejected
thee, but they have rejected me, that I should not reign over them.*

*. . . howbeit yet protest solemnly unto them, and shew them the
manner of the king that shall reign over them.*

*. . . And ye shall cry out in that day because of your king which
ye shall have chosen you; and the Lord will not hear you in that day.*

I Samuel 8:4-18

MONETARY policy refers to the attempt by rulers to achieve certain economic goals by increasing or decreasing the total money supply of a
country through banking institutions. This policy is usually implemented
through a central bank which holds commercial banks' legally required reserves. **Fiscal policy** refers to the attempts of civil governments to achieve similar economic goals through their taxing and spending power. In almost every
case, monetary and fiscal policy are used in conjunction with each other.[1]

The topic of monetary and fiscal policy is almost always treated by
economists on a purely positivistic basis, at least as far as the economists'
allow themselves to be objective. That is, economists accept the fact that civil
governments do indeed establish national policies concerning monetary and
fiscal matters. The economists simply describe **how** such policies are implemented through various tools of control. Such a positivistic approach
shortchanges the student of economics because it completely ignores some
very important normative issues of which the student should be aware. Also,
by accepting without question the status quo of civil rulers' intervention in the
economic affairs of citizens, a purely positivistic approach serves to imply
acceptance—that is, it gives the mistaken idea that no viable alternative other
than government control is workable. This is certainly **not** true. Before we investigate the matter of how monetary and fiscal policy are implemented, let us

---

[1]For a graphic presentation of monetary and fiscal policy see Tom Rose, *Economics: Principles
and Policy* (Milford, Mich.: Mott Media, 1977), pp. 216-217.

deal with the broader normative issue of whether or not the civil authorities should attempt to manipulate the overall economic activity of a country through monetary or fiscal policy. Doing this will provide us with a broader perspective from which to judge both the **idea** and the **effectiveness** of such manipulation.

Let us start by recognizing the status quo: It is impossible to escape the fact that the rulers of every nation in the world have both a responsibility and an authority for conducting the civil polity of their country. Refusal to recognize this fact would put us in opposition to the clear teaching of Scripture. It is also true that these same rulers have taken upon themselves an un-biblical responsibility to oversee the economic well-being of the people, for where in the Bible are civil rulers given such power? This is the status quo — this is the way things are. In recognizing "what is," let us also recognize that the grave responsibility of overseeing a people's economic welfare cannot be embraced without the rulers also grasping whatever powers they deem are needed to implement whatever national economic policies they happen to select. This raises some normative questions. It raises the important question of whether it is morally right, or even wise, for rulers to wield such grand power. The study of economics can perhaps answer the question of whether or not such a course is wise, but a person must turn to theology to determine its morality.

The implementation of such vast power to control an economy necessarily entails a shifting of economic decision-making from the people to their rulers. It entails a shift from decisions being made by widely dispersed individuals at many different points of purchase and production to government-controlled boards which centralize decision-making at the national level. Two normative questions arise for Christians to consider: One question has to do with **biblical** authority. The other question has to do with **constitutional** authority.

Is control of, or the power to directly influence, the economic activity of citizens a proper role of civil government from a biblical perspective? If Christians really believe that the Bible is God's revelation concerning not only salvation but also the moral principles on which to build a godly society, then the Bible can and should be resorted to for guidance in answering such a question. Nowhere does the Bible even suggest that power over the economic affairs of a people should be granted to the civil authorities. Contrariwise, the Bible clearly teaches that we should not put our trust in men (Ps. 118:8-9, 146:3-5). It also teaches that civil rulers have a tendency to rebel against God's moral law-system (Ps. 2:1-3) and that rulers invariably pervert the use of such power towards their own evil ends.

Is the idea of manipulative monetary and fiscal control by civil rulers in harmony with the Constitution of these United States, which established a **federal republic** made up of politically sovereign and independent states? Or has the present degree of centralized government control been unconstitutionally arrogated by rulers at the national level by their ignoring or misinterpreting the clear provisions of the Constitution?

What, for instance, did Article I, Section 8 of the Constitution mean to the founders of the American Republic?

> Congress shall have Power . . . to coin Money, regulate the Value thereof, and of foreign Coin, and fix the Standard of Weights and Measures; . . .[2]

Surely "regulate the value thereof" meant, at that time, to determine the amount of gold and silver content of coins, which thereby would serve indirectly to regulate their value relative to each other as well as to foreign coin. Can this clause be stretched to warrant the establishment of a central bank such as the Federal Reserve System, which attempts to "fine tune" the economy through constant monetary manipulation? Different people will, no doubt — as they already have — come up with different answers. Whatever answer a people as a whole arrive at, the choice will predetermine the kind of economic system and social institutions that result from following the implication of the answer.

Why do we digress from "pure economics" to make these points? We do so simply to show that the science of economics cannot be practiced in a test tube or a vacuum. The study of economics cannot be simply a positivistic science; economic systems and institutions are necessarily based on, and are the result of, normative theological and political presuppositions. In short, in our positive analysis of economic institutions and systems, we must always be aware of the normative framework within which our analysis is made.

Policy Goals

The broad economic goals that American civil rulers aim at on the national level are:

(1) to maintain a high level of employment,
(2) to maintain stable price levels,
(3) to promote rapid economic growth and
(4) to maintain equilibrium in our foreign balance of payments.

We raised the normative question as to whether rulers **ought** to be given the vast powers needed to achieve such policy goals through monetary and fiscal intervention and manipulation. Let us lay the normative issue aside at this time and raise the question of **how** the set goals might best be accomplished. Another practical question raised by the establishment of such broad goals as those listed above is upon what assumptions are the goals based? For instance, the proponents of government control fall into two broad categories:

---

[2]Alfred H. Kelly and Winfred A. Harbison, *The American Constitution; Its Origins and Development,* 5th ed. (New York: W. W. Norton, 1976), pp. 1053-1054.

monetarists and **fiscalists** (the latter are known as neo-Keynesians).

Monetarists generally feel that the policy goals stated above can best be achieved with the least overt interference in the economy by implementing the various tools of monetary policy discussed in the chapter on banking systems. These are: Changing the level of required reserves that commercial banks maintain at the central bank (Federal Reserve Bank), changing the discount rate and engaging in open market operations.

Monetarists claim that monetary policy is quick, efficient, impersonal and general. They point out that changes in the total money supply quickly pervade the whole economy from within a few weeks to a few months.

Fiscalists deny the monetarists' claim. They correctly point out that the effectiveness of monetary policy is dependent on **how** businessmen, bankers and the general public happen to react to monetary stimuli. From the fiscalists' viewpoint, monetary policy is not forceful enough. Fiscalists remind us that bankers held on to excess reserves during the Great Depression of the 1930s and that monetary policy may therefore prove to be ineffective in stimulating economic activity because of people's varying reactions, depending upon their particular circumstances. Therefore, since bankers and businessmen may choose **not** to respond to monetarily induced stimuli through the banking system as the rulers wish, fiscalists opt for a more direct means of stimulating the economy; that is, through the implementation of fiscal policy. If the civil authority taxes and spends, they say, the economy will respond more certainly than to monetary policy because the government has firm control over the public purse. By this statement the fiscalists mean that if the governing authorities directly engage in spending programs, the money thus spent will be positively injected into the economy and start circulating. Their complaint against monetary policy—which is implemented through the banking system by making excess reserves available to commercial bankers—is that profit-seeking bankers, for some unforeseen reason, might not use the excess reserves to extend loans to businessmen.

In one respect, both monetarists and fiscalists have a similar mind-set. Both groups agree that the civil rulers **should** attempt to influence and control the level of economic activity in a country. Their only point of disagreement is on **how** such control can best be applied.

Only a very small minority of economists take a free market or a hands-off approach as far as the government is concerned. The author is among this small group. The reasons for opposing government control or government intervention in the economy are varied. Opposition can be based on biblical principles, on ideological fears of oppressive governmental tyranny, or they can simply be based on pragmatic economic reasoning. Opposition on biblical principles is based on the view that the Bible limits the proper role of civil government in society to that of simply maintaining law and order so people can peacefully go about their private affairs (I Tim. 2:1-2). Those who oppose government intervention on ideological grounds point out that, historically, more people have been oppressed and enslaved by their **own** rulers than by foreign powers. The pragmatists argue from carefully reasoned economic logic that government intervention in the market place produces adverse economic effects which are counterproductive. The school of Austrain economists would be included in this last group. The author opposes government intervention for all three reasons: the biblical, the ideological and the pragmatic.

Fiscalists today are generally considered to be neo-Keynesians, that is, followers of the ideas popularized by the British economist John Maynard Keynes. His ideas were actually neither new nor radically different from the ideas held by some earlier economists, but Keynes happened to present them at a more politically opportune time. Also, he couched his ideas in terms that were politically attractive. These two facts—the opportune timing and the political attractiveness of his government interventionary ideas—account for Keynes' sudden widespread appeal. Professor Alvin Hansen, who became Keynes' strongest advocate in these United States has this to say about Keynes' *opus magnum, The General Theory of Employment Interest and Money:*

> The book under review is not a landmark in the sense that it lays the foundation for a "new economics.". . . The book is more a symptom of economic trends than a foundation stone upon which a science can be built.[3]

An economist will begin his analysis of economic problems or his building of economic models from different assumptions, which are an outgrowth of his underlying presuppositions or world-view of life. The rest of this chapter will be devoted to helping the student understand some different ways of looking at monetary and fiscal problems.

The Controlist vs. Non-Controlist Debate

The goals a person chooses and the means deemed appropriate for achieving them are largely determined by one's presuppositions. Now, presuppositions are ultimately a matter of faith, which produces a person's world-and-life view. It is one's world-and-life view which conditions one's insights, feelings or hunches rather than science. In short, the application of science is built upon a person's non-scientific presuppositional view of life and the world which surrounds him. In attempting to understand the on-going debates which divide one school of economics from another, it is important to gain an understanding of the presuppositional agreements and disagreements among economists.

Any economist who does not consciously attempt to understand economic

---

[3]Alvin Hansen, "Mr. Keynes on Underemployment Equlibrium," *Journal of Political Economy,* July 1936, p. 686 quoted in Bruce R. Bartlett, *The Keynesian Revolution Revisited,* Monetary Tract, no. 20 (Greenwich, Conn.: Committee for Monetary Research and Education, 1977), p. 11.

science in light of God's word is guided ultimately only by his own power of reason. By definition, such a person is technically a humanist; since a humanist is a person who allows his thoughts to supplant God's word. Obviously, the large majority of economists falls into this category. Certainly those economists who share the presuppositional views of the monetarists and neo-Keynesians would be so categorized. Neither group thinks in terms of what God's plan of economics might call for; therefore, they make no attempt to view economics relative to God's word. Both groups tend to think purely in positivistic terms and tend to overlook the moral and ethical aspects of the policies they recommend. It is only natural, then, that both schools of thought would tend toward the humanistic solution of imposing various forms of government control over the economy in attempting to build their Utopia. They just differ, as previously stated, over the **kind** of government control they claim is needed and **how** it should be applied.

The Neo-Keynesian Assumption

Neo-Keynesians start their reasoning from an economy that is assumed to be operating at less than full-employment, and they presuppose that the economy, if left to itself, is liable to stagnate. By this, they mean that the free market economy might well establish an equilibrium balance of supply and demand at a level of economic activity far below the so-called "full-employment" level. There is no inherent reason, they contend, for the economy to equilibrate naturally at the full-employment level. They see a need for the interventionary hand of the civil authorities to stimulate the economy whenever it falls short of the desired full-employment level. In order to avoid the "liquidity trap" that made government monetary policy ineffective during the Great Depression of the 1930s, neo-Keynesians say that a positive program of spending by the civil government through fiscal policy is needed.

Also, the Keynesian approach takes a "mild" view of money. By this we mean that they do not think the amount of money in circulation or the rate at which the money supply is being increased or decreased has very much impact on the economy. Just why they reason this way is explained in our discussion of the Keynesian Income-Expenditure Model. In recent years, the early Keynesian view that money does not matter at all has been softened to the point where more neo-Keynesians now admit that the total money supply does matter to a certain degree; but the quantity of money is still relatively unimportant to them until the latter stages of an economic boom.

Before going on, we might note that there is no general agreement among economists on what the so-called full-employment level actually is. Some economists regard it as being achieved with a 3-percent level of "frictional" unemployment. Others choose a 6-percent level of "frictional" unemployment. Frictional unemployment is defined as that level of unemployment which is "normal," for it simply reflects the normal on-going process of people quitting one job in order to take another or the normal process of being fired. Economists recognize that a certain level of unemployment is needed in a free labor market in order to allow people free movement from one job to another.

Note also that we have already referred to the "liquidity trap" of the 1930s without actually using the term. When the Federal Reserve finally did make additional reserves available to commercial banks in order to "reflate" the economy during the depression, bankers did not energetically move to expand loans to business firms. Neither did businessmen show great interest in borrowing to make job-creating capital investments. Monetarists explain the depression era liquidity trap by pointing to the perverse monetary policy bankers had experienced just previously at the hands of the Federal Reserve Board during 1929-1933. The Federal Reserve Board had held back in supplying needed credit to the banking system and thereby forced many banks into insolvency. Bankers, the monetarists explain, were simply taking careful precautions against getting caught in **another** liquidity crisis that might well have been brought on by a similar perverse action by the Federal Reserve. As for businessmen failing to borrow money to create new jobs during this period, the Austrian and other free market economists explain that businessmen had become worried about the bad business climate created by the socialistic policies that were increasingly being followed by the Roosevelt Administration. Except for these disturbing factors, a properly implemented monetary policy, they claim, would have worked.

The neo-Keynesian assumption of a stagnated economy stems from a view held by some of the early Classical economists (David Ricardo, Robert Malthus and Karl Marx, who is viewed by some as the last of the Classical economists). This view of a stagnated economy saw the free market economy as eventually reaching a point where markets would become glutted and the level of unemployment would become persistently high. John Maynard Keynes did not accept the glutted market view in the early 1920s, but he gradually came to accept it in the 1930s with the advent of the Great Depression and the resulting high level of unemployment among British labor union members. His view changed, no doubt, because of the strong role that labor unions played in the British economy.

Keynes saw that the British labor unions' insistence on wage levels that were above the free market level was what created such a persistently high level of unemployment in England. He also assumed the unions would not peacefully agree to a reduction in nominal money-wages, so he prescribed a different scheme. "Why not solve the problem of high unemployment," Keynes reasoned, "by allowing workers to retain their present **nominal** wages which admittedly are above the free market level, but gradually reduce their **real** wage level by engaging in deficit government spending? As newly created money is injected into the economy through various government spending programs," he reasoned, "the general price level will tend to rise. As price levels rise, the purchasing power of the existing wage will decrease in real terms because it will buy less and less."

Government control over the money supply could thus be used unobtrusively as a tool to insidiously debauch the purchasing power of wage earners' paychecks. As employers paid workers less and less in **real** terms relative to the prices employers received for the goods and services sold, the real cost of wages paid by employers would fall. Employers would then recall laid-off workers, and the rate of unemployment would subsequently fall.

Keynes believed that workers would surely strike and create widespread economic and political chaos and possibly bring an end to the capitalistic system if employers attempted to get unions to agree to widespread cuts in nominal wages. He reasoned that militant union members would have no one to strike against if their incomes gradually lost real purchasing power bit by bit. He also thought that laboring people would not even notice the gradual loss of purchasing power of the monetary unit.[4]

Keynes' scheme, of course, was a government-directed exercise in duplicity; and this is exactly why his plan was so politically appealing to bureaucrats and civil rulers. Keynes' scheme promised to relieve civil authorities from the unpleasant task of telling labor unions that they must stay within the boundaries of the law in case of strikes. In short, the civil rulers jumped at the chance of avoiding the nasty job of enforcing the law and punishing those workers and unions who might break the law in their coercive strike activities. Keynes' scheme promised an easy route of **seemingly** going along with the militant labor unions, but in reality the scheme was designed to surreptitiously cheat workers out of the wage gains they thought they had gotten through union activity. His prescription was based on the fragile assumption that economists call "money illusion"—that the public in general, and labor unions especially, remain unaware that the purchasing power of their wages is decreasing as a result of monetary inflation. This, in fact, turned out to be a very naive assumption; for the public rather quickly discovers such government duplicity. Labor unions usually lead the public in awareness, for they can hire well-trained economists to advise them on how to keep ahead of the game. Thus, a long-time trend of a recurring wage-price spiral is likely to ensue.

The basic dishonesty of this Keynesian approach is, of course, quite evident; and the evil economic effects produced by it are now evident in most economically advanced countries in the world. Remember the maxim introduced to you earlier in this text: Good theology produces good morals and ethics, which in turn produce good economics. Widespread economic problems are caused by wrong decisions based on wrong morals and ethics, which are in turn based on wrong theology.

Keynes' prescription of having the British government engage in deficit spending to stimulate employment (at that time it was called "reflating the

---

[4]John M. Keynes, *The General Theory of Employment, Interest and Money* (New York: Harcourt & Brace, 1936), pp. 9, 267-268.

economy") was specifically designed to combat the high unemployment problem of the 1930s. It was supposed to be only a **temporary** policy to solve a specific problem during a period of high unemployment. Keynes thought that he had enough political influence to induce Parliament to respond to different signals from him so that, at the time he deemed proper, the country could again turn to a non-inflationary monetary and fiscal policy. Political leaders in America warmly embraced the "new Keynesian economics" for the same reasons that British politicians did — Keynes' scheme promised a seemingly painless way of solving a knotty problem that was too unpleasant to approach straightforwardly. But once embraced, the practice — like an addictive drug — was too attractive to politicians to be easily set aside. The deficit spending concept, especially wrapped in such a deceptive package, proved to be an extremely sophisticated means of giving the people what they demanded without the unpleasantness of imposing higher taxes. Shortly before Keynes died in 1946, he repudiated the failure of governments to **stop** using his prescription, but his repudiation has received very little publicity.

The Monetarist Assumption

Monetarists start their reasoning from an economy that is assumed to be already operating at a full-employment equilibrium level. They make this assumption because they presuppose that the economy, if it is not interfered with, will naturally tend toward full-employment equilibrium. If, by chance, the economy happens not to be operating at the full-employment level, then this is *prima facie* evidence that some outside force — usually some coercive force such as the civil government or militant labor unions — is disturbing the economy and thus impeding its natural movement towards full-employment equilibrium. Therefore, say the monetarists, all that is necessary to restore economic order is to eliminate whatever force or forces are doing the disrupting. Free market economists, including the Austrian School, would be in general agreement with this assumption.

At this point, the focus of attention between the monetarists and neo-Keynesians shifts to labor unions, which both groups agree are one of the basic causes of continued high levels of unemployment.

The monetarist view is this: Labor unions use the threat of force to impose their higher-than-free-market wage demands on employers. This forceful action ultimately produces unemployment when consumers refuse to "validate" the unions' excessive wage demands through their purchases. Let the civil authorities do their duty by punishing anyone who imposes force on another, reason the monetarists, and then the militant unions would not be in a position to impose unrealistic wage demands on employers. Any union which succeeds in getting an employer to raise wages, beyond what consumers will allow him to recoup in the prices they pay, will have to endure the resulting unemployment until the union workers agree to accept lower wages. This, by the way, is a perfect picture of the underlying cause for the high levels of unemployment that unionized industries suffered during the 1980-1983 recession: steel, auto, rubber and others. Unions in these industries had forced wage levels to heights that consumers refused to validate by their purchases in the marketplace. This caused sales to plummet and unemployment to shoot upwards.

The neo-Keynesian view is this: Keynesians also recognize that high wages brought about by militant labor unions are the major cause of widespread unemployment. Because of unions' militant refusal to take wage cuts, wages tend to be "sticky" on the down-side. Wages can move upward during periods of high demand, but they cannot easily move downward during periods of slack demand. Keynesians reason that it is politically unrealistic to imagine that labor unions will ever agree to widespread reductions in wages in order to restore full-employment. Therefore, reason the Keynesians, let us accept this harsh reality and seek some other route to solve the unemployment problem. The easiest way to solve the problem, they recommend, is to have the national government stimulate the economy through large public expenditures of money financed through budget deficits. Doing this will "sop up" the existing high levels of unemployment. Full-employment equilibrium will be restored because the injection of government-created money into the economy will induce consumers to validate the higher prices employers must receive for their products in order to keep workers on the payroll. As a result of the new influx of government money into the economy, consumers will buy out the employers' previously accumulated inventories. As inventories drop, employers will call back laid-off workers, thus causing a return to full-employment equilibrium.

Free market economists are quick to point out the inherent duplicity and inequity involved in such a scheme. When the government validates the unions' excessive wage demands by creating new money to finance government spending programs, the resulting rise in prices is what saves union members from the folly of their own actions. While the unionists are able to pay the higher prices which result in the economy, there are many who cannot and who thereby suffer a reduced standard of living: the elderly on pensions as well as others living on fixed incomes. Finally, if the process of validation continues long enough, other economic maladjustments such as excessive consumption, reduced levels of capital investment and diverted streams of spending and malinvestments begin to occur.

The two contrasting views of how changes in the money supply affect the economy are shown in Charts 10:1 and 10:2. A comparison of the Keynesian Income-Expenditure Model with the Monetarist Cash Balance Approach will help us understand why the two groups are almost sure to recommend divergent policies to cure the problem of widespread unemployment.

The Keynesian Income-Expenditure Model

In their view of how money works in the economy, neo-Keynesians focus primarily on interest rates. They believe that an increase in the money supply will cause the market rate of interest to fall. This drop in interest rates will make job-creating investments more profitable for businessmen who will therefore decide to increase their investment expenditures. As more people are employed by the expanding business firms, consumption expenditures by workers will rise, and national income will also rise. Thus, **real** GNP will expand as the economy moves toward the full-employment level.

A graphic presentation of how neo-Keynesians view the outworking of increases or decreases in the money supply is shown in Chart 10:1.

Chart 10:1

Keynesian Income-Expenditure Model

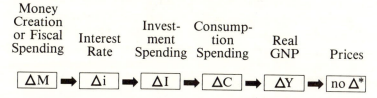

*Until full-employment is reached.

An easy way of remembering the step by step process envisioned by neo-Keynesians is to picture this abbreviated scheme:

$$\Delta M \Rightarrow \Delta i \Rightarrow \Delta I \Rightarrow \Delta C \Rightarrow \Delta Y$$

where:

$\Rightarrow$ = causes, brings about or leads to
Δ = change in
M = money supply
i = interest rates
I = capital investment by business firms
C = consumer spending (consumption expenditures)
Y = GNP = Gross National Product (the national production of goods and services in real terms)

In their view of how the economy reacts to government injections of money, neo-Keynesians assume that increases or decreases in the total money supply do **not** affect saving. They also assume that the first impetus of money injections is on business investment and only secondarily on consumer expenditures through what they call the "multiplier effect." Finally, they believe that an increase in the money supply will permanently reduce interest rates. This is the most important point to remember, because there would be no permanent increase in real GNP if interest rates rose later, for higher interest rates would serve to dampen business investment and thereby reduce the level of employment.

This illustration of how neo-Keynesians view money working in the economy helps us understand why they tend to recommend deficit spending to solve the problem of unemployment. If an increase in the money supply will permanently lower interest rates and serve to expand employment without causing prices to rise, then government spending programs are indeed the ideal solution to reaching a full-employment equilibrium. The only problem, as the neo-Keynesians see it, is to cut off government spending just before the economy reaches the estimated full-employment level, lest the economy become "overheated" and price levels begin to rise. It then becomes a practical question of "fine tuning" the economy in order not to "overshoot the mark." This is why the concept of fine tuning is inherent in the neo-Keynesian world-and-life view by implication. The economy must constantly be fine tuned in order that just the right amount of government spending can be implemented. In practice, of course, the attempt to fine tune the economy has not worked—the economy is too complicated and too diverse to be successfully manipulated by a group of centralized planners.

The Monetarist Cash Balance Approach

Monetarists focus primarily on what they call the real cash balances held by individuals and business firms. By real cash balance, they mean the purchasing power of a given cash balance expressed in terms of the real amount of goods and services it will purchase. If one's cash balance has increased by 10 percent but price levels have also gone up by the same percentage, then there has been no change in one's real cash balance.

Monetarists operate on the assumption that people feel comfortable with a certain real cash balance and that monetary disturbances which upset this status quo will make people feel uncomfortable, thereby inducing them to bring their portfolio of assets back to the desired balance. An injection of new money into the economy will cause money to flow into the pocketbooks of the public. They may decide to keep part of the increase, but the rest they will use to acquire other assets they value more highly than the extra cash received.

This cash-balance reaction applies to both the general public and businessmen. An increase in the money supply will directly produce an increase in consumer spending (instead of only indirectly as in the neo-Keynesian model) and will directly produce an increase in business investment (rather than working through the interest rate mechanism as in the neo-Keynesian model).

Monetarists assume that an increase in the money supply will have its first impact on consumer spending and that producers then respond to consumer spending by expanding their operations to produce the goods and services that consumers are demanding. It is primarily this response to consumer spending which brings about the increase in capital investment by business firms.

As far as interest rates are concerned, monetarists believe that an increase in the money supply will cause interest rates to fall in the short run. This is easy to understand. If interest rates are the result of the interaction of the supply of capital funds with the demand for capital funds, then an increase in the supply of funds will force interest rates downward. But eventually interest rates will start rising to compensate for prices which have also started rising. The increase in prices occurs because an increased number of dollars is chasing the same limited supply of goods; thus, prices are bid upwards. Because people will come to expect prices to continue rising, they will discount future rises in price levels by requiring an interest rate premium when extending loans to borrowers. An extra premium in interest is demanded by lenders in an inflationary era to compensate for the loss in purchasing power they will experience when borrowers later repay their loans—each dollar received a year later will buy less in real goods and services. Interest rates will rise in the long run, and this rise in interest rates will serve to dampen new capital investments by business firms. The high cost of interest will cause business entrepreneurs to defer some capital expenditures. Thus, in the long run, the economy will not expand in real terms, and total employment will not go up as in the Keynesian model. The only long run effect of increasing the money supply will be an increase in the general price level. A graphic presentation of how monetarists view money working in the economy is shown in Chart 10:2.

Chart 10:2

Monetarist Cash Balance Approach

Money Creation	Real Cash Balances	Spending (Consumer and Business Investment)	Prices
ΔM	ΔCB	$\Delta (C+I)$	$\Delta P*$

*When price levels rise, real cash balances will fall back to their original level because the larger nominal balances will buy no more in real terms than smaller balances bought at lower prices.

The monetarist view of cause and effect can be shortened into this scheme:

$$\Delta M \Rightarrow \Delta CB \Rightarrow \Delta D \Rightarrow \Delta P$$

where:

M = money
CB = real cash balances held by the public
D = demand = (C + I)
P = general price level
Δ = change in

Problems of Fine Tuning

It was just a small step for the followers of Keynes to progress from the idea of stimulating the economy through government deficit spending to the idea of attempting to "fine tune" the economy by "reflating" it during periods of slack demand and "deflating" it during periods of excessive demand. This, after all, is exactly what Keynes hoped to do through his influence with the British Parliament on a "hip pocket" basis. But when the practice of fine tuning is resorted to, some practical problems soon appear. It is one thing to theorize about reflating and deflating the economy in order to smooth out business cycles, but it is another thing to know exactly where the economy is in the business cycle at any given moment, to know exactly what contra-cyclical steps should be taken and to know exactly how much stimulation or dampening should take place. Furthermore, different sectors of the economy may respond differently to the same general monetary or fiscal stimuli, thus responses are certain to be erratic.

In addition to the problem of discerning where the economy is, what steps to take, when to take them, how different sectors may or may not respond and how much to inflate or deflate, there are additional problems. Every business cycle is somewhat unique in that its component impetuses vary from cycle to cycle. What worked last time (and there are always conflicting opinions as to whether or not certain policies actually **did** work) might not work next time. Or, to state it differently, the policy which failed to work in one instance might also fail to work in another. For instance, there is still an on-going debate about whether or not the famed tax cut of Congress in 1964 accomplished what it was designed to accomplish. Neo-Keynesians say that it did; monetarists and free market economists claim that it did not. The neo-Keynesians point to the total GNP which the tax cut supposedly generated, while critics point to the rising price level which subsequently occurred and which they predicted would occur. Another fine tuning argument revolves around the "mini-recession" that was produced in 1970 when the Federal

Reserve Board suddenly reversed in 1969 the expansive monetary policy it had been following for a number of years.

Free market economists complain that neither monetary nor fiscal policy has helped but has actually hurt by causing the economy to become more unstable than it would be in the absence of artificial stimulation.

Critics of fiscal policy say it is too cumbersome to implement because fiscal policy involves congressional action which is very time consuming, unpredictable and always political. A desired spending program may possibly come "on stream" long after it is needed. The spending it generates may come at a time when the economy is already in a period of full-employment. If so, hyperinflation may occur. Perhaps the prize example of fiscal policy delay is the St. Louis Gateway Arch located on the waterfront next to the Mississippi River. The idea of building the 630-foot stainless steel arch was concocted by a Scandinavian architect during the Great Depression of the 1930s as a "make work" program. It was authorized by Congress after repeated delays and was finally completed in 1967!

Critics of monetary policy claim that the record of the monetary "experts" is none too good either because their actions have been bumbling and have therefore affected the economy adversely. The critics remind the money managers of their biggest fiasco, the perverse monetary policy followed by the Federal Reserve Board in 1929-1933. The Federal Reserve money managers have finally admitted their error, but they count it as one of the "costs of learning." Then the critics point to other miscalculations such as the sudden money contraction of 1969. Another is the miscalculation that produced the "credit crunch" which occurred in 1973-1974. It would be better, claim the critics, if the authorities would stop trying to manipulate the economy at all and just let it stabilize so private entrepreneurs and bankers can do their own planning free from the disturbing influence of unpredictable monetary manipulations by governmental authorities.

Another problem of fine tuning the economy is that there are conflicting opinions as to what full-employment really is, as we have already indicated. Such conflicts can lead to contrasting assumptions and, therefore, to contrasting policy recommendations. An example of this conflict was brought to light in a study by Citibank of New York.[5] Citibank assumed a "natural" level of unemployment of 3.5 percent in the study while the President's Council of Economic Advisors (CEA) assumed a 6-percent level of unemployment. Because of their differing assumptions as to what constitutes full-employment, the two entities arrived at contrasting policy recommendations. Citibank's version of full-employment led to the conclusion that the economy had been consistently overstimulated from 1970 to 1978, except for a brief period between 1974-1976. The CEA's version concluded that the economy needed almost constant stimulation since 1970 to bring it up to full-employment except for a

---

[5]Citibank, *Monthly Economic Letter,* July 1978, p. 13.

brief moment in 1973. Who is right? The fact that the general price level rose by 63 percent from 1970 to 1978, an average of 7 percent per year, would indicate that the economy truly had been overstimulated. For, a sustained rise in the general price level over a period of years is almost always the result of new money having been consistently injected into the economy.

This synopsis gives us only a brief insight into the many problems that policy-makers face when they attempt to become the people's caretakers in the economic arena. The humanistic drive to control others in order to remake the world in man's image is so strong that politicians and bureaucrats move from one failure to another in the midst of criticism and countercriticism. The fiscalists and monetarists argue with each other, as well as among themselves, as to whose particular policies work or do not work. Someone is constantly coming forward with a "new plan" which he promises will do a better job. In the midst of all these claims and counterclaims stand the too-few free market economists who insist that **any** kind of government control will produce adverse effects which will be counterproductive.

Tools of Fiscal Policy

The tools used by governing authorities in attempting to control the overall level of economic activity are, first, specific taxing and spending programs which must be passed by Congress and, second, so-called "automatic stabilizers."

Specific Taxing and Spending Programs: Whenever Congress passes a bill to increase or decrease taxes or to initiate new "job-creating" or spending programs, it is implementing **fiscal policy** through its power to tax and spend. Spending programs may also be financed by deficit spending through the creation of new money. To the extent that new money is created and injected into the economy to finance its spending programs, Congress engages in a combination of fiscal and monetary policy. This is why we mentioned earlier that most government spending programs use a combination of the two policies.

Let us digress for a moment. Unless there is some mysterious "magic" in the taxing and spending process or in the money-creating process, it is, of course, impossible to really create new jobs through such government programs. All that happens when the civil authority taxes and spends is this: There is a net transfer of jobs from the private sector to the public sector, or there is a redistribution of jobs in the private sector in response to the rechannelled money-flows that government spending induces. There can be no net gain in output or in employment. Actually, there will most likely be a net decrease in output if we assume (and many years of history support this assumption) that government production is less efficient than private production.

Automatic Stabilizers: There are certain long-term programs which are regarded as "automatic stabilizers." These are programs such as:

(1) the graduated income tax
(2) social security
(3) unemployment compensation

These are called automatic stabilizers because they operate contra-cyclically to offset the major trend of incomes. As incomes rise, people move into higher income tax brackets; and more income is siphoned off into government coffers. The same effect occurs with social security and unemployment compensation. As more people are employed, the total amount of money siphoned off into the social security and unemployment compensation funds increases. When incomes fall as a result of people being laid off, the monies "accumulated" in these funds are supposed to be paid out.

If these additional tax revenues were indeed accumulated and not immediately recycled back into the economy, the previously listed government programs would indeed tend to serve as contra-cyclical forces. But in reality, the monies that are siphoned off are almost immediately reinjected into the economy. Thus, it is doubtful that these government programs really serve effectively as automatic stabilizers at all.

The greatest criticism of relying on specific taxing and spending programs for evening-out the ups and downs of business cycles is the extreme variableness in time between their introduction as bills before Congress and their final implementation (remember the St. Louis Gateway Arch, which was designed in the 1930s but not built until the late 1960s). To solve this problem neo-Keynesians have pushed the idea of having a number of standby programs that could be automatically implemented when the level of unemployment reaches a predetermined level. They claim that such standby programs would help alleviate the long lag-times between government's recognition of a problem and getting geared up politically and economically to solve it.

Tools of Monetary Policy

The tools of monetary policy have already been discussed to some degree in the chapter entitled The Banking System. Our objective here is to focus on the **impact** caused by applying various tools of monetary policy, while our discussion in the earlier chapter focused on the **process** of implementation. The three primary instruments of monetary control are:

(1) changes in the discount rate that banks must pay when borrowing reserves from the Federal Reserve Bank.
(2) changes in the percentage of reserves that banks are required by law to keep on deposit at the Federal Reserve Bank.
(3) open market operations.

Changes in the Discount Rate: Changes in the discount rate are implemented by each Federal Reserve Bank in the district it serves, subject to approval by the Federal Reserve Board in Washington, D.C. Such changes generally follow the market rather than lead the market rate of interest. Each district Federal Reserve Bank adjusts to the interest rate in its specific area, but this rate quickly tends to stabilize countrywide; otherwise massive flows of money would occur from one part of the country to another as lenders sought the highest rate of interest available.

The discount rate can be used to stimulate or to dampen the economy by making it less costly or more costly for commercial bankers to acquire additional reserves to expand loans. Perhaps the greatest effect caused by changing the discount rate is the psychological impact the change has on businessmen. A change in the rate serves as an open public announcement to both bankers and businessmen that the availability of money is becoming "looser" or "tighter." Businessmen are thus psychologically predisposed to expand or contract business investments because they are able to discern the trend of interest rates. The same applies to bankers who are the intermediaries who create the funds loaned to business firms.

Changes in the Legal Reserve Requirement: Changes in the legal reserve requirement are implemented by the Federal Reserve Board in Washington, D.C., for the nation as a whole. This action tends to have somewhat of a "sledgehammer" impact, and it affects every bank's reserve position directly. The real and psychological impact is even greater than changes in the discount rate. Because of its great shock effect, this tool is used sparingly.

Open Market Operations: The least obtrusive and most insidious tool of monetary policy is the buying and selling of government securities in the open market by the Federal Open Market Committee (FOMC), which is physically located at the Federal Reserve Bank in New York City. This tool can be used to inflate or deflate the economy with practically no public notice at the time of implementation. The open market operation (OMO) has come to be the most-used tool for implementing monetary policy. As you remember, the purchase of government securities serves to inject money into the economy because the Federal Reserve Bank actually creates new money with which to make its purchases. On the other hand, the sale of securities serves to withdraw money from the economy because purchasers of the securities pay the Federal Reserve Bank with earned dollars, which are thus taken out of circulation, and which the Federal Reserve Bank then destroys by bookkeeping entries. In order to understand how the Federal Reserve can inflate and deflate the supply of money through the OMO, it is necessary to always bear in mind that the Federal Reserve Bank has an open-ended power, that is, unlimited power, to create new money by simply making bookkeeping entries on its records and exchanging these entries for whatever it buys. Money can be destroyed by simply reversing the process.

When the Federal Reserve Bank increases or decreases the total supply of money through its OMO, it has a direct impact on the real cash balances held by every citizen in these United States as well as the dollar-value of all assets owned by the public. Few citizens realize the great impact that such a quiet operation as the OMO has on their economic status. If citizens did realize what great impact the OMO has on their day-to-day economic health, it is doubtful that they would allow such power to be wielded by either the Federal Reserve authorities or by the government itself. It is a power that has been abused in the past, which abuse has generated unwanted cyclical abberations; and this power is certain to be abused again and again in the future, to the detriment of both the liberty of the people and the economic health of the country.

An International Perspective

We have already pointed out that the drive of civil rulers to fine tune the economy stems from a humanistically based drive to control others and to remake the world according to unregenerate man's image of what the world should be. This drive leads to ever-increasing levels of taxation and, finally, to massive inflation of the money supply when rulers persist in spending more money than the people are willing to pay in taxes. As a result of such monetary inflation, price levels start spiraling upward.

This domestic process of deficit government spending spills over into the international arena very quickly because each country is tied to every other country through international trade. A country that engages in massive deficit spending will first experience a rise in domestic price levels. Then it will experience a flood of imports as its citizens turn to lower-priced foreign products. This, in turn, produces a short-term drop in domestic employment because, when the public buys a higher percentage of imported goods, domestic employers lay off workers as sales drop. Reduced sales is the public's way of disemploying workers and managers in firms whose production costs have gotten too high relative to foreign producers. Usually unionized industries such as auto and steel are hardest hit by falling employment because their unions have aggressively pushed wages higher whenever the opportunity arose.

Since no ruler has political power to reach individuals and firms in foreign countries, rulers compensate by imposing restrictions on their own citizens in order to solve economic problems. The final outcome is that the rulers of countries which have followed inflationary policies soon take steps to cut off the free flow of imports which they wrongly blame for the problem of rising unemployment. They do this either through import controls or by raising tariff levels to protect domestic industries. Sometimes cooperative arrangements to control imports are reached between the rulers of various countries through "voluntary" quotas such as the agreement between these United States and Japan to limit importation of Japanese autos. In any case, the real objective rulers have in mind is to restrict the free flow of goods and to insulate their country's economy from the full force of foreign competition so that the rulers can have a free hand in implementing whatever domestic monetary and fiscal

Table 10:1

Destruction of Paper Money
1950-1978

Country	Percentage decline in purchasing power	Country	Percentage decline in purchasing power
Chile	99	Norway	78
Argentina	99	Sweden	78
Uruguay	99	Philippines	78
Brazil	99	Ecuador	78
Bolivia	99	Pakistan	77
Indonesia	99	Nepal	76
Viet Nam	99	India	75
S. Korea	99	S. Africa	75
Israel	98	Austria	75
Paraguay	98	Morocco	74
Iceland	98	Thailand	73
Peru	96	Netherlands	73
Ghana	96	Syria	70
Turkey	96	Costa Rica	70
Colombia	96	Burma	69
Yugoslavia	92	Belgium	66
Taiwan	91	El Salvador	66
Spain	89	Tunisia	66
Mexico	88	Canada	66
Finland	84	Dom. Republic	63
Ireland	84	United States	63
Iran	83	Haiti	63
Portugal	83	Egypt	62
United Kingdom	82	Switzerland	59
Greece	82	Guatemala	58
New Zealand	82	Iraq	58
Japan	82	Sri Lanka	57
Sudan	81	W. Germany	57
Italy	81	Venezuela	54
France	80	Malaysia	50
Denmark	80	Panama	47
Australia	80		

Source: H. F. Langenberg, *Fall Notes,* 1980, p. 15. (The statistics were given in the June 27, 1980, seminar at the Hotel Pierre in New York by Dr. Franz Pick.)

policies they desire. In short, political rulers want to rule the market just as they want to rule the people instead of being subservient to them. This is what the deadly serious game of politics is all about: Does the civil government exist to serve the people, or do the people exist to serve the political rulers?

The situation that results from such "economic insulation" from foreign competition is called **autarky**. That is, the rulers of each country seek autocratic control over their citizens without having to fear interference from outside competitive influences. In seeking autarky, the rulers' desire is to have a country that is economically self-sufficient with themselves in control. A country that has a government-issued fiat money, rather than a gold- or silver-based money in the hands of the public, can easily be insulated by the rulers from competitive forces originating in other countries. The rulers become relatively free from discipline which might be imposed either by their own people domestically or by foreigners, and they end up having a free hand to inflate and inflate as they strive to build their earthly Utopia. The extent to which rulers all over the world have destroyed the purchasing power of fiat monetary units can be seen in Table 10:1.

A Biblical Perspective

A biblical perspective concerning the power that civil rulers now wield in implementing monetary and fiscal policy to manipulate and control citizens can be gained by a diligent search of the Scriptures. The author suggests that you search the Scriptures to determine answers to these questions:

(1) What is the proper role of civil government in society? (See: I Tim. 2:1-2; Rom. 13:3-4; I Pet. 2:13-17.)

(2) Do rulers have a tendency to become tyrannical and to rebel against God's lawful order? (See: I Sam. 8:9 & 18; I Kings 21:1-17; Ps. 2:1-3; Isaiah 1:21-23; Acts 5:28-29; Eph. 6:11-12.)

(3) Does man have a sinful nature? Is there a danger of trusting in the authority of man over man instead of in God's mercy and providential care? (See: II Sam. 24:1-14; I Chron. 21:1; Ps. 118:8; Jer. 17:5-9.)

(4) Is God sovereign over the economic sphere of man's life? Does God have the ability to bring about His will through the voluntary and mutual cooperation of individuals who stand free and self-responsible before Him? (See: Ex. 8:1; I Chron. 29:11-12; Eccles. 5:19; Jer. 17:10-11; Jer. 18:6.)

(5) How can the love of God be translated into love for our fellowmen? What does this imply in a free society? (See: Matt. 22:37-40.)

(6) Where in God's word are civil rulers ever given power to interfere in the economic life of citizens? Where is even a hint of such power given? Can it be that civil rulers who arrogate power to themselves to

control prices — even in periods of emergency — or to engage in manip-ulative fiscal and monetary policies are in rebellion against God's law? (See: II Kings 6:24-33; II Kings 7:1-16.)

Many other Bible verses could be suggested for the student to investigate, but the above list will serve as a starter.

Humanists who insist on maintaining a dichotomy between the positive and normative spheres of economics would ask, "What does the Bible have to do with economics?" Christian economists believe that the Bible provides the moral and ethical foundation upon which a godly economic system can be built. (Deut. 5:29; Ps. 33:12.) Any other system will be faulty in its basis and immoral in its operation and will ultimately produce widespread social dishar-mony and economic chaos.

One Christian economist has this to say:

> Because God is supreme and sovereign, His divine norms and standards of justice, truth, goodness, beauty, mercy and love must have the final control and motivation in everything the Christian thinks, wills and does. These norms rather than those of an apostate political, legal and economic science must become the directives by which the Christian is guided as a citizen, as a worker, as a teacher, as a businessman and as a parent; and they alone must constantly enlighten him or her in solving the problems with which he or she is faced in **all** areas of life.
>
> . . . If Christians in America accept the neutralist principle, not only will Christ's cause go by default but also Christians themselves will inevitably become traitors to God's Kingdom. In fact, all that is now necessary for the complete triumph of apostate secular human-ism in the United States and its attendant revolutionary conse-quences is for Christians in America to sit back in their church pews, sing hymns and do absolutely nothing outside in the workaday world of business, education, labor and politics.
>
> We must seek to show the tremendous relevance of the Biblical view of man-in-society for American politics and economic life. Our Lord is giving us an opportunity to study through the economic and political implications of our discipleship. Let us then pray that the Holy Spirit will guide us into a further and deeper understanding of the unsearchable riches that are in Christ Jesus our Savior and let us pray that we may be determined to make Christ's Kingship real in every aspect of our lives. As the Lord of history and of space and time, Jesus Christ can be satisfied with nothing less than the Chris-tian reformation of American society as a whole, and it therefore becomes our bounden duty and glorious privilege as His disciples to struggle for a condition of modern society which will give the max-imum opportunity for all Americans to live a full, free and more

abundant life. We are to make sure that we are never controlled by an apostate and rebellious world, but that we might control that world in the strength and power of our mighty God.[6]

To this statement dedicated Christians can only say, "Amen!"

Questions

1. "The implementation of monetary and fiscal policy as a means of influencing the people's economic activity is beyond the proper role of the civil authorities." Attack or defend this statement:
   (a) from a biblical standpoint, citing appropriate passages.
   (b) from a constitutional standpoint, citing appropriate clauses.

2. List the four broad economic goals that have been set up as policy goals by the U.S. Congress. What specific powers do you think are needed by civil rulers to achieve these goals? Which powers would you grant to the rulers: (a) willingly? (b) reluctantly? (c) not at all?

3. What criticisms do neo-Keynesians levy against monetary policy? What criticisms do monetarists levy against fiscal policy? Evaluate their claims and counterclaims and state your view point from your perspective as:
   (a) a government bureaucrat.
   (b) a citizen.

4. What is the "full-employment" level?

5. What is "frictional" unemployment?

6. What is the "liquidity trap" that was supposed to have occurred during the Great Depression of the 1930s? Why do you think the "liquidity trap" occurred?

7. Describe and evaluate J. M. Keynes' view of the unemployment problem in Britain and the cure he prescribed. Would you recommend the same cure or another? Explain.

8. What practical problems do policy-makers face once they decide to embark on "fine tuning" the economy?

9. Contrast the assumptions and views held by neo-Keynesians and monetarists concerning:
   (a) the economy.
   (b) "full employment."

---

[6]E. L. Hebden Taylor, *The Great Myth in Politics* (Memphis: Christian Studies Center, n.d.), pp. 8-10.

(c) labor unions.

(d) the role of government in the economy.

(e) the solution to the problem of unemployment.

10. Contrast how neo-Keynesians and monetarists view the working of money in the economy.

11. Graphically depict how money works in the economy according to the Keynesian Income-Expenditure Model vs. the Monetarist Cash Balance Approach.

12. Both neo-Keynesians and monetarists are government-interventionist-minded. Explain.

13. What key factor causes neo-Keynesians and monetarists to disagree on the long-term effect of increases in the money supply?

14. Is it possible for the civil authorities to create jobs? Explain.

15. What are "automatic stabilizers"? Do they really stabilize the economy? Explain.

16. List the three tools for implementing monetary policy and discuss their impact.

17. Describe what happens when a country's rulers persist in following a long-term inflationary policy.

18. Examine the "Destruction of Paper Money (1950-1978)" tally of world currencies.

    (a) In how many countries has the purchasing power of money lost 50 percent or more of its purchasing power?

    (b) What lesson do you learn from this observation?

19. What do you think is a proper biblical perspective concerning the role of civil government in society? Relate this to the current practice of civil rulers' implementing monetary and fiscal policy to "fine tune" the economy. Search the Scriptures in developing your answer. Write a one-page summary and discuss it with others who may hold different views. Take care to cite appropriate Bible passages.

11

International Trade

*And say unto Tyrus, O thou that art situate at the entry of the
sea, which art a merchant of the people for many isles, . . .*
*. . . Tarshish was thy merchant by reason of the multitude of all
kind of riches; with silver, iron, tin, and lead, they traded in thy
fairs.*
*. . . Syria was thy merchant by reason of the multitude of the
waves of thy making: they occupied in thy fairs with emeralds, pur-
ple, and broidered work, and fine linen, and coral, and agate.*

Ezekiel 27:3, 12, 16

I F we view the world from a **political** perspective, we see it divided into approximately 170 separate nations. Each nation views itself as politically sovereign and independent from all other nations. Each is capable of exerting
political authority (hegemony) over the people within its borders.

If we view the world from an **economic** perspective, we see that it is not
naturally divisible into isolated compartments as appears on a political map.
Rather, the world is an economic whole. It is a "one-world market" in which
economic relationships are interdependent, even across political boundaries.
The world consists of some 4.5 billion self-interested individuals who are constantly and busily engaged in producing and consuming the diverse range of
goods and services needed, not simply to exist, but also to enjoy the bountiful
blessings of their God-given freedom. World population is expanding at the
rate of about 1.7 percent per year. Man, if not inhibited by an outside force,
will naturally seek to maximize his own economic welfare by purchasing as
cheaply as he can and by selling as dearly as he can. There is nothing inherently evil in this tendency, it is just an economic outworking of man's nature as
created by God. Man's tendency to higgle and haggle to gain personal benefit
should not be squelched; rather, it should be fostered, for voluntary trade
leaves each trading partner better off after the trade than before.

An Overview of World Trade

The principle of voluntary trade is the same whether it takes place between a
man and his next-door neighbor or between a man and his "neighbor" who
lives in the next town, the next county or in a distant country on the other side

of the earth. In each instance, the parties to the trade are voluntary participants who seek a personal gain through mutually beneficial exchange.

These United States contain some 6 percent of the world's population and about 7 percent of the earth's land area. In the recent past, we have produced and consumed about 30 percent of the world's output of goods and services. Critics of free market capitalism have a habit of attempting to generate a feeling of mass guilt by pointing out that Americans consume such a large percentage of wealth. But note that we **produce** as well as consume this percentage. ("For the scripture saith, Thou shalt not muzzle the ox that treadeth out the corn. And, The labourer is worthy of his reward," I Timothy 5:18.) The people of these United States supply approximately 15 percent of the world's exports and about 20 percent of the world's manufactured goods. In 1980 American farmers produced 22.6 percent of the world's grain but accounted for 58.2 percent of all grain exports.[1] Truly, America has become the world's bread basket. Thus, the degree of economic freedom enjoyed in these United States of America has been a real blessing to people all over the world! America has served as a dynamic market for raw products produced in distant lands as well as a ready source for the machinery, equipment and technology that people in other lands so sorely need to improve their own standards of living.

Tables 11:1 and 11:2 indicate the role played by these United States in foreign trade and their dependence on it.

Table 11:1

U.S. International Transactions
(Billions of dollars)

Year	Merchandise Exports	Merchandise Imports	Service Exports	Service Imports	Current Account Balance	Direct Investment Abroad	Direct Investment in U.S.
1960	19.7	14.8	9.2	9.0	2.8	2.9	.3
1965	26.5	21.5	14.6	11.3	5.4	5.0	.4
1970	42.5	39.9	23.2	20.2	2.3	7.6	1.5
1975	107.1	98.0	48.6	34.8	18.3	14.2	2.6
1980	224.0	249.3	120.7	84.6	3.7	18.5	10.9
1981	236.3	264.1	136.6	97.7	4.5	8.7	21.3
1982	211.1	247.3	139.0	103.0	-8.1	-2.2	9.4

Source: Federal Reserve Bank of St. Louis, *International Economic Conditions*, 22 January 1982, p. 7 and 21 April 1983, p. 6.

---

[1]U.S. Dept. of Agriculture.

Table 11:2

World Trade
(1977 Estimates)

American Exports (as a percentage of
U.S. Production):

Soybeans	60%
Oil-field Machinery	51
Wheat	44
Cotton	41
Construction Machinery & Equip.	39
Metal-forming Machinery	35
Tobacco	32
Computers	28
Corn	27
Agricultural Chemicals	26
Mining Machinery	20
Photographic Equip. & Supplies	16

American Imports (as a percentage of
U.S. Consumption):

Diamonds	100%
Chromium	89
Tin	86
Nickel	70
Gold	60
Shoes	49
Petroleum	43
Iron Ore	33
Color TV Sets	30
Autos	25
Steel	18
Aluminum	8

Source: U.S. Dept. of Commerce and U.S. Dept. of Agriculture.

Expanding Investment Across National Borders

By 1965 direct investment overseas by Americans had reached a total of $49.5 billion; and by 1980 it had grown to $212.6 billion. During the same period, total direct investment in these United States by foreigners had grown from $8.8 to $61.3 billion.

In 1977 foreign-owned firms in these United States had sales of $181.8 billion. They employed 1.1 million Americans (about 2 percent of the non-financial work force) and paid wages of $17.5 billion. Foreign-controlled firms accounted for 20 percent of U.S. exports and 28 percent of U.S. imports.

The above data indicate the growing mutual economic dependence of the peoples of the world. There is an old saying in support of free trade among nations which goes like this: "The people of the world have two alternatives. Either freely traded goods and services will be sent across political boundaries, or bombs and bullets will." The data in Table 11:3 indicate the source and destination of investment funds in these United States at the beginning of 1980.

Table 11:3

Source of Funds (billions)		*Where Funds Are Invested* (billions)	
Netherlands	$12.5	Retail/Wholesale Trade	$11.2
Great Britain	9.4	Petroleum	9.9
Canada	7.0	Chemicals	7.1
W. Germany	5.0	Financial	3.7
Japan	3.4	Insurance	3.5
Switzerland	3.3	Machinery	3.3
Netherlands Antilles	3.3	Metal Products	3.0
France	2.2	Food Products	2.6
Belgium/Luxembourg	1.7	Real Estate	1.6
Sweden	1.2	Other	6.4
Panama	.6		

Source: U.S. Dept. of Commerce.

The Principle of Trade

The economics of international trade may seem complicated because of the fact that different currencies are involved. In truth, the principle of mutually beneficial trade is the same whether such trade takes place between citizens of the same country or between citizens of different countries. In both instances, each party seeks to maximize his well-being by giving something he values less to get something he values more. The end goal of engaging in voluntary trade, though we ususally do not stop to consider the point, is to be able to enjoy more of the good things of life than if each individual tried to be 100 percent self-sufficient. This fact holds for individual persons, and it also holds for individual countries.

In order to clarify the principle of trade, let us focus our attention on two individuals in the same locale. Then we will separate them with an artificial political barrier which will necessitate the use of different currencies. By doing this, we will remove the "mystery" of international trade by showing that the **principle** of free trade does not change just because the trading partners live in different countries which use different currencies.

The Principles of Absolute Advantage and Comparative Advantage: Suppose you have two friends, Ken and Ben. Both go into business producing two commodities: wheat and high-quality stereo sets. Suppose, also, that each devotes 50 percent of his time in producing each commodity. After one year their total production looks like this:

	Wheat	*Stereos*
Ken	40,000 bu.	40 units
Ben	10,000 bu.	30 units
Total	50,000 bu.	70 units

We can see that Ken is more productive in both lines of endeavor. He has what economists call an **absolute advantage** in producing both wheat and stereos. In wheat, Ken can out-produce Ben by 4:1 (or by 300 percent), and in stereos by 4:3 (or by 33⅓ percent).

Suppose that Ken and Ben consider the possibility of trading with each other with the hope of boosting their production. If they come to us for advice, what should we tell them? Should we say that, since Ken has an absolute advantage in producing **both** wheat and stereos, it would be to his benefit to "go it alone"? If we should give this kind of advice, we would make a grave error, for it certainly is to Ken's and Ben's mutual advantage to trade with each other.

On what basis do we say this? We say it because of what economists call the **principle of comparative advantage**, which is a universal principle. This principle holds that, even though one producer may have an absolute advantage in producing both commodities, he has a comparative advantage in producing only one of them **if** the relative cost ratios of producing the commodities differ between the two persons. (Read that again! and then continue.)

Here is a formal statement of the principle of **comparative advantage**: Total output will be maximized when each person specializes in producing what he can produce with the greatest comparative advantage or the least comparative disadvantage. Another way of stating this principle is: A gain in total output is possible from specialization if the cost ratios of producing two commodities are comparatively **unequal** between two persons.

Take a preview of what is to come: The principle of comparative advantage, when applied to countries, reads almost the same as when applied to individuals. A gain in total output is possible from specialization if the cost ratios of producing two commodities are comparatively unequal between two countries. We have used Ken and Ben, who are individuals instead of countries, because we believe the principle can be grasped more easily this way. But the principle remains the same whether it is applied to persons, firms or countries. Total output will be maximized when the people in each country specialize in what they can produce with the greatest comparative advantage or the least comparative disadvantage.

At this point in our discussion, let us make an important point just to make sure we really understand the difference between absolute and comparative advantage. In determining absolute advantage, we compared Ken's production of wheat with Ben's production of wheat; and we compared Ken's production of stereos with Ben's production of stereos. We did this before when we stated that Ken outproduced Ben on a 4:1 ratio in wheat and on a 4:3 ratio in stereos.

But in calculating their relative comparative advantages, we do not compare wheat with wheat and stereos with stereos. Rather, we first note Ken's cost of producing stereos in terms of his **own** production of wheat; second, we note Ben's cost of producing stereos in terms of his **own** production of wheat. Then we compare each person's cost ratio of stereos in terms of wheat with the other person's.

	Wheat	*Stereos*		*Comparative Cost Ratio*
Ken	40,000 Bu.	40 units	=	1,000 : 1
Ben	10,000 Bu.	30 units	=	333 : 1

We see here that Ken's cost of producing one stereo is 1,000 bushels of wheat, while Ben's cost is only 333⅓ bushels. Apparently, we have turned an absolute disadvantage on Ben's part into a comparative advantage! Is this not interesting? It sheds a whole new light on the situation by opening up an avenue for mutually beneficial exchange. Even though Ben is at an absolute disadvantage in producing either commodity when compared to Ken, he has a relative advantage in producing stereos because his own cost of producing stereos in terms of wheat is less.

As already indicated, we can expand this into a general principle of trade and economic cooperation. Individuals, firms and even countries will find it mutually beneficial to cooperate with each other in the specialization of effort as long as their comparative cost ratios of production between goods are unequal.

After shifting their production in order to specialize in the line where each has a relative or comparative cost advantage (Ken would shift into wheat, and Ben would shift into stereos), the new arrangement would look like this:

	Wheat	*Stereos*
Ken	70,000 bu.	10 units
Ben	0	60 units
Total	70,000 bu.	70 units

By the simple process of allowing each to specialize in what is relatively less costly for him to produce, total production has been increased with no additional input of labor. The end result of specialization is a net increase of 20,000 bushels of wheat which Ken and Ben can divide according to agreement. The important point to make is that the practice of free trade has increased total output through specialization of effort.

We cannot resist at this point to glorify our great God and Creator for His wonderful works to the children of men (Psalm 107:8). If each person — and therefore each aggregate of persons in business firms and nations — were identical and equal in their abilities, gifts and interests, there would be no need nor opportunity for men to engage in mutually beneficial trade and economic cooperation. But, praise God, He has created each person as a unique individual with distinct and unequal capabilities and interests! Thus, mutual economic cooperation is both possible and beneficial among men because of their diversity. It is this built-in **inequality** which makes economic systems, such as Christ's church, dynamic organisms. There is a worthwhile economic role for each person to play in God's scheme of voluntary economic cooperation — the scheme we call the free enterprise system. The principle of comparative economic advantage ultimately rests on the diversity of gifts that God gives to individuals. Economically, the principle is the same as the diversity of spiritual gifts Paul speaks of in I Corinthians 12. We can go one step further: Since voluntary exchange is based on the unique gifts God has bestowed on mankind, free trade should always be fostered and never squelched by civil rulers. This holds for free trade between individuals within the same country or between citizens of different nations. Governments which restrict free trade serve to suppress the natural outworking of God's rich gifts to mankind.

Now let us imagine that Ken and Ben live across the road from each other, and let us draw a line down the center of the road to indicate an international boundary between two countries. By doing so we have suddenly internationalized their trading arrangement. But creation of a political boundary does not change the economics of their relationship. The only surface change is that if Ken and Ben use money instead of barter, then their monetary units will be called by different names and will have different values (dollar, pound, franc, peso, yen, etc.). This will then make it necessary for them to engage in what is called foreign exchange.

Foreign Exchange

When two individuals or firms located in different countries want to buy or sell to each other, they cannot transact business without engaging in what is called foreign exchange. The reason is obvious. The currency of each country generally circulates only within its own political borders. American dollars do not generally circulate in Britain, and German marks do not generally circulate in France.

In some instances, the currency of one country will be accepted by a few merchants in another country; for example, merchants who sell to tourists. But foreign currency does not circulate generally. Rather, it is taken to a local bank which then converts it into local currency for the merchant. The bank then uses established banking connections to deposit the foreign currency at an overseas branch of a bank from the country that issued the original currency. American tourists' dollars spent in France, for instance, are quickly deposited in an American bank with offices in France. The French bank that accepted the American currency in exchange for French currency then ends up owning a deposit of dollars in the branch of an American bank located in France. These dollar deposits are called **Eurodollars,** a term used to designate dollars on deposit in any foreign country in the world. Deposits of one country's currency at a bank in another country (for example, Italian lira deposited in Switzerland) are called **Eurocurrency.**

When an American consumer purchases an automobile from Japan his dollars are not actually sent overseas. What happens is this: (1) The American consumer pays dollars to his local auto dealer. (2) The dealer then deposits the money at his own bank. (3) The order for the auto is sent overseas, but the dollar-denominated check which the auto dealer writes for the order is sent to an American bank which has a branch in Japan. This bank accepts the dollar-denominated check and then credits the dollar amount to the account of the foreign manufacturer located in Japan. Thus, a foreign business firm becomes the owner of dollar deposits in the American bank. (As we indicated above, the overseas ownership of American dollar deposits anywhere in the world are called Eurodollars.) The only thing that has happened is that ownership of the dollar deposit has changed from a U.S. citizen to a firm in Japan.

Banks that do not have a foreign banking connection for the currency being traded use the services of foreign exchange dealers who specialize in trading foreign currencies, but this does not change the basic process described. Modern foreign exchange dealers perform the same service today that money-changers provided to foreign visitors in biblical times: When Jews who lived in foreign countries journeyed to Jerusalem to visit the temple, their currency was changed into local currency. Today most transactions are done by transferring bank entries instead of physically exchanging coins.

There is only one place where American dollars will be generally accepted in exchange for goods and services, and that is in these United States. The payments of American consumers for imports generate demand for exports from our country. The people of one country cannot long continue to buy the products of another country unless its citizens reciprocate by using their accumulating currency credits to purchase imports from the first country. Foreign trade is indeed a two-way street.

Let us take an example so we can understand the concept of foreign exchange. First, let us define the term. **Foreign exchange** is simply the trading of one currency for another. If we assume that one U.S. dollar is worth two German marks, then this foreign exchange ratio can be defined in two ways: either as dollars worth a certain number of marks or as marks worth a certain number of dollars.

U.S. dollar = two marks
German mark = 50 cents

This, in effect, is no different than saying that a ladies' blouse is worth $20 or that a dollar is worth one-twentieth of a ladies' blouse. We usually do not use the latter expression, for we are in the habit of valuing things in terms of money. But while Americans are in the habit of mentally valuing everything in terms of dollars, Germans are used to valuing things in terms of marks.

Graph 11:1

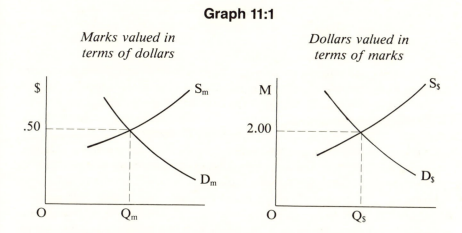

Note the typical demand-supply curves shown in Graph 11:1. This is because the demand-supply forces are exactly as explained in micro-economics textbooks.[2] When dollars are used to buy marks in the foreign exchange market, two things occur: First, the demand for marks increases; that is, the demand curve for marks moves to the right. Second, the supply of dollars increases; that is, the supply curve for dollars moves to the right. (See Graph 11:2.)

What happens to the existing foreign exchange rate of 50 cents per mark when Americans purchase more goods from Germany than Germans purchase from us? If we remember that only marks can be spent in Germany, it becomes clear that Americans must purchase marks on the foreign exchange market. The price-effect of this process is shown in Graph 11:2.

---

[2]See Tom Rose, "Demand, Supply and Prices," in *Economics: Principles and Policy* (Milford, Mich.: Mott Media, 1977), pp. 223-276.

Graph 11:2

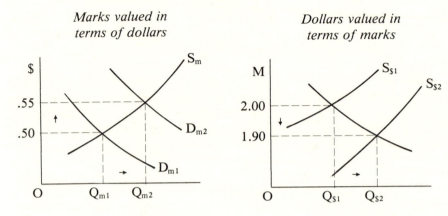

Marks valued in terms of dollars

Dollars valued in terms of marks

What really happens in the previous transactions is this: Americans, on a net basis, exchange ownership of dollar-deposits for mark-deposits. The exchange is made at whatever exchange ratio (price) happens to exist between the two currencies at the moment. Net purchases of marks will increase the demand for marks, thereby causing the price (exchange ratio) of marks, expressed in terms of dollars, to rise. Since the purchases are made with dollars, this causes the supply of dollars to increase on the exchange market, thereby causing the price (exchange ratio) of dollars in terms of marks to fall.

Day-to-day changes in foreign exchange rates are usually very slight — varying from a fraction of a cent to a few cents. If the demand for marks (supply of dollars) is great, the price of marks in terms of dollars rises; thus, we say that the mark has appreciated in value while the dollar has depreciated in value. We can see from Graph 11:2 that if the price of the mark rises by 10 percent the price of the dollar falls commensurately.

Flexible vs. Fixed Exchange Rates: When one country's currency appreciates relative to another, this means that its products become more expensive in terms of the depreciated currency. There is, therefore, a decrease in demand for goods from the country whose currency has appreciated. Over the last number of years, the German mark and Japanese yen generally appreciated in value relative to the American dollar. And, as the prices of German- and Japanese-made autos rose in terms of dollars, some American consumers who would otherwise have bought these foreign autos refrained from doing so.

Civil rulers, in their humanistic drive to control every aspect of men's lives — as already indicated in the chapter entitled Monetary and Fiscal Policy — often intervene in foreign exchange markets in order to "stabilize" foreign exchange rates. Illogically, rulers often develop a sense of national pride in the price of their country's currency on the foreign exchange market. But their usual motive in interfering is generally more pragmatic: They want to be free to follow an inflationary monetary policy internally in their own country without being affected by competitive pressures from foreign countries. So, the rulers buy or sell currencies on the foreign exchange market to maintain a **fixed** rate—that is, they freeze the price of their currency vis-à-vis other currencies.

What rulers attempt to do in maintaining a fixed exchange rate is to buy or sell currencies in the market so as to keep the exchange ratio for their own currency within a very narrow range of fluctuation. If we take the previous example of the American dollar and the German mark where the price of the mark was rising in terms of dollars, the German central bank could buy American dollars with marks. This would increase the supply of marks in the foreign exchange market, thereby bidding up the price of dollars in terms of marks. Another way the same objective could be reached would be for the U.S. Federal Reserve Bank to sell some of its holdings of marks to buy back dollars. This offsetting action is limited in effectiveness because the Federal Reserve Bank's holding of marks is limited. Once the fund of marks is depleted, the monetary authorities would be forced to either devalue the dollar or to let it float. That is, the fixed exchange rate would be lowered so that a dollar would buy fewer marks at the official rate, or the fixed rate would be abandoned entirely. In this latter situation, the government would not intervene in the foreign exchange market at all; and the various prices of currencies would settle at their free market level.

One argument extended in favor of fixed exchange rates is that it allows businessmen to engage in foreign trade without running the risk of losing money in case the exchange rate should change between the time businessmen place orders or receive orders for goods and the contracted date of delivery. The time lag between order placement and receipt of goods may take a number of months, depending on the commodity involved. However, this is a rather specious argument; for businessmen can take adequate precautions against unexpected changes in foreign exchange rates by "buying or selling forward." What this means is that a businessman can offset a **future** sale or purchase of goods by purchasing or selling **today** the right to purchase or sell foreign exchange at a future date at today's price. The only cost involved is the relatively small premium paid for such "forward" contracts.

Sometimes the complaint is lodged that the cost of buying forward can be substantial if foreign exchange rates are especially volatile, and this is true. But, if governments would not create instability in the foreign exchange market by engaging in deficit spending or by attempting to "stabilize" the market through massive purchases and sales of currencies, then there is no reason to expect the exchange rate to be volatile; for price movements would generally tend to occur in small increments and thereby move smoothly. In short, instability—when it does occur—is most likely to be the result of government manipulation. A manipulated market tends to be unstable, while a freely fluctuating market tends to be relatively stable.

The possibility of non-government-induced price changes raises another issue. There admittedly is more risk in doing business across national boundaries. Both the political and economic risk are greater because the domestic businessman is not familiar with political and economic happenings in distant lands. Who, then, should shoulder this extra risk of engaging in foreign trade? Should the business firm which freely chooses to engage in foreign trade as a means of increasing profits (which is certainly a legitimate goal) bear the additional risk? Or should the general public, who are the ones that ultimately pay the cost of guaranteeing fixed exchange rates through their country's central bank, bear the additional risk? The point on which to focus is this: There most certainly is an extra cost involved when one chooses to engage in foreign trade. Either this extra cost must be built into the cost structure of the firm's foreign trade business, or it must be paid for by the general public.

One practical argument against fixed exchange rates is that so-called "fixed" exchange rates are not really fixed at all. Rather, they are only temporarily "pegged" by political fiat until prevailing economic and political pressures force the monetary authorities to establish a new set of "fixed" rates. Then the new rate is only temporary as well. Such changes in official exchange rates always involve arbitrary judgments and a high degree of political consideration as well as secrecy, lest the monetary authorities "tip their hand" in advance to speculators who deal in foreign exchange. The average citizen is usually uninformed, and even more sophisticated people may also be unwary of what is going on. The uninitiated tend to be caught off guard and thereby suffer losses when government authorities unexpectedly announce a new official exchange rate. When the official exchange rate for the U.S. dollar was suddenly pegged at a different level in the early 1970s, for instance, a number of American firms with international operations were caught off-guard. Some of these firms experienced windfall profits or losses, depending on whether they were net holders of American dollar-deposits or of foreign currency-deposits. From this we see that the power of political authorities to alter foreign exchange rates by fiat can impose unexpected gains or losses on the public. How much better it is for companies and individuals to recognize existing uncertainties at the beginning so adequate precautions can be taken through the privately operated futures market in advance. Such timely planning would allow businessmen to count necessary costs by buying forward. Such a practice would enhance wise planning instead of short-circuiting the best laid plans through arbitrary actions of monetary authorities. ("For which of you, intending to build a tower, sitteth not down first, and counteth the cost, whether he have sufficient to finish it?" Luke 14:28.)

The Impact of Monetary Inflation: In a world of free and uncontrolled markets, long-continued balance of payments problems are not at all likely to occur. Why not? Because if the people of one country start accumulating currency credits of another country, two reactions set in: First, people in the accumulating country will naturally tend to use their accumulated credits to purchase imports from, or to make investments in, the deficit country. Secondly, prices will fall in the deficit country because its people are purchasing goods from overseas instead of from domestic suppliers. Falling price levels will tend to speed up purchases by foreigners, especially by those who live in the surplus nation. Therefore, equilibrium will be quickly restored.

If the deficit country and the surplus country have a flexible exchange rate between their currencies, a depreciation of the deficit country's currency vis-à-vis that of the surplus country is what makes prices sink lower in the deficit country in terms of the surplus country's currency. But if the monetary authorities of the two countries maintain a fixed exchange rate — meaning that the monetary authorities stand ready to interfere in the foreign exchange market — the needed price adjustments can be delayed for as long as the deficit country has holdings of foreign currency to sell. But the day of reckoning must finally come if imports continue greater than exports. The longer the needed adjustment is delayed, the more drastic it will be when the adjustment finally occurs.

We must understand one thing: It is usually not an imbalance of trade, in and of itself, that causes one country to continue for long periods of time in a chronic deficit position. Rather, it is usually the domestic monetary policy that the political rulers follow which causes the deficit position. What we are saying is this: If one country continues a long time in a deficit position, we should look, not at the buying habits of the people (in that they seem to prefer foreign goods to domestic goods); but we should suspect that the monetary authorities have been following an inflationary policy and that the resultant increase in the domestic money supply is what has caused domestic prices to rise vis-à-vis foreign prices. It is this government-induced price differential which motivates citizens of the deficit country to seek lower-priced goods from overseas. The people, in effect, seek to protect themselves from rising price levels by purchasing lower-priced foreign goods.

To make sure we understand, let us examine how the whole process works: Initially, civil rulers follow a domestic inflationary monetary policy because they want to spend more money than they receive in taxes. This monetary inflation causes domestic prices to rise relative to the price of foreign goods. The public then turns to purchasing lower-priced foreign goods. This causes an outflow of ownership claims on the domestic currency. The foreign exchange rate would rise, except that the deficit country's central bank intervenes in the exchange market to keep the price of foreign exchange at the "pegged" rate. The political rulers are thereby able to continue their inflationary course domestically as long as their central bank has enough ownership claims on foreign currency to keep offsetting the imminent price adjustment in the exchange market, or as long as the central banks of surplus nations are willing to keep lending their currencies, or as long as borrowings of currency can be made from some international institution such as the International Monetary Fund (IMF).

It was finally the breakdown of all these alternatives which forced these United States off a pegged or fixed exchange rate and onto a flexible or floating exchange rate in the early 1970s. As long as these United States were on a pegged rate, American political rulers had to choose between stopping their present inflationary policy — and they refused this choice — or devaluing the American dollar. The latter choice was resorted to twice — once in 1971, and again in 1973. Finally, the decision was made in 1973 to let the American dollar float against other currencies. American civil authorities continued an even more inflationary policy since that time, with the predictable result of soaring domestic prices. The prices of foreign goods also rose as the American dollar depreciated in value in the foreign exchange market.

The Question of Oil Imports

Some economists and politicians who favor a continued inflationary policy contend that the underlying cause of America's chronic imbalance of payments and rising domestic price levels in the recent past is not excessive money creation. They claim, rather, that the cause was an increase in domestic production costs brought about by the Arab oil cartel, the Organization of Petroleum Exporting Nations (OPEC). They claim it was the resulting outflow of dollars, which represented business costs that had to be recouped, that caused domestic price levels to rise. They claim it was this outflow of "petro dollars" that caused the chronic balance of payments deficits.

Upon first consideration, this argument appears to be a plausible explanation. Certainly it shifts the blame for rising prices from domestic policymakers to foreigners. But two facts contradict this view: First, the OPEC nations rechannelled their dollar-claims to these United States in the form of orders for goods, direct investments and the purchase of securities. Between 1970 and 1980, the annual rate of foreign investment in our country rose from $1.5 billion to $13.7 billion.[3] Second, both Germany and Japan import more oil as a percentage of their GNP than our country, and these two countries had chronic surpluses after OPEC became effective rather than the chronic deficits in foreign trade we experienced. So, the explanation for chronic balance of payments deficits must lie elsewhere. The comparative percentage of oil imports from 1970 to 1977 is shown in Table 11:4.

---

[3]Federal Reserve Bank of St. Louis, *International Economic Conditions*, Annual edition: June 1983, p. 4.

Table 11:4

Total Oil Imports
(as a percent of GNP)

	1970	1971	1972	1973	1974	1975	1976	1977
U.S.	.3%	.3%	.4%	.6%	1.7%	1.6%	1.8%	2.2%
Germany	1.3	1.5	1.3	1.6	3.3	2.8	3.1	2.9
Japan	1.1	1.3	1.3	1.5	4.2	4.0	3.8	3.4

Source: Federal Reserve Bank of St. Louis, *Review*, August 1978, p. 3.

The Gold Standard

During the greater part of the nineteenth and the early twentieth centuries, most countries were on what was called the international gold standard. This means that each country designated the value of its currency in terms of gold (by weight) and stood ready at all times to redeem it for gold upon demand.

If the people in one country increased their imports, they could do so only as long as their gold supply lasted or if they could convince people in the net-exporting nations to loan or invest their export earnings in the net-importing nation. Gold itself was not usually shipped between countries, for it is expensive and risky to do this. It was merely the ownership of gold claims that was transferred from the people of one nation to those of another. The price of gold varied between buyers in one country and sellers in another by only one or two percent to account for the transportation cost of shipping gold. This spread in price was known as "gold points."

The gold standard worked excellently as long as the rulers of each country were willing to abide by the simple "rules of the game." These were:

(1) Currency must be readily convertible into gold upon demand.
(2) Domestic price levels and the level of employment must be allowed to fluctuate in response to the competitive pressures of world trade.

The rules of the game, in effect, required the civil rulers to take a "hands-off" or a non-interventionary policy regarding their domestic economies. Rulers were to keep the peace and nothing more. Their role was to let the people be free to serve each other by engaging in profit-seeking trade and economic activity within their borders or across the political boundaries which divide nation from nation.

During the gold standard era, the rulers of most countries generally did follow a non-interventionary economic policy. World trade and economic activity in individual countries responded accordingly. A never-before-experienced era of general economic growth and prosperity occurred all over the world. It was also an era of general international peace, for mutual trade tends to unite countries via common interests. Remember the old saying referred to earlier: Either economic goods will cross national boundaries, or armies will.

However, civil rulers did not remain willing to adhere to the rules of the international gold standard. Doing so conflicted with their own political aspirations which included winning and keeping the political support of their citizens by vote-capturing deficit spending programs.

As long as civil governments were required by terms of the gold standard to pay out gold upon demand in exchange for currency they issued, the amount of new money political authorities were able to create was very limited. It was limited to a certain multiple of the gold held as official monetary reserves. The total world supply of gold increased only about 2 percent per year on the average as new gold was mined. It was this conflict—the desire of political authorities to create and spend new money versus the built-in protection the gold standard provided citizens by guaranteeing the gold-content of their currency—which led political leaders the world-over to sabotage and eventually repudiate the gold standard.

World War I afforded civil rulers a convenient excuse to go off the gold standard. After the war, a number of countries returned to a quasi-gold standard (called the gold-exchange standard). The rulers, however, persisted in interfering in their economies during the 1920s. We have already explained how Federal Reserve officials inflated the money supply in these United States in order to help Britain return to a quasi-gold standard in 1924. It was this long-continued inflationary policy which set the stage for the financial crash in the fall of 1929. (See the chapter supplement entitled "All About Gold" at the end of Chapter 6.) By 1933, in the depths of the Great Depression, most major countries had left the gold standard entirely so they could "reflate" their economies without fear that their citizens would take newly created money to the banks in exchange for gold. In summary, the gold standard imposed a noninflationary monetary policy on civil rulers. They just were not willing to endure such a healthy discipline, so they sabotaged the system. Today many uninformed people fear a return to the historic gold standard, which guarantees the people's right to cash in paper dollars and receive gold coins in exchange, because the people have been wrongly told that the gold standard did not prevent the 1929 crash and the subsequent depression. But in truth, the countries of the world did **not** return to the historic gold standard after World War I. Instead, the leading countries of the world adopted the gold-exchange standard at a conference in Genoa, Italy, in 1922. This quasi-gold standard allowed monetary inflation to occur between 1924-1929, which, in turn culminated in the financial crash of 1929.

Arguments for Protection

There are a number of arguments which can be given in favor of protecting firms in a domestic economy against the rigors of foreign competition by imposing high tariffs or import restrictions. Most of these arguments are espoused by persons who have a vested interest in the protective policy being suggested. By "protecting the domestic economy," the partisans of protection usually mean having the government protect that segment of the economy in which they have a particular interest.

The "Infant Industry" Argument: One of the most persuasive arguments favoring protection from foreign competitors is the cry for "temporary" protection to give a new industry time to get on its feet. Afterwards, the new industry can supposedly compete effectively with foreign producers. American history is replete with such demands. These infant United States provided English manufacturers with a vast market for their goods. The growing manufacturing industries in the northeastern part of our country clamored for protection against the flood of "low-priced" goods from England. Higher tariffs, of course, would ultimately be paid by the people in the agricultural west and south in the form of higher prices for the protected domestic products. An early sectional contest developed in our young Republic, and this contest has continued into present times.

The problem with the "infant industry" argument is that so-called infant industries never seem able to grow up to adulthood and become independent. In the eyes of each producer in the protected industry, the need for protection seems to persist. Also, protected industries are slow to adjust to new methods of production because the lack of competition does not force them to modernize as quickly as non-protected industries.

The "National Self-Sufficiency" Argument: Perhaps a less partisan argument for protection can be made by those industries which supply arms and other goods necessary for national defense. (Is it not interesting that pro-protection arguments are always advanced by the industries concerned?) The argument goes like this: "It is necessary to subsidize or protect certain key industries today in order to assure a domestic supply of war material tomorrow in case of war, for we certainly do not want to be dependent on foreign suppliers for armaments, do we?"

One response is that existing manufacturing plants can be converted to wartime production very quickly if the desire to do so is there. The rapidity of such changeovers during World War II was surprising to everyone concerned. Most developed nations have a wide range of diversified industry which can provide the necessary base for such changeovers.

Another response against the self-sufficiency argument, more on the philosophical side, is that the rulers of any one nation may be more reluctant to involve their citizens in the terrors of war if their nation is economically dependent on foreign suppliers. Some European nations which are dependent on foreign sources for many strategic materials—Switzerland is the outstanding example—have long followed a conscious neutralist policy with great success.

The "Diversified Economy" Argument: Another argument in favor of protectionism is that a country, if not insulated from international competition, will tend to specialize in only a few major commodities because it is more efficient in producing them. The argument is that the resulting specialization will make the nation subject to wide economic swings that it cannot control because its economy will be too dependent on foreign markets. Therefore, continues the argument, it is good insurance to subsidize and protect certain domestic industries in order to provide the country with a broader base to promote economic stability.

This argument is similar to the two prior arguments in that the protected industries always seem to need continued protection. And, because the seeming need for protection never ends, the increased costs to consumers never end either.

The "Favorable Balance of Trade" Argument: This argument contends that protection is needed to insure a country's "favorable balance" of trade. A country's trade balance is said to be "favorable" if its total exports exceed total imports. Its balance is "unfavorable" if imports are greater than exports.

This argument is a holdover from the Mercantile Age (1500-1800) when a more or less continuous state of war existed between the major European nations (mainly England, France, Spain and Holland). Each mercantile nation tried to be self-sufficient because it was on a continual war footing. Trade was regarded, not as being mutually beneficial to the trading parties, but as a win-lose proposition in which one trading party bested the other. The national goal of mercantile nations was to amass as large a cache of gold and silver as possible in order to help finance military and commercial ventures against enemy nations.

In reality, a nation that has what is considered to be a favorable balance of trade (whose exports exceed imports) accepts claims on the currency of the foreign nations to which it exports. The exporting nation receives these claims in exchange for real wealth it has sent overseas as exports. From a real economic wealth basis, we might ask how receiving IOUs in exchange for shipping out real wealth can be considered favorable! For many years, from the early 1600s to the late 1800s, these United States of America generally had an unfavorable balance of trade. We continued for many decades to receive more real wealth in the form of imports than we shipped overseas as exports. The difference was made up by claims on wealth (IOUs, bonds, stock certificates, etc.) which were held by foreigners, mostly in England, but also in France and Holland.

In short, our present capital base was largely built on European capital that we borrowed in the past. Europeans were willing to invest their export earnings in America because our laws insured the safety of property and because they expected to earn large profits on their investments or high interest on their loans. Every other less-developed country in the world today must also go through the same "unfavorable" balance of trade process unless its people wish to go through the more painful and tedious process of generating capital out of their own savings. Building capital out of domestic savings alone is a foolish and needlessly difficult process if capital can be had on more favorable terms from more developed countries. In a free market situation, such international borrowing and investment will naturally occur to the mutual benefit of all concerned. All that is needed is that the governments of less-developed countries follow a laissez faire policy.

The "Protect Our Home Industry" and the "Protect Our High Wage Level" Arguments: The arguments to protect our home industry and our high wage levels are very similar in nature. The one is used by managements and owners of business firms. The other is used by labor unions.

The basic idea is that foreign competitors are more efficient producers for one reason or another. Today, for example, many foreign steel producers have more efficient plants because their old plants were destroyed in World War II. New plants were built in the post-war era with help from our country, using the latest and most efficient technology. Many foreign plants are now, there-fore, lower-cost producers than competing American plants. The argument is that American steel producers should be protected from such competition as well as from the practice of "dumping." The term "dumping" means the selling of products overseas at prices that are lower than the actual costs of producing them in the economy where they are manufactured. U.S. steel companies com-plain, with some justification, that foreign governments subsidize steel exports and that this amounts to unfair competition. So they seek import restrictions.

Unions use a similar argument against the lower wage levels that are gener-ally paid to workers in foreign countries. "How can high-paid American labor compete with low-paid foreign labor?" they ask.

Both labor and management in these instances propose high tariffs or restrictive quotas to keep competing foreign goods out of the country. Such protection slows down the rate at which domestic firms are forced to modern-ize. It also allows unions to demand and get higher wages from protected firms than they could otherwise get in a more competitive situation because higher labor costs can more easily be passed on to consumers in the form of higher prices for the protected commodities. This explains why union leaders and management spokesmen often present a common front on the protection issue. Their interests coincide: Protection would result in higher profits for stockholders and higher wages for unionized workers, but also higher prices for consumers.

All protection arguments propose to insulate domestic industries — at the expense of the public — for the benefit of owners and workers in the protected industries. As you can see, this situation is not materially different than the issue of licensing certain professions and trades. It is relatively easy for those with a vested interest favoring protection to militate together for concerted political action calling for protection. But it is more difficult for the public to organize effectively in opposition. Why? Because the benefits of protection in any certain industry go to a relatively few; therefore, the benefits are relatively great to those who receive them. But the cost of protection, even though great in total sum, is spread thinly across the broad consuming public. Individual costs, therefore, on any one item are relatively small to those who pay. However, the total cost on all protected items can be very substantial.

Accordingly, it is usually not very economical to organize a substantial opposition movement among members of the public to counter cries for protection in specific industries. A good example of this is the domestic sugar industry. The world price for sugar at the time of this writing was about 8 cents per pound, but the domestic wholesale price was 13.5 cents because a 5.5 cent import tax (tariff) is imposed on sugar brought into the country. Domestic sugar producers have pushed for a protected price of 15 cents per pound. If the tariff should rise to 7 cents per pound, the extra cost to each consumer for a five-pound sack of sugar would be 35 cents. What housewife will go to the trouble of organizing a free-trade consumer group to resist paying 35 cents extra per bag of sugar, even if she were to use 10 or 20 five-pound sacks per year? Yet, when we consider the millions and millions of pounds of sugar consumed annually in this country, this seemingly insignificant levy really amounts to a great fortune! Thirty-five cents per five-pound sack of imported sugar goes into government coffers, but the 35 cents for each sack of domestically produced sugar goes into the coffers of the protected domestic producers. The protective tariff on sugar, which has been in effect for over 40 years, is just one of many anti-consumer schemes which line the pockets of protected domestic producers and their employees. The total annual cost of protection to the consuming public, like a leaking water line when one pays for the use of water by a meter, can be substantial. The fact that one does not notice the small cost on a day-by-day basis is irrelevant.

The argument for or against protection finally boils down to the question of what is the proper role of the civil authority in society. If power to levy tariffs is given to the civil authority, should tariffs be for revenue only, or should they be used to protect certain segments of society at the expense of the general public? This is a normative issue which can be answered only by considering the issue from a moral or ethical standpoint.

International Monetary Cooperation

Since World War II, numerous attempts have been made by civil rulers to secure monetary cooperation on an international basis. Unlike the international gold standard, which was an informal working arrangement without a supranational organization, the post-World War II efforts have tended to shift monetary authority from the national level of government to international organizations. We discuss some of these below.

The International Monetary Fund: As World War II was drawing to a close in 1944, representatives of most countries allied against Germany, Italy and Japan met at Bretton Woods, New Hampshire. Since that time, the meeting has been called the Bretton Woods Conference. The purpose of the meeting was to work out some orderly system of international payments for the postwar era. These United States, at that time, were in an extremely powerful situation relative to other countries. We had a vast gold reserve and a productive economy which had not been damaged by the ravages of war. We were, in fact, the world's supply-house for food, manufactured goods and financing.

The Bretton Woods Conference produced a large body of rules and understandings for regulating international transactions and payments of trade imbalances. Out of this conference was formed the International Monetary Fund (IMF), which was designed to help participating countries maintain fixed exchange rates.

The idea was to help countries meet currency drains when imports exceeded exports on a temporary basis. Each country was to maintain, within a narrow range, a fixed price on its currency relative to all other currencies. The IMF was to lend either gold or dollar reserves to a deficit country when called upon so that the deficit country could support its fixed exchange rate by purchasing its own currency in the foreign exchange market. Later, after the "temporary" emergency was passed, the deficit country was supposed to repay the IMF. Capital to start the IMF was supplied by cooperating nations, with these United States contributing the largest share. Any country that faced a continuing long-term deficit would, of course, eventually have to devalue its currency relative to other currencies; but devaluations in excess of 10 percent were to be approved by IMF members in advance.

The Bretton Woods Agreement did not work out the way it was intended (as its critics predicted). After 1950, various countries devalued their currencies without receiving prior agreement from other nations. While the IMF did no doubt help some countries survive temporary deficits without their being forced to devalue their currencies, the ready availability of borrowed funds on a supposedly short-term basis proved to be too tempting for the long-term. Why? A long-term is simply a number of short-terms strung together, and who can tell when a "short-term" begins or ends? So, the net result of being able to borrow "short-term" was, in practice, an easy means of allowing a deficit country to help finance its chronic long-term deficits. In summary, each country was tempted to follow a short-term inflationary monetary policy internally, always hoping that the long-term problem would somehow go away during the interim in which it borrowed reserves from the IMF. In the long run, easy credit from the IMF helped deficit countries to insulate their economies from foreign competition while their rulers recklessly engaged in massive deficit spending programs. With the discipline of foreign competition removed, it is no wonder that governmental rulers acted in an undisciplined manner.

One especially weak point of the Bretton Woods System is that it was based on the U.S. dollar, which other countries used in place of gold as a monetary base for their own money supplies. Thus, when foreign countries accepted dollars instead of gold as a means of balancing international accounts, there was a multiple expansion of money on a worldwide basis. That is, instead of a foreign country expanding its own money supply on a certain multiple of the actual gold it held as bank reserves, it used U.S. dollars. To that country, the U.S. dollar was "good as gold" because dollars could be converted into gold on demand — or at least until these United States repudiated their promise of redemption in 1971. But the dollars such foreign countries held as bank reserves, and upon which they based their own money supply, were **already** based on a multiple of the gold held as bank reserves for a monetary base in these United States. In other words, the Bretton Woods Agreement operated on what is called the gold-exchange standard; that is, the gold reserve used to support the domestic supply of U.S. dollars was **also** used to support the fractional expansion of money in the foreign countries that held U.S. dollars as part of their own gold reserve base. In short, the same gold reserve base in these United States did "double duty" by supporting twice as much money — once in our country and yet again in foreign countries. This doubly multiplied expansion of money on an international basis largely explains the worldwide inflationary binge during the post-World War II period. (The degree of worldwide monetary inflation and its effect on price levels was referred to in the chapter on money.)

One additional step designed to supply countries with even more credit was the creation of so-called **Special Drawing Rights** (SDRs) by the International Monetary Fund (IMF) in 1970. SDRs are nothing but bookkeeping entries which were dubbed "paper gold" by international banking propagandists. Of course, gold is gold, and paper is paper; but these so-called "paper gold" credits were created by IMF officials and handed out to IMF members on an allocated basis. As a result, countries which had already used their full borrowing capacity were enabled to borrow even more. Two separate allocations of SDRs have already been handed out to IMF members, and more can be made any time the decision is made to make more fictitious bookkeeping entries. On a domestic basis, this would be equivalent to the banking authorities of a country deciding to increase every person's checking account by crediting an extra $1,000 of "paper gold" to his bank account in order to increase his ability to spend. The result, seen in this light, is obvious. Price levels would zoom upward, and there would be no increase in real purchasing power or in real wealth created.

It seems that no institution has less ability to discipline itself to balance spending with income than the agency called civil government, especially at the national and international levels. One of the greatest challenges facing any freedom-loving people is how to discipline their rulers to live with balanced budgets, for political rulers are extremely adept at devising sophisticated schemes to allow them to spend more than the people are willing to pay in taxes. Such schemes always call for some form of monetary inflation that is not readily understood by the mass of ordinary citizens such as the "paper gold" illusion of the IMF.

In summary, the net result of the Bretton Woods Agreement has been:

(1) an undermining of the strong financial standing of these United States during the post-World War II period,

(2) massive monetary inflation on a worldwide basis which produced rising price levels all over the world,

(3) a boost towards the development of autarkic economies throughout the world, and

(4) a final breakdown of the Bretton Woods System when the U.S. dollar was no longer able to serve in place of gold for the monetary reserves of foreign countries.

In the post-war period, the gold reserves of these United States dropped from over $24 billion in 1949 to about $11 billion (valued at $35 per ounce) in August, 1971, when we repudiated our promise to foreign governments to redeem dollars for gold.

The U.S. government closed the "gold window" to foreign governments on August 15, 1971. On March 31, 1972, our government changed the official price of gold stated in terms of dollars from $35 to $38 per ounce (i.e., the dollar was officially devalued). The dollar was again devalued on September 21, 1973, to $42.22 per ounce of gold. Except for reducing U.S. liabilities to the IMF by $7.22 per ounce of gold, these devaluations were meaningless actions since the dollar was no longer convertible into gold anyway, and because the free market price of gold had already soared far above the officially set price. The free price of gold reached $195 per ounce by the end of 1973 in the European market.

As you will recall, our federal government had closed the "gold window" (i.e., repudiated its promise to redeem dollars for gold) to U.S. citizens 40 years earlier in 1933 when President Roosevelt nationalized gold. (See the supplement "All About Gold" at the end of chapter 6.) His action then caused dollars held by U.S. citizens to become fiat dollars. The action taken in August, 1971, now caused the dollars held by foreign governments to also become fiat dollars. When these United States "floated" the U.S. dollar in 1973 by cancelling the fixed exchange rate between the dollar and other currencies, the Bretton Woods System of fixed exchange rates collapsed. Since that time, all countries have been on a flexible exchange rate basis.

The World Bank: Another outgrowth of the Bretton Woods Conference of 1944 was the creation of the International Bank for Reconstruction and Development, or as it is commonly called, the World Bank. Cooperating nations contributed necessary capital so that the Bank could make low-cost loans to less-developed nations. (These United States contributed 25 percent of the capital.) The World Bank also guarantees loans made by other institutions to developing nations.

The World Bank has to some degree replaced private international loans that used to be made during the gold standard era. Because the World Bank is a supranational, quasi-governmental agency, it has made loans where private investors would fear to risk their own funds. As might be expected, the long-term results have been of questionable benefit economically; for World Bank funds are loaned only to governments rather than to private profit-seeking organizations. Critics claim that World Bank funds tend to be wasted or to be used for projects that civil rulers of developing nations prefer for reasons of personal gain. Defenders of the World Bank, who usually value government projects more highly than private projects, claim that the Bank has been successful for the purpose designed. Critics claim the Bank has helped spread socialism (government ownership and control of the means of production) all over the world at the expense of private capitalism.

The European Economic Community: International economic cooperation began in Europe in 1948 with establishment of the Organization for European Economic Cooperation (OEEC). Its purpose was to coordinate the allocation of Marshall Plan aid sponsored by these United States in order to accelerate the economic recovery of Western Europe. During the 1950s, import quotas and intercountry payments restrictions on intra-OEEC trade were rapidly eliminated. Thus, after the war, European nations grew accustomed to cooperating with each other in trade and other economic matters.

Out of the OEEC grew the idea of creating a vast "United States of Europe" which would establish a large competitive common market area. It was hoped that such a broad market area without tariffs would facilitate mass production and cost-saving economies of scale by producing a more efficient allocation of labor, capital and raw materials.

In 1952 the European Coal and Steel Community (ECSC) was formed. This created a common market for coal, steel and iron ore among six nations: France, Germany, Italy, Belgium, the Netherlands and Luxembourg. In 1957 these countries established the European Economic Community (EEC) or Common Market, as it is called. Its main purpose was to create, in planned stages, a customs union for both industrial and agricultural goods. All internal trade barriers were to be removed and a common external tariff was planned. The ultimate objective is the possible political union of member countries.

France originally opposed the entry of Britain into the EEC, so Britain established the European Free Trade Association (EFTA) with Norway, Sweden, Denmark, Switzerland, Austria and Portugal. In 1973 Britain, Denmark and Ireland became members of the EEC. Other EFTA members made arrangements to cooperate with the EEC without becoming full members.

One great advantage enjoyed by these United States is that their uniting under the Constitution of 1787 provided a vast free trade area which stimulated the efficient production and distribution of mass produced low-priced goods. This vast market area, combined with the great degree of economic and political freedom enjoyed by American citizens, created a business climate in which individuals were free to mutually serve and compete with each other. This "American experiment" produced steadily rising incomes and living standards for two centuries. Whether or not the EEC will ultimately produce similar results remains to be seen, but the economic union created by the EEC has already created a vast free trade area similar to the one in these United States of America.

The General Agreement on Tariffs and Trade: Twenty-three nations joined together in 1943 in an agreement to reduce trade barriers. The resulting agreement was called the General Agreement on Tariffs and Trade (GATT). Members of GATT have participated in multinational negotiations to resolve trade conflicts and to plan freer trade policies. This has produced a number of tariff reductions in broad categories of products. Reductions in tariffs are applied on a non-discriminatory basis to all members. The GATT agreement also prohibits most import quotas. Today, GATT has more than 80 member nations.

To the extent that trade barriers can be eliminated between nations, the principle of comparative advantage will have greater application, and people all over the world will benefit from increases in production that result from the specialization of effort.

The U.S. Export-Import Bank: In 1934 the Congress of these United States established the U.S. Export-Import Bank (Eximbank). Under a law of 1945, the Eximbank is empowered to aid in financing U.S. exports. This government-owned bank lends money directly and also guarantees loans made by private banks in order to facilitate the expansion of exports. The Foreign Credit Insurance Association (FCIA), a group of some 50 large insurance companies, has a working arrangement with Eximbank to cover commercial risks for export. Also, more than 250 commercial banks provide some private funding to help facilitate exports. FCIA members and the commercial banks are guaranteed by Eximbank against all political risks as well as against 90 percent of commercial risks to which the insurance companies and banks are exposed.

A further source of private funding for promoting exports is provided by the Private Export Funding Corporation (PEFCO). This organization was formed in 1970. It is owned by 54 commercial banks, 7 industrial firms and an investment banking firm. Most of the banks and all of the industrial firms are very large, and each has a particular interest in either producing goods for export or in financing export sales. Eximbank protected PEFCO against funding risks during the early years of its formation. PEFCO extends loans to both private and public borrowers outside these United States. All loans are unconditionally guaranteed by Eximbank.

Eximbank was originally funded with government money contributed by U.S. taxpayers. At the end of its September 30, 1982, fiscal year, the total worldwide risk exposure of Eximbank was slightly over $38 billion. During 1982 Eximbank authorized loans of $3.5 billion, extended loan guarantees of $.7 billion and extended insurance authorizations of $5.1 billion. The total number of authorizations (loans, loan guarantees and insurance) totalled 3,067. These amounted to a total financial commitment of $9.3 billion for the year, which supported export sales of $12.1 billion.

Eximbank no longer depends on **direct** capital subsidies from taxpayers to obtain needed working capital to finance exports. However, it does so **indirectly** because it is enabled by law to borrow from the U.S. Treasury and the U.S. Federal Financing Bank when its loan repayments are insufficient to provide it with the necessary flow of capital to underwrite new export loans. By the end of its 1982 fiscal year, Eximbank had borrowed a total of $17 billion from the U.S. government. During that year the average cost of Eximbank's borrowed funds exceeded the average interest received on loans by 3.4 percent; that is, U.S. taxpayers subsidized the Bank's lending operations by 3.4 percent times $17 billion. At present Eximbank is authorized to lend, guarantee and insure up to a total of $40 billion. By the end of 1982 it had committed $38 billion of the total allowable. In 1982 a total of 158 countries had loans outstanding of over $34 billion, and 21 countries were delinquent in loan repayments totalling $1.4 billion. Countries with delinquent loans of more than $25 million in 1982 were: Argentina, Bolivia, Brazil, Red China, Cuba, Dominican Republic, Iran, Poland, Romania and Zaire.[4]

If you read the previous information carefully, you will see that the U.S. Export-Import Bank amounts to a sophisticated scheme of allowing private firms to sell exports on credit—the risk of which is ultimately shifted onto U.S. taxpayers. Eximbank and its cooperating banking and insurance organizations allow private firms to "sell" on credit to foreign buyers where existing or expected political and commercial risks would make it either more expensive or impossible to do so privately. There is a saying that goes like this: "If it is too risky for **my** money and too risky for **your** money, let us do it with **government** money!"

You can judge whether or not the adage applies to Eximbank. What happens, in effect, when an exporter makes a "sale" to a foreign buyer that is financed through Eximbank is this: The foreign buyer receives a shipment of real wealth with a partial downpayment. The selling firm receives an IOU which it then hands over to Eximbank and which is to be paid off by the party in the importing country with interest over a term of years (usually 10 to 20 years). The exporting firm in these United States receives cash from Eximbank—cash that has been provided by U.S. taxpayers either in the form of the original cash grants or by borrowing from the U.S. Treasury or the Federal Financing Bank. In the event of default, it is U.S. taxpayers who stand the loss.

An example of how a default works can be seen in the case of Laker Airways Limited, a British airline which declared bankruptcy in February, 1982. At that time Eximbank's exposure on loans for five DC-10-30 aircraft totalled $147.2 million (a $86 million direct loan by Eximbank and $61.2 million loan made by PEFCO which was guaranteed by Eximbank). When Laker declared bankruptcy, Eximbank took possession of the mortgaged aircraft and set

---

[4]U.S. Export-Import Bank *Annual Report,* 1982, p. 24.

about to sell them. It paid PEFCO $12.2 million in principal and $3.5 million in delinquent interest installments, then it gave PEFCO a promissory note for $48.9 million with the same installment dates as carried by PEFCO's loan to Laker.[5]

Eximbank can be criticized on this basis: If the political and economic risks are too great for large private firms, banks and insurance companies to underwrite, then are not the economic and political risks also too great for U.S. taxpayers to assume? After all, the role of Eximbank is **not** to reduce the risk but only to **transfer** the risk that already exists from one party to another.

Proponents of government-sponsored agencies such as Eximbank, on the other hand, can point to some four decades of seemingly profitable operations. They claim that only a relatively few very large losses have occurred (see the previous listing of defaults of greater than $25 million). Two loans that have been repudiated by revolutionary governments are the $49 million loaned to mainland China before 1947 (the communists took over in 1949) and $71.2 million loaned to Cuba (the communists took over in 1959).

An evaluation of Eximbank must rest, not on the apparent success of the bank's historical operations, for this kind of socialist enterprise can be made to operate so that it seems to be beneficial to all (an illusion). Rather, Eximbank must be judged according to its underlying economics and according to the normative question of who should bear the risks of engaging in foreign trade. The underlying economics show very clearly that the bank is a sophisticated mechanism for shifting the risks of doing business from those parties who stand a chance of reaping profits (large exporting corporations) onto a third party (U.S. taxpayers) who are not really involved in the business deals being made. This leaves us with a normative question: Should the additional risks involved in foreign trade be borne by those firms and financial institutions who stand to earn profits from foreign trade, or should such risks be shifted onto taxpayers? The free market approach is that those who stand to gain from an undertaking should also bear the burden of risk in the event of failure. The biblical approach would also dictate that profit-seekers should undergo their own risks of adventure rather than foisting them off onto disinterested third parties.

A Biblical Perspective

We have seen that the potential for trade—both within the same nation and between nations—is the result of God's making each person a distinct and unique individual with differing abilities and interests. It is man's differing gifts and abilities which produce the economic phenomenon we call specialization of effort, and it is this phenomenon which makes voluntary exchange between individuals economically beneficial. This uniqueness of individuals is a fact of

---

[5]Ibid., p. 26.

God's original creation, and it would exist even if man had not fallen into sin. After Adam fell and sin increased on earth to the extent that man attempted to build a humanistically oriented one-world government (as exemplified in the Tower of Babel), God took steps to lessen the outworking of man's evil nature in human society by confusing the language, dispersing the people and even dividing the continents (see Gen. 10:25, 11:1-9). This dispersement of man to the four corners of the earth made it incumbent on man to engage in trade and commerce as a means of maximizing his economic well-being in a world of scarce resources. Let us recall the historical sequence: Before man's fall into sin, he was charged with the pleasant task of dressing the Garden of Eden, which readily gave of its fruit. But when man rebelled against God's constituted law-order, God cast man from the garden and cursed the ground for man's sake (Gen. 3:17). After man was driven from the Garden of Eden and migrated to various parts of the earth, men indulged exceedingly in wickedness (Gen. 6:5). So God sent a deluge which obliterated all but the eight persons of the godly family of Noah. Once again God instructed man to multiply and to replenish the earth (Gen. 9:1). This they did, and the whole earth was of one language (Gen. 11:1). However, man's sinful nature soon turned the way of all humanism: Under Nimrod's totalitarian rule men built the Tower of Babel, which was an attempt to dethrone God and His law-order by attempting to elevate man and his puny power of reasoning above God. So, God thwarted man's sinful intent by confusing his tongue and physically dispersing him all over the world. The result, politically, was to create small, dispersed nations where political power would not be so concentrated as to unduly impinge on man's freedom. The result, economically, was to place men in varying climates and in lands with varying resources so that men could engage in the mutually beneficial process of voluntary trade and exchange of goods and services based on the principle of comparative advantage we discussed earlier. Free trade among men — trade between next-door neighbors as well as trade between men of different nations and languages — thus appears to be the direct result of God's working out His plan for mankind in general and for His people in particular.

The principle of dividing men physically into the lowest common denominator as a means of restraining evil seems to apply politically as well as economically. If our grasp of this principle is correct, then it appears that God's design for economic and political organization is to keep man **out** of one-world type organizations which would lead to the building of another international Babel. Supranational organizations such as the United Nations and the World Bank must be judged according to this God-given light.

When it comes to the use of government-sponsored organizations which serve to transfer the risk of doing business from private business firms to the general public — either through tax-supplied government guarantees or by thrusting higher prices onto consumers by imposing tariffs or import quotas — then the moral question of the commandment "Thou shalt not steal" seems to apply. Christians should recognize that fallen man will have a natural inclination to escape his responsibilities by cleverly using the civil authority as a means of foisting entrepreneurial risks or business costs onto others. It is from this moral perspective that such national or supranational organizations as the U.S. Export-Import Bank and the World Bank should be weighed. Moral judgment must also be used in evaluating the practice of imposing protective tariffs and import quotas which help a select few at the expense of many. By attempting to be guided by moral principles, some practices and institutions that may seem to function adequately on the surface may then be seen for what they really are—nothing but very sophisticated schemes for shifting the legitimate risks and costs of doing business onto the unsuspecting public who should really be the ultimate beneficiaries of all economic production and trade.

Voluntary organizations that are privately funded—in contrast to government-sponsored or government-underwritten organizations which exist on enforced tax levies—do not have it within their power to forcibly shift costs onto others. The enhancement of foreign trade through voluntary private organizations will tend to stimulate the growth of self-responsibility to the ultimate benefit of all concerned. Let those who stand to profit from entrepreneurial activities also stand the risk of engaging in them. The practice of forcibly shifting the risks of business from the profit-seekers onto the general public cannot be condoned either economically or morally. The principle that applies here, which is the same that applies to all human activity, is that of accepting personal responsibility for one's own actions: "And be it indeed that I have erred, mine error remaineth with myself" (Job 19:4). (See also: Deut. 24:16; Jer. 31:30; Ezek. 18:20; Gal. 6:5).

Questions

1. Critics of free enterprise capitalism complain that Americans, who constitute about 6 percent of the world's population, consume about 30 percent of the world's output of goods and services. Does this place a burden on the people who live in less-developed nations? Explain.

2. Look at the lists of goods imported into and exported from these United States. What do these lists tell you about our exporting and importing strengths and weaknesses?

3. What is the primary motivation for engaging in voluntary trade?

4. Explain the difference between absolute advantage and comparative advantage. If you have an absolute advantage in the production of both corn and autos, might it still be to your advantage to engage in trade with another person? Explain, giving an example.

5. If you had an absolute advantage in the production of two goods that I could also produce, when would it not be to your advantage to trade with me?

6. How does the fact of inequality in God's creation affect the potential for trade between countries?

7. When you buy a foreign import, where do your dollars go? Explain what happens.

8. What are "Eurodollars"?

9. Suppose Americans import more from Japan than the Japanese import from us. As a result, the price of the Japanese yen rises by 10 percent in terms of the U.S. dollar. Show what happens graphically.

10. What motive do civil rulers generally have for intervening in the foreign exchange market and attempting to stabilize exchange rates?

11. What argument could a businessman give in favor of fixed exchange rates? How can "buying forward" achieve the same goal? Which would you recommend as a policy to follow? Why?

12. Is the foreign exchange rate ordinarily likely to be volatile? What is its biggest source of instability?

13. What practical argument can be put forward against fixed exchange rates? Do you prefer fixed or flexible exchange rates? Why?

14. What two reactions occur when Americans import more than they export? How does price adjustment take place if exchange rates are: (a) flexible? (b) fixed?

15. How does an inflationary monetary policy by civil rulers lead to an increase in imports? Outline the process step by step under a fixed exchange rate.

16. What forces caused these United States to devalue the dollar and go off the fixed exchange rate for a flexible exchange rate in 1973? What happened afterward? Explain in detail.

17. Has the so-called outflow of "petro dollars" caused a chronic balance of payments deficit in these United States?

18. Explain how the international gold standard worked. What "rules of the game" did civil rulers have to adhere to in order to make the gold standard work?

19. Why were civil rulers throughout the world not willing to adhere to the gold standard?

20. List six arguments in favor of protection against foreign imports. Comment on them pro or con.

21. A so-called "favorable" balance of trade gives foreigners real wealth in exchange for IOUs. Comment on whether or not this is really

favorable. If you were the ruler of Communist Russia and had the goal of "burying" these United States, would you regard the receipt of real wealth in exchange for IOUs as favorable or unfavorable?

22. Why is it relatively easier for protectionists to join together for support than it is for those who favor a free trade policy?

23. Describe the background, goals and operation of the International Monetary Fund.

24. What was the especially weak point of the Bretton Woods Agreement? What did it produce on a worldwide scale?

25. Explain what an SDR is.

26. What is the purpose of the World Bank? Who financed it?

27. What is GATT?

28. Describe the operations of the U.S. Export-Import Bank and its related organizations. Who originally funded it? Who benefits from it? Who stands the risk?

29. What loans have not been repaid to Eximbank because of political upheavals?

30. On what basis must an evaluation of organizations such as Eximbank and the World Bank be made? Present your evaluations and discuss them with someone who holds an opposite view.

31. What political and economic application can we make concerning God's method of limiting the expression of evil in society, as at the Tower of Babel?

12

Economic Development

And it shall come to pass, if thou shalt hearken diligently unto the voice of the Lord thy God, to observe and to do all his commandments which I command thee this day, that the Lord thy God will set thee on high above all nations of the earth:

And all these blessings shall come on thee, and overtake thee, if thou shalt hearken unto the voice of the Lord thy God.

Blessed shalt thou be in the city, and blessed shalt thou be in the field.

Blessed shall be the fruit of thy body, and the fruit of thy ground, and the fruit of thy cattle, the increase of thy kine, and the flocks of thy sheep.

Blessed shalt be thy basket and thy store.

But it shall come to pass, if thou wilt not hearken unto the voice of the Lord thy God, to observe to do all his commandments and his statutes which I command thee this day; that all these curses shall come upon thee, and overtake thee:

Cursed shalt thou be in the city, and cursed shalt thou be in the field.

Cursed shall be thy basket and thy store.

Cursed shall be the fruit of thy body, and the fruit of thy land, the increase of thy kine, and the flocks of thy sheep.

Cursed shalt thou be when thou comest in, and cursed shalt thou be when thou goest out.

Deuteronomy 28:1-5, 15-19

ECONOMIC growth can best be defined as the process of people increasing their production of real welath on a per capita basis over a period of time. In an agricultural community, this involves making two blades of grass or two ears of corn grow where only one grew before. In an industrial community, it means producing more autos, refrigerators, shoes or other manufactured goods. In short, economic growth entails raising a people's standard of living. This can take place by increasing the input use of one or more of the three basic factors of economic production—land, labor and capital. It can also take place by increasing the efficiency with which these inputs are used in order to reduce production costs. This almost always involves a gradual improvement in labor education and in agricultural and industrial technology.

A good example of real economic growth can be seen in the U.S. automobile industry by comparing the autos of the 1930s with those of today. A buyer of an auto in the 1930s might have expected his new car to last perhaps 60,000 miles before it was junked. Today, buyers expect much more mileage out of cars because the technology of building engines and other components has improved tremendously. Materials have improved; and tolerances, because of automation, are much closer. This produces less vibration and less wear. Lubricants have also been improved. Another point is that more autos are produced per ton of steel today than in the 1930s because improved steel technology allows the use of thinner but stronger sheet metal. This same kind of economic growth can be seen in every industry—from the production of food, clothes and machines to the production of entertainment and banking services.

The theory of economic growth deals with these questions: How does economic growth occur? Why have some countries lagged behind others in developing high standards of living? What factors influence economic growth? What can be done to foster economic growth in the less-developed countries (LDCs)? Who should be responsible for fostering economic growth?

There is broad agreement among economists on the answers to some of these questions, but there is also disagreement. There is broad agreement on what must be done for economic growth to occur, but there is strong disagreement on how best to achieve what needs to be done and on who should be responsible for fostering economic growth. The large majority of economists today, for instance, are strongly inclined to recommend a careful regimen of central government planning and control over the economy in order to ensure the attainment of governmentally established objectives. The socialist/communist economies of the U.S.S.R. (Soviet Union), Red China and Cuba are prime examples of this line of thinking. Many Western nations and practically all LDCs now follow this course of centralized government control. Only a small minority of economists still hold, today, to a strict laissez faire policy in which governmental authorities do not consciously attempt to influence either the direction or the rate of economic growth. This government "hands-off" policy coincided with—and some of us would say was responsible for—the great worldwide economic growth which occurred all through the nineteenth century and up into the first decade of the twentieth century.

Problems of Less-Developed Countries

An economically less-developed country[1] is characterized by a number of

---

[1]The terms **underdeveloped country** and **less-developed country** are interchangeable. In some respects, a less-developed country can be regarded as an underdeveloped country that is somewhere along the road toward becoming economically developed. The main reason for using the term less-developed is simply not to cause offense, for people in some underdeveloped countries do not like the term being applied to their country.

problems which must be overcome before sustained economic growth can take place. These problems are listed below and can be grouped into one or more broad categories for the purpose of analysis:

(1) Religious, cultural and educational
(2) Social barriers
(3) Physical or "real" problems
(4) Political philosophy

Now let us look at some of the specific problems which characterize less-developed countries:

Poverty: Large masses of the population live in real poverty. The margin between actual starvation and survival is very thin. A very small wealthy class may exist. Even if all the property of the wealthy class were to be distributed among the poor, the problem of poverty would not be alleviated in the least because there are so many poor and so few rich. The long-term need is to increase the general level of people's income so that a greater margin of savings can take place. If income cannot be increased, then savings must somehow take place from present income so that capital investment can be financed. This would require a temporary drop in consumable income. We might ask, how can the seemingly eternal circle of poverty be broken so as to raise people's incomes and thereby finance needed savings and investment? Perhaps the quickest solution is to investigate governmental policies which may be inhibiting people's incentive to engage in economically productive work. It is amazing how a phlegmatic population can suddenly become intensely work-minded with a sudden change in economic and political climate.

A perfect example of such a sudden changeover occurred in West Germany after World War II. From 1945 to 1948, West Germany seemed unable to pick herself up after being defeated by the Allies. The streets of her cities remained a shambles. In June, 1948, before the impact of U.S. economic aid, Germany, under the leadership of Chancellor Ludwig Erhard, implemented a currency reform which based the German mark solidly on gold. This was done, by the way, against the express wishes of the Allied nations, including these United States, who did their best to lead Germany along the lines of a fiat monetary policy.

Immediately upon returning to a soundly based currency, German citizens propelled themselves into action. Shop windows that had long been empty were filled practically overnight. Streets that had been deserted soon swarmed with busy traffic. Almost miraculously, new buildings were seen rising from the rubble and the air was filled with the sound of hammers and steam shovels. Men who previously had been looking unsuccessfully for work now found jobs readily available. A sound monetary policy generated widespread economic activity, and this happened before the impact of U.S. economic aid reached Germany after World War II.[2]

---

[2]Elgin Groseclose, *America's Money Machine* (Westport, Conn.: Arlington House, 1980), p. 242; Ludwig Erhard, *Prosperity Through Competition — The Economics of the German Miracle* (New York: Praeger, 1958).

In some respects West Germany was different from the usual less-developed country because it had a history of industrialism, while the usual LDC does not even have a trained work force. But the point to focus on is that post-war West Germany was following the typical LDC path of economic stagnation **until** proper governmental policy was implemented to establish a healthy economic climate. That was all that was needed to galvanize the people into a self-help frenzy of economic activity.

Lack of Education: The masses are generally illiterate. Productive skills are very low. The low level of productivity helps contribute to the problem of illiteracy, for parents are not able to support their children even if schools were available; so children must scrounge or work to produce their own food. In short, investment in human capital, like investment in non-human capital, requires a margin of saving before it can take place.

Overpopulation: The land is apparently not productive enough to produce enough food to sustain the existing population. If the margin of food is expanded, population tends to increase even more. There is, therefore, a chronic tendency for population to outrun the food supply. Importing food for free distribution only seems to worsen the problem by stimulating further increases in population growth.

Lack of Capital: There is a dire shortage of capital investment and tools of production. Existing tools are crude and simple, and the methods of production are highly labor-intensive and inefficient. Most productive effort comes either from humans using crude hand tools or from animals pulling crude agricultural implements. This lack of capital is the result of a lack of profit incentive, which may be caused by a number of factors such as failure to respect private property or restrictive governmental policies.

Low Level of Technology: Productive techniques, both in agriculture and industry, are crude and of low output. This problem goes hand-in-hand with the educational problem.

Agriculturally Based Economy: The large majority of the population is tied directly to the land for sustenance—either as growers of crops, hunters and scavengers of the land's natural produce or as tenders of livestock. The key to raising incomes is that workers somehow must be released from the land to work in factories where low-cost mass production can take place. This cannot be done until an agricultural surplus is generated to feed the workers who will shift from farm to factory work. This calls for increased productivity in agriculture as a starting point.

Barter Economy: Trade is conducted mainly by barter or on a farm-to-market basis where, if money is used, buyers and sellers spend much time higgling and haggling over prices. The volume of sales per outlet is thus very small and often barely capable of supporting the trader or seller.

Absence of Credit and Savings Institutions: Banks and other financial intermediaries are either non-existent or they are not trusted; therefore, they are not used by large segments of the population. This inhibits the pooling of small savings into the formation of capital investment, so the rate of capital growth is slow.

Low Level of Savings and Investment: The large masses of people consume practically all that they produce each year. The amount of savings available for capital investment is very small. Often, what little **is** saved is invested in gold or silver coins and then hoarded or worn as necklaces or other ornaments. This type of non-productive investment occurs because the people do not trust governmental policies or because they are unfamiliar with savings-type institutions that pay interest.

Inaccessibility of Natural Resources: Natural resources may be abundant in some instances, but they are inaccessible to the large masses of people because they lack the ability to find and exploit them. The reason is that they lack the necessary capital and technological know-how. Government land policy may also be responsible for keeping large segments of the population disenfranchised from the land by vesting control of the land in a relatively few large landholders who do not exploit existing resources.

Lack of Infrastructure: Facilities for transportation and communication are crude and undeveloped. Roads are usually pathways that turn into quagmires during the rainy season and into dust bowls during dry periods. Because of the slowness of communication and the costliness of transportation, one part of the country may be out of contact with other parts. A temporary local shortage of food or water can quickly develop into a real crisis while other parts of the country have surpluses. This explains the many deaths due to famines and droughts in underdeveloped countries.

False Religions: The people do not believe in the true God of the Bible — the One who created the world and sustains it moment by moment according to His instituted law-structure. The people are given to superstitious beliefs and are easily controlled by witch doctors, seers and necromancers. The people's failure to recognize the true God and His created universe prevents them from developing or adopting a scientific cause-and-effect habit of thinking and of analyzing problems, which is a necessary precondition for technological development to take place.

Feudal Society: Social and economic relationships are based on status and one's historic role in the social structure. This inhibits the performing of economic services on a contractual or pay basis. People do not serve each others' needs as a means of realizing a gain or profit but because a certain service is **expected** from them. This inhibits the performance of economic services between individuals because the services are limited by a static culture. On the other hand, because man's wants are unlimited, services provided by profit-motivated entrepreneurs would always tend to be expanding.

Non-sanctity of Private Property: Property is not safe. The property of individuals is not adequately protected by law or custom. Stronger individuals or the community may dispossess the weaker or less influential members of society from their property. Government practices may follow confiscatory policies. The rulers themselves may regard the property of others as subject to be taken by whim or for the "good of the state." The relatives of a more successful individual may envy his material success. In some cultures, it is not unusual for such relatives to move in with the more successful person and to live off his accumulated wealth until it has been consumed. When he is reduced to their same level of poverty, they move out. The incentive to accumulate wealth is thereby destroyed or at least inhibited.

Lack of Profit Incentive: Individuals feel little incentive to engage in economic production or trade in order to accumulate wealth. This might be the result of false religions which teach that material things are "bad" while spiritual things are "good." It may be the result of adverse governmental policies such as socialistic collectivism or the arbitrary rule of men instead of rule by law. Anything that contributes to the non-sanctitiy of property will result in a lack of profit incentive, and the universal result is the failure of an entrepreneurial class to develop.

Lack of a Trained and Disciplined Labor Force: Low levels of education retard the gaining of salable skills. Workers are not reliable because they have not learned the discipline of dependability which is so necessary to production-line work in manufacturing and processing. When paid at the end of a week, such workers may disappear or go on an extended drunk until their money is gone. Also, because they come from a slower-moving culture which sets time by the sun, they are not sensitive to time increments of 15 or 30 minutes. Therefore, they do not report for work punctually each day. However, a production line cannot operate until **all** needed workers are on the job. This lack of time-awareness and working discipline takes a generation or two to develop.

Poor Health and Lack of Energy: Superstition and poor sanitary conditions cause many persons to become listless and enervated by poor nutrition, disease and parasites. This produces a general lack of vitality and an unwillingness and inability to engage in sustained effort.

Poor and Unproductive Soil: Ignorance of physics and soil chemistry leads to an abuse of existing natural resources and to the "mining" of the soil by wasteful agricultural practices. This reduces soil fertility and limits the output of food.

Corrupt and/or Unstable Civil Government: Government officials often regard their positions as a means of furthering their own private goals and self-enrichment. Corruption, bribery and graft abound and become an accepted way of life. Legal rule is by arbitrary men instead of by the impartial rule of law. Government policies, because they are often corrupt or not understood by the populace, are not generally accepted. The rulers must therefore rule by outright force instead of by general consent of the population. This produces political instability which fosters a revolutionary climate; such a climate is not conducive to private entrepreneurs making long-term investments in the hope of earning profits. Those venturesome entrepreneurs who do earn profits tend to hide them in unproductive caches or to export them because they do not trust the governmental authorities.

Lack of Foreign Investment: Governmental instability as well as other problems already listed cause foreigners to be reluctant to make capital investments. Wherever the arbitrary rule of men exists and/or where private property is not adequately protected, the resulting bad business climate retards capital investment. This holds true, not only for domestic residents, but primarily for foreign investors who might otherwise be willing to undergo more risk in the hope of earning higher profits.

Barriers to Social Mobility: In some countries, the existence of rigid caste systems and other social barriers inhibit the vertical social mobility of the more able and successful individuals. This serves to dampen individual initiative and to retard the growth of latent entrepreneurship. In extreme cases, such social barriers may even inhibit certain groups from doing any business at all with individuals of other castes or social groups.

Lack of Respect for the Individual: In non-Christian countries, individuals are not generally regarded as precious in their own right. People are regarded as chattel. They are expendable. Human life is regarded as almost valueless. This is the result of not accepting the biblical view of man. This feeling tends to pervade very aspect of society. Government officials regard the masses as pawns to be manipulated at will to achieve whatever goals the civil rulers establish. Economically, human life is readily sacrificed to gain or save physical wealth. This low regard for the worth of an individual encourages practices that are both autocratic and manipulative.

Brain Drain: The relatively few individuals who are able to gain an education do not find enough challenge and opportunity in their homeland. Most high-paying and prestigious positions are usually government related, but the number of government positions in the ranks of the ruling elite is limited. Therefore, a large percentage of the more highly educated persons emigrate to more industrialized countries.

Chronic Balance of Payments Deficit: Desire of the masses to enjoy the niceties that can be imported from more developed countries causes imports to exceed exports by a wide margin. Lack of foreign investment causes a deficit which is not offset by compensating payments. The country lacks claims on foreign exchange with which job-creating tools and machinery could be imported.

The Land Problem: In most less-developed countries, there is an abundance of suitable land on a per capita basis for enough food to be produced to adequately feed the population. In many such countries, large masses of people are effectively excluded from access to the land by ancient land tenure policies or by politically bestowed land grants which were given to a very few politically favored families. The economic effect of such policies and historic land grants has been to disenfranchise masses of people from the land and to inhibit agricultural production. Two classes of people develop: The relatively few landed families whose wealth is based on large land holdings and the many unlanded masses — some of these work for the landed aristocracy, and the rest do whatever they can to eke out a subsistence living. Politically, such a system creates a powder-keg situation that is ripe for exploitation by communists and other radicals.

Obviously, some type of land reform is needed so that the unlanded masses can be restored to the land and agricultural production can be expanded. The problem is **how** needed land reform can take place so that vested property interests are respected. If present property rights are frozen at the status quo, the problem is likely never to be solved. Some Central and South American countries have particularly explosive situations at this time: On the one hand are the rich landed classes who strongly resist any encroachment on their historic right to title which can be traced back hundreds of years to the time of the Spanish conquistadors. On the other hand are communist agitators who rouse the people behind them with the revolutionary's promise of distributing free land. The ignorant masses do not relize that the communists are not sincere in actually following through on their promise to redistribute the land. The revolutionary struggles now going on in Central and South America cannot be understood without an understanding of the underlying land problem.[3] In the Soviet Union, the state is the sole owner of all farm land except for the small private plots of an acre or two which peasants are allowed to farm privately.

The land problem appears to be almost insolvable when one considers the intense radical polarization of the landed elite versus the unlanded masses. How can the status quo be changed without destroying the rights of those who own land today — even though their present rights are based on wrongs imposed centuries ago? How far in the past can or should a government reach to restore dispossessed rights? Should it go back one day? one year? ten years? a hundred? three hundred? a thousand? There are some possible solutions discussed later, but the main points we want to make at this time are: (1) The land problem is both real and pressing because it creates present misery for millions and continued fodder for revolutionary agitators. (2) The solution of the problem is a knotty one because long-established vested interests are threatened. Therefore, resistance to change is certain to be very strong. Before passing on to a general treatment of all the problems listed above, we can make note of the following points: First, the land problem was met and at least partially solved in Tsarist Russia in the mid-1860s; so an historic precedent exists to serve as a guide. The solution was ended when Lenin and his communist followers forcibly overthrew the government and seized power in 1917. (See "The Russian Tsarist Experience" below.) Secondly, God provided a

---

[3]Throughout the world the blueprint for communist subversion follows this procedure: Discover some real or alleged social problems. Then promise to solve the problems as a means of gaining popular support in coming to power. Finally, once in power, do whatever is necessary to remain in power. Any previous promises can then be ignored.

means of preventing the land problem from occurring in Old Testament Israel through the institution of the Year of Jubilee; so there is also a biblical principle available for our guidance.

Searching for a Solution

The long list of problems we have just reviewed seems to create a vicious circle that apparently dooms LDCs to an unending series of crises which seemingly cannot be solved. Every economically developed nation has somehow managed to find a solution, so we know that these problems are capable of solution. Let us pause to make one point here: It is inaccurate to say that the less-developed countries or nations face these problems, for it is generally the **rulers** of such countries who have taken it upon themselves to improve the lot of the masses. The masses of citizens, if left to themselves, lack a national concept as well as a vision of how things might be different 10 or 20 years in the future. The people of less-developed countries tend to relate to each other on a tribal — or at most, on a regional — basis. They are more interested in eating and providing for their families today, tomorrow and next week than in building a nation. This is not necessarily to imply that the masses do not plan for the future. It is only to say that their perspective is different and that their time frame is shorter. It is also safe to state that any plans developed by government officials to implement a national project will no doubt conflict with the private and personal plans of the people. Any national project must be forcibly imposed in some way on the masses — either by outright taxation and fiat or by deception. This poses an ethical or moral question: To what extent, if any, do the rulers of a nation have a right or duty to impose their desire for economic development onto their people?

It is understandable why rulers, in the face of such circumstances, almost invariably turn towards a socialistic type of centralized planning and control to implement their ideas. First, the rulers conceive that the achievement of goals through persuasive leadership and voluntary compliance is uncertain and unnecessarily time consuming. The illusory promise of speed and efficiency in accomplishing things by government mandate speaks strongly to well-meaning bureaucrats. Also, man by his fallen nature easily tends toward the use of power instead of toward persuasion in his relationships with others. It seems so much easier and quicker to order someone to do something immediately than to spend hours, days or months to convince them that it is to their own benefit to do so. Also, positions of power are irresistably attractive to those ever-present personalities who regard themselves as being above the law and inherently superior to the masses. Such persons either see government positions as power opportunities to force others to do what the elite ruler assumes is best for the masses, or these persons see government positions as golden opportunities to enrich themselves at public expense.

The second reason rulers of less-developed countries invariably turn toward centralized control of the economy is that they or their advisors have received technical training which leads them in this direction. Most of these rulers and their supporting bureaucrats have been exposed to or have received their training in economics and civil government in secular universities of the more-developed countries. While the developed countries where they studied did not generally achieve their own economic and political greatness by following the socialistic centralized control route — but rather by following the free enterprise route — the professors who teach at the universities are generally committed to the idea of centralized government planning. Therefore, the rulers and bureaucrats of less-developed countries are usually indoctrinated to follow a general philosophy of economic development which has not been successful historically and which has not stood the test of time.

Centralized Controls as a Solution

Because most LDCs have adopted the government-control philosophy of economic development, we will discuss this policy first. We will evaluate it as we go along and then consider the laissez faire or free enterprise alternative which most government planners consider no alternative at all.

What civil rulers do under the centralized control route is to group around them a conglomeration of "experts" who set about developing a series of long-range economic plans. These "experts" are made up of foreign advisors plus a contingent of indigenous persons who probably received their training in economics, finance and civil government overseas. A carefully laid out five- or seven-year comprehensive plan is set up — much like the five-year plans that the central planners in the Soviet Union set up but not quite so detailed.

The plan will include the building of infrastructure (transportation and communications networks, power grids and other utility services such as water and sewage) that is deemed necessary for supporting the modern factories which are planned. Quite often the planners are overambitious, for it is easy to spend money that one has not personally worked for and accumulated through the slow and difficult process of self-denial. Government planners do not count the cost of their planned capital investments in terms of the personal cost of saving through self-denial. Less care in choosing potentially profitable investments is a natural result of centralized planning. The planners are in a hurry to industrialize; for they know that in order to grow economically, workers will have to be shifted out of agriculture into industry. There seems to be a built-in tendency for central planners to plan large expensive facilities such as massive dams (the Aswan Dam in Egypt, for example) or large manufacturing plants that call for skills that people do not yet have and which produce goods that the internal domestic market cannot yet absorb (the large steel mills that were built in India during the 1960s with American foreign aid, for example). Often the end result is high-cost production of poor quality goods which produces, contrary to the expectations of the planners, a disappointingly low rate of return on invested capital. In short, many such investments actually turn out to be mal-investments because a much higher rate of return can be had elsewhere (in simple agriculture, for instance).

Since less-developed countries are primarily agriculturally based, a more natural — but less exciting — plan of development would be to make the first investments in primary agriculture: providing small independent farmers with improved hand tools, small motorized tractors and rototillers, better seed, fertilizers and insecticides. Such a plan would provide many people throughout the less-developed country with tools that are sorely needed to increase the food supply and thus develop a wider margin of income over outgo. As we have indicated, this route of economic development is less ostentatious than the "big project" fever that usually circulates at the top planning level; but the potential food surplus through such primary agricultural development is tremendous. It takes relatively little planning expertise — which is one reason top-level planners do not choose it! Choosing less centralized planning instead of more centralized planning would tend to eliminate their role as bureaucratic planners. The basic farming route would also put spendable and investable funds directly into the hands of the populace, but this is exactly what the central planners do not want. Why? Because the planners correctly assume that the masses will want to spend their money on different things than the planners envision.

A number of Christian denominations as well as independent Christian groups currently support foreign "economic missionaries" who devote their time to helping people in backward courtries develop modern farming methods. They teach them how to use better tools, how to irrigate and how to breed improved livestock that will produce more weight or more milk per unit of feed. They even teach farmers how to pool their resources to purchase machinery that can be used by members of voluntary cooperatives. This is done in addition to teaching the gospel of Christ which will lead the people to conform their private and social lives and institutions to biblical precepts. These economic developers lead the people by persuasion and by example rather than sitting at the central seat of government and imposing their ideas on the people by fiat.

Indeed, it is true that people in less-developed countries will generally choose to spend their savings on imported "luxuries" such as foreign-made clothes, pocket-size transistor radios or some other item they can enjoy **now**, unless they are prevented from doing so or convinced to do otherwise. This is where the issue of voluntarism versus government fiat comes in. Do the masses know what is best for themselves or not? It not, should they be forced or persuaded to do differently? Who is in a position to decide what is best for the people anyway — the people or their rulers? The central planners would, of course, say they are looking 20 to 40 years in the future; but so would the Christian missionaries who follow the route of persuasion in their religious and economic ministries. In finality, the issue boils down to a choice between reasoning with people to spend less on themselves **today** with the expectation of providing their children with more to enjoy **tomorrow.** Who is to say how much should be consumed today versus how much should be invested for the future? The government-control route forcibly bottles up the desires of the populace by fiat to achieve government-mandated goals. Government planning necessarily short-circuits the desires of the populace—otherwise, there would be no need for a central plan!

Governmental action can be implemented in various ways, some of which are so sophisticated that they provide rulers with means of imposing their will on the people without their being able to discern what is happening. Let us investigate some of the methods that can be used:

Central Bank: One way of overruling the wishes of the populace is to establish a government-controlled central bank. Such a bank can issue printed money which, by government fiat, must be accepted on a par basis with silver and gold coins. Deposit money can also be created for use by the more sophisticated citizens in the capital city or other large cities, but the masses will generally come to accept paper money as long as it can be freely exchanged for silver and gold coins which they regard as real money. After this partial acceptance, the rulers can then attempt to get on a 100-percent fiat money basis as quickly a possible. When this stage is accomplished, there is no practical limit to the amount of money the rulers can create.

Once widespread use of paper money is instituted, government authorities can start the process of gradual monetary inflation, that is, debauchment of the currency. As new money is created, the governing authorities use it to purchase labor services and real wealth from the people. Labor services and real wealth thereby gradually come under governmental control. Laborers can be hired with printed money to work on government projects, and wealth purchased with the newly created money can also be used on government projects. General price levels, of course, soon begin to rise in response to the systematic creation of new purchasing media by the governing authorities. The general rise in prices amounts to a "hidden tax" levied on the people, who are not sophisticated enough to realize what is happening.

This money-creation means of transferring control of labor and wealth from the hands of citizens into the hands of civil rulers is highly preferred by central planners over outright taxation. It is effortless and very efficient when viewed from a governmental standpoint. It is much easier than collecting taxes either in money or in kind.

A government-controlled central bank can be used to systematically debauch the currency as a means of quietly forcing the masses to consume less than they produce even if the existing margin of surplus is very thin or nonexistent. The yearly percentage in price increases amounts to forced "savings" that are siphoned off from the private to the public sector.

Taxation: Direct and hidden taxes can be raised to whatever level the people will endure or to the extent that the cost of collection remains less than the revenue produced. However, because the government collection machinery in less-developed countries is crude and inefficient and because the people have not yet been conditioned to paying income taxes, the "hidden tax of inflation" through the central bank mentioned above is preferred by the rulers.

Tariffs and Import Controls: Very high tariffs can be imposed, especially on those items the authorities consider "luxuries." Sometimes the tariff rate is three or four times as much in value as the article being imported, thus placing it out of reach of all but the very wealthy.

Import quotas can also be used to drastically limit the amount of goods the populace can legally import. These and high tariffs tend to create an artificial profit potential which stimulates smuggling.

Tariffs generate additional revenues which the authorities can use in fulfilling their centralized plan for national development. Import controls serve to limit imports and the amount of foreign claims which would otherwise accumulate against the domestic currency.

The imposition of high tariffs and restrictive import quotas, in addition to creating smuggling opportunities, also creates profit-making opportunities which bureaucrats and rulers themselves find difficult to resist. While the general populace is not in a position to get around bureaucratic regulations, those who are familiar with the operation of governmental machinery are in such a position. The following United Press International (UPI) news release gives only one instance of the many ways government officials can evade rules and regulations which ordinary citizens must obey:

> SÃO PAULO, Brazil (UPI) — In most Latin American countries, where foreign cars are either heavily taxed or banned, an enterprising diplomat can turn a tidy profit by selling local residents automobiles that his diplomatic prerogatives allow him to import duty free.
>
> Just how profitable this practice is in Brazil, and how many diplomats engage in it, became evident recently when federal officials announced they had impounded 23 luxury Mercedes Benzes they said were sold illegally to wealthy Brazilians by diplomats from at least 15 countries and one international organization.
>
> Investigators for São Paulo's federal police now say they are searching for 43 more Mercedes sold to individuals who could afford prices up to $75,000 — $25,000 of which was pocketed by the diplomats as commissions.
>
> Brazil banned car imports in 1966. The only way a Brazilian can legally obtain a Mercedes or other foreign-make automobile is to buy a used car from a diplomat returning home.
>
> But police say at least three car rings found an ingenious way around the laws. They sold wealthy Brazilians new Mercedes

through diplomats willing to import cars in their own names.

After three years the cars would be classified as used vehicles that could be sold legally, and the Brazilian owners would have been able to register them under their names without paying stiff import duties.[4]

Summary of State Planning

If we were to summarize the philosophy of centralized economic planning in the hands of governing authorities, it would amount to this: Though rulers may be men of high ideals, their world-and-life view is that the land and people over which they exert hegemony constitute so much "raw material" which they desire to develop according to whatever national plan they happen to conceive. Economic and government institutions are established to assist the rulers in achieving their overall projects, whether or not the general populace agrees. The rulers regard themselves as an intellectual elite whose judgment is superior to the people's. They think they know what is necessary for improving the people's welfare. In many respects they may indeed be better judges, but they impose their judgment by fiat instead of by persuasion.

Eventually, such control by fiat becomes quite personal. It must become so, unless rulers are willing to allow the masses to diverge from the national plan. Such divergence, however, would upset the grandiose plans of the planners and therefore cannot be tolerated. Take, for instance, the matter of population control. Many ruling regimes attempt to solve the persistent problem of overpopulation by reducing the birth rate through government distribution of contraceptives, forced or voluntary sterilization programs and abortion clinics.

India: In 1961 the census bureau of India was shocked to learn that the real birth rate was much higher than planners had estimated. A government program of voluntary sterilization which paid people to be sterilized was begun. When this voluntary plan did not produce the desired results, Prime Minister Indira Ghandi announced a program of **forced** sterilization in the mid-1970s. The adverse public reaction which resulted from this program and other stringent measures helped contribute to her temporary political downfall. The very imposition of such a program shows to what extent humanistically oriented rulers will go in their attempt to play God.

Red China: The ruling authorities in mainland China also make contraceptives available and promote abortions to limit population. In addition, they encourage young people to delay marrying (28 years for males and 25 for women) and promote wider spacing of children (5 years apart). There has also been some discussion of imposing collective "baby quotas" on villages and urban communities. A recent report from a commune in Shansi indicates that

---

[4]*Dallas* (Texas) *Morning News,* 2 November 1978.

this policy has been brutally put into effect. Twenty-eight pregnant women were forced to undergo abortions (two who were eight months pregnant died). One of the husbands incited the rest of the commune to kill 38 members of the birth-control team, then he committed suicide when captured by the Chinese police force.[5]

Taiwan: The authorities in Free China, who also follow a centralized planning route to some degree, initiated a milder "family planning" program in 1963 as a means of population control. Interestingly enough, the birthrate had **already** trended downward before the government plan was implemented. Between 1951-1966 the birthrate per 1,000 women aged 14-49 had dropped from 211 to 149.

Taiwan's birthrate experience is characteristic of a people whose standard of living has steadily risen. The people voluntarily decide to limit their offspring; and they do this even without the use of modern contraceptives. Scientists have noticed that animal populations tend to stabilize naturally when population densities reach certain levels. Demographers and economists have likewise noted similar tendencies among humans. Apparently, God's plan motivates humans to do consciously what non-human creatures do unconsciously.

While we are considering Red China and Free China (Taiwan) and the attempts to control population, we should not pass up the opportunity to debunk one aspect of the population myth — the myth that dense population, so-called "overpopulation," and poverty go hand-in-hand. From the data shown in Table 12:1, it should be evident that economic freedom versus lack of economic freedom is the key issue relating to economic prosperity, not relative population densities.

Table 12:1

	Red China	Free China (Taiwan)
Population (total)	1 billion	17.9 million
Population per square mile	280	1,323
Literacy rate	25%	90%
Total output per capita	$535	$2,238
Energy consumption per capita (coal equivalent)	1,845lb.	4,853lb.
Steel consumption per capita	69 lb.	586 lb.
Cement production per capita	85 lb.	1,410 lb.
Workers in agriculture	75%	25%

Source: *U.S. News & World Report,* 14 December 1981, p. 35.

---

[5]American Aid Society, Dallas, Tex., and the Conservative National Committee, Vienna, Va., *World Affairs Brief,* March 1983, [p. 1.]

326 ECONOMICS: THE AMERICAN ECONOMY

Both countries are more agriculturally intensive than these United States, for instance, where only 3 percent of the workforce is employed in agriculture. A higher percentage of workers in Free China has found release from farm work and moved into factories than in Red China.

One might ask: Does God have a plan and a built-in law-structure which, if man is left free, will work beneficially to all according to His sovereign design? The secular economist and social scientist would scoff at such a suggestion. They will opt for imposing government control over even the most private aspects of life, including procreation. This is a natural reaction of humanistically oriented man. Control over population is a natural conclusion of government economic planning, for broad economic controls logically devolve into minute controls over every aspect of life. After all, how can the secular god called the State implement a national plan without planning the component **parts** of that plan? If the State is to be sovereign nationally, it must necessarily be sovereign throughout; and this approaches the point where the State is elevated to the position of a secular god. The Christian economist and the Christian ruler—if they are consistent with biblical teaching concerning the sovereignty of God—must opt for an alternative other than centralized government control. (See Matt. 6:25-34, 10:29-31; Luke 12:6-7).

The Free Market as a Solution

Is there a viable alternative to vesting control and direction of economic development in the hands of governing authorities? The answer, though not popularly endorsed in this day of humanistic secularism, is a definite "Yes!" Adam Smith's book, *The Wealth of Nations,* though not written from an overtly Christian perspective, was a critique of the type of early government planning and control which was called **mercantilism**. Modern types of centralized government planning, both in less-developed and developed countries, can be accurately regarded as a form of **neo-mercantilism**.[6]

Adam Smith's book was instrumental in convincing political leaders in Britain and these United States to follow a free trade policy, though no civil government has been refreshing enough to follow a 100-percent laissez faire policy. To the extent the civil authority left people free to follow their own ways by limiting itself to guaranteeing the impartial rule of law instead of imposing the arbitrary rule of men, less-developed nations have miraculously blossomed into highly developed industrial giants. These United States of America are perhaps the outstanding example throughout history of a people who very quickly passed through the various economic stages from less-

---

[6]Every country, even the most advanced economically, is always in the process of developing economically. Treatment of the principles of economic development logically apply to our own country today. These United States are practicing, through nationally imposed controls and regulation, a similar form of neo-mercantilism that the rulers of presently underdeveloped countries practice.

developed to highly developed. Let us look at them historically as a brief case study.

The American Experience

The early colonists, who emigrated to New England in the early 1600s, came to America primarily for religious reasons. They came to establish covenant communities based on the rule of God and to obtain political and economic freedom. That the primary motivation was religious is attested to by the well-known history of the Pilgrims who first fled from England to Holland to escape religious persecution. There in Leyden, the Pilgrims were economically successful; but they were concerned about the unchristian atmosphere to which their children were exposed. They gained financial backing from some London merchants and formed a collective business partnership, and 102 émigrés sailed in the Mayflower for the New World in the fall of 1620. How the Mayflower was blown off course and landed off the rocky shore of New England instead of Virginia is known to every American schoolboy and girl. The Mayflower Compact testifies to this staunch people's dedication to build a covenant community based on the Bible as their rule and guide for every aspect of life, including civil government and economics. The settlement at Jamestown, Virginia, was even earlier (1608). However, the Bible was not as highly regarded there. It is not surprising that economic development at Jamestown lagged behind the fast development that took place at Plymouth.[7]

During the first and second years, the Pilgrims came close to starvation. Food remained in scarce supply because the community pooled the produce of the people's labor in common storehouses. The produce was regarded as belonging to the collective partnership, which included the London businessmen who provided the risk capital; so stores were rationed out to individual families on a need basis. This system of collective effort and ownership did not work satisfactorily at all. It ran counter to man's acquisitive nature. Apathy and languishing in the face of dire necessity prevailed. Early in 1623, the Pilgrims changed to a system of **individual** ownership in which each family controlled a specific tract of land and privately owned what was produced on it. The immediate and long-lasting results were amazing.

The Thanksgiving of 1623 was their first feast of plenty. Miraculously, the stimulus of private enterprise and the hope of private gain motivated the previously apathetic settlers into a regimen of dedicated hard work. After the institution of private property, entire families went out to plant corn and to work in the fields (thankfully, the Pilgrims did not have child labor laws). Of this experience, Governor William Bradford wrote:

---

[7]See Peter Marshall and David Manuel, *The Light and the Glory* (Old Tappan, New Jersey: Revell, 1977).

All this while no supply was heard of, neither knew they when they might expect any. So they began to think how they might raise as much corn as they could, and obtain a better crop than they had done, that they might not still thus languish in misery. At length, after much debate of things, the Governor (with the advice of the chiefest amongst them) gave way that they should set corn every man for his own particular, and in that regard trust to themselves; in all other things to go on in the general way as before. And so assigned to every family a parcel of land, according to the proportion of their number, for that end, only for present use (but made no division for inheritance) and ranged all boys and youth under some family. This had very good success, for it made all hands very industrious, so as much more corn was planted than otherwise would have been by any means the Governor or any other could use, and saved him a great deal of trouble, and gave far better content. The women now went willingly into the field, and took their little ones with them to set corn; which before would allege weakness and inability; whom to have compelled would have been thought great tyranny and oppression.

The experience that was had in this common course and condition, tried sundry years and that amongst godly and sober men, may well evince the vanity of that conceit of Plato's and other ancients applauded by some of later times; that the taking away of property and bringing in community into a commonwealth would make them happy and flourishing; as if they were wiser than God. For this community (so far as it was) was found to breed much confusion and discontent and retard much employment that would have been to their benefit and comfort. For the young men, that were most able and fit for labour and service, did repine that they should spend their time and strength to work for other men's wives and children without any recompense. The strong, or man of parts, had no more in division of victuals and clothes than he that was weak and not able to do a quarter the other could; this was thought injustice. The aged and graver men to be ranked and equalized in labours and victuals, clothes, etc., with the meaner and younger sort, thought it some indignity and disrespect unto them. And for men's wives to be commanded to do service for other men, as dressing their meat, washing their clothes, etc., they deemed it a kind of slavery, neither could many husbands well brook it. Upon the point all being to have alike, and all to do alike, they thought themselves in the like condition, and one as good as another; and so, if it did not cut off those relations that God hath set amongst men, yet it did at least much diminish and take off the mutual respects that should be preserved amongst them. And would have been worse if they had been men of another condition. Let none object this is men's corruption, and nothing to the course itself. I answer, seeing all men have this corruption in them, God in His wisdom saw another course fitter for them.[8]

If one principle can be said to be truly characteristic of these United States — both during the 150-year Colonial Era and the 200 years since our independence from England — it is the principle of private property controlled by free men who are directly answerable to God. It is only during the last couple of generations in our country that this principle has been seriously weakened by the persistent growth of centralized government at the national level. The whole law-structure of these United States and all of her social and economic institutions were built on this one central principle, which is **theologically** based. Man's right to property is God-given. He was created by God, and God bestowed on man inalienable rights; and these rights are to be conscientiously protected by the rule of law. Americans, by their heritage and by their constitution, are not to be subjected to the arbitrary rule of men. The right to property, and this includes the effective control of wealth, is a fundamental precept in these United States.

Nowhere in the world had so many men enjoyed such an extent of freedom as they did in America. It is crucial to the student of economics to note that this never-before-experienced degree of freedom was **religiously** based. Freedom, in the final analysis, must rest on theological presuppositions that involve a people's whole world-and-life view. Men in America responded to this theologically based freedom enthusiastically. Wealth was produced with such energy that it appeared to pour freely out of a cornucopia. Ordinary men were stimulated to make extraordinary efforts to save, accumulate and invest. Small and large fortunes and a steady accumulation of productive capital occurred all over the country. Capital accumulation was widely engaged in by the entire populace rather than being concentrated in the hands of just a few of the elite. There was no mass of impoverished citizens. This economic miracle happened in America with a minimal degree of governmental attention. Complete freedom was never achieved, of course, for we live in an imperfect world in which there is an ever-present tendency for rulers to impose controls and regulations on the people. However, the degree of economic, political and social freedom enjoyed in America was much, much greater than men had experienced in any other country in the world except in Old Testament Israel before the advent of the Kings.

After Americans won their freedom from Great Britain in the Revolutionary War, observers were amazed at the solid economic progress being made in the young Republic. One European visitor to America in the 1830s wrote:

---

[8]William Bradford, *Of Plymouth Plantation: 1620-1647* (New York: Knopf, 1970), pp. 120-121.

I sought for the greatness and genius of America in her fertile fields and boundless forests; it was not there. I sought for it in her free schools and her institutions of learning; it was not there. I sought for it in her matchless constitution and democratic congress; it was not there. Not until I went to the churches of America and found them aflame for righteousness did I understand the greatness and genius of America. America is great because America is good. When America ceases to be good, America will cease to be great.[9]

Never before in the history of mankind had so many people owned so much. Before the War Between the States, ownership of wealth was very widespread; and real incomes rose steadily. The advent of the War Between the States and creation of the National Banking System, which was designed — as we saw in an earlier chapter — to help finance the war, served to concentrate the control of wealth into fewer hands. Even so, ownership of wealth in these United States was more widespread than in other countries. This characteristic, though weakened during this century by socialistic practices, has remained up to the present time.

When more and more wealth is accumulated in a country, this means that productive capital becomes more abundant, too. When this happens, labor becomes relatively less abundant than capital. Since the higher margin of return always goes to the productive factor which is less abundant, this means there will be a tendency for wages to rise relative to the return received by the owners of capital (profits). Strictly speaking, the return paid to the owners of wealth is really **interest.** From a bookkeeping standpoint, most of the return to wealth is called **profit.** It is in this bookkeeping sense that we use the term profit here, which lumps interest and economic profit together. Let us remember that much of what is considered as corporate profit is really interest earned on invested capital.

As profit-seeking entrepreneurs earn profits and reinvest them in their businesses, they increase the amount of capital in existence relative to the amount of labor. As a result, labor becomes relatively less abundant; and the margin of payment shifts from capital to labor. This explains why wages trend upward in countries as capital investment increases. It is a natural process. The process is shown in Graph 12:1.

In this present day, the rulers of many less-developed countries take a Marxian view of profits as being something capitalists get by unfairly exploiting workers. They therefore tend to follow misguided policies which limit profits under the illusion that they are helping the working class. In doing so, they tend to stymie the growth of capital investment which, in the long run, is the best guarantee of rising wage levels. Their anti-capitalist policies actually end up hurting workers.

---

[9]Alexis de Tocqueville: Paraphrased in Frank Abbott Magruder, *American Government: A Textbook on the Problems of Democracy* (Boston: Allyn and Bacon, 1949), pp. 12-13.

Graph 12:1

The Marginal Return of Labor vs. Capital

150 Years Ago: The marginal return went to the owners of capital because capital was relatively less abundant than labor. This means that profits were relatively high and that wages were relatively low:[10]

| *Total Supply of Labor* | *Marginal Return* | *Total Supply of Capital* |

Today: The greater marginal return goes to the providers of labor because labor is relatively less abundant than capital. This means that wages will be relatively high and that profits will be relatively low:

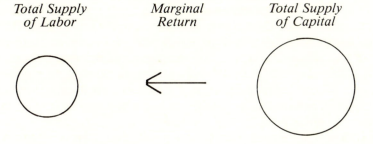

| *Total Supply of Labor* | *Marginal Return* | *Total Supply of Capital* |

In developing these United States, the ruling authorities never considered —at least until recent years—that they had the rightful power to limit profits. This was a wise policy to follow, for it spurred the earning of profits by profit-seeking entrepreneurs who continually reinvested them. This, rather than the growth of labor unions, explains the steady rise in real wages in these

---

[10]It is important to recognize that low wage levels are a natural phenomenon in capital-scarce countries, and not a result of "brutal capitalists" who "unfairly exploit poor defenseless workers." High profits are the cure for low wages; for as profit-seeking entrepreneurs continue to reinvest their profits, the resulting increase in capitalization creates a demand for more workers to employ the capital, which in turn increases output. The increased output, on one hand, and the increased demand for labor, on the other, work hand-in-hand to raise real wage levels.

United States. As the total supply of productive capital increased relative to the total supply of labor, wages in the free market could not go anywhere but up. It is important that we recognize that the major spur to the accumulation of productive wealth and the subsequent tendency of wages to rise is the result of a **theological** concept that has been stressed in America: The God-given right of individuals to work for themselves and to enjoy the fruit of their own labor — in short, the principle of private property.

> *And also that every man should eat and drink, and enjoy the good of all his labour, it is the gift of God.*
>
> *Ecclesiastes 3:13*

> *Every man also to whom God hath given riches and wealth, and hath given him power to eat thereof, and to take his portion, and to rejoice in his labour; this is the gift of God.*
>
> *Ecclesiastes 5:19*

Rulers of less-developed countries should be taught this biblical principle and its long-term economic effect on the accumulation of capital and on rising wage levels. Those rulers who will humble themselves to the rule of Christ and to the law-structure given in His word (Isa. 45:23; Phil. 2:10) will find that they will naturally implement policies which are conducive to economic growth.

The Russian Tsarist Experience

Before the mid-nineteenth century, Russia was a very backward nation both politically and economically. The tsar ruled as an autocrat over the church and state. Some 95 percent of the population was tied directly to the land — most as serfs, who were the equivalent of slaves, plus a very small percentage of large landowners.[11] The extreme lack of political and economic freedom dampened individual initiative. The result was a hopelessly backward nation with a static, almost non-progressing economy. When Nicholas I was Tsar (1825-1855), the Russian state and the Russian economy was based on serfdom and state socialism.

This static, non-progressing situation had existed for centuries; but it began to change drastically during the reign of Alexander II (1855-1881). Tsar Alexander II decreed the abolition of serfdom in 1861. Household serfs were freed within two years, and peasant serfs (farmers) received their personal freedom with allotments of land from a 50-percent portion taken from the large estates. The decree allowed the serfs to purchase their plots of land on credit through a 49-year bond. Some 85 percent of the large landowners sold 50 percent of their holdings to the peasant serfs.

---

[11]Statistics for this portion are largely taken from George Vernadsky, *A History of Russia* (New Haven, Conn.: Yale University Press, 1969).

While land thus sold was held on a communal-ownership basis, each peasant privately owned the produce that was raised on the particular plot he and his family worked. The stimulus generated by this move toward private ownership was tremendous. Between 1850 and 1900, the population doubled (without immigration). Between 1900 and 1915, the population increased by another 30 percent to 170 million.

In 1815 only 3.5 million people (5 percent of the total population) lived in towns and cities. By 1897 the urban population had risen to 16.5 million (13 percent); and by 1914, just before the outbreak of World War I, it had risen to 25 million (15 percent). This shift in population provides evidence that a substantial rise in agricultural productivity took place in Tsarist Russia. This was the natural result of giving people greater economic freedom and the assurance that what they produced was their own. By 1905 the area under cultivation expanded to about 100 million hectares (one hectare equals two and one-half acres). By 1914 the cultivated area had expanded to 120 million hectares.

As we would expect with the increase of freedom, agricultural harvests zoomed upward. During 1861-1870, grain harvests yielded an average of 0.5 tons per hectare. During 1901-1910, the average had increased by more than 50 percent to 0.8 tons per hectare. In 1913 the grain harvest reached 92 million tons. It was during this period of relative economic freedom, from 1861 to 1914, that Russia became a great exporter of grain.

One little-realized fact about Russia is that Tsarist Russia was a consistent net exporter of wheat during the latter part of the nineteenth century. But since the Communist Revolution of 1917 and the resultant loss of freedom, the Soviet Union has been a consistent net importer of wheat. In spite of tremendous advances in agricultural technology and labor-saving machinery, Communist Russia has failed year after year of being able to feed itself.

Up to the time of Alexander II, industrialization did not bound ahead because of the lack of personal freedom and the resulting general apathy of the Russian people. Foreign investment, as we would also expect, was minimal; for little hope for profit exists in such a stagnant economy. This, too, started to change during Alexander II's reign because he initiated a free trade policy which stimulated private initiative:

• Private companies were invited to build railroads on a concession basis.

• Government-owned factories in the Ural Mountains were sold to private individuals.

• Foreign investment, attracted by the sudden potential of earning profits in Russia, increased greatly. By 1913, 25 percent of capital investment was foreign: Britain, France, Belgium, Germany, Sweden and these United States were all represented. This large percentage of foreign investment testified to the fact that foreigners felt confident that the tsarist regimes provided adequate protection to private property.

• Domestic investment also increased substantially. Before the reign of Alexander II, most large industries were government-owned. By 1900, ownership of the 50 largest industries was distributed as follows:

> 29% by descendants of peasants
> 8% by descendants of small merchants
> 5% by descendants of noblemen

• Industrialization continued to expand at a rapid rate right up to the advent of World War I:

(1) Production of cotton increased from 179,000 looms in 1905 to 220,000 in 1911. In 1890 per capita consumption of cotton was 2.3 pounds; by 1910 it had doubled to 4.6 pounds.

(2) Iron production increased from 1.5 million tons of pig iron in 1900 to 3.5 million tons in 1914.

(3) Oil production expanded from a mere 160,000 tons in 1860 (when the oil industry was just beginning) to seven million tons in 1905. This amounted to 27 percent of total world production. In 1913 it was nine million tons, which was only 17 percent of world production because production in other countries had expanded more rapidly.

In 1864 the *zemstros* (local governmental bodies) began overseeing matters concerning education, health, charity and even fire insurance. The number of hospitals, schools and cooperative societies increased drastically. Twenty-five percent of the population was literate by 1897.

We have gone into some detail concerning the remarkable economic development of Tsarist Russia because it presents an excellent case study of how an extremely backward nation was suddenly transformed into an agricultural and industrial dynamo. This miraculous transformation occurred with the granting of more liberty and private ownership of productive effort to the masses. Within one generation, the Russian economy was dynamically expanding on all fronts. This expansion continued at a rapid pace until World War I suddenly interrupted it.

It was the very chaotic situation caused by World War I that led to conflict between Nicholas II and the Duma (legislative council) in 1916. On March 14, 1917, the Tsar voluntarily abdicated; and a democratic socialist Provisional Government was set up with Alexander Kerensky as Minister of Justice.

It is important to note that economic growth under tsarist rule advanced rapidly—from the mid-1860s right up to 1914 when World War I started. Few people are aware of this fact. Fewer still realize the close correlation between the expanding freedom of a people and the expanding production of the economy. The tsarist period in Russia from 1861 to 1914 presents an ideal study of economic development from which the less-developed countries of today might well benefit. There is little doubt that present-day economic planners in less-developed countries would discover that a laissez faire policy, if consistently followed, would generate more capital investment—from both domestic and foreign sources—than the popular but misguided policy of centralized government planning and control.

Now we come to a startling contrast. What happened to post-World War I Russia?

Post-World War I Russia

The democratic Kerensky Provisional Government was forcefully overthrown by the Bolsheviks in November, 1917, under the fanatical leadership of Vladimir Ilyich Lenin (1870-1924). A terrible period of civil war followed while the communists ruthlessly seized and extended their tyranny across the nation.

An even worse period followed during which the communist rulers murdered and purposely starved millions of peasants who resisted the government's policy of eliminating private property and socializing all means of production. It is estimated by reliable sources that this cold-blooded genocide and other systematic extermination of human life has, to date, cost in excess of 60 million lives. This "price" was willingly exacted by the communist leaders for two reasons: The "price" is counted in **other** people's lives, not their own; and persons are regarded by communists only as "matter in motion"; so there is no moral restraint against the taking of life when doing so serves the purposes of those in power.

Even today, more than ten million political prisoners are kept in 1,000 slave-labor camps which are widely distributed throughout the Soviet Union. This vast pool of forced labor constitutes a considerable portion of the Soviet Union's effort in building infrastructure. Slave laborers are forced to work on large government projects such as clearing dam sites, building roads and railroads, moving rock and dirt, mining gold and cutting trees in the trackless wastes of Siberia and laying of gas pipelines. The prisoners' life span is pathetically short—only a few months on the average—because they are purposely kept on starvation diets and are poorly clothed and housed even in sub-zero weather. The average slave laborer succumbs within a few months, being literally worked to death, though some have managed to survive for a number of years. Probably the most-noted survivor of the slave-labor camps is Aleksandr I. Solzhenitsyn, author of *The Gulag Archipelago,* who won the Nobel prize in literature in 1970 for his exposé of the communist slave-labor system. Economists tend to overlook the existence of these ten million slave workers in evaluating the Soviet economy; but this is a mistake, for the slave-labor system is an integral part of the Soviet economy today.[12]

Contrary to Tsarist Russia, when increasing freedom motivated the Russian populace to scramble in pursuit of personal gain, the communist rulers set up a highly centralized system of controlling the economy. Instead of con-

---

[12]U.S., Congress, Senate, Committee of the Judiciary, *U.S.S.R. Labor Camps.* 93d Cong., 1st sess., February 1, 1973.

sumer wants being satisfied at the same time that agricultural and industrial expansion was taking place, the communist rulers have systematically starved the consumer and farm sectors of the economy in order to boost production in the military and heavy machinery sectors. For some 65 years, since the take over in 1917, consumer production has purposely been held to the bare minimum that Soviet citizens will endure without actually rising up in open rebellion.

Investment in the agricultural sector is also restricted, which partially explains the continuing need of the Soviet Union to import grain on credit from the West. Consumer goods that are available at state-owned stores are generally of poor quality and are heavily taxed by what is called a "turn-over tax"—equivalent to an excise tax. The surpluses that are siphoned off by the turn-over tax and from starving these other sectors of the economy are then used to expand the heavy industry and military sectors of the economy.

The forcible take over of the Kerensky Provisional Government, the bloody civil war and mass killings that followed during the next decade and a half and the blundering attempts to force rapid growth in heavy industry at the expense of other sectors of the economy have created a pattern of almost constant chaos and gross inefficiency in the Soviet economy. A series of Five-Year Plans has been implemented, starting in 1928, to steer the Soviet economy in the direction the leaders desire. The official policy of refusing to recognize the important role of profits and interest in economic calculations has severely impeded Soviet planning. The lack of proper cost allocation has led to gross inefficiency in all sectors. There is a continual need for importing Western capital and technology. Today the communist rulers have finally achieved partial success in building the large heavy industry and war materials sectors, but this has been accomplished at the gross expense of human life and a consistent degradation of human values that would have been impossible in a free country.

A Comparison of the American and Russian Experiences

If we compare the American and Tsarist Russian experiments of economic development with the post-communist experiment, we find a study in contrasts. The two former experiments achieved a broad-based dynamic economic growth by releasing the latent energy of millions of self-directed individuals. This was done without bloodshed and without the imposition of tyranny. In fact, progress in both instances was gained as a result of increasing people's freedom and self-responsibility rather than by decreasing them. The latter experiment under communism has achieved a narrow-based growth in only a very few sectors of the economy by forcibly harnessing the energies of millions of hapless citizens and by ruthlessly exterminating those who resisted. The contrast in methods reveals a divergence of policy in economics and civil government based on the contrasting world-and-life views which underlie the two approaches. The contrast also shows what is bound to happen when a false dichotomy is made between the so-called application of "pure" economics and the moral and religious values which should guide man in his actions.

The American experiment from its very start recognized the biblical view of man as being a precious, God-created being who has an inherent right to freedom. The tsarist regime, beginning in the 1860s, moved strongly towards the American pattern with amazing results. In contrast, the communist experiment is built on the anti-Christian, humanist view of man as being a chance product of organic evolution, with the logical result of turning citizens into pawns. The communist view of man as being no more than "matter in motion" removes any moral restraint against the using, abusing and disposing of "this worthless matter" when the ruling authorities have wrested all they can from "it" for the "good of the State."

There is a conflict here. It is not so much a conflict of economic and political systems, which are **results**, but a conflict of the underlying philosophies of man and views of God. Man's view of God cannot help but affect the outworking of his world-and-life view and the political and economic systems he sets up.

In December, 1977, Professor Wladislaw Krasnow, a former propaganda broadcaster for Moscow Radio who defected to the West in 1962, wrote about the contrasting American Revolution (1776) and the Communist Revolution (1917):

> The American Revolution established religious freedom and separated church from the state; the Communist Revolution replaced the pre-eminence of Orthodox Christianity with total monopoly by a new secular religion, Marxism-Leninism, which became the essence of the communist state.
>
> The former reaffirmed respect for private property and individual enterprise; the latter expropriated virtually all private property and in favor of the total state control over Russia's economy.
>
> The former reaffirmed and enhanced political liberties; the latter did away with them.
>
> The former was against a monarch who mistreated the Colonies; the latter, against a democratic, socialist-leaning, provisional government that had just abolished the czarist monarchy.
>
> The former confirmed its legitimacy through ballot power; the latter through bullet power.
>
> After a bloody civil war was over, the communist victors had no Lincoln among them to proclaim "malice toward none." The reign of the communist malice just began. First, against the defeated. Then, against their own allies: the social democrats, socialist-revolutionaries and anarchists. Finally, it turned against the Communists themselves, such as Trotsky's supporters, so that under

Stalin more Communists were done in by their own comrades than by all the czars, capitalists and imperialists put together.

Down the drain went millions of peasants and workers who never could figure out to what "ism" they belonged. The communist holocaust against Soviet citizens took — in peace time! — even more lives than the Nazi holocaust against the Jews. (Read Robert Conquest, "The Great Purge.")

Thus, the cost of the 60 years of communist rule in Russia is the heaviest investment in blood, sweat and tears that mankind has ever known. Although I cannot imagine the magnitude of the achievements that would conceivably justify even one-hundredth of this cost, the Soviet Union can show precious little to its credit.

In industry it has one of the lowest productivities among industrialized nations. In agriculture, it employs 15 times as many peasants as American farmers, but cannot feed the country. Its standard of living is closer to Portugal and Spain than to Germany or Japan, the defeated countries of World War II.

. . . The only indisputable communist achievement of 60 years is then its unsurpassed ability to put on a front, to bluff and fool foe and friend alike, and to bully the world into giving up all human rights.[13]

The Land Problem

Earlier we pointed out that the existence of a small landed elite coupled with large masses of unlanded peasants produces a potential for revolutionary activity in some less-developed countries. The crux of the real problem is how to go about putting the peasantry in touch with land so that private economic production can take place.

In Tsarist Russia the problem was approached by the autocratic ruler simply issuing a decree that the landed nobles were forced to follow — half of the nobles' lands were sold to the serfs, and the nobles were paid by bonds that were to be paid off over a period of years. This, of course, is a form of forced dispossession; but it was a more humane way of freeing serfs than the Union used in The War Between the States to free Negro slaves. Negro slaves were freed, but the large majority remained landless.

Some peaceful solution to the long-existing land problem might possibly be worked out by the leaders of countries faced with revolutionary foment if a voluntary means of purchase could be arranged which would adequately compensate existing landowners. Before any steps are taken to sell large privately owned plots to the unlanded, all government-owned land should certainly be distributed to the masses. This step alone might be enough to solve the problem.

---

[13]*Dallas* (Texas) *Morning News*, 13 December 1977.

In an earlier chapter, we noted that these United States of America also have a growing land problem; for the federal government still owns over 30 percent of the land in our country. There is no good reason for this government ownership. Much of this land, we pointed out, is being withheld from economic production, thereby causing the total supply of production to be less and consumer prices to be higher than they otherwise would be. It is dangerous to both the liberty and economic welfare of the American people for the civil authority to own such vast areas of land. Remember the economic stimulus that occurred in Tsarist Russia when vast areas of land were turned over to the people? Imagine, then, the dynamic economic stimulus which would certainly occur if the federal government took similar steps to divest itself of its vast land holdings. Profit-seeking entrepreneurs, both large and small, and millions of individual householders would immediately be galvanized into action. As economic activity surged, unemployment would plummet; people now on welfare roles would find employment opportunities beckoning to them.

It is appropriate at this point to turn to the Bible in order to learn what provision God made to keep men from being disenfranchised from the land. First, we learn from the early chapters of Genesis that all that is needed for economic production to occur are the two primary factors of production: land and man (Gen. 2:15-16, 9:1-3). With free access to land, man is fully capable of developing the third factor of production, capital (tools), with which to multiply his human effort in producing whatever he needs to live and to do his God-appointed work.

In Genesis 47:13-26, God shows how the loss of private ownership of land and its transfer of ownership to the ruler resulted in enslavement of the Egyptians and then to enslavement of the Israelites. This was an important object lesson for God's people. When the Israelites crossed the Jordan River and entered the Promised Land after their 40 years of wandering in the desert, God had them divide the land, by tribes and by family, into privately owned plots. Each family thus had private ownership of land. God made ample provision to assure man's economic independence. Man's political freedom, too, is dependent on his economic independence; for in Old Testament Israel, God set up what would be equivalent today to a democratic republic populated by a large body of freemen.

In this democratic republic, what provision did God make to prevent the appearance of the land problem, that is, to prevent men from becoming disenfranchised from the land in one manner or another? The answer is noteworthy: God commanded that no man had the right to sell or dispose of his birthright (the land is God's gift to man, Ps. 115:16) permanently and thereby dispossess his progeny. Every 50 years was the Year of Jubilee, and in this year the land—if sold or lost to others for indebtedness or for any other reason—was to be returned to the original family (Lev. 25:10-28). Each new generation was guaranteed that it would have access to the land so that each individual's economic freedom would be preserved. Any land holder was free to sell, to dispose of or to lose his land, but not beyond the next Year of Jubilee. Land was **privately** owned but the essential idea that no father could dispossess his children from the benefits of God's gift to men (the earth) was built into the God-given law-structure of society. Old Testament Israel, before the time when the people asked for a king "like other nations" (I Sam. 8:5), was a private property-based society. There was no taxation, by the way, for government-imposed taxation was a curse God warned the Israelites would come as a consequence of their asking for a secular king (I Sam. 8:7-18).

The Israelite community was an agriculturally based society without a civil ruler that imposed taxes. Is there any way that the Year of Jubilee principle of safeguarding men against being disenfranchised from the land can be implemented in modern societies which have secular rulers and for societies which may not always remain agriculturally based? The answer is yes, but great care must be used; for sinful men can pervert any system in order to enslave their fellow men.

One way of guaranteeing that people will always have individual access to land, so as not to disenfranchise large masses of people, is to change existing tax policies. On one hand, both labor and capital should be untaxed; this will uphold the private property principle that what man produces through his own effort is his and his alone—that no other party, even the civil authority, has any proper interest in it. On the other hand, the tax on land sites (i.e., on the unimproved value of the land, which has value only because of its God-given status) should be raised. As we have seen in an earlier chapter, raising the tax on land provides an economic incentive for landowners to put their land into economic use to meet the demands of the marketplace. Individuals who hold land for speculative purposes instead of for producing goods and services for the benefit of others, would sell unused land to entrepreneurs who would make better economic use of it.

The implementation of a site-value land taxation policy in all countries— both economically developed as well as in less-developed countries—would spur production, reduce unemployment and eliminate the alleged need for government welfare programs. The role of government in society would be greatly reduced, and the ratio of privately oriented production versus government-mandated production would be increased.

Are there any criticisms of a site-value taxation policy on land? Yes. Some free-market advocates claim it is socialistic. This is an invalid criticsm, for **any** tax amounts to a socialization of people's wealth or income. A site-value tax is no more a socialization of wealth than is a tax on labor or on capital. In the chapter on taxes, we pointed out that the **ideal** situation would be not to allow the civil authority any power to tax at all; but, to be practical, we must recognize that civil governments have already taken such authority. The second best tax policy, if the civil authorities are to be given authority to tax, would be a flat head tax on each citizen. The worst taxes, in the author's opinion, are those on labor or capital because taxes levied on these sources require a vast horde of tax collectors who are both expensive to maintain and who violate the people's liberties by snooping into their private affairs.

Collectivists generally do not like the idea of untaxing labor and capital and raising taxes on land-sites for two reasons: First, they correctly claim that a tax on land-sites will not generate nearly enough income to support the existing level of government programs and services. Secondly, collectivists realize that, if government's power to tax is limited only to the relatively small amount of income generated from the unimproved value of land-sites, the economy will naturally be directed more towards private enterprise and less towards government-directed activities. To both of these criticisms the author would say, Amen! That is why he recommends untaxing labor and capital and uptaxing land.

Finally, is there a danger to a site-value taxation policy? Yes, there are always dangers men face whenever power is delegated to the civil authority; for in the course of history, more people have been enslaved by their **own** rulers than by foreign enemies (see the Egyptian example in Gen. 47:13-26). No tax should ever be imposed at the national level, for at this level the tax imposers are too far removed from the taxpayers. Site-value taxes should be levied only at the county level, and from there the needed funds passed on (in these United States) to the state and national levels of government. This would — beneficially for the sake of freedom — **reverse** the existing centers of government power. Instead of a tyrannically strong central government which now dictates to the states, counties and local governments, political power and influence in these United States would be strongest at home, next strongest at the state level and least powerful at the national level. This need not weaken the nation's stance toward foreign nations.

The same shifting of economic and political power would also be found, through a site-value taxation policy, in the less-developed countries. Right now, every LDC in the world is characterized by strong central governments which regard their role as that of directing and manipulating citizens toward whatever Utopia the rulers happen to envision. Usually their Utopia is some kind of socialist-oriented economy and society. Thus, the rulers of such countries can be expected to oppose any policy which decreases their power role and increases the economic freedom and political self-direction of the citizens.

Needed land reform policies in less-developed countries could be carried out much easier through a mild change of site-value taxation (untaxing labor and capital and uptaxing land sites) than by forcibly redistributing land from large landowners to the unlanded masses. A policy of site-value taxation that would peaceably restore men to economic contact with the land would do much to defuse revolutionary activities of the radical communists who are now fomenting rebellion and anarchy. The fact that present regimes would oppose a change does not negate the beneficial points explained earlier. Since each country has the right of self-determination, the only step outsiders can take is to point out the wisdom of following sound policies and the folly of following unsound policies. Then the people and rulers of each less-developed country must live with the consequences of the policies they choose.

A Biblical Perspective

In evaluating how best to overcome the various economic, political and social problems that less-developed countries face, it is necessary to consider two aspects of the problem: the **cause** of the existing problems and the various **solutions** that are possible.

Some problems that less-developed nations face are clearly the result of transgressing the word of God as revealed in the Bible. Sinful man finds himself directly opposed to the law-structure through which God rules the universe. Go back to the section of this chapter where we listed the various problems that exist in less-developed countries. Study them and discern which are the result of breaking the Ten Commandments (Ex. 20:1-17; Deut. 5:1-21) and of failing to heed God's promise of blessings and cursings (Deut. 28 and 29).

If we do this, we can see that many of the existing problems that plague less-developed countries would soon vanish if the people would embrace the Gospel and begin systematically to order their personal and social lives according to biblical precepts. In short, economic problems are many times simply the outworking of moral evil; or they may be the result of well-intentioned acts which contravene God's law through ignorance. Starvation in India in the midst of millions of "sacred" cattle is perhaps the prime example. (Rom. 1:22-23). Apathy of the people in the voluntary collective experiment of the early Pilgrims and of the Russian peasantry before the reign of Alexander II are other examples (I Thess. 4:11-12; II Thess. 3:8-13). Any amount of economic planning implemented by centralized rule will not and cannot possibly change the underlying causes which produce the visible problems (curses). What is needed, rather, is staunch recognition of man's inherent right as well as duty to stand individually free and self-responsible before his Maker (Ex. 8:1; Rom. 14:4), and a godly law-structure which adequately protects man's God-given right to property. Implementing such biblically based principles in society would immediately release an explosion of dynamic activity that could not possibly be held in check by civil rulers short of imposing absolute tyranny. This is both the secret of free market economic development and the solution for many of the problems which currently beset less-developed countries.

Once the causes of the problems (curses) that beset LDCs are analyzed from a biblical basis, then — and only then — are we ready to consider possible solutions. Various possibilities must be evaluated in light of biblical precepts to insure that proposed solutions do not rob citizens of their individual responsibility before God nor allow the authority of the state to extend beyond its biblical limits, thereby establishing the state as a secular god. It is also necessary to keep in mind the sinful tendency of rulers to pervert judgment and to plunder the people who are entrusted by God to their care (I Kings 21:1-16; Isa. 1:23).

If the Bible is used as a normative guide, as suggested above, in evaluating and developing political and economic policy, we will find that the condition of economic underdevelopment suffered by many countries today is the result of rejecting the clearly revealed law-order in God's word. Most of the problems that civil rulers wrestle with would vanish if economic and governmental policies were changed to conform with biblical principles. There is a great need to bring people of less-developed nations to a saving knowledge of Jesus Christ and then instruct them how to consistently order their personal and social lives according to biblical precepts. Finally, there is less need for top-level government planners, whose job it is to impose government programs on the masses, than there is for Christian missionaries who will work with the people at the grassroots level and lead them to establish a godly and productive economic order.

In summary, while we recognize that it is possible for a less-developed country to advance economically by imposing centralized plans on the masses by government fiat, the cost of doing so is very great when counted in terms of involuntarily imposed human sacrifice. Also, we must discern that the current popular trend of centralized economic planning runs directly counter to God's revealed word because it denies man's self-responsibility before God. Central planning invariably turns the civil authority into a lawless plunderer by breaking the commandment "Thou shalt not steal" through government expropriation and transforms the agency of civil government into a secular god. The historical record shows that free market voluntarism coupled with the principle of private property produces a more dynamic economic expansion than collectivization of the economy, and this is accomplished by enhancing human life instead of degrading it. This economic and social blessing is exactly what we would expect by following the law of God.

Blessed is the nation whose God is the Lord[!]

Psalm 33:12

Questions

1. Define economic growth. Give three examples of economic growth in your own country and in two other countries.

2. List the problems that economically less-developed countries face.

3. Investigate a LDC of your choice and list the problems you find in it. If you were asked for advice, what solutions would you recommend to alleviate the problems? How would you suggest they be implemented?

4. Review the list of problems from question #2. Do you find any common causes? Explain how they can be solved.

5. Why would we expect a conflict between the rulers and the masses of people concerning the rulers' plans for economic development?

6. Why do rulers of developing nations usually embrace the idea of centralized government planning instead of free market voluntarism?

7. Why is there a tendency for mal-investment to occur through central government planning in less-developed countries?

8. Discuss the pros and cons of big government projects versus investing in primary agriculture to foster economic development. Which course would employ more people and make better use of their skills? Which course do government planners usually follow? Why?

9. Assume you are either a Christian "economic missionary" or a central government planner. Present your case to the ruler of a developing nation as to why your approach to economic development should be followed. Is your argument based primarily on positive economic principles or on normative points involving moral and ethical values? Explain.

10. Rulers must somehow gain control of citizens' wealth if they hope to implement their top-level plans for economic development. What three ways of doing this were explained? If you were the ruler of a developing nation, which would you prefer? Why?

11. For whom do import controls create artificial profit potentials? How?

12. Summarize the philosophy or world-and-life view held by economic planners in civil government. Is this view in conformity with or in conflict with your understanding of scriptural principles? Explain and substantiate your statement with appropriate Bible references.

13. Should civil rulers concern themselves with birth rates and population control? Why or why not? Is there a biblical principle involved? Explain.

14. Does sovereignty over the whole imply sovereignty over the component parts which make up the whole? If Christians do not object to God's sovereignty over the whole universe and its various parts (including themselves), should they object to rulers in civil government attempting to control the economy of their country and its component parts? Explain. Be ready to defend your views in class.

15. Why did the amount of labor expended in farming lag during the first two years of the Pilgrims's stay in America? What caused the sudden change, and what was the result?

16. What theological principle concerning property was characteristic of early America? What effect did it have economically and in civil government?

17. What did Alexis de Tocqueville have to say about the greatness and genius of America? Does it still apply? Explain.

18. Critics of the free market often complain that wages were too low and profits too high in these United States during the nineteenth century. Do you agree or disagree? Explain how high profits can be the very cause of rising wage levels. Show this graphically.

19. Assume you are invited to serve as economic advisor to the prime minister of a less-developed country. His previous advisor was a Marxist who convinced him that business profits are the result of businessmen unfairly exploiting workers. Therefore, the country has been following a policy of levying high taxes on corporations in order to eliminate profits, plus setting a high legal minimum wage in order to raise the general level of wages. Write the prime minister a memo which either (a) supports the existing program or (b) opposes it. In either case, explain the economic principles at work. Finally, evaluate the previous program and your own recommendations biblically.

20. Briefly describe the Russian economy before and after the 1860s. What differences were there? What caused them?

21. Is there a lesson in economic development that present-day rulers of LDCs can learn from the Tsarist Russian period of 1860-1914? Explain.

22. Substantiate or refute this statement: In 1917, the Bolsheviks overthrew the Kerensky government. The downtrodden masses cooperated with Lenin and his followers because the masses had not been progressing economically.

23. Why do the communist rulers of the U.S.S.R. not consider 60 million lives as too high a price to pay in fulfilling their state plan?

24. What policy do Soviet rulers follow to maximize growth of their military and heavy industry sectors of the economy?

25. Contrast economic development in Tsarist Russia from 1860-1914 with economic development in Communist Russia after 1917. Under which regime would you prefer to live? Why?

26. What is the real conflict between the historic American and Communist systems of civil government and economics? Be ready to discuss your statement in class.

27. What is the so-called "land problem"? What policy did God command in Old Testament Israel to prevent it from occurring? Can the principle be applied in modern times? Explain.

28. Write a short statement in which you defend or attack the policy of site-value taxation and the untaxing of labor and capital. Then defend your position against someone who holds the opposite view.

29. Evaluate Professor Krasnow's article concerning the American and Communist revolutions. In what way are his remarks pertinent to the causes and solutions to problems that less-developed nations face?

30. What problems in less-developed nations do you see as the result of transgressing God's word? Give some specific examples. Would conformance to God's law-structure cause the problems to vanish without centralized government planning? Explain.

31. If the civil rulers of developing nations do develop plans to eliminate some of the problems, what precautions should they take concerning proposed solutions?

32. In what ways does the current popular trend of centralized economic planning run contrary to God's revealed word? Do these points apply only to less-developed countries, or do they also apply to these United States of America? Explain.

13

Christ's Kingdom: How Shall We Build?

And in the days of these kings shall the God of heaven set up a kingdom, which shall never be destroyed: and the kingdom shall not be left to other people, but it shall break in pieces and consume all these kingdoms, and it shall stand for ever.

Daniel 2:44

IMMEDIATELY before ascending to heaven to reign at the right hand of His Father, Jesus made an astounding statement and left His disciples with explicit kingdom-building instructions:

. . . All power is given unto me in heaven and in earth.
Go ye therefore, and teach all nations, baptizing them in the name of the Father, and of the Son, and of the Holy Ghost:
Teaching them to observe all things whatsoever I have commanded you: and, lo, I am with you alway, even unto the end of the world.

Matthew 28:18-20

If we, as ambassadors for Christ, are to clearly understand our kingdom-building assignment, then we must start with a clear view of what Christ's Kingdom is. We must envision all that His Kingdom encompasses so that we may occupy it for Him till He returns in power and in glory.

Many in the Church of Christ view the Kingdom primarily as a future event that will be realized only at the second coming of Christ. To them the Church is just a small occupying force in a strange and foreign land. It will never conquer the land this side of heaven, so its greatest work is to preach the gospel in order to usher in new saints and to teach them how to live personally holy lives in the midst of evil. Christians, according to this view, are a salting (preserving) influence, but they are more in a "holding" role culturally than in a conquering role. Christ, according to this view, reigns over His spiritual kingdom; but the rest of the world in this sinful age belongs to Satan, and not much good can really be expected from it.

But, if we ponder Christ's statement and instructions, we soon come to realize that His Kingdom is all-encompassing. Jesus said that **all** power is given to Him in both heaven and in earth. Thus, Christ is indeed King of Kings and Lord over all (I Tim. 6:15; Rev. 17:14). We are to go, therefore, to all nations preaching the saving Gospel of Christ. And we are to teach all nations to observe whatsoever Christ has commanded. But this assignment entails much more than simply edifying the saints so they can personally live holy lives. Christ's instructions to teach them to observe all things whatsoever He has commanded must be seen, if indeed Christ is King of Kings and Lord of Lords, as a strong cultural mandate. Holy personal living, alone, is not enough; nor is simply being a salting influence to those whom our personal lives touch. In addition to living holy lives personally and being a salting influence on earth, we are to **occupy** until our Lord returns (Luke 19:13). Our mandate is not simply a passive holding action, but it is rather an **active and expanding dominion action**. Note that the two servatns who increased the talents given to them were rewarded, but that the passive servant who did not increase his holdings was condemned. As Christ-followers we are to establish dominion — we are to establish Christ's Kingdom which is to consume all other kingdoms (Dan. 2:44, 7:18-27). In short, we who are Christians are to boldly declare the fact that Christ's suzerainty extends over all creation and that every knee shall bow and every tongue shall swear to Him (Isa. 45:23; Rom. 14:11; Phil. 2:10-11).

But, in practical terms, what does Christ's cultural mandate mean? Among other things it means that we must bring all man-made institutions into conformity with the mind of Christ. We are to pull down the ungodly strongholds of this world and we are to erect godly institutions in their place by bringing every thought into obedience to Christ (II Cor. 10:4-5). We are to carefully investigate the social institutions of the family, the church, business and civil government; we are to carefully evaluate the various processes of social interchange: education, care of the poor and needy, economic intercourse, economic growth and care of the environment. In each instance, we must ask, "What ideal did God have in mind for man to follow when He created the universe and established His moment by moment sustaining rule over creation? Is God neutral concerning how man is to engage in economic exchange? Is God neutral concerning how man is ruled politically or how man engages in social activities? Or does God's word provide us with a sure guide as to the ideal manner in which we are to engage in social relations?"

Recently this author read a paper at a faculty forum at the college where he teaches. The essence of the paper was that the voluntary free market system is the only system of economic exchange that is in conformity with biblical precepts. One faculty member, a sincere Christian, strongly disagreed. He contended that God gives man freedom of choice concerning economic exchange. Thus, according to him, socialist/communist systems of exchange are just as moral inherently as free market capitalism if the people involved choose by majority vote which system they are to live under. To arrive at such a conclusion, one would have to view such things as a person's right of property and one's personal responsibility to God for his actions as subject to being overruled by majority vote. The fallacy of such a position can be brought into sharp focus by posing a question in an area where it is perhaps easier to see black and white: Does God give man freedom of choice in marriage? Is it all right for man to institute "open marriage" or "group marriages" if the majority of people so vote? Clearly, no Christian would admit such gross immorality as being in accord with Scripture! But if God gives man no choice concerning the commandment against **adultery**, why does not the same rule apply concerning the commandment against **stealing**?

Can it be against God's law to share another man's wife by majority vote (adultery), yet in accordance with God's law to share his property against his will by majority vote (stealing)?

The problem that develops in the area of economics is that wrong practices usually start out in very small ways, thus their basic immoral essence tends to escape recognition until the practices have become solidly established socially. Once a practice has become socially accepted and woven into the fabric of social custom, it becomes very difficult to eradicate, even though the practice may be producing some very deleterious effects. Most Christians can easily recognize collective adultery as being immoral, even in the beginning stages (take, for example, Hitler's statist program to develop a super-Aryan race by mating "ideal" male and female types). But, it takes a very discerning Christian to see the inherent immorality in such government-sponsored programs as Social Security, Medicare, Medicaid, Food Stamps, Welfare Payments, Aid to Mothers With Dependent Children, Tax-Supported Education, Farm Subsidies, Business Subsidies, etc. Each of these government programs entails the forcible taking of wealth from some citizens and distributing it to others. Each is a form of "legalized theft," and the fact that such programs are imposed on citizens by popularly elected representatives or by direct majority vote (in the case of tax-supported education) does not change their essential immoral character.

The biblical argument favoring the decentralized system of voluntary exchange, which is characteristic of free market capitalism (over centrally controlled collectivist systems, which deny man economic freedom) is simple and straightforward:

Man is created in the image and likeness of God and has been given a viceregency dominion over the earth (Gen. 1:26-28). Accordingly, man has a **right** to be free because he is an image bearer of God, who Himself is free. Since God is free by His very nature, man shares in this freedom aspect of God's nature. As God is free to impute value into things and make alternative choices (He set His love upon Israel), so is man.

The whole study of man as an economic being rests on his God-given ability to impute value and to act on his value imputations as a responsible rational being. Man thus has a **duty** to remain free so that he can act responsibly as God's vice-regent here on earth (Gen. 1:28) and so that he can serve God (Ex. 8:1). This is an important aspect of freedom which is often overlooked.

While it is true that man has a right to freedom based on his being created in the very image and likeness of God, man's duty to God as vice-regent **requires** that he be free in order to stand as a free and self-responsible agent before his Creator. How else can man offer willing sacrifices of righteousness to God (Ps. 4:5)? Any political/economic system which subverts man's personal reponsibility to God, as all socialist/communist systems of collectivism do, are clearly violations of biblical precepts because they attempt to break God's direct lordship over man. They forcibly relieve unwilling citizens of control over property which self-responsibility to God requires them to maintain.

The entire Law and Prophets generally support the concept of personal responsibility that is inherent in the free market system, and the Decalogue does so specifically. God declares it morally wrong to steal or covet another's property because property is the physical means God has given man to offer willing spiritual sacrifices to Himself. And the civil authorities have no moral or legal right to set aside the protection God afforded man by His commandments against stealing and covetousness any more than they have a right to set aside any other of God's commandments. Nor can this be done rightly by majority vote. Rather, the civic authority is bound to uphold and administer **all** of God's laws (Deut. 17:14-20), for the civil magistrate is **not** the **source** of law, but only the **administrator** of God's existing laws.

Paul clearly indicates that the proper role of civil government is simply that of a keeper-of-the-peace, and not that of an activist economic controller (Rom. 13:3-4; I Tim. 2:1-2). Nowhere in the Bible is the civil ruler given authority to engage in charitable works or economic intervention and regulation. God has not given civil government an open-ended power to invade any sphere of life it chooses because only Christ has all power over every sphere. To give government such power is to set it up as an idol. One principle runs consistently throughout the Bible, and it is that no social institution administered by sinful men is ever given anything but a very limited sphere of power. In this age of big government and expanding bureaucracy, Christians need to be aware of this principle; for, as the kingdom of power-seeking humanistic civil government expands, the effective outworking of Christians in building the Kingdom of God will be commensurately pushed back. God's cultural mandate to us calls for the reverse process to happen: We are to expand God's work, and the dominion of secular humanistic government is to recede.

Current Social Practices

Let us investigate some current practices in these United States of America and then attempt to discern the mind of Christ concerning them, for our cultural challenge as Christians is to faithfully build only those institutions which meet with God's approval. All others we are obliged to tear down and rebuild according to God's plan.

Recently a pastor in Tulsa, Oklahoma, told me of an instance which shows modern-day Christians' lack of understanding about Christ's mandate to build His Kingdom. The pastor received a phone call from a woman who had car trouble while travelling through town with her two young children. Being a Christian, she sought help from local churches listed in the telephone directory. The pastor immediately went to her aid with a deacon. When they arrived where the woman was stranded, she said, "Praise the Lord you came! Do you know you are the fourteenth church I called? All the other pastors referred me to a government agency, but I want help from God's people."

The pastor and deacon arranged to have the woman's car repaired, and they supplied food and lodging as well as some funds to help her on her way. But what about the other 13 pastors? What kind of kingdom-building vision do they have? What kind of kingdom-building vision do Christians have who encourage people to turn to the State for help instead of inviting them to turn to God's people for charitable aid?

Such a government-oriented attitude, if followed by Christians generally, would result in an ever-decreasing influence of Christ's church in society and an ever-expanding role for civil government. Such an attitude evidences a gross misunderstanding of what true charity is, as well as a misunderstanding of our Lord's command to love our neighbor as ourself (Lev. 19:18; Matt. 22:39; James 2:8). True charity necessarily involves both **voluntarism** in giving as well as the giving of one's **own property** — two requirements which state aid is absolutely incapable of fulfilling. It is technically impossible for the state to perform a charitable act because the civil authority always acts through force (i.e., by the mandate of law), and the largess distributed by the civil authority is not its own but is forcibly wrested (by law) from the taxpayers. Few Christians today seem to take these facts into consideration.

Let us consider some economic needs of men and how they are currently being met. Next, let us consider the harmful social effects that result from such handling. And, finally, let us consider the implications of Christianity for meeting men's needs and the beneficial social effects that would result from a proper biblical restructuring of society:

Education: An overwhelming majority of American children are now taught in tax-supported schools. This was not always the case, for early education in America was both private and Christian. It is not an overstatement to say that the early character of these United States of America — much of which still endures in our world-and-life view — was formed and molded by Christian education. But, early in the history of our country, religious apostasy caused influential people to turn to statist education as a means of furthering their humanistic world-and-life views.

Professor Samuel L. Blumenfeld gives this picture of early American education: Early in the Puritan Commonwealth, common schools (i.e., grade schools) were established as a means of insuring the transfer of Calvinist Puritan theology from one generation to the next. These were our country's first public (tax-supported) schools. They were **religiously** oriented rather than secularly oriented. However, privately operated Calvinistic schools sprang up to teach the more practical commercial subjects; and by 1720, Boston, the center of public education, had more private than public schools. By the close of the American Revolution, many towns in Massachusetts had no public schools at all. At this time, Boston was the **only** town in the entire nation that had public schools. All else were private. But, in 1805 the Unitarians took over Harvard College and expelled the Calvinists.[1]

The Unitarians rejected the Calvinist world-and-life view that was so successfully being promulgated in the majority of private Christian schools, so they pushed for a law to reinstate the defunct public school sector, which they hoped to control in order to make tax-supported public schools the vehicle for pushing their own humanistic ideas. To quote from Blumenfeld:

> . . . Their [the Unitarians] first organized effort was the campaign in 1818 to create primary public schools in Boston.
> Why only public schools and not private or charity schools? Because private schools were run and controlled by individuals who might have entirely different views concerning the nature of man. Besides, private owners were forced by economic reality to concentrate on teaching skills rather than forming character. As for the church schools, they were too sectarian, and the charity schools were usually run by Calvinists. Only the public schools, controlled in Boston by the affluent Unitarian establishment, could become that secular instrument of salvation.[2]

Tax-supported education was furthered in the mid-1840s when Horace Mann became the first state superintendent of schools in Massachusetts. He fashioned schools in Massachusetts after the statist schools he had become enamored of during a trip to Germany. Gradually, every other state in the Union established a statist, tax-supported school system after the pattern initiated by Mann. By the 1920s, tax-supported education had become a well-accepted social institution in America. It was about this time that the socialist educator John Dewey's influence was being strongly felt. He and his collectivist associates at Columbia University in New York were instrumental in placing their protégés in key positions at various state teachers colleges throughout the nation. Their success in planting followers in key spots helps explain the socialistic drift of statist tax-supported education over the last half-century.[3]

---

[1] Samuel L. Blumenfeld, "Why the Schools Went Public," quoted in *Reason* (Santa Barbara, Calif.: Reason Foundation, 1979), pp. 18-23. For a fuller treatment of this subject, see Blumenfeld, *Is Public Education Necessary?* (Old Greenwich, Conn.: Devin-Adair, 1981).

[2] Ibid., p. 21.

[3] For those who are interested in reading the frank statements of Dewey and his associates to make these United States of America into a socialist nation, read the *Fabian Tracts* and publications of the League for Industrial Democracy of the 1940s. They are available at some university libraries and larger metropolitan libraries.

What has been the result of America's turning from voluntarily supported private education to statist tax-supported education? The resulting effects have been very harmful:

(1) Parents have lost effective discretionary control over their children's education. Parents have been emasculated, economically speaking, because they cannot cut off support for educational practices and policies they do not like. Each local tax-supported school system is a government-created monopoly which parents, as taxpayers, are forced to support whether or not their own children use the public education services. Parents are, in effect, "captive consumers" who have no effective voice in what their children are taught, the books their children are required to read, or the required courses their children must take. Any parent who has had occasion to complain to local school authorities about not wanting his or her child to be exposed to immoral required-reading books or to sex-education programs knows the truth of this statement. Tax-supported educational bureaucrats feel no economic pressure to cater to the wishes of parents because their tax income is assured whether or not parents are satisfied customers. The attitude taken by the tax-supported educator is that he or she is the professional expert, so parents should peacefully acquiesce to his or her professional knowledge. Parents who complain are regarded as radicals and of being somewhat un-American.

(2) There has been a gradual drift of control in tax-supported education to the highest and most centralized political level—from the local school board, to the State Board of Education and, finally, to the U.S. Department of Education in Washington, D.C. With each successive step, parents have had less and less control as individuals; and public education has become more humanistic, more socialist oriented and less godly. Economically, politically and socially the tenets and ideas of collectivism are inculcated in many insidious ways on young minds from kindergarten through graduate school. This is done blindly, for the most part, because the teachers themselves are usually so indoctrinated that they do not even recognize the humanistic world-and-life view they hold. Is it any wonder that our young people graduate from high schools and colleges as budding collectivists? The author has been teaching in private Christian colleges for 16 years and has worked closely with educational leaders for even more years, so he speaks from first-hand experience when he says that tax-supported education turns out young collectivists who have been unknowingly conditioned to mentally and emotionally accept the idea of a state-controlled society headed by a humanistic elite.

A few years ago the author spoke at a large state university's "Free Enterprise Day" sponsored by its College of Business Administration. The head of the Business-Education Department approached him after the presentation and asked, "How can we teach our students a consistent free enterprise philosophy?"

The question was excellent, and the man's motivation was sincere. He had responded favorably to the thesis that the free market system is the practical outworking in society of man's God-given freedom and self-responsibility.

The author replied, "It is highly improbable that you can teach a consistent philosophy of free enterprise for two reasons. First, your school is a tax-supported educational institution. As such, it is a perfect example of practical socialism in action—the state owns and controls the means of production. How can you hope to teach consistent free enterprise ideals in an institution where the state owns and controls the means of producing educational services? Second, what world-and-life view does your institution hold? Does it not view man as a chance evolutionary happening rather than as a precious God-created individual? Since the whole ideal of free enterprise rests on the individual freedom and self-responsibility of man as a precious God-created being, and since your institution, holding an evolutionary view of man, denies this fact, it is again impossible to teach a consistent philosophy of free enterprise. To do so will eventually bring you into conflict with your institution's humanistic world-and-life view."

The man was at first dismayed to hear such a straightforward reply; but, after discussing the points at greater length, he agreed that the points made were accurate. He indicated he would do the best he could, recognizing his institutional limitations.

(3) Because parents have lost effective economic control over tax-supported education, such education has grown increasingly expensive while becoming less and less effective in real educational content. This result is characteristic of socialist enterprises generally; for, when the state controls the means of production, managers of state-owned enterprises soon cease to be responsive to consumer needs.

One of the gravest concerns of tax-supported educators is the steadily deteriorating quality of their graduates' ability to read, write and do math. Employers commonly complain that too many young people cannot read and write properly and have neither the needed skills nor the necessary work disciplines to be profitable employees. College administrators have noted a steady drop in college-level entrance exam scores over the last two decades. For instance, the Educational Testing Service reports that SAT scores for college-bound high school seniors have dropped from 466 verbal and 492 mathematical in 1967 to 424 verbal and 466 mathematical in 1980—and this in spite of the fact that the median number of years spent in school has increased during the same interval from 12.3 to 12.6.[4]

As for the exorbitant cost of tax-supported education, we see the effects in a number of ways. Approximately 80 percent of people's local property tax bill goes towards support of the local public school monopoly. If we figure that the average homeowner directly pays about $800 to $1,000 per year in local school taxes, and assume he pays this amount for each of his 40-odd

[4]Educational Testing Service National Report, *College-Bound Seniors,* (Princeton, N.J.: ETS, 1980), p. 5.

years of working life — but, in reality, school taxes continue into retirement until death — the grand total reaches between $32,000 and $40,000. That is a lot of money; and it would buy approximately twice as much education if it were spent privately instead of publicly. The author is well aware of this fact, for he has worked in private educational institutions whose very existence depends on frugality coupled with high quality.

The direct local property tax, however, is not the only cost of tax-supported education loaded onto the public. The state also levies an education tax which falls directly on the taxpaying public. So does the federal government. And, finally, all three levels of government — local, state and national — also levy educational taxes on business firms who must, if they are to stay in business, pass the costs on to consumers in the form of higher prices for the goods and services they sell. These are, of course, hidden, but they are substantial in totality. Thus, once again the consumer pays. If all business tax levies for education were eliminated, the overall price of goods and services would drop commensurately. There should be no doubt in anyone's mind that tax-supported education is exceedingly expensive.

(4) Spiritually and intellectually the control of American education is largely in the hands of the humanist elite who wield political power at the local, state and national levels. Thus, American education naturally tends to build the kingdom of Satan rather than the Kingdom of God. And it will remain in such condition until the fast-growing private Christian school movement again overtakes the increasingly ineffective statist schools as they did in the 1700s.

The Bible nowhere delegates responsibility for educating young people to the civil authority. Rather, the Bible places such responsibility with parents, for education is a covenant religious duty (Deut. 6:4-9). In short, we can confidently state that the education of our children is such an important kingdom-building work that parents **dare not** leave it for the state to do, lest the godly intent of education be subverted into furthering the destructive work of Satan. The clear implication for Christians is that our statist schools should be dismantled and that the control of education should be returned to the **individual** control of each family. This does not call for compromise solutions of giving parents tax credits or chits that can be spent where parents choose, for such compromise solutions retain a deadly element. They improperly recognize the state's unwarranted role in financing education through taxes; and the compromise solutions invite continued statist control, for the state **will** control that which it finances.

Care of the Aged: There is a popular fiction that social security was started because Americans were not taking adequate care of the elderly. The truth is that the social security program was started during the Roosevelt Administration (whose pump-priming efforts to stimulate the economy were not working) in order to induce older people to leave the job market and thus vacate jobs for younger persons who were unemployed. This represents poor economic reasoning because it was based on the supposition that only a finite number of jobs exist in an economy and that individuals must compete against each other for the fixed number of jobs available. But, since human wants are insatiable, so is the potential number of jobs.

It is appropriate at this point to dispel another popular myth: that the financial crash of 1929 and the ensuing 10-year depression can rightfully be blamed on the system of free market capitalism; and, specifically, that the crash was caused by stock market speculation and that the depression was a result of the business community's failure to do its "social duty" to provide needed jobs, thus the need for the civil government to step in and save the people from the neglect of businessmen.

The simple truth is this: From 1924 through 1928, the Federal Reserve Board followed an expansionary monetary policy in order to keep interest rates low in these United States with the intent of helping Britain stay on the quasi-gold reserve standard she returned to in 1924. Lower interest rates in this country would induce people to keep their funds deposited in England, thus reducing the outflow of gold from that country to ours. Much of the excess money created by the Federal Reserve in attempting to keep interest rates lower here than in England went into ostentatious expenditures and into speculative ventures such as buying stock on margin and Florida real estate deals. The point to keep in mind is that a country's central bank, the official monetary arm of the government, can **create** excess purchasing media, but **cannot control** what people do with the newly created money once they get it in their hands.

Federal Reserve officials had been concerned about the growing speculative fever ever since mid-1928, but they did not know how to deal with the problem their inflationary monetary policy had created. Finally, in May, 1929, the Federal Reserve precipitately raised the discount rate by a hefty amount to put a damper on speculation. As you will remember, the discount rate is the rate Federal Reserve Banks charge member-banks when they secure short-term loans from the Federal Reserve Bank in their district. The higher discount rate forced commercial banks that had loaned "call money" to stock market speculators to call in their loans. Keep in mind that, when a commercial bank extends a loan to a customer, new money is actually created and the overall money supply is thereby expanded. When bank loans are repaid by borrowers, money is thereby destroyed and the overall money supply is contracted.

The result of this precipitate Federal Reserve action was a sharp reduction in the price of stocks because borrowing speculators had to sell their stocks in order to generate cash to pay off their call loans. This selling of stocks culminated in a wave of panic selling in October, 1929. Then, when panic set in, Federal Reserve officials, instead of making needed reserves available to member-banks with liquidity problems, as good monetary policy would have dictated, began a **perverse** policy of restricting the money supply even more drastically by **refusing** to accept discounted notes offered by member-banks.

Thus, from 1929 to 1933 the money supply was contracted by approximately 35 percent, and the people of our country found themselves in the midst of the worst depression in history.

It is important to recognize the chain of cause-and-effect which led to the depression: (1) The initial financial panic was set off in 1929 by official **government** action. This happened **after** the same government had set the stage for a financial panic by following 5 years of inflationary monetary policy. (2) Once the financial panic occurred, official **government** action acerbated the problem by **further** monetary mismanagement and thereby pushed the country into the 1929-1933 depression. Anyone who does not grasp these two very important points has no chance of understanding what really happened in the 1920s and 1930s.

Now comes the ironic part of this bit of financial history. The American public turned to the civil government to "solve" the depression problem—they turned to the very culprit that had **caused** the problem in the first place. The Roosevelt Administration moved in with socialist programs that had popular appeal, but which badly frightened many in the business community. Potential entrepreneurs became fearful about committing funds to job-creating investments. This led the Roosevelt Administration, which was heavily infiltrated by socialist/communist elements, to point the finger of blame at the business community and to claim necessity for the federal government to move in and fill the void. It was against this dreary background that the Social Security program was spawned.

As first envisioned, social security was designed to be a government plan which forced people to save—they were to be forced to set aside funds during their working years and then draw out the funds after retirement. Each citizen was to have a "personal account" like an insurance policy. The personal account was fictitious, of course, for the money paid in by each social security participant was immediately spent on various government programs and was backed up only by IOUs (bonds) issued by the federal government. The only backing for the IOUs was the general taxing power of the national government.

But even the illusory "personal account" idea was dropped because, when social security went into effect in 1937, it had already been changed to a "pay-as-you-go" plan. Under this arrangement, the national government taxed away some of the earnings of younger persons who were employed and transferred them to older persons who had retired. Thus the term "transfer payments," which is a euphemism for something that really is not very nice—a program of legalized theft directed by the government itself in which the government simply enacts a law that makes it legal to take wealth from one citizen in order to give it to another. In short, the term "transfer payment" is just a euphemism for collectively breaking the commandment "Thou shalt not steal."

Once a person understands the economics of social security, it is easy to see that the program represents a clear breaking of the eighth commandment

(Ex. 20:15) as well as a deviation from the biblical rule that parents are to lay up for their children and not the children for their parents (II Cor. 12:14).

The problem with such governmentally sponsored transfer payment programs is that they begin in such small ways that their inherent immorality tends to go unnoticed until the programs grow and begin to produce obviously harmful effects in society. When social security began in 1937, the maximum payment withheld from a worker's paycheck was only one percent of $3,000 in wages, or a maximum of $30 per year. This was only a trifle, even according to depression standards. This $30 was matched with a tempting popular subterfuge—a matching $30 to be paid by the employer. Of course, the employer's "matching contribution" is a wage cost which must be recouped from the price of goods and services sold. Accordingly, the **entire** cost of social security comes out of the wage earner's pocket, for all wage earners are also consumers. In summary, the total maximum cost of social security in 1937 was only $60 per year, and half of that was disguised to make people think employers were really paying it—hardly enough to cause people to scrutinize the morality of the program very closely. Besides, who would be so bold as to speak out against a popular program designed to help old folks!

But today the social security program has mushroomed into such a financial monster that its harmful economic effects can hardly escape notice by even the most undiscerning. The total tax base has grown from $3,000 in 1937 to $37,800 in 1984, and the combined employee-employer tax rate has increased from 2 percent to 14 percent. In short, total maximum payments per worker have soared from $60 to over $5,000 annually. By 1990 the tax base is scheduled to rise to $57,000, and the combined employee-employer tax rate will be 15.3 percent which will produce over $8,700 in social security taxes per worker per year. This sum is adequate enough to motivate people to reconsider the worthwhileness of social security economically as well as to impel them to re-evaluate its moral soundness.

Here is a principle to remember: The practice of good morals produces good economics. Therefore, whenever we come across policies or practices that produce harmful economic effects, it behooves us to investigate the underlying morality of the offending policy or practice.

What are some of the harmful economic and social effects of social security?

In the first place, social security serves to pauperize our nation as a whole because it stimulates consumption **before** saving and investment take place. Under a voluntary private retirement program, a person would gradually build up a retirement nest egg through life insurance and pension plans all during his productive working life. During this 40- to 50-year span, the funds saved would contribute considerably to building the productive capital base of our country. The efficiency of output would thereby rise, and the production of even more wealth would be stimulated. This would in turn cause people's standard of living to rise generally. This is an example of free market capitalism in action. Elderly people would tend to be more highly regarded in society because they would be the owners of considerable capital funds over which they had discretionary control.

But under the social security "wealth transfer" scheme, the situation is much different. Funds withheld from a worker's paycheck are **not** productively invested. Instead, they are almost **immediately transferred** to a retiree who spends the funds for consumable goods and services. This explains, for instance, the high percentage of elderly persons boarding and unboarding airplanes at airports all across the nation. If we can make an analogy, we can say that social security uses government coercion to force Farmer Brown to set aside seed corn, but that the government then takes the seed corn and gives it to Mr. Jones to eat. In short, social security sets in motion a vast government-sponsored program of systematic decapitalization which leads assuredly towards national impoverishment. Recently a dear old Christian lady at a Thanksgiving Day "thank service" at church got up and said, "I thank the Lord for social security! Without it I would have a hard time getting along." This same dear soul planned to make a trip to the Holy Land in order to spend some excess savings in order to decrease her assets to qualify for entering a government-sponsored old folks home. If this dear saint understood the economics of social security, she would realize how sacreligious it is to thank God for such an immoral monstrosity. In 1980 a total of $136.5 billion in social security transfer payments were siphoned off from workers and funnelled into retirees' income.[5] In 1984 the amount rose to $210.6 billion, or 32 percent of the federal budget.[6]

The author might add at this point that social security is only one of various wealth transfer programs enforced by government edict. It is important to recognize the subtle threat of force that lies behind each such government scheme, for the strong arm of the law will be quickly used against anyone who decides not to "contribute to the pot." Wealth transfer schemes are truly a brutal business when seen in their true light. Today almost half of the American population is in some way or another dependent on government handouts in the form of pay, welfare, pensions or business and farm subsidies.[7] The total amount of so-called government transfer payments (federal, state and local) mushroomed from $5.6 billion in 1945 to $283.9 billion in 1980;[8] and by 1984 it reached $393.1 billion.[9] If America can be accused of a national economic sin, it is the massive and prolonged breaking of the eighth and tenth commandments through an all-powerful humanistic government.

These critical comments about social security are **not** directed at the millions of elderly people and presently employed workers who are caught up in it, for they, by and large, are either ignorant participants or feel trapped

---

[5]*U.S. News & World Report*, 26 January 1981, p. 74.
[6]Ibid., 14 February 1983, p. 73.
[7]Ibid., 9 March 1981, p. 73.
[8]Ibid., 2 March 1981, p. 26.
[9]Ibid., 14 February 1983, p. 73.

into it by law. Rather, the comments are directed at social security as an institutional program. Most people are still under the illusion that any program duly enacted into law by their political representatives must be lawful from a moral and ethical standpoint. It has been only during the last few years that growing numbers of the general public have begun to question the inherent morality of governmental acts; and this is a healthy indication, for ungodly rulers lead the people astray in their humanistic drive to build a Utopia on earth (Isa. 9:16; Prov. 28:10).

A second result of humanistically oriented wealth transfer programs such as social security is to develop powerful political blocs which become monolithically unified in single-purpose goals — that is, to protect the existing level of government-bestowed benefits and to work at increasing benefits at the expense of all other competing blocs. The development of special interest blocs allows political demagogues to establish themselves in office by playing on the people's fears and larcenous hearts. We see evidence of this development in every election for political office. People with good memories will be able to recall the series of ads on television during the 1964 Johnson-Goldwater presidential campaign which depicted elderly persons voicing their fear that social security benefits would be cut off if Barry Goldwater were elected president. The large number of votes cast by the elderly in response to these fears contributed materially to Goldwater's resounding defeat.

Let us now ask: What would be a godly way of providing for the aged? If the present "American plan" is ungodly, what is God's alternative?

A godly plan of caring for the aged would call for the civil authorities to follow a non-inflationary monetary policy that would protect the integrity of the monetary unit. This, in turn, would call for a non-interventionary government which would be limited to its biblical role of serving only as a keeper of the peace (I Tim. 2:1-2). A stable money supply would produce a healthy, long-term gradual decrease in the general price level which would steadily increase the purchasing power of people's savings.

Over the last 100-150 years, productivity (i.e., the efficiency of economic output) has grown approximately 2.5 to 3.0 percent per year. If such a trend were to continue unaccompanied by monetary inflation, the result would be that a dollar saved today would buy $1.03 worth of real goods and services next year, plus whatever rate of interest might be earned. In 10 years the value of today's dollar in terms of real purchasing power, exclusive of interest earnings, would be $1.34; in 20 years it would be $1.80; in 30 years $2.42; and in 40 years $3.26. Remember that these values apply only to the original dollar that was saved and do not include accrued interest.

Instead of following our present inflationary policy which insidiously robs older people of their hard-earned savings — thus stimulating them to spend instead of to save — such a non-inflationary policy as recommended would strongly motivate people to accumulate savings through efficiently run financial intermediaries such as life insurance companies, savings banks and pension funds. Another benefit of letting people arrange for their own accumulation of retirement funds is that there would be no need for the vast numbers of tax-supported social security personnel now employed by the government.

But what about those citizens who persist in being spendthrifts and who do not have the personal discipline to save consistently for retirement? And what about those frugal souls who do save, but who handle their funds unwisely and end up old and destitute? This brings us to the second biblical point: Such persons are proper cases for charity, which is the proper realm for individuals, the church of Christ and voluntary social-aid organizations. Nowhere does the Bible give the civil authority responsibility for caring for the poor or aged. Think of the Christian's responsibility for shedding forth the love of Christ through charitable outreach that is now being usurped by an aggressive and activist civil authority! To the extent that the state taxes away citizens' wealth and income, each Christian's ability to support God's kingdom-building work is weakened. God's plan calls for people to be individually responsible for providing for their own declining years. Those who have failed to meet this responsibility, either by neglect or by bad fortune, must either continue to work or be dependent on charity freely bestowed by other individuals or organizations. Individual responsibility, of course, does not preclude acting voluntarily in concert with others (insurance, savings banks, etc.), but it definitely precludes any kind of coercive wealth transfer scheme mandated by the civil government.

Care of the Poor and Needy: The same line of argumentation that applies to social security can also be applied generally to the poor and needy. Great masses of people in our country have become institutionally poor because of various government programs that direct people toward idleness instead of motivating them toward job hunting and the acquisition of new skills. Man, by his very sin nature, will tend to seek the easiest short-term course, even though it may ultimately lead toward long-range economic impotency. For instance, how many individuals have we seen happy to receive government-bestowed "rocking chair money" instead of seriously looking for income-producing work?

The minimum wage law also serves to disemploy persons who have only marginal skills. The minimum wage law thus inhibits low-skilled persons from gaining worthwhile job-market experience that would lead to other employment opportunities at higher pay. As strange as it may seem, doing away with the minimum wage law would **help** the poor instead of hurt them. The absence of such a law would allow employers to pay low-skilled persons whatever they were worth in the marketplace. This would open up many jobs that are now closed because the legally mandated pay level is too high to hire people to fill them. But, more importantly, it would provide low-skilled persons job opportunities to learn new skills and to develop the required job disciplines to qualify for higher paying jobs. In short, once again we can see how the civil authority, through its economic intervention, has acerbated the problem of poverty rather than cured it. In addition, our civil authorities have created large political blocs of people who are institutionally committed to idleness. The minimum wage law destines them to long-term unemployment, so the civil authority steps in and provides government-bestowed wealth transfer incomes as a sop.

Biblical charity, on the other hand, is both **voluntary** and **short-term**. It motivates people in need to quickly become self-supporting because the voluntary donors have the power to cut off funds to the lazy and indolent. The biblical way of caring for the poor and needy would be, first, **not** to price them out of the market institutionally through a minimum wage law. Secondly, privately supplied self-help opportunities through work would help the poor and needy remain socially useful rather than causing them to lose their own self-esteem through government-mandated idleness (Ruth 2:15-23). For the civil authority to accept the responsibility of caring for the poor and needy is to arrogate a power **not** given to government by God. It is to usurp the God-given responsibility of individuals and the church.

The High Cost of Energy: The 1970s introduced a new problem to Americans in general and to many people the world over—the shortage of energy and its commensurate high cost. Two questions can be raised: Why are we suddenly faced with shortages and high cost of fuel? And how should the problem be met?

The second question can be found by answering the first. The cause of high-priced energy in these United States is not greedy businessmen who wrench profits out of the poor and downtrodden. Rather, the problem has been caused by mismanagement in the area of civil government. To understand what has happened, we must go back to 1955, the year Congress passed legislation to control prices in the oil and gas industry.

In 1955 there were approximately 20,000 wildcat drillers exploring for oil and gas in the continental United States. And even though our usage of oil and gas was increasing each year, the total known reserves of these energy sources were growing at an even faster rate. The more rapidly increasing supply relative to the less rapidly increasing demand helped keep prices low. But, with the imposition of federal price controls on interstate gas in 1955, much of the profit incentive needed to induce wildcat drillers to risk their capital in exploration disappeared. So, many of these risk-taking entrepreneurs turned to other activities. Soon oil and gas usage began to surpass the lower rate at which new reserves were being discovered. By 1971 the number of wildcat drillers had dropped to about 8,000, and the energy supply situation in our country had grown critical.

Leaders in the oil and gas industry repeatedly warned congressional committees and other high-placed politicians and bureaucrats about our dwindling reserve situation, but it was politically unpopular to return to a free market policy because the public is generally ignorant of supply-demand economics.

The public wanted cheap energy **today,** let tomorrow take care of itself; the federal government therefore continued its interventionary policy of fixing prices.

The inability to earn adequate returns on capital invested in a government-controlled price situation explains why leading oil companies began to search for cheaper oil sources overseas. As we now know, these cheaper oil supplies were found in the Mid-East. Thus, gradually, our country became more and more dependent on foreign sources of energy. And when Congress extended price controls to oil in 1971, even more pressure was added to make our country dependent on foreign oil.

The Arab oil boycott which precipitately occurred in 1973 shocked Americans; for, somehow, America had passed from being a net exporter of oil to a net importer. Government officials pointed the finger of blame for the sudden shortage of oil at profit-seeking oil companies, at the American public who were dubbed "energy hogs" and at the fact that the earth has only a finite amount of fossil fuels which were being depleted at much too fast a rate.

Not one of these claims stands the test of reason.

Some years ago, in the very midst of the oil shortage problem, this author publicly claimed in his syndicated newspaper column and in taped radio programs that the world is awash in oil and gas. While it is true that God created the universe with a finite amount of resources, we must also recognize that our gracious Lord is the author of history. He not only foreknew the course of events in world history and the growth of world population, but he is the dynamic **cause** in bringing these events about. To accuse God of putting man on an earth which He inadequately supplied with the needed economic resources for man to fulfill his destiny is equivalent to saying that our Creator and Father is stingy and miserly. It is a gross denial of the scriptural truth that a gracious and loving God has abundantly supplied man with all his needs. Actually, the finite resources of the earth are so vast relative to world population that, practically speaking, the earth's resources are almost limitless. The only factor that is lacking to tap the earth's almost limitless resources is the **incentive** to search out and develop them. It is in this crucial aspect of incentives that the federal government has erected innumerable barriers.

To continue our historical narrative, let us remember that the number of domestic wildcat drillers dropped from 20,000 in 1955 to 8,000 in 1971. Thus, the 1973 Arab boycott caught us in a very tight supply situation — a tight supply situation created by our own civil rulers. It is not unfair to say that the energy pricing policy followed by the federal government created the very situation that, not only encouraged a boycott by the Arabs, but which guaranteed its success.

Happily, at the present time, leaders in our national government have seen some of the error of their ways and have taken steps to deregulate the oil and gas industry, in spite of some special interest groups who continue to push for continued government controls. The deregulation process started a number of years ago by letting energy prices creep upward, and it has continued with various interruptions and delays toward the goal of removing all price regulation. What has been the result? Large advances have already been made in rebuilding proven reserves of oil and gas. Why? Because by the early 1980s the number of wildcat drillers exploring for oil and gas expanded from 8,000 to 15,000. They have been attracted by the higher profit potential now allowed by the removal of federal price controls. Not only did new entrepreneurial wildcatters move in to find new fields, but they used advanced technology to drill deeper in order to discover new reserves in existing oil and gas fields. The higher allowable prices also motivated the application of new technology to squeeze out additional supplies from fields which were once considered depleted at the lower price controls that existed earlier.

What is the problem that the oil and gas industry faces today? It is the problem of oversupply! The price of oil has tumbled to the point where the earlier massive flow of "petrodollars" has dwindled so much as to threaten the economic viability of the OPEC nations. By early 1984 the price per gallon of gasoline at service stations dropped to $.99 in some parts of the country, down from a high of $1.35 a few years earlier. It is interesting to note that the price of natural gas has **not** fallen but has continued its climb. Why the difference? Continued government interference in the market for natural gas has suppressed competition, so lower costs have not been passed on to consumers.

As an economist the author is particularly fond of pointing out that the best cure for high prices and limited supplies, in a free market, is high prices. What do we mean by such a statement? Simply that high prices, in a free market environment, produce a two-fold effect: First, high prices motivate consumers to cut back on consumption. Statistical data show that, between 1979 and 1981, there was a 15.4 percent decline in gasoline consumption.[10] In recent years, total gasoline usage dropped at an average of 4 percent. Secondly, high prices stimulate profit-seeking competitors to enter lines of economic activity where prices are high. This explains the increase of wildcat drillers from 8,000 in 1971 to 15,000 in 1980, and it also explains why large companies have purchased major oil companies (U.S. Steel Corporation bought Marathon Oil and DuPont bought Conoco, just to mention two instances).

But, before we turn away from the currently improving energy supply situation, let us go back and see what other actions the federal government took to acerbate the energy crisis. During the 1960s Congress passed additional legislation which loaded automobiles down with anti-pollution control devices. These caused a reduction in average miles per gallon of gas from 15-16 in 1963 to approximately 10 in 1973. That amounts to an increase in consumption of approximately 33 percent. Then, in addition, Congress passed legislation that required new autos to use unleaded gasoline. This necessitated about 15 percent more crude oil to be used in refining a gallon of gasoline.

---

[10]Ibid., 6 April 1981, p. 7.

There is one other development to consider. During this time when the federal government was, on one hand, dampening the supply of oil and gas by imposing price controls, and stimulating demand on the other hand by mandating gas-guzzling anti-pollution controls, a vast new oil field was discovered in Alaska. This seemed like God's answer to a sorely distressed nation, but what happened? Our political leaders did not welcome this new find as a boon to hard-pressed consumers and as an answer to our growing dependence on foreign oil. Rather, Congress became the tool of politically powerful ecology groups which strove to preserve the pristine purity of the Alaskan wilderness which few had ever seen or would ever see. These ecology interests valued the free wanderings of fauna in Alaska more than the need of their fellowmen for new energy sources, so they plagued the oil companies with one politically initiated delay after another. The net result of the ecologists' political influence was more than a 6-year delay in building the Alaskan pipeline plus multibillions of additional costs which consumers would eventually have to bear in higher prices for gasoline and fuel oil.

Recently the author gave a series of talks on the biblical basis of the free market at a large annual Christian conference. The executive director of a Christian outreach ministry in a northeastern city approached him after the talks. He was against the idea of a free market in energy because, in his opinion, greedy capitalists had forced the price of fuel up in order to line their pockets at the expense of the poor people he ministers to. His feeling of alienation had led him, without realizing it, to accept the socialist/communist theory of exploitation. Therefore, he and his organization do all they can to help the subjects of his ministry to get all the government handouts that are available.

By mistakenly thinking that the high price of energy was caused by greedy capitalists instead of by institutional disturbances of supply and demand by civil authorities, the missionary turned to the humanistic forces for help that were the very cause of the problem! As we can see from the historical account of the oil and gas industry given above, it was misguided governmental action that served to drastically reduce our domestic supply of energy through the unwise imposition of price controls. It was also misguided governmental action that served to increase the overall demand for gasoline by requiring gas-guzzling anti-pollution devices on new autos. The governmental mandate to use unleaded gasoline further dampened supply. And, finally, it was political pressure on the government that caused the 6-year delay in bringing the newly discovered Alaskan oil on stream. No one who understands what really happened can honestly blame free market capitalism for fuel shortages and high prices, for the free market works in the opposite direction — it serves to increase supply and to lower prices.

This, of course, is a communications problem for the news media take keen pleasure in making the business community the scapegoat for social problems. The unthinking public, many Christians among them, easily fall prey to publicly disseminated misinformation; and this mentally conditions them to look to the civil government as a solver of problems rather than the cause of them. The whole series of ill-conceived governmental interventions in the oil and gas and auto industries has been a tremendous disservice to the public, but too few citizens understand what really happened. Our Christian brother who is the executive director of the inner-city mission, as well as other Christian brethren who have fallen for anti-capitalist propaganda, would be better advised to place the blame for the high cost of fuel where it rightly belongs — on the humanistically oriented intervention of civil government in men's economic affairs.

It is not at all characteristic of free market activity to produce widespread social problems or to produce massive misallocations of economic resources. Free market activity, because it takes place without coercion and is directed towards the objective of satisfying consumers' needs on a one-to-one basis, does exactly the opposite — it tends to solve problems while they are still small enough to be manageable. So, whenever widespread problems such as persistently rising price levels, widespread unemployment or massive shortages or surpluses do appear, we must search for the underlying causative force. Almost always, the underlying cause will be found to be some kind of structural problem effected by some unwise governmental policy which has interfered with man's natural tendency to serve his neighbors' needs at a profit to all concerned. And it is here that we must make a theological point: Without exception, the unwise governmental interference will be found to be the result of fallen man's inherent rebellion against God and His instituted law-system. Fallen man attempts to dethrone God and God's law and to set himself up as the ultimate authority in society in his sinful attempt to build a Utopia on earth.

How can we summarize the points we have made, and what implications can we draw concerning how men are to go about serving their mutual needs? Especially, we might ask, what implication is there for Christians concerning how they are to deal with others?

A search of Scripture fails to turn up any guideline that condones the use of force in economic transactions either singly by individuals or collectively by the civil authority. For example, even when Samaria was under seige, there was not the slightest hint that the civil ruler had rightful authority to impose price controls in order to keep food prices low (II Kings 7). Neither does Scripture anywhere even hint that the civil authority has rightful power to direct and manipulate the economic or social affairs of men in order to achieve desirable national goals. Thus, it is of no concern to political authorities whether price levels are high or low, whether the level of employment is high or low, whether or not economic growth is taking place or whether a country's balance of payments to foreign nations is stable or not. The only biblical authority given to civil rulers is that of keeping the peace so that justice will reign and free men will be able to act self-responsibly before God, to whom they ultimately must answer.

Not enough Christians have seriously attempted to discern the mind of God about how they should comport themselves in economic affairs. Thus, many Christians have an unbiblical tendency to turn to an activist civil government in seeking quick solutions to alleged social and economic problems. In doing so they err in two ways: First, they tend to load onto the civil authority duties which are really their own personal responsibilities or which are responsibilities of the church. The unfailing result of this error is that humanistically oriented civil government tends to grow at the expense of the church of Christ. Jesus wants his followers to actively beat down the gates of hell, not to passively acquiesce in the growth of Satan's secular sphere.

Secondly, Christians who encourage or condone the civil authority's provision of "charity" to the needy are guilty of institutionally breaking the eighth and tenth commandments through the collective agency called civil government. Such sins, even though done collectively through ignorance, cannot escape God's notice and judgment, for He created a world of cause and effect. Many of the social ills cited above can be traced to unwise and basically immoral and unethical government policies. But, Christians are required by God's word to live godly and lawful lives — lawful, not according to legally imposed man-made laws, but lawful according to God's higher law. This requires a careful commitment to conform our every thought and action to the mind and heart of Christ. It also requires a special care not to be enticed into social customs or into politically imposed policies that are antinomian (lawless) in their essence.

We as Christians must turn away from the inherently coercive and immoral wealth transfer schemes being promoted by our government leaders, and we must turn to the voluntary private policies of helping others which are upheld by the Bible. There is a seeming risk in turning from coercive collectivism to free market voluntarism, for we cannot predict in advance just how people's needs will be met in the voluntary sphere. But this, in itself, calls for an act of faith — faith that God, in His all-knowing and all-loving role as Creator and Sustainer of the universe, will work out His plan in our lives individually and socially if we will but follow faithfully in His footsteps and obey His laws. God's word simply calls for us to offer up the continual sacrifice of righteous adherence to God's law-system and then to place our trust in Him for the outcome (Ps. 4:5). This is what the study of economics is all about, and this is how Christ's Kingdom is to be built.

Questions

1. What is your view of Christ's Kingdom? How does your view influence your long-range plans and your day-to-day economic activity?

2. What is Christ's cultural mandate? What does it mean to Christians

concerning the social institutions of the family, the church, business and civil government?

3. Do you think God is neutral about how man is to provide for his economic wants? Explain. Be ready to discuss and defend your view in class.

4. Is there a valid biblical argument favoring:
    (a) a decentralized system of voluntary exchange?
    (b) a centralized system of involuntary exchange?

    Be ready to discuss and defend your view in class by referring to appropriate Bible verses.

5. Attack or defend: The Bible upholds the practice of government transfer payments as a means of helping the poor and the aged.

6. A needy person becomes stranded in a strange community. Whose duty is it to render help? Does the person have a right to help? Trace the economics of help rendered:
    (a) voluntarily through the church or other private sources.
    (b) by tax-supported government agencies.

7. Attack or defend: All education should be provided privately and none by the civil authority.

8. Briefly review the development of tax-supported education in early America and the motivation of those who supported it.

9. What have been the economic effects of tax-supported education?

10. Your advice is asked on how to improve the SAT scores for college-bound high school seniors. If given the three options below, which would you choose? Why?
    (a) Eliminate all private schools.
    (b) Eliminate all tax-supported schools.
    (c) Increase educational expenditures in tax-supported schools.

11. Discuss the economics of social security (i.e., how does it work?).

12. Attack or defend: During his working years a worker builds up a social security "nest egg" which is drawn out during his retirement years.

13. What do you think is the biblical way of taking care of old people and the poor and needy? Give examples with appropriate Bible verses.

14. Attack or defend: It is impossible for the civil authority to perform a charitable act.

15. Briefly relate the history of the oil shortage during the 1970s. What policy recommendations would you make to insure against a reoccurrence?

Selected Bibliography
And Suggested Readings

Anderson, Clay J. *A Half-Century of Federal Reserve Policymaking, 1914-1964*. Philadelphia: Federal Reserve Bank of Philadelphia, 1965.

Bach, George L. and Teece, D. J. *Economics*. 10th ed. Englewood Cliffs: Prentice-Hall, 1980.

Bahnsen, Greg L. *Theonomy in Christian Ethics*. Nutley, New Jersey: Craig Press, 1979.

Buer, Mabel C. *Health, Wealth and Population in the Early Days of the Industrial Revolution, 1760-1815*. London: Routledge & Sons, 1926.

Burstein, Meyer L. *Money*. Cambridge: Schenkman Publ., 1963.

Cameron, Rondo, ed. *Banking and Economic Development*. New York: Oxford Univ. Press, 1972.

Campbell, Colin D. and Campbell, Rosemary G. *An Introduction to Money and Banking*. 5th ed. Chicago: Dryden Press, 1983.

The Center for the Study of Economics. *Incentive Taxation*. Indiana, Penn. Monthly.

Chilton, David. *Productive Christians in an Age of Guilt Manipulators*. Tyler, Texas: Institute for Christian Economics, 1981.

Chodorov, Frank. *The Income Tax: Root of All Evil*. New York: Devin-Adair, 1954.

Clapham, John. *The Bank of England*. London: Cambridge Univ. Press, 1944.

DeRoover, Raymond. *The Rise and Decline of the Medici Bank*. New York: W. W. Norton, 1966.

Dilts, David A. and Deitsch, Clarence R. *Labor Relations*. New York: Macmillan, 1983.

Dolan, Edwin G. *Basic Economics*. 2d ed. Hinsdale: Dryden Press, 1980.

Dwinnell, Olive Cushing. *The Story of Our Money*. Boston: Meador Publ. Co., 1946.

Elliott, J. Walter. *Money, Banking, and Financial Markets*. St. Paul: West Publ., 1984.

Federal Reserve Bank of St. Louis. *Review*. Monthly.

Federal Reserve System, Board of Governors. *Federal Reserve Bulletin*. Washington, D.C. Monthly.

Garrett, Garet and Rothbard, Murray N. *The Great Depression and New Deal Monetary Policy*. San Francisco: CATO Institute, 1980.

George, Henry. *Progress and Poverty*. New York: Robert Schalkenbach Foundation, 1962.

Groseclose, Elgin. *Fifty Years of Managed Money*. New York: Books, Inc., 1966. Rev. ed.: *America's Money Machine*. Westport: Arlington House, 1980.

_____. *The Monetary Services of Silver*. Washington: Institute for Monetary Research, 1965.

_____. *Money and Man: A Survey of Monetary Experience*. 4th ed. Norman: Univ. of Oklahoma Press, 1976.

_____. *A Survey of Western Currencies, 1912-1962*. Washington: Institute for Monetary Research, 1962.

Gruchy, Allan G. *Comparative Economic Systems*. 2d ed. Boston: Houghton Mifflin, 1977.

Henning, Charles N.; Pigott, William; and Scott, Robert H. *Financial Markets and the Economy*. 4th ed. Englewood Cliffs: Prentice-Hall, 1984.

Hollander, Paul. *Political Pilgrims*. New York: Oxford Univ. Press, 1981.

Howard, Irving E. *The Moral Alternative to Socialism*. Chicago: Citizens Evaluation Institute, 1971.

The Institute for Contemporary Studies. *Tariffs, Quotas and Trade: The Politics of Protectionism*. San Francisco: 1978.

Johnson, George E. "Economic Analysis of Trade Unionism." In *American Economic Review*, vol. 65, no. 2, May 1975.

Kamerschen, David R. and Klise, Eugene S. *Money and Banking*. 7th ed. Cincinnati: South-Western Publ. Co., 1980.

Kemmerer, Donald L. and Jones, C. Clyde. *American Economic History*. New York: McGraw-Hill Book Co., 1959.

Kershner, Howard E. *God, Gold and Government*. Englewood Cliffs: Prentice-Hall, 1957.

Kidwell, David S. and Peterson, Richard L. *Financial Institutions, Markets, and Money*. 2d ed. Chicago: Dryden Press, 1984.

Kolko, Gabriel. *The Triumph of Conservatism*. Chicago: Quadrangle Paperbacks, 1967.

Kravchenko, Victor. *I Chose Freedom*. Garden City: Garden City Publ. Co., 1946.

_____. *I Chose Justice*. New York: Chas. Scribner's Sons, 1950.

Kreps, Clifton H. and Pugh, O.S. *Money, Banking and Monetary Policy*. 2d ed. New York: Ronald Press Co., 1967.

Labin, Suzanne and Lyons, Daniel. *Fifty Years: USSR versus the USA*. New York: Twin Circle Publ. Co., 1968.

Lepage, Henri. *Tomorrow Capitalism*. LaSalle, Ill.: Open Court Publ. Co., 1978.

Lipsey, Richard G. and Steiner, Peter O. *Economics*. 6th ed. New York: Harper & Row, 1981.

Lipson, Eric. *The Economic History of England*. London: Adam & Charles Black, 1943.

Luckett, Dudley G. *Money and Banking*. 3d ed. New York: McGraw-Hill Book Co., 1984.

Lyons, Eugene. *Workers' Paradise Lost*. New York: Paperback Library, Inc., 1967.

McFadden, Charles J. *The Philosophy of Communism*. Boston: Benziger Brothers, Inc., 1963.

Madeleine, Grace. *Monetary and Banking Theories of Jacksonian Democracy*. Philadelphia: Dolphin Press, 1943.

Marshall, Peter and Manuel, David. *The Light and the Glory*. Old Tappan, New Jersey: Fleming H. Revell, 1977.

Marshall, Roy; Briggs, Vernon M., Jr.; and King, Allan G. *Labor Economics: Wages, Employment, Trade Unionism, and Public Policy*. 5th ed. Homewood, Ill.: Irwin, 1984.

Martin, Rose L. *Fabian Freeway*. Santa Monica: Fidelis Publ., Inc., 1968.

Marx, Karl. *The Communist Manifesto*. With Introduction by Stefan T. Possony. Chicago: Henry Regnery, 1954.

_____. *The Communist Manifesto*. With Introduction by A. J. P. Taylor. New York: Penguin Books, 1979.

Mayer, Thomas; Duesenberry, James S.; and Aliber, Robert Z. *Money, Banking, and the Economy*. 2d ed. New York: W. W. Norton, 1984.

Mises, Ludwig von. *Human Action*. New Haven: Yale Univ. Press, 1963.

_____. *Omnipotent Government*. New Rochelle: Arlington House, 1969.

_____. *Socialism*. Indianapolis: Liberty Classics, 1981.

Monetary Tracts. Greenwich: Committee for Monetary Research and Education, Inc.

North, Gary. *An Introduction to Christian Economics*. Nutley, New Jersey: Craig Press, 1973.

_____. *Unconditional Surrender*. Tyler, Texas: Geneva Press, 1981.

North, Gary. ed. *The Journal of Christian Reconstruction*. Vallecito, Calif.: Chalcedon.
Symposium on Christian Economics, vol. II, Summer 1975.
Symposium on Education, vol. IV, Summer 1977.
Symposium on Politics, vol. V, Summer 1978.
Symposium on Social Action, vol. VIII, Summer 1981.

Novak, Michael. *The Spirit of Democratic Capitalism*. New York: Simon & Schuster, 1982.

Palyi, Melchior. *A Lesson in French Inflation*. New York: The Economists' National Committee on Monetary Policy, 1959.

Patterson, Robert T. ed. *Why Gold?* Great Barrington, Mass.: American Institute for Economic Research, 1964.

Polo, Marco. *The Travels of Marco Polo*. New York: Library Publ., n.d.

Quigley, Carroll. *Tragedy and Hope*. New York: Macmillan, 1966.

Rand, Ayn. *Capitalism: The Unknown Ideal*. New York: The New American Library, 1966.

Rauschning, Hermann. *Time of Delirium*. New York: D. Appleton-Century Co., 1946.

Rees, Albert. *The Economics of Work and Pay*. New York: Harper & Row, 1973.

Richards, Richard D. *The Early History of Banking in England*. London: P. S. King, 1929.

Ritter, Lawrence S. and Silber, William L. *Money*. 5th ed., Rev. ed. New York: Basic Books, 1984.

Robertson, Ross M. and Walton, G. M. *History of the American Economy*. 4th ed. New York: Harcourt, Brace Jovanovich, 1979.

Röpke, Wilhelm. *The Economics of a Free Society*. Chicago: Regnery, 1963.

_____. *A Humane Economy*. Indianapolis: Liberty Fund, Inc., 1971.

Rogers, James E. T. *Six Centuries of Work and Wages; The History of English Labour*. London: Allen & Unwin, 1884.

Root, Franklin R. *International Trade and Investment*. 4th ed. Cincinnati: South-Western Publ. Co., 1978.

Rose, Tom. *Economics: Principles and Policy (from a Christian Perspective)*. Milford, Mich.: Mott Media, 1977.

_____. *Free Enterprise Economics*. Dallas: The Institute for Free Enterprise Education, 1974.

_____. *How To Succeed In Business*. Dallas: The Institute for Free Enterprise Education, 1975.

_____. *When the Union Organizer Knocks*. Plano, Texas: American Enterprise Publ., 1972.

Rose, Tom and Metcalf, Robert M., Jr. *The Coming Victory*. Memphis: Christian Studies Center, 1980.

Rothbard, Murray N. *America's Great Depression*. Princeton: Van Nostrand, 1963.

_____. *Man, Economy and the State*. Princeton: Van Nostrand, 1962.

_____. *What Has Government Done to Our Money?* Los Angeles: Libertarian Publishers, 1976.

Rushdoony, Rousas J. *The Institutes of Biblical Law*. Nutley, New Jersey: Craig Press, 1973.

_____. *The Politics of Guilt and Pity*. Nutley, New Jersey: Craig Press, 1970; reprint ed., Tyler, Texas: Thoburn Press, 1978.

_____. *This Independent Republic*. Nutley, New Jersey: Craig Press, 1964; reprint ed., Tyler, Texas: Thoburn Press, 1978.

Schnitzer, Martin C. and Nordyke, J. W. *Comparative Economic Systems*. 2d ed. Cincinnati: South-Western Publ. Co., 1977.

Schwarz, Fred. *You Can Trust the Communists*. Englewood Cliffs: Prentice-Hall, 1960.

Schumpeter, Joseph A. *Capitalism, Socialism and Democracy*. New York: Harper Torchbook, 1962.

Simon, Julian. *The Ultimate Resource*. Princeton: Princeton Univ. Press, 1981.

Singer, C. Gregg. *From Rationalism to Irrationality*. Phillipsburg, New Jersey: Presbyterian and Reformed Publ. Co., 1979.

Smith, Goldwin, *A History of England*. 3d ed. New York: Charles Scribner's Sons, 1966.

Sprague, O. M. W. *History of Crises Under the National Banking System*. Reprints of Economic Classics. New York: Kelley, 1968.

Sutton, Anthony C. *Wall Street and the Bolshevik Revolution*. New York: Arlington House, 1974.

_____. *Western Technology and Soviet Development*. Stanford: Stanford Univ. Press, 1968.

Taylor, E. L. Hebden. *Economics, Money and Banking*. Nutley, New Jersey: Craig Press, 1978.

Taylor, George R. ed. *Jackson vs. Biddle's Bank*. 2d ed. Lexington: D. C. Heath & Co., 1972.

Tocqueville, Alexis de. *Democracy in America*. 2 Vols. New York: Vintage Books, 1945.

Tucker, Robert C. ed. *The Marx-Engels Reader*. 2d ed. New York: W. W. Norton, 1978.

U.S. Congress. Senate. Committee of the Judiciary. *U.S.S.R. Labor Camps*. Washington: Government Printing Office, 1973.

Vernadsky, George. *A History of Russia*. New Haven: Yale Univ. Press, 1969.

Vetterli, Richard and Fort, William E., Jr. *The Socialist Revolution*. Los Angeles: Clute International Corp., 1968.

William, Maurice. *The Social Interpretation of History*. New York: Sotery Publ. Co., 1921.

Name Index

Subject Index

Scripture Index

OLD TESTAMENT

NEW TESTAMENT